"No CGI can match what Vic can accomplish."
STEVEN SPIELBERG

"Vic Armstrong is, of course, a legend in the film world."
MARTIN SCORSESE

"No one does better action sequences than Vic. Some stunt co-ordinators are good with explosion scenes, some are good with car chases or gun battles. But Vic is a master of them all."
ARNOLD SCHWARZENEGGER

"I'd call Vic a mild-mannered man, like Clark Kent, but under that he's Superman. It was a pleasure to work with Vic on the Indiana Jones pictures… he really was a great addition to our team."
GEORGE LUCAS

"Vic has evolved from a stuntman to a filmmaker, and one of the best."
HARRISON FORD

"He knows what makes a great action sequence, and where to put the camera so you get bigger bangs for your bucks. He's the man."
PIERCE BROSNAN

"Be warned, whenever Vic says 'I've got an idea', something dangerous is about to happen. That's why we love him."
ANGELINA JOLIE

"He is one of the greatest ever stuntmen, a top second unit director, a top stunt co-ordinator, and also a director in his own right. He's had a great career and deserves it."
SIR CHRISTOPHER LEE

THE TRUE ADVENTURES OF THE

WORLD'S

My life as INDIANA JONES, JAMES BOND,

GREATEST

SUPERMAN and other movie heroes

STUNTMAN

THE TRUE ADVENTURES OF THE WORLD'S GREATEST STUNTMAN
MY LIFE AS INDIANA JONES, JAMES BOND, SUPERMAN AND OTHER MOVIE HEROES

ISBN: 9780857689146

Published by

Titan Books

A division of Titan Publishing Group Ltd.

144 Southwark St.

London

SE1 0UP

This updated paperback edition: May, 2012

1 3 5 7 9 10 8 6 4 2

Designed by Martin Stiff

Production by Bob Kelly

Did you enjoy this book? We love to hear from our readers. Please e-mail us at:
readerfeedback@titanemail.com or write to Reader Feedback at the above address.

To receive advance information, news, competitions, and exclusive offers online,
please sign up for the Titan newsletter on our website: **www.titanbooks.com**

A CIP catalogue record for this title is available from the British Library.

Printed and bound in the UK by CPI Group (UK) Ltd, Croydon, CR0 4YY

THE TRUE ADVENTURES OF THE WORLD'S GREATEST STUNTMAN

My life as INDIANA JONES, JAMES BOND,

SUPERMAN and other movie heroes

VIC ARMSTRONG

with ROBERT SELLERS

Introduction by
STEVEN SPIELBERG

TITAN BOOKS

DEDICATION

TO

BOB ARMSTRONG, MY FATHER AND MY FRIEND.
HIS GUIDANCE AND INSPIRATIONAL LESSONS IN LIFE
MADE ME WHO I AM TODAY.
ANN, MY MOTHER FOR HER LIFELONG SUPPORT.
WENDY, MY WIFE FOR HER NEVERENDING LOVE AND PATIENCE.
MY BROTHER ANDY AND SISTER DIANA FOR ALWAYS BEING THERE.
BRUCE, NINA, SCOTT, GEORGIE AND
ROBERT MY GRANDSON BECAUSE I LOVE THEM.

WITH SPECIAL CONTRIBUTIONS BY

LORD ATTENBOROUGH

KENNETH BRANAGH

PIERCE BROSNAN

HARRISON FORD

RENNY HARLIN

ANGELINA JOLIE

RAFFAELLA DE LAURENTIIS

SIR CHRISTOPHER LEE

GEORGE LEECH

GEORGE LUCAS

ARNOLD SCHWARZENEGGER

MARTIN SCORSESE

RICHARD TODD

and MICHAEL G. WILSON & BARBARA BROCCOLI

CONTENTS

Steven Spielberg, myself and Harrison on the set of Indiana Jones and the Temple of Doom.

INTRODUCTION
By STEVEN SPIELBERG

I have astonishing memories of Vic Armstrong, from the early days of *Raiders of the Lost Ark* right up to *War of the Worlds*. What Vic means to me, and to many of my contemporaries, is his capacity to do the impossible. He can make the wildly improbable seem totally credible. He can perform amazing feats, as well as planning them for other people to do safely.

I'll never forget the scene in *Indiana Jones and the Last Crusade*, one of the most reckless things he ever did. The scene involved a fantastic leap from a galloping horse onto a speeding tank. Like so much of his work, that seemed totally outrageous at the time, and yet he did it himself with what I call courage, but he would simply say nerve!

There were many more great moments in his work on my movies. But one of the greatest came when Harrison Ford suffered a bad back injury in a big fight scene in *Indiana Jones and the Temple of Doom*. It put him out of action for three weeks – and the picture would have ground to a halt if Vic hadn't stepped forward. He stood in for Harrison and saved the picture from a pretty disastrous shut-down.

And of course he's still at it. He was as cool and indomitable as ever on the very complex *War of the Worlds*, where the world seemed to be coming to an end with Vic's help. I remain deeply impressed by his very British cool – a response to any challenge, however difficult or dangerous it might be, that is always casual, easy and amiable. Whatever I ask he sets about it without fuss.

It's no wonder that Vic was given a lifetime achievement award by his peers. He certainly gets another one from me. No CGI can match what Vic can accomplish.

TAKE ONE

For several weeks, five or six times a day, I threw myself onto a manure heap.

I guess I should elaborate a little. I was training a horse to run and hold a straight line, while I stood up on his back at a gallop, and leapt off. I was measuring how far I could leap, and also testing the horse's honesty. I was pretty sure the horse would be reliable, because he was an old friend called Huracán that I had ridden many times before; it was my ability to get the timing right and achieve a constant distance that was the biggest concern.

Cut to two months later and I'm suited up in the famous garb of Indiana Jones, battered jacket, fedora and trusty whip at my side, galloping along looking between Huracán's ears, judging his speed. I get a sudden flashback to when I was nine years old, perched on the back of Roy, my first racehorse, flying up the gallops at home. I settle Huracán down as we race up a slope to arrive parallel with a rumbling, circa WWI tank. We stay at the same pace as this metal monster, and as close to the edge as possible without slipping into the yawning chasm between us. My heart rate picks up as I start counting the horse's stride pattern in my head, 'one, two, three, four...' judging the amount of strides to the position we've agreed is the best spot for the camera to capture the action.

Totally in rhythm, I count the final 'three, four' and in time with the horse's stride I kick my feet out of the regular stirrups, pull my knees up to my chin and crouch momentarily on the stunt stirrups, up by the saddle. On the next beat, which is the 'up' stride for Huracán, I straighten my legs from the squat position and kick as hard as I can sideways. Huracán runs straight as an arrow and I'm airborne... but in a split second I realise I'm in big trouble.

I've mistimed the jump minutely, not getting all of the impetus I needed, and from being a heroic, dashing figure flying through space, I turn into a Tom & Jerry character, bicycling and clawing my way through the air, trying desperately to clear the gap, the revolving tank tracks and certain injury to land any way I can on the machine. I make it – just. Disaster has been averted. But even as I'm getting my breath back, it's time to dust myself off, catch my horse and go for take two.

Welcome to the world of a stuntman.

STARTING GATES

I always feel a broken bone is a failure, but accidents do happen. Over my years as a stuntman I've broken my shin, my arm, my nose and my collarbone, busted my ribs and knackered one heel. The shin was a nasty one. I was in Morocco, and a horse I was riding did a somersault. My stunt friends drove me around Marrakesh to find a hospital and they even had to inject me with morphine. The next thing I knew, I was waking up in a hospital mortuary next to a dead body. The glamorous life of a stuntman, eh?

Movie stunts have been my life for the past 40-plus years, and when I look back on some of the things I did I think I must have been a little crazy, although they were all calculated. I once fell 100 feet off a viaduct for one of the *Omen* films; I've jumped off a 340-foot building on a wire, fallen out of a helicopter onto the side of a mountain, and yes, leapt off a horse onto a moving tank as Indiana Jones.

All the same, it was a sheer accident that I got into the business in the first place, as it is for most stunt people. I originally wanted to be a steeplechase jockey. Since I can remember I've loved horses and before I could even walk I was riding them. My parents owned a donkey and as a baby they used to put me in a Victorian basket saddle that's just like a chair made out of wicker, but with a girth that lets you attach it to the horse or donkey like a saddle. They let the donkey graze in the garden with me on its back. It helped that I grew up in the country, in Farnham Common near Pinewood Studios. I was born at a place called Collingswood nursing home, which is even closer to Pinewood. I guess it was destiny that I ended up working at that famous studio so much.

I inherited this love of horses from my Dad, Robert Armstrong, who was farrier to the British Olympic team from 1948 through five Olympic Games to the Tokyo Olympics in 1964, travelling around the world shoeing Olympic gold medal-winning horses and helping with the training. He was an absolute genius;

At the family home, Hawkins Farm in Farnham Royal, Buckinghamshire.
My sister Diana is in the cage. I think she locked me out for some peace and quiet.

they say he had a rubber hammer because he could shoe any horse without the animal ever getting fractious. Dad had a great way with horses; like the Horse Whisperer, he could touch any horse and it would be calm with him. He became very famous in his field and knew the Queen; he met her lots of times. Mum and Dad got invites to cocktail parties at Windsor Castle with the Queen and Prince Charles and Princess Anne. Dad was also an honorary member of the British Horse Society and a Fellow of the Worshipful Company of Farriers, an honour bestowed on him by the Lord Mayor of London. People all over the world knew him from his travelling with the British Olympic team. He was even a guest on *What's My Line?* once with Eamonn Andrews, and I remember crowding around a tiny television set to watch it.

I still have a memento from those days which was presented to Dad: one of the shoes which Dad had made and nailed on for Foxhunter to wear when he won the Olympic gold medal at the Helsinki games in 1952. It is now chromium plated and mounted on a plaque inscribed 'To Bob Armstrong, without whom we would

I'm about 3 or 4 years old in this photograph.

not have won the gold medal.' Foxhunter and his rider Sir Harry Llewellyn were national heroes back then.

Dad grew up in the Gorbals in Glasgow, Scotland, in incredibly austere times, and then my Granddad came down south during the 1914-1918 war. He was a farrier sergeant major with the remounts, which were the horses that got wounded during the war and were shipped back to England to get patched up, before being sent back to the Somme. He was based at the stables in Datchet in the grounds of Windsor Castle. Granddad then bought a blacksmith shop on the corner of Slough high street, behind the Crown Hotel, and Dad started working there aged nine years old. His first job was shoeing the pair of Oxen that travelled around advertising OXO cubes, because he was the only person small enough to be able to get underneath the Oxen to shoe them. He worked really hard, and eventually he took over the business.

I remember my Dad telling me a story about shoeing this one particular horse when it kicked out before he'd finished – the nail went in the back of his hand and ripped all the tendons out. He looked at the damage, trying to fish out these pieces of what he thought were filings off the horse's foot from the back of his hand, but in fact they were bits of tendon sticking out. He finished shoeing the horse, then cycled from Slough with his hand in the air to try and stop the bleeding, all the way to Windsor hospital where they bent his hand right back to shorten the tendons and stitched them all back together. That's the sort of people they were in those days, tough and hard working.

Dad also used to train with all the top boxers of the day, such as Eric Boon. Dad would run with them in the mornings then go into the blacksmiths and start work while the boxers had a rest. Later in the day the boxers would come into the forge to work with the striking hammer, which is a seven pound hammer, and they would hit the hot iron in rhythm to help them with their punching power.

Mum and Dad were incredible adventurers too and in 1955, when I was nine, they sold all their belongings, uprooted and went to live in Kenya. It was a huge step for a young family; my sister Diana was 11 years old and my brother Andy was just eight months old at the time. A friend of Dad's owned some riding stables out there and wanted him to be a partner and run them. We sailed out from Southampton and went through the Bay of Biscay where everybody was terribly ill because of the mountainous seas. Then we stopped in Aden and saw the local tribe coming out of the desert. We also went through the Suez Canal, and I'll never forget waking up and seeing a camel walking by the porthole of the boat as we were going up through it; amazing memories.

We got off the boat at Mombassa and continued our journey by train through the National Park where you'd see elephants, rhinos and giraffes walking around. Unfortunately, when we arrived at our final stop we discovered that the woman who wanted Dad to work with her was actually going through some kind of mental breakdown and didn't have all the facilities she said she did, it was all pie in the sky. We'd also arrived in the middle of the Mau Mau uprising, terrorists who were trying to drive out the white settlers. Sadly this woman was subsequently murdered. They found her with her arms and legs broken, and think the Mau Mau killed her.

With no work, we lived in the Queen's Hotel in Nairobi for three months, burning up all our savings. Then salvation arrived in the form of the Jockey Club, who were opening the racetrack in Nairobi and wanted Dad to move up country to a little village called Enjuro, to manage 300 racehorses on this huge spread of land. Dad trained them and we shipped the horses down to Nairobi to race every weekend. The remnants of the British Empire were still largely visible, all the tea plantations were still there and even now when I smell wood smoke I'm instantly

*One of our annual family photographs, at Hawkins Farm before we went to Kenya.
I have my treasured air gun that Dad brought back from abroad.*

taken back to Kenya as a nine year-old, and I can still taste the red dust.

It was freezing cold in the mornings and I tried to be like the local kids and walk barefooted, but by ten o'clock you couldn't walk on the ground it was so hot. I got into trouble with my Mum once when I swapped my new leather sandals for a pair of shoes made from car tires that the local kids used to wear. Another time we came home from the races to be met by my sister Diana, who being the only one at the farm was asked by one of the African riders to help him because a horse had stamped on his foot and mangled the toes. Diana did not have any antiseptic so she put toothpaste on the foot and bandaged it and he went off very satisfied.

I certainly believe that this trip ignited the adventurous spirit in me, plus the fact that throughout my childhood Dad was always travelling and he'd bring us sweets and gifts and photographs from all over the world. I've retraced some of his steps. I went to Nice in the South of France and found the old hotel he once stayed at, and where the stables were, and imagined what they were like when he was there with the British Olympic team. So I guess my lifelong love of travelling started as a kid sailing out to Africa, images I can still remember to this day, even though it's over 50 years ago.

The Mau Mau troubles were still going on and neighbouring farms were being destroyed. Dad's friends said he ought to get a gun to defend himself. But even though he was a tough man, Dad was a pacifist and said he couldn't shoot

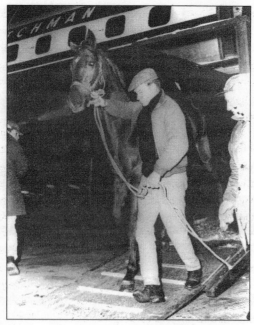

My dad returning home from the Helsinki Olympics, having won the gold medal with Foxhunter.

anybody. Besides, all the black people that worked for us had a great love for Dad and Mum, and while everybody got burnt out around us we were left alone. They were very dangerous times but incredibly exciting, and wonderful for a nine year-old to have no school for a year and just live wild and play with horses and the local kids all day long.

The 1956 Olympics in Sweden were coming up and the British show jumping society called Dad asking him to come back and work for them. It was a big decision to make, should he stay out in Kenya or move everything back to England? We weren't making a lot of money out in Africa so we came back home and basically started again from scratch, which was a huge undertaking. But Dad would always manage to buy somewhere, we'd renovate it and then sell it and move on; it drove my Mum mad because we were always moving from house to house. We used to live out of tea chests, because in those days all your packing was done in tea chests.

While he was shoeing horses and travelling with the British Olympic team Dad loved his racing, buying and selling horses. Dad travelled to many different yards shoeing, and would see a horse they wanted to sell because it was no good or had a bad leg. Dad was a great veterinary blacksmith, he could cure all sorts of ailments with feet; he made some incredible surgical shoes which I've kept as mementoes. So he'd buy these horses very cheaply – we always bought cheap – and correct them with his shoeing, get them better and then race them. He trained all of them himself, getting up an hour early, about four o'clock, before going to work. And he had a few winners, too.

After a while Dad expanded the training side of his business to training other people's horses, and that's how we met Richard Todd. In the 1950s Richard Todd was one of the biggest film stars in the world. I took him back to Pinewood Studios in 2001 when I was preparing *Die Another Day* and the whole place came to a standstill. We went into the restaurant and everybody's head swivelled round as though the Queen had walked in; we couldn't eat for people coming over and shaking his hand. And I was telling him about the Bond film and the plans for the car chase in Iceland and he said, 'Oh, we trained there before the Second World War, doing our arctic training.' When I was filming there, dressed in all the best clothes modern technology could provide, I imagined Richard there with leather boots and canvas windproofs rehearsing arctic warfare. He was actually the first officer to parachute into Arnhem; an amazing character.

RICHARD TODD

I owned a racing stable and Bob Armstrong was our farrier, he was one of the top farriers in Britain. But he was more than just a farrier, he was also a horse master and a good horseman, he understood horses and had a way with them. And from being our farrier he eventually took over the training. He was a super chap, a splendid man. I was a great respecter of Bob's unique skills.

Whilst I knew Bob in all those early years in the '50s and '60s Vic was around with his sister Diana, they were just a couple of kids, and both were horse experts, like their father. I've heard that because I was filming and I always did my own stunts, I never allowed anybody to do a stunt for me, Vic was determined to be a stuntman himself eventually, and it gave him his interest in filming and stunt work. And I watched his career grow to him becoming the leading stuntman in this country.

Richard Todd turned out to be a great patron of Dad's and kept us going for

The Village boys' football team in Marsh Gibbon, Bucks. That's me, bottom left.

years and years bringing over his horses for us to train. And that's when I started dreaming of the movies. Richard Todd would tell us of the films he'd worked on, *Robin Hood, Rob Roy*, and then I'd go and see them. As a kid I used to play cowboys and Indians and throw myself off my ponies, which drove my Dad mad. 'Never throw yourself off a horse,' he'd say. He was a bit like a pilot watching parachutists jumping out of a perfectly good plane. They just could not see the logic in it. I used to go to the movies and recreate what I saw back at home. I rode Richard Todd's horses in all their races as an amateur after that, which was wonderful.

I was always a dreamer, always fantasising and playing games and that's helped me as a stunt co-ordinator. That's all you do when you co-ordinate something, a fight or an action sequence, you fantasise, you play cowboys and Indians, except somebody gives you a few million pounds to do it with, and all the toys and the equipment you need.

Because Dad was always moving around, I ended up going to 23 different schools. I'll never forget we had a horrible maths teacher at this one school. I hated this guy, he was a horrible bastard, and I was bottom of the class; 34 of us and I was bottom. When he left, a new teacher came in that I also did technical drawing with, and I did very well in technical drawing, and the next term I came top in maths. But when this teacher left, the nasty bastard came back and I dropped to 34th again. But that was a great lesson, it proved to me that I wasn't an idiot, that if I put my mind to whatever I wanted to do, I could reach the top.

In those days I just wasn't interested though, because I knew exactly what I wanted to do for a living: I was going to be a steeplechase jockey and that was it. I didn't figure I needed higher education. I think all the travelling I did gave me more of an education than I could ever have got from school anyway. I was a great reader, too. I used to devour the *National Geographic* magazine and books. That was my film training, reading books. I loved visualising what was going on. I had a great imagination and used to write these fantastic stories for my English lessons, which is what I do now, but put them on film.

My life totally revolved around horses. I'd get up at six o'clock to help out at the stables and then cycle to school absolutely pumped up. The other kids coming in had just got out of bed. I felt so much older and so much more advanced than they did. I'd come home for dinner and then it was back to the stables. Weekends were even busier because the jockeys all came down for training sessions with the horses; it was all hands on deck. All this taught me great responsibility. My school mates would go off on weekend trips but I couldn't because I had horses, I had responsibilities, the horses had a training schedule, somebody had to feed them, we couldn't afford anybody else to do it, I would do it.

Working with horses also instilled in me great discipline. I've always been a real disciplinarian and a believer in mind over matter. Even as a kid I was a big lad. When I left school I was six foot plus and used to starve myself to death to get down from 14 stone (210lbs) to ten stone (140lbs) just to ride racehorses (with riding the height doesn't matter, it's just what you weigh), that's getting on for a third of your body weight, but I did it. You force yourself to do these things. It builds character. You force yourself to do things you're frightened of, heights and falls and stunts. It's mind over matter. I think that's what I learnt from working with horses and racing. And it's bred in me, it's in the family; Dad would never give in, he'd always keep going and going. He'd never take time off for illness; the only reason you don't turn up for work is because you're dead. That's why I'm a bit hard on my film crews if somebody doesn't turn up because they've got a runny nose, it's because I come from a different world to them, totally different principles and values.

I was just nine when I rode my first racehorse. At the time we had a little semi-detached house that backed onto the gallops and Mum stood at the end of the garden to watch me. It was on a horse called Roy and I sat perched up on his

At our stables in Sussex. Andy is riding our donkey Harold Wishbone,
and Dad is shoeing Fixture, a horse I later rode in races. I'm about 13 here.

neck staring straight ahead between his ears and just went for it, it was an amazing feeling. After that Roy became my horse to look after, and in the summer holidays we'd go down to the West Country, to Exeter and Newton Abbot in Devon, for race meetings. In the evenings it was a trip to the movies and then a fish and chips supper before going back to sleep in the straw in the horsebox, we couldn't afford a hotel. Then we were up at five working the horses. I used to lead Roy round in the parade ring at the racetrack before the jockey got on, and felt so proud and grown up.

Then at 11 years old an accident almost scuppered any hopes I had of being a jockey. I was out riding a lovely but lively racehorse of Dad's called Bell of Andrum when a pig ran up to a fence and the horse reared up. It was my fault, I hung onto its head and pulled him over backwards and he fell on top of me, bashed me up pretty bad and that scared me from riding racehorses for over a year. Then when I was 12 Dad sold the horse that fell on me, and which so terrified me, to a local guy called Jeff Robinson, who used to help out at our stables when he was a teenager. And that really fired me up to get back into riding. I thought, my God, if he can ride that horse so can I, because I always figured I was streets ahead of Jeff as a rider. And I never looked back after that. I'd ride horses from before dawn till after dusk, not bothering to go to school. The school inspector would visit my Mum at home saying, 'Where is he? He hasn't been at school.' And Mum would say, 'Oh he's got a terrible cold. He's in bed.' Then I'd actually go galloping past the guy in a pack of other riders and he'd think I was a man; I was growing up so fast.

Just before the 1960 Rome Olympics I went with Dad and the British team to Dublin; it was their last big show jumping event before they went off to do the Olympics. During our visit the Ballsbridge sales were on, so Dad and I went to have a look. While we were there a horse came up for sale that went on to become one of the most famous racehorses in history: Arkle.

Right before Arkle in the sale ring was a little broken down horse called Trebor that Dad fancied, but he was beaten in the auction by his good friend Fred Broome, the father of David Broome, the famous show jumper. The Broomes raced Trebor but both of his front legs broke down, the tendons just went, and Dad was able to buy him for £100 (along with a donkey we called Harold Wishbone which my brother Andy learnt to ride on). We kept Trebor all through that winter, starved him down, got him skinny, which lightens the load on the damaged tendons and thins the blood down, and I then hunted with him, which got him really strong and fit.

On 20 March 1960 we went to the Hursley Hunt races at Pit Manor near Winchester; I rode him in the members' race and we just ran away with the race and won. And I won that same race three years running. I was 14 and I'd already ridden my first winner, it was so exhilarating. That's when I decided to leave school, I just didn't go back. After that race there was nothing else in my mind, I wanted to race horses for the rest of my life.

Trebor, which ironically is my Dad's name spelt backwards, was one of the greatest horses I have ever sat on, and it broke my heart when one day after we had finished a race at Exeter he died of a heart attack as I was walking back to the weighing room. It was so typical of his courage to have finished the race when he obviously was not well.

I was coached in race riding by Michael Haines, who was our stable jockey and one of the classiest riders I have ever seen on a racehorse to this day. I think Mick was as excited as I was when I won that first race. I would have loved to have been a professional jockey, but my six foot, one inch frame was against me, so I stayed an amateur.

Soon I was riding regularly in races and it was great because Dad and I worked as a team. I was the rider and he was the guy on the ground and there wasn't a horse that we couldn't work between us, wild young horses, crazy horses that we'd get cheap because they were a handful or had some problem, but we'd train them and race them, because that's all we could afford. I continued to race even when I became a stuntman. My movie pay basically funded our racing. We were a very democratic family – what I have, everybody else has. When I first started driving a car (legally) and wanted to go out one night, the whole family had a whip round to buy a gallon of petrol. And I'll never forget when I first got the opportunity to join the Actor's union Equity and I didn't have enough money to pay the £22 fee, a huge amount in those days, my sister Diana, who had a job at Liberty's store in London, lent me the money. So I grew up with a great respect for money because I knew how hard it was to get and to keep. What money we had was usually spent on the horses. Whenever we bought a new house the first thing that was renovated was the stables.

Unless you've lived and grown up around horses it's difficult to relate to that way of life because you don't actually make any money out of horses. You might sell a horse for more than you paid for it, but it has cost you a bloody fortune to run up until then. You do it for the sheer love of horses. When it gets in your blood, it just consumes your whole life. And you've got to have that passion. I love movies, but horses are my real passion. Any stunt I've done and been proud of doesn't compare with the sensation of galloping into a steeplechase fence with 20 other horses and jockeys thundering along beside you in the environment of a race. It's incredible the rush you get, and the sense of achievement, whether you win or lose, is fantastic.

It's also the association of man and animal, it's working together as a team, it's the danger, it's the noise, it's the whole essence of it, and the competitiveness, just the mixture of everything. Horse racing is like the film business, it's a small community and you're all competitive but you all have respect for each other, even though you also think you're better than each other. I couldn't bear to sell any of my racing saddles, each one has a memory, and they're so dry they'll probably snap if you use them now, but they all have incredible memories. Horses have got me where I am today. I've got nice cars, beautiful homes, all through being able to ride a horse, which isn't bad.

I carried on racing right through into the 1970s in between my film work, and Dad and I would still wheel and deal together, sell and buy horses. One day when I was working on *Superman* I could not lose the usual amount of weight I would

Here I am racing at Horseheath in Cambridgeshire.

have to in order to ride one of our horses in an upcoming race, because of my commitment as Chris Reeve's stunt double. I said to Dad that we needed to find a good amateur jockey to ride this particular horse and Dad turned to me and said, 'For two pins I'd love to ride it myself.' And suddenly the penny dropped – all through those austere years as a blacksmith and training his own horses, he'd have given anything to ride them in a race himself.

He was always a great horseman and taught me so much, such as the gift of having light hands, which would control an unruly horse far better than heavy hands. And when I came into the business as a jockey he was always generous in his encouragement and pride towards me and loved me riding his horses, but deep down he really wanted to do that himself and had never mentioned it once, until that moment when I could tell from his voice that he'd always dreamt of racing. 'Well,' I said, 'why don't you go for it, Dad?' And he went, 'I think I will.' He was 69 years old. He had to go to Weatherbys, the governing body, the licensing people for the jockeys, to have a medical, which he passed with flying colours. In fact the doctor said, 'Good heavens, I wish I was as fit as you and I'm 20 years younger.'

Dad's first race was at Lingfield in Surrey and it made headlines in *The Sporting Life* newspaper because the cumulative age of the horse, jockey and trainer was 124. Because it was a flat race, which needs a special licence, we had the horse in training with a wonderful old lady called Norah Wilmot; she trained horses for the Queen and the Queen Mother and was one of the first women to be granted a trainer's licence by the Jockey Club. And then he rode up at Redcar and was never less than as cool as a cucumber; he wasn't flustered or nervous at all. My heart was thumping like mad!

Dad never retired, he kept on going. He had great strength of character. I saw times when it was rough, not much money and bills to pay, but Dad never worried too much. He'd worry about it inwardly but never worried the rest of the family about it, and we'd always get through it, and we did pretty well in the end. And Mum was always there and supported Dad. She was real salt of the earth, a hard-working woman. Not really a horsy person, she'd had a couple of riding accidents that put her off a little bit. She'd been in the land army during the war and drove a lot. She taught me to drive when I was six years old.

Both Mum and Dad were always very proud of my racing. I think it was the proudest day of Dad's life when I won my first race. And he was tremendously proud of my stunt career. He came out on a couple of movies, he knew the film business pretty well and was proud of what I was doing in it. He didn't like the idea of me falling off horses though. When I broke my leg in Morocco on a film he was a bit worried about that, as I would be. I often think about it now, with kids of my own; I would worry to death if that had happened to them, but both my parents had total trust and faith in my decisions, and that was wonderful.

Dad was the biggest inspiration on my life. His entrepreneurship, the bravery of him going out and trying new things, experimenting with life, his knowledge and the respect people had for him, all of that came together to give me confidence to go and be a stunt co-ordinator and a second unit director. My father reached the top of his profession and that really drove me to want to be the best. When I started in the business I wanted to be the best stuntman in England. And that kind of drive came from Dad. He was the most amazing guy I've ever met and also my best friend.

BREAKING INTO MOVIES

E ven in the crazy world of show business, the leap from steeplechase jockey to movie stuntman is a considerable one. But I'd long fancied the chance to get into films, especially when I heard about the sort of money you could earn, between ten and 15 pounds a day, which was phenomenal. I was earning two pounds a week if I was lucky as a jockey. So it all sounded great.

Back in the '60s Johnny Rock was the country's biggest horse supplier to the film industry, and I was always in and out of his stable yard because Dad used to buy and sell horses from him. One day Rock hired me to drive some horses up to Elstree studios, and that was the first set I remember going on. It was an episode of *The Avengers* (called 'Silent Dust', I think). They were shooting a hunting sequence and these stunt guys had to do a fight rolling under the horses that I'd brought over. I watched and was fairly disgusted. 'Is that horse safe?' they whined. 'Is he going to kick me?' I thought, who are these wallies? I can do that ten times better. And that's probably what spurred me on.

Later I heard that Johnny Rock's stables were being used to audition stuntmen for the Charlton Heston epic *Khartoum*, so I trawled over, more out of hope than expectation. And so it proved. No one was going to hire a raw rookie on so prestigious a production. But it really frustrated me that most of the guys going were just regular stuntmen and not riders. Then the lucky break arrived courtesy of a family friend, Jimmy Lodge.

Jimmy was the best riding stuntman around, and was hard at work on a spy film called *Arabesque* with a bunch of horses, hired from the 'top' horse supplier at the time, that as far as I was concerned were straight out of Southall market; useless old dogs. They were supposed to jump gates and hedges while being chased through fields by helicopters and Land Rovers with people firing machine guns at them and these things couldn't even jump over their own shadow. In fact

Just starting out on my journey as a stuntman.

Pam de Boulay, the stuntwoman doubling Sophia Loren, broke her knee when her horse refused to jump a two-foot fence and slammed her into the gatepost. So Jimmy phoned me up in absolute desperation asking to borrow one of our horses, to which I agreed, and then called again saying he had a job for me as a rider doubling one of the leads. I went down there and started riding and that was it, I'd landed my first film, at £20 a day, fantastic. I met Gregory Peck and Sophia Loren, who were icons in those days.

As well as stunt doubling, one of my jobs was to hold the horse while the stars did their close-ups. Peck was in the saddle with Sophia holding on behind. Crouching down out of camera range I led the horse in, but it started bucking because Sophia was basically sitting bareback behind the saddle on its kidneys. Pulling up, Sophia looked at me. 'Veek, Veek, why is the horse bucking?' And without thinking I replied, 'Sophia, if you were riding me bareback I'd be bucking, too!' Oh no, what have I said? Luckily she burst out laughing. 'Naughty, naughty, naughty.' I just said it out of the blue. I couldn't stop myself. But she was absolutely gorgeous Sophia, just breathtaking.

After that experience I thought, this is the life for me, I can work on movies and in between jobs carry on racing and one would finance the other. So I looked for advice from people I knew in the film business, but they all shut the door, nobody wanted me in it. It's a notoriously tough business to break into and that hasn't changed in 40 years. Thank God Jimmy Lodge gave me my start.

So I went up to London thinking, the only way I'm going to get on in this game is to have an agent. In the mid-'60s there was only one stunt agency, HEP, originally formed by Frank Howard, Rupert Evans and Joe Powell. Tragically Frank Howard was killed on a movie in Morocco when a horse rolled over him, so his wife Gabby ended up running the agency and I became the youngest stuntman on their books. My greatest asset then was my youth. I was the young kid on the block. You'd go to auditions and line up against a wall with all these old stunt guys and the actor would walk in and see me and say to the director, 'Oh, I think the young man on the left is the best double for me.' You might not look anything like them but their egos kick in. So I got a lot of work very quickly.

Back in the '50s the majority of stuntmen came from a military background, they'd been commandos and the like in the war, and weren't really classified as stuntmen, just glorified extras who did the odd bit of riding and stunt work. Then people like Joe and Eddie Powell, George Leech, Bob Simmons, Jock Easton, Ken Buckle, Alf Joint, Paddy Ryan and others built up reputations and started getting paid extra for stunt work, but still a pittance compared to America, where it had begun much earlier and in a much bigger way. Cut to the '60s, and nobody new was coming in apart from the odd mini cab driver, ex-boxer and doorman drafted in to play a heavy and be in a fight, so they became stuntmen. But that's all it was in those days. So when I arrived in 1965 there was nobody else in the stunt business except this old brigade. I was really one of the first of a whole new generation, along with people like Rocky Taylor, Martin Grace, Bill Weston and Marc Boyle.

Pretty soon I'd set myself the target of becoming the top stuntman at the HEP agency. Gabby was terrific with me, getting auditions, introducing me to the right people, and jobs quickly came along. I'll never forget one of them. It was for a TV show and I had to double this guy vaulting over a 12-foot chain link fence. The director yelled 'Action' and I ran, took one jump, hit the fence halfway, bounced over the top and was gone (like a early version of Parkour). The director was astonished that somebody could fly over a fence as easy as that, so didn't need another take, and wrapped. In those days you were paid on the day in cash and I got seven pounds, ten shillings. 'I thought I was on £15 for the day,' I said. 'Yes, but we finished by lunch time so we only have to give you half.' I phoned Gabby, who was livid. 'They contracted you for a day and you should get all the money.' She eventually managed to get my other seven pounds, ten shillings out of the company. Great lady, Gabby; she was very sweet and whenever I was in her office hustling for work she would always reminisce and tell me how much I reminded her of her Frank.

Other small jobs followed until, early in 1966, I was sent along for an audition at the old MGM studios in Borehamwood. It was for a First World War picture called

The Bells of Hell Go Ting-a-Ling-a-Ling, again starring Gregory Peck and financed by the Mirisch Corporation, who were behind such hits as *The Magnificent Seven* and *The Pink Panther*. I was to double for Ian McKellen (now Sir Ian of course) in his screen debut. 'You're perfect,' they said. 'But we're waiting to see one more stuntman.' I came back an hour later and he still hadn't showed; another hour, still no show. Third hour there was a heavy bang on the door and this guy walked in, who has been a lifelong friend ever since, and godfather to my eldest son Bruce, Bill Weston. He had long hair and a scruffy beard and looked like the wild man of Borneo, and here we were supposed to be doubling clean-cut young pilots. 'I'm terribly sorry I'm late,' he boomed. 'Just got in from the Bahamas, been crewing a yacht out there.' The producers stared with incredulity at him, trying to visualise what he looked like without half a haystack of hair. Old Bill said, 'If you give me the job I'm willing to shave it off.' And he held up a razor in one hand and a shaving stick in the other. 'We'll let you know,' said the producers.

Outside Bill introduced himself and cadged a lift back to Slough train station. 'I think you've got the job,' he suddenly announced. I wasn't so certain, this being my first big audition. 'I can't do it anyway,' he went on. 'I'm up for this thing called *2001: A Space Odyssey.*' Arriving home the phone rang and I was told the job was mine. Bill was right. Even better, it was ten weeks in Switzerland at £75 a week. I was really excited.

The Bells of Hell Go Ting-a-Ling-a-Ling was about an Allied mission to carry aeroplanes which had been dismantled in parts small enough to fit into horse-drawn hay carts through German occupied territory, where they would be reassembled in order to bomb enemy targets, namely the Zeppelin bases in Friedrichshafen. Believe it or not it was all based on a true story. And the budget matched its epic scope. I flew out to Switzerland on an old charter plane from Gatwick, propeller job. I had no money at all and had to borrow a pound off my Dad to buy the duty free cigarettes. I didn't know anybody either and was totally green about the movie business, but a guy named Eddie Powell quickly took me under his wing. Eddie was famous as Christopher Lee's stunt double on the Hammer horror pictures and was also Peck's regular double. He was a lovely man.

When the picture started it was quickly apparent that it was doomed from the outset. It rained, it snowed and the weather forecasts were horrendous; everything went wrong. One day we drove these vintage trucks up a mountain to wait for a camera helicopter to do some aerial shots of us, but by dusk it hadn't arrived and as we drove back down into the valley the assistant director John Peverall met us. 'It's a wrap guys,' he said. 'We know it's a wrap,' we answered back. 'We can hardly see our hands in front of our faces.' He said, 'No, they've cancelled the whole movie.' The Mirisch brothers had come out to see what was going on. We only had a minute of footage to show them for almost seven weeks' work and as they sat watching it the projector broke down, so they said, 'That's it, pull the plug.' The next day everyone was flying back to London. The film never got finished. Nevertheless, it was an important film for me because not only was it my first location, I also met many people that would be influential on my career, people like Paul Ibbetson who was the 3rd assistant director, Basil Appleby the production manager and many more that employed me over the years. It certainly made me aware of the importance of networking.

THE FIRST NINJA

Back in London I phoned Bill Weston to tell him how the Swiss job went. His reply was typical Bill. 'I've got a contract here which you can have. I can't do it.' He was doubling Keir Dullea on *2001* and it was going on forever, while meanwhile this movie at Pinewood was underway called *You Only Live Twice*. 'All you do is just go up there and tell them you're replacing me.' I couldn't believe it. 'Fantastic Bill. Thanks a million.'

I tore up to Pinewood and was directed to the back lot, where the famous 007 stage stands today. Back then it was just barren ground, out of which had temporarily sprouted a mass of scaffolding so high it could be seen from the main London-Oxford road some three miles away. Within the construction was a masterpiece of set design, a volcano rocket base; the new headquarters of Blofeld and SPECTRE, where the explosive climax to the new James Bond epic was to take place. I was gobsmacked. Inside it was like the Albert Hall. I haven't seen a set to this day as big as that one. It had its own monorail, a helicopter could fly in and out and the roof slid back. It was phenomenal. My jaw hit the floor. I met legendary action co-ordinator Bob Simmons, who was hiring people to be the ninjas who attack this base. Pointing up to the roof he said, 'We want somebody to slide down there on a rope firing a gun, think you can do that?' I said, 'Piece of cake.' Bob smiled. 'All right, you've got the job.' I thought, this is going to be fantastic.

Virtually every stuntman in England had been brought in for this battle sequence, and others besides. There were mini cab drivers, strong-arm men, drug dealers, spivs, everyone you could think of – real tearaways, but fantastic characters. They brought in girls by pretending they were holding auditions for the next Bond movie and filmed them doing the most outrageous things. And they got away with it! You'd be locked up and they'd throw away the key these days.

The first thing everyone had to learn was how to slide down 125 feet from the roof ninja-style, land safely, un-sling their guns and start firing. Bob Simmons came up with this great idea of using a piece of rubber hose that we could squeeze on the rope like a brake shoe to slow the fall. To reduce the friction and try and keep the rubber cool, I used to put talcum powder inside the pipe, but you went *really* fast at the beginning of the drop until the talc burnt off! Because I was still racing horses my power to weight ratio was tremendous, so I used to roar down and stop at the last minute. But some of these guys were overweight or not strong enough. On one take this guy came hurtling down, whoosh, and straight into the ground. The director yelled, 'Cut, cut!' The gunfire stopped, the dead people got up and went back to their starting positions, all except this one guy who was still moaning, 'Arghhh.' I thought, he's a good actor. We walked over and he'd broken both ankles. The poor fellow was in agony.

Handling the descent was easy for me; it was getting up there in the first place that caused the biggest problem. I didn't like heights in those days and to reach the top of the set you had to climb ladders and scaffolding, which took you ten minutes. Once you were up there it was scary as hell, scrambling along girders, bent over and just three feet below the roof, to get to your drop position, holding onto the rope, just your toes on the girder, with 125 feet of space below you and your arse just hanging out over nothing. Plus you weren't attached to any safety lines climbing out there or when you came down. When you finally got to your position, if you let go of the rope or slipped, you were a goner.

With the master shots completed Bob Simmons selected 20 of the best stuntmen to handle the more difficult task of zooming down one-handed whilst firing a machine gun. I was amongst the team. Whereas before it was pure strength that held you onto the rope, this time we were attached by a metal device that when pulled on the rope sliding through your hand it slowed your fall. One of the stunt guys, an ex-paratrooper called Tex Fuller, was asked to demonstrate this gadget, which was called a descendeur, at his parachute regiment's annual reunion in a village hall. He was on a beam ready to slide down when this thing snapped from metal fatigue and he fell ten foot onto the deck. 'Oh my God,' he said. 'I was 125 foot up this morning doing this.' We all were!

It was discovered these aluminium devices were dangerous because they'd get invisible fractures in them, so ultimately they were junked. The next day at work while we were all discussing the prospect of having to go up onto the girders again with these now suspect devices, one of the stunt guys said that he had heard of these new devices called figure eights. So being the youngest I was sent off to

As one of the ninjas in You Only Live Twice. *That's me coming down first.*

Thomas Black's, the climbing shop in Gray's Inn Road in London, to try and find some of these new tools. I bought all the figure eights that they had in the shop and came back to Pinewood triumphantly. The figure eights were thin pieces of metal in the shape of an eight that were much safer than the old descendeur, but bear little resemblance to the thick alloy figure eights that are around today. Ours were so thin that when they got hot sliding down, they would burn through the rope if you did not disconnect them immediately.

Joe Powell, another legendary stuntman, was our team leader and he took responsibility for tying our ropes onto the girders. He had a wicked sense of humour and you could hear him muttering under his breath – deliberately loud enough for you to hear – as he tied the knot, 'Is it left over right, or back again, or under there? Oh, that will be all right I think!' And all this while you are hanging onto a cold and slippery girder 125 feet in the air, about to entrust your life to that knot when you launched yourself off.

By far my biggest job in movies to date, *You Only Live Twice* was a massive learning curve for me, just being around so many stuntmen like Joe Powell, Richard Grayden, George Leech, Rupert Evans, Paddy Ryan, Peter Brace, Gerry Crampton, Bill Cummings, Jack Cooper, Eddie Eddon, Tim Condren and many more, soaking up their experience and how they went about things. I learnt so much from Bob Simmons, the way he delegated by forming us all into little groups with team leaders taking on responsibility, so he only had to deal with a few people. It was a very simple way of working, but nobody had ever done it before and few do it even to this day. But it was the way I used to think as well and I've used that system ever since. That volcano battle was a huge co-ordinating job and my hat went off to Bob Simmons. I was so awe-struck by it. And I've always kept how Bob handled that sequence in my mind whenever I do big movies. It's certainly stood me in good stead. It was a golden key.

On that movie I also caught my first sighting of a star I'd work with many times in the future, Sean Connery. But I was nobody in those days and movie stars often walked on rarefied air away from the workers. So I never met Sean face to face back then. He was just God, being brought in and out of the set like the Pope arriving at the Vatican for a service. In he'd come in his little cart and then whizz out again, only stopping for a few Hail Marys.

Even today when I see that volcano sequence I get a huge kick out of knowing that the first ninja coming down guns blazing is me. I also bought my first car with the £90 I earned as a stunt adjustment for sliding down the ropes on that film. (A stunt adjustment is the extra money you get paid for performing a particular stunt, over and above your normal wages.) The car in question was a Ford Anglia 105E, like Harry Potter's car. I was so proud of it and kept it for years. I'll never forget that old car, and when you think our wages were £65 a week, it was a lot of money. Now every time I go and negotiate a fee, I remember those days when the most I could ever afford for a car was £90.

STUNTMAN FOR HIRE

Following *You Only Live Twice* I picked up small bits of work on other large studio movies. Terry Marcel, who I had worked with on *The Bells of Hell...* called me to work on *The Assassination Bureau*, which was a delightful period romp with Telly Savalas and Diana Rigg, fresh from *The Avengers*. I had to get hit in the head by this block-and-tackle swung by Oliver Reed and fall into a gondola dock. In make up I dozed off and waking up there was this young lady sitting in the chair next to me, with her feet up. It was Diana. Wow. Her legs were as long as mine and I'm six foot one! A very sexy lady.

It was horses next, literally hundreds of them for *Mayerling*, an historical drama with Omar Sharif and Catherine Deneuve. A bunch of stunt guys, Tim Condren, Bill Weston, Martin Grace, Reg Harding, Roy Street, Peter Pocock, Barry de Boulay and myself, were called out to Vienna for five days but ended up staying nearly four weeks because the film's major set piece, the Hapsburg army's clash with rioting students, took so long to shoot due to the freezing weather. I was a cavalryman and my mate Peter Pocock was a student who had to dive off this statue and bulldog me; that's when you're hit and taken off a horse. The ground was frozen solid and so were the crash pads. I was notorious for always missing them anyway. So Pete jumped me and I landed so hard it knocked a filling out of my tooth. The weather got so bad we spent more time partying than riding horses. There were hundreds of extras just hanging around freezing to death. I'll never forget sitting next to Barry de Boulay, this wonderful old stunt guy who'd been a Motor Torpedo Boat commander in the war, and seeing an icicle hanging off his nose.

Then it was over to Pinewood for *Chitty Chitty Bang Bang*, the classic family picture brought to the screen by 007 producer Albert R. Broccoli. I was one of the Child Catcher's cavalrymen, and on the castle turret with a big old cannon in the scene where they're trying to shoot down Chitty as it flies past. They built a replica

An early publicity photograph, trying to endear myself to prospective employers.

of mad King Ludwig's famous Neuschwanstein castle at the back of the studio and I actually went over and tapped the wall because I couldn't believe it wasn't real. It was amazing. But this was a massively expensive production. I remember when the stage version opened in the West End we were filming *Die Another Day* and two coach loads of us came down from Pinewood to the opening night. 'Of course, I was in the original movie,' I told them. 'You what!?' They couldn't believe it.

While undoubtedly these were big movies, the jobs on them didn't last long and generally work was thin on the ground. So I was carrying on with my other career as an amateur steeplechase jockey. But I'd always be on the lookout for film auditions. At the time I was living about five miles from Pinewood, and a mile from where I was born. I've always been based around the same area and as luck would have it that was close to the studios. So I'd pop in occasionally to see what was going on. Every Friday lunchtime at the bar in Pinewood there was an unofficial stuntman's club. You'd walk in and there would be a dozen stuntmen in there all punting for work.

A few jobs did trickle in, but in very hit-and-miss movies that nevertheless provided valuable experience and a good quota of laughs. *Subterfuge* was a bog-standard spy thriller. The stunt co-ordinator was Derek Ware, later famous for his stunt team HAVOC who did action sequences for *Doctor Who* in the '70s. He called me in to drive a motorbike and sidecar. Fine, except I'd never ridden a motorbike and sidecar in my life, just motorbikes. Nowadays with health and safety regulations I'd have to sign a dozen forms before they'd even let me near the thing. Back then nobody asked any questions and nobody was around to teach you these things. You just did it. The business has changed so much. So I just kept quiet. My passenger was Derek Martin, then a stuntman but later an actor (he's now best known as Charlie Slater on the TV soap *EastEnders*). Because I could ride motorbikes I thought I must be all right with sidecars, but they're terrible things, you lean one way and they flip over on you. The scene called for us to run and jump into the motorbike and take off fast. So I really opened this thing up and it started veering all over the place as I alternately shut down and opened up the throttle trying to get control. It was hysterical. I'll never forget Derek hanging inside for dear life, looking up at me asking, 'Have you ever done this before?' I could only answer, 'No!' He wasn't too impressed.

Vehicles were part of my next job too, but the stakes were considerably higher. *The Chairman* was an action thriller starring Gregory Peck and directed by J. Lee Thompson, who had films like *The Guns of Navarone* and *Cape Fear* to his credit. But I remember him as an incredibly nervous character that used to get call sheets and tear them up into little strips all day long. Better than biting your fingernails or smoking I guess. Again I was over at Pinewood's back lot and thrilled to be doing my first big vehicle stunt, because it all added to your resume. I had to crash a truck into a wall and bail out before it burst into flames. Doing crashes is actually very difficult because it goes against all your instincts. That's why racing drivers don't necessarily make great stunt people, because in stunt work you have to do everything against your better nature and judgement. And in those days you had to consider the guy that supplied the truck who's going, 'Don't hit it too hard because I can't get the spare parts any more.' While the director's saying, 'Crash, bang, wallop it!'

From big budget to no budget at all with my next assignment: *Zeta One*, a bit of science fiction hokum about some girls from outer space who are like the sirens on the rocks and entice men by wearing lingerie and suspender belts and then beat the crap out of them. It was as weird as it sounds, and really cheap. But in those days you were very grateful to get the work. I was teamed up again with Peter Pocock, with whom I'd also worked on the filmed inserts for TV's *Not Only, But*

Also, with him doubling Dudley Moore and myself doubling Peter Cook. We did a whole season of those and had a great time. He was a real extrovert was Peter Pocock, and also something of a ladies' man in his day. In this scene for *Zeta One* we were dressed as gamekeepers, a bit *Lady Chatterley's Lover*-esque, trying to hunt these women down. Peter had to crawl through some bushes and stick his head out. Looking left he saw a leg, looking right another naked leg and then clunk, the legs crushed his head and he had to turn and look up, basically right up this girl's crotch. Peter got so embarrassed he couldn't do it. And here was this suave ladies' man in real life. God, it was funny.

Years later, I had a builder working on my house and when I came in he said with reverence, 'Hello Mr Armstrong, I saw one of your films last night,' so I stuck my chest out and said, 'Oh great,' thinking it would be a Bond or something, and he said '*Zeta One*'! My chest deflated.

BOND ON ICE

My next movie was a real breakthrough and came about purely by luck. I was visiting my Dad's farm and parking the car when the phone rang. 'We're looking for Vic Armstrong,' a voice said. 'Yeah, that's me,' I said. 'Are you available next week?' I went, 'Yeah.' 'OK, we'll get back to you.' I put the phone down thinking, great, I've got a job. That night they called again. 'You're flying out Tuesday to Switzerland.' 'What's the movie?' I asked. 'It's Bond.' I realised I was just an A on their list. If I hadn't been there to answer the phone, they would've gone to the Bs, Cs or Ds. There's so much luck involved in this business.

The film was *On Her Majesty's Secret Service* and I found myself doubling the brand new James Bond, George Lazenby. I only went out to Switzerland for two weeks to do the climactic raid on Piz Gloria, Blofeld's Alpine base, where we all jump out of helicopters firing guns, but I wound up staying on with the second unit for months; fabulous. The biggest problem we encountered out in Switzerland was the awful weather. It just snowed and snowed and the second unit shot nothing for weeks. I suppose the second unit director got the blame for the inclement weather (it must be someone's fault!) so they fired him and got a new second unit director, John Glen, and when he arrived the weather behaved and we started shooting. It was fate. Glen would later direct five consecutive Bond movies, a record unlikely ever to be broken.

The ski sequences in *Secret Service* are superb and a lot of that is down to Luki 'Lucky' Leitner, who doubled Lazenby. You see him going down a mountain on one ski and jumping off chalet roofs; amazing stuff. And what a playboy! I love people like that – they're larger than life. The crew stayed at the tiny village of Mürren, perched on the side of the Schilthorn mountain. I remember once when we were up the Schilthorn we'd been snowed out all day, and by late afternoon, with no chance of shooting, it was a wrap. We started drinking hot Glüwein, and

Playing one of Blofeld's henchmen in O.H.M.S.S.
From L-R George Cooper, Eddie Stacey, Reg Harding and me. Eddie and I are the only two still around.

in this stupid moment I said, 'Come on Lucky, I'll race you down.' He went, 'Ja,' then stood up and did not appear as drunk as I hoped he was. Shit, I shouldn't have said that. Now I've challenged this world champion skier to a race. But I'm thinking, how much can he beat me by on a gentle slope like this?

We lined up and someone began the countdown. 'Three… two…' Lucky put his hand up. 'Wait a minute,' he said, and turned around to face the other way. I knew I was in trouble then. 'OK, here we go, three… two…' Again Lucky stopped the count, this time he took one of his skis off. Oh shit, I thought. 'Three… two… one, go!' Skiing as fast as I could I was just aware of this thing going whoosh past me, three times faster. How he got the speed racing backward on one ski I don't know, but he kept up the pace all the way down to the bottom. I was completely out of control and crashed into the ticket shed for the ski lift and all the snow came off the roof – everyone thought it was an avalanche. And there was Lucky laughing at me; great days.

Besides doubling Lazenby in some of the fights, I performed the stunt at the end of the big ski chase when Bond ends up hanging over the edge of a cliff. I was going to be secured by a safety cable but watching a previous stunt, which used cable from the same roll, gave me second thoughts. Joe Powell nearly got killed doubling Telly Savalas as Blofeld in the bobsleigh where his head hits a forked tree and rips him off the sled. They put a snatch-back cable on Joe but at the crucial moment it broke and Joe crashed head-long into the tree branch across the track, and then went sprawling back onto the track, cracking his head on the ice and sliding unconscious down the bob run. Everybody panicked, but all I was thinking was, when they tie that cable round my leg to go over this cliff I hope the bloody thing doesn't snap again.

Perhaps the worst thing about the whole stunt was the fact that I couldn't walk out to see over the edge because you couldn't have footprints in the virgin snow. It was going to be a leap of faith, almost. I prepared myself, hooked the cable round my ankle and ran like hell, hurtling into space. As I neared the precipice, the layer of snow beneath me gave way and I dropped suddenly, a few feet more than planned, but I thought it was the cable that had broken because all I saw was this 1500-foot sheer drop. That was a real heart-stopping moment.

After climbing back and gaining his composure, Bond is disturbed by one of Blofeld's thugs and a vicious fight takes place resulting in the baddie being thrown to his death. Along with all the physical action in the film, George Leech choreographed this. With the unavailability of resident Bond stunt arranger Bob Simmons, the obvious replacement was George, who'd worked on all five previous Bond movies as Simmons' assistant and knew the job backwards. That was the first time I'd worked with George and the first time I'd really rehearsed a proper fistfight. I learnt a lot from him doing that, and funnily enough years later he became my father-in-law because my second wife, Wendy, is his daughter.

GEORGE LEECH

I had to pick a dozen stuntmen for *Secret Service* and Vic was one of them. I picked them and I was responsible for them and being stunt arranger on that movie was like being in charge of a gang of unruly schoolboys. A phone call came through from the office one day. 'Please control your men. One is climbing the Eiger, another is skiing across a table while hotel guests are having breakfast and Lazenby is shooting at animals on the Alps with a pistol and driving the insurance people and producers mad.' I said, 'You can't keep a gang of virile men sitting on their arses waiting.'

Since that film I've seen Vic progress and he's progressed all the time, using his experience to good effect. If Vic were weak on any

Filming the stock car race sequence. I think I just made it out in time before the thing blew up. Well, in the movie anyway!

subject, like boxing, he would get a professional guy to train him. On *Secret Service* that was George Cooper, and they'd have sparring sessions in order for Vic to brush up on that activity. He's always learning and challenging himself. I think that's the key to his success.

Apart from George Leech and Lucky Leitner, I met other big personalities on that shoot. Lazenby was very good, very professional about his job. And Cubby Broccoli was a lovely guy too. He'd see us off at five o'clock every morning on the cable car going up to the top of the Schilthorn, just to give us a bit of moral support. The film was a memorable experience all round. One day, shooting just beneath the Eiger we became aware of another film crew in the next valley and skied over to discover it was Robert Redford making *Downhill Racer*. Evenings were fun, too. Every night we had champagne, woke up with the most atrocious hangovers and then went to work. Christ, in your twenties you could do it standing on your head. Great party picture that one.

Besides the fun and thrill of doing a Bond movie, being associated with 007 brings huge kudos. Coming back home the industry grapevine is alerted to the fact you've done a Bond, and work seems somehow easier to come by. It needed to be, as the British film industry was about to face one of its recurring recessions. It was going to be survival of the fittest.

SURVIVING THE RECESSION

The industry was in the doldrums as the '60s drew to a close and the 1970s rolled in. The big American companies who'd bankrolled British films in their mid-'60s heyday had gone, and taken their money with them. Big movies were still being made in the UK but far fewer of them, so to be working you had to be the cream of the crop because everybody was available. To help my job prospects I produced some photographs with my contact details. I'd noticed at Equity actors handing them out, so I thought why not stuntmen. It seemed an obvious idea, except I was the first one to do it. They featured a montage of stunt and portrait shots and I'd send them to producers and studios. I got great feedback, people would ask, 'Which film is that stunt from?' As a result they got me a lot of work. Then that work got me more work and it snowballed. So I got a reputation very, very quickly.

One of those jobs was to go out to Ireland for *Alfred the Great*, an historical epic starring David Hemmings and Michael York. I hopped into my trusty Ford Anglia and sped off to the Emerald Isle, chosen for its trademark bogs, but then experiencing the hottest summer in living memory. We ended up spraying the ground green because it was all burnt brown like Spain. You'd do a stunt fall off a horse and come up with green paint all over you. But *Alfred the Great* was a big film. It's a piece of rubbish, but it was a big, big film in its day. I ended up doubling Michael York and doing loads of saddle falls. I was working alongside Jimmy Lodge and so I learnt an awful lot. It was a good experience.

Unfortunately while in Ireland I missed out on a chance to be in one of the all-time great British films, *The Italian Job*. Because of my experience driving horse trucks, the producers wanted me to drive the coach that in the famous climax crashes and hangs over the edge of the mountain. Ironically I left *Alfred the Great* prematurely anyway with Jimmy Lodge to go straight onto another picture, *Hell Boats*, filming in Malta, working under stunt co-ordinator Joe Powell. This was a

Working on Hammer's Twins of Evil. *I'm fourth from the right, planning the next shot.*

Boy's Own Paper-style war adventure and I was hired because I was a good physical double for American star Jimmy Franciscus. Plus I was blond so I could play plenty of Germans running around and getting shot. I actually killed myself in one scene. I played the guy that fired the gun and the other bloke that got the bullet and died. That's the movies for you.

In amongst the big movies was straightforward bread-and-butter stunt work, for example a day horse riding on *The Vampire Lovers* for the famous Hammer company. I love watching those old Hammer horror movies. They were done superbly well. In fact I did another one for them about a year later, *Twins of Evil*. That was a fun movie, real gothic stuff. It has stayed lodged in my memory because of the cast – not Peter Cushing, but two stunning real-life twins, real sexy girls and former *Playboy* models, Madeleine and Mary Collinson. They were gorgeous little things. I remember a mate of mine went out with one of them, I couldn't believe it. I was so jealous. But that movie is also quite important to me because it was the first time I'd seen prosthetics used (although the technique has been around forever).

In one scene a guy gets his arm chopped off and what they did was find a real amputee, stick a false forearm on him, nail it to this pike he was holding and then slash it off. I was very impressed and it's stuff I used later in *Gangs of New York*, so it stayed with me all those years. The old techniques are the best. But it's far trickier than you might think because you have to hit exactly the right spot, otherwise you'd cut into his real arm. I've seen that done a few times. So even something as relatively simple as hacking an arm off, you have to get the timing and positioning just right, and the guy has to react realistically, as if his arm really *has* been cut off. That's what it's all about, selling those moments to the audience.

DAVID LEAN

I t's always the same in this business: you hang around doing nothing waiting for a job but the minute you book a holiday or something you're guaranteed a film will come along. I was about to get married to my first wife Jane and, sod's law, I suddenly got a call to go to Ireland for two weeks on *Ryan's Daughter*, to work on what became the famous storm sequence. It was September and as I wasn't getting married till the end of November I thought there shouldn't be a problem. David Lean had already shot the storm sequence, it was the first thing he did on the movie, but now he thought it was very weak and wanted to re-do it. So off I flew to Ireland.

Anyway, those two weeks turned into a month, then six weeks, and then two months. The first unit upped and left to go to South Africa to shoot beach scenes with Sarah Miles. We stayed on. In all I was there nearly five and a half months! We wouldn't even go to work unless a force ten gale was forecast; amazing. And we had wind machines going full blast, too. It was absolutely horrendous. We'd spend our days sitting in trailers playing poker, waiting for the right gale. Five and a half months for that one sequence and it was the second time around, but what a sequence. So I got married in between it all. And the crew, who had been there over a year, had married local people and were having babies. Complete madness.

My wife Jane was an accomplished horsewoman, which is how we met as she lived next door to me in Farnham Common, and we had two great sons together, Bruce and Scott. Sadly Jane and I later parted, through no fault of hers.

Lean's meticulousness is legendary, but for that storm on *Ryan's Daughter* it reached near-lunatic proportions. Sometimes the crew would spend all morning just rigging one little set-up. But seeing Lean at close quarters I couldn't help but be impressed. He was so elegant, like a God. When I think back on those days we did treat the Leans of the movie world like icons. The whole business was different, the pecking order was different, there was the aristocracy (which was the stars, the producers, and the directors), and then you had the workers. Now it's much more democratic; and if I'm honest, not as good really.

Lean had a prop man called Eddie Fowlie – or foul Eddie as he was affectionately known – he did *Lawrence of Arabia* and Lean loved him, gave him his Rolls Royce. One day on *Ryan* they were setting up the aftermath of the storm, putting washing-up liquid in the waves so they'd get this foam. Eddie was walking up and down the beach doing nothing in particular, but all the time looking over his shoulder in case Lean turned up. I just happened to be watching. Even in those days I loved observing what was going on. Suddenly Eddie did a double take and dove straight into the water and started working furiously. I was then aware of this entourage approaching. 'Eddie, what on Earth are you doing?' It was Lean. 'Just sorting all this out, somebody's got to bloody do it,' said Eddie. 'You're wet through! Go back to the hotel man and have a warm bath.' 'No, it's all right guv, don't worry.' 'I insist,' commanded Lean. 'I'm not going to shoot a foot of film until you're off this set.' 'Oh all right, guv.' Off Eddie went, and I thought, there's one who knows how to play the game. I have subsequently worked with Eddie on many movies, and he is still a great character.

HOW TO FALL OUT OF A HELICOPTER

Figures in a Landscape was an odd, gritty drama directed by Joseph Losey about two men, played by Robert Shaw and Malcolm McDowell, on the run from the local militia in a nondescript country. Though it sunk without a trace upon release it was another breakthrough for me because it was my first ever stunt co-ordinating job – only three years after I'd started.

Getting the job in the first place was a total fluke. I was visiting Peter Pocock and he was on the phone to this Hollywood producer, John Kohn. 'No I can't do it, I'm doing *Cromwell*.' I grabbed Peter's attention. 'I'll do it.' But he shook his head. 'They want me to double this really short actor.' I said, 'I'm not that tall.' So Peter arranged the interview for me and I shot up to London, cut the heels off my shoes, bent my knees, all to look as short as I could, and ended up as Malcolm McDowell's double. It was only his second movie, just after *If....* The next thing I knew Jane and I were driving down to the location in Malaga, Spain, and in the hotel there was Robert Shaw, wearing a cravat and looking very smart. Next to him was McDowell. Introducing myself, Shaw laughed and turned to Malcolm, who had this sort of squashed face, and said, 'Good God, look, the bloody stunt double's better looking than the actor!' which was rather embarrassing to say the least.

Jimmy Lodge was our stunt co-ordinator, but halfway through he left to work on *Kelly's Heroes* and I managed to persuade the producers to allow me to take over. Having worked on the Bond movies I knew a little about what to do because I was like a sponge in those days, absorbing information. As well as co-ordinating the show, including arranging all the fight scenes, I carried on performing stunts. I must have doubled everybody.

In one scene Bob Shaw shoots me off a church roof. One of the toughest things about doing stunts is negotiating fees. I learnt on this film to get the negotiator to see the stunt from your perspective, because if he's below looking up he thinks, that's not very high, but stand him on top of the roof looking over the edge, and it's suddenly very different. So I was on top of this church, lining up my fall into a heap of boxes, when our assistant director Dave Tringham arrived to have a look and lark about. Suddenly he looked down, and dropped to his hands and knees going, 'Jesus Christ, get me down!' Before helping him off I said, 'While we're up here Dave, we should talk about the money.' 'Yeah, whatever you want!' So I got £25. I was on £120 a week, but this was the bonus 'stunt adjustment.'

Doing big pressurised stunts like high falls for the first time, it's almost so you can say 'done that' and you tick it off the list. You do that to earn your spurs, and also so later, when you're setting them up yourself as a co-ordinator, you know what you're talking about, what you're dealing with, and what the stuntman is going through.

On *Figures* I also performed one of the craziest stunts of my early career – falling out of a helicopter onto the side of a mountain, all without the aid of airbags or safety nets. And I'd never even been up in a helicopter before. We were up in the Sierra Nevada mountains and the only stunt equipment I had was a padded life-preserver jacket. With a fall like that, you've got to be careful to manoeuvre yourself in the air so you don't land on your head (which would obviously mean a broken neck or smashed skull), but you've also got to keep your arms out of the way so you don't snap them. It was about a 35-foot drop, so I found the steepest gravel slope (the theory being the longer it takes to slow down and stop, the less the impact – within reason) and got to look at it from the helicopter to make sure there weren't any big rocks underneath. Don't forget you also have to act when you do stunts; you can't look prepared or rehearsed, you have to just get shot, arrghh, and fall out in a totally realistic way. That's the hardest part.

So the cameras started to roll. 'Action!' I bailed out, turned over in mid-air, landed flat on my back, bounced off and rolled down to the bottom. Dave Tringham turned to Losey and said, 'If you're not happy Joe we can do it again. Vic's OK, he's getting paid for it.' Joe went mad; he was paranoid about someone getting hurt. 'It's too bloody dangerous. I'm never going to do it again.' He was a nervous wreck while we were shooting it. So I got a reputation for doing dangerous stunts, which gave me a leg up. Sadly our helicopter pilot Gilbert Chomat died a little while afterwards on *The Red Baron* in Ireland. I think eight or nine pilots that I've flown with, as well as great aerial cameramen like Johnny Jordan and Skeets Kelly, have all died on movies; tragic.

What with falling out of helicopters and bell towers, it's not hard to guess that *Figures* was a very physical film. Robert Shaw was a lovely guy, but he was

One of my more reckless early stunts, a 35-foot drop onto a mountainside in Spain's Sierra Nevada.

tremendously competitive. He was a keen runner and so was I – I had run for my county as a kid. One sequence had both men escaping from a helicopter across a riverbed. I was doubling McDowell, so it was going to be Shaw and me. We did a first rehearsal and Bob edged in front, so I went a bit faster. After lunch he challenged me to a race. The cameras were rolling but this was personal between him and me. It was a quarter of a mile and we ran like hell, we ran our hearts out. And I beat him. For an actor, he could run (I think he ran for the Amateur Athletic Association as a young man), but when he crossed the finishing line he threw up everywhere, as he'd been drinking red wine all through lunch.

Working as stunt co-ordinator on *Figures* gave me an appetite for more of the same. Very early on I started thinking I'd like to be a stuntman, that's a great job. Then, I'd like to be a stunt double because you get to work on all that star's films. Then I thought, stuntman is all right but that guy over there, pointing the finger and employing me, that's the best job, I'd like to be a stunt co-ordinator. And then when I became a stunt co-ordinator I started thinking, that guy telling the stunt co-ordinator what to do, that's the best thing. And that was the director. And that's the way I've always looked at the business.

LEARNING FROM THE BEST

On my next picture I was re-acquainted with Bob Simmons, who was stunt co-ordinator on *When Eight Bells Toll*, a 007-wannabe thriller from the pen of Alistair MacLean and starring a pre-fame Anthony Hopkins. I was involved in the film's shoot 'em up climax that took place in a subterranean cavern built at Pinewood. I was there purely as a stuntman, to run around and get shot, but very grateful for it. In those days any job was another line on your resume and another few quid in your pocket. And any chance to work with the maestro Bob Simmons was a privilege.

Bob was the top man in those days, the first one that really opened the stunt business up in Britain, so to land a job with him meant you were getting somewhere. He had his own preferred team (like I later did), guys like Dickie Graydon and Ken Buckle, but they were always falling out and then getting back together again, like school children in the playground. There's a tremendous amount of jealousy and back stabbing in the stunt business, and it's very competitive, which means when the work's as thin on the ground as it was in the early '70s it made the fighting all the more keen. I never really got in with Bob's gang – maybe instinctively he saw me as a threat – but I learnt a lot of choreography from him, like how he broke down fights. And when I employed a stunt crew, they either got on, or got out – I wanted no in-fighting.

In my view Bob never really got the credit that he deserved. In his memoirs he wrote, 'I've lived like a king and spent every penny and don't regret a minute of it.' Quite rightly so. Bob lived the life of the 1940s. I think he was born 20 years too late because he was another Errol Flynn. I've got so much admiration for him, although we weren't that close and didn't work that much together. It was sad when he died. But he spent every penny he had. You've got to admire the guy, a wonderful attitude to life.

Someone else I learnt an awful lot from was Alf Joint. I'd gone to Bracknell to play a part and do a bit of car driving for a robbery sequence in the tough British gangster flick *Villain*. Alf was co-ordinator. He was amazing. There was great attention to detail in the way he worked out routines and he always came up with truly original ideas. My mate Rocky Taylor was on it too and we'd rehearse crashing cars and throwing people over bonnets and then just play cricket all day while we waited to go back to work. It was like being at school.

Alf also doubled the film's star, Richard Burton. *Villain* was the only occasion I worked with the great Burton, but he made a lasting impression on me. Burton was so aloof, like this untouchable figure. He'd only come out of his trailer every now and again to sit in the car and say his lines and then go back, leaving Alf to do the rest. And I'll never forget, at lunchtimes Elizabeth Taylor would turn up with the Rolls Royce. The boot would open and there'd be a Harrods hamper in there with champagne, and old Richard would get so hammered he'd be unable to work any more.

It was on to a very different kind of British legend next in Frankie Howerd. The film was *Up the Chastity Belt*, a spin-off from his successful BBC comedy show *Up Pompeii*. Alf Joint was supposed to double Frankie in a jousting sequence but wasn't the greatest horseman in the world so suggested I do the riding doubling, which was fine by me. In those days any job was a great job. Dave Prowse, who later played Darth Vader in the *Star Wars* films, was my opponent.

Frankie Howerd left an indelible mark on my memory. I think he fancied me, bless him, and he chased me round everywhere. 'Get the double in,' he'd say. 'Oh hello darling, let me help you with your leggings, ooh!' He was so funny, though.

Not long after my 'close encounter' with Howerd I had the opportunity to work opposite another British comedy icon, Tommy Cooper, on his TV show. I'd always been a fan of Tommy Cooper. What a natural comedian he was, just brilliant. In this comedy sketch fellow stuntman Martin Grace and I acted as raw army recruits. Well, I've never been in the army and couldn't march to save my life. At one point I had to say to this sergeant major, 'I'm having a bit of a problem with this march.' He replied, 'Son, you were born with a problem.' Of course Tommy Cooper messes the whole thing up, turning left instead of right, marching off in the opposite direction, that kind of thing. I just couldn't take my eyes off him, this six foot four bloke with a nose like a Belisha beacon who was always sneaking round the corner to sip his brandy. Once he needed a pee and said, 'Just going to have a word with my agent.' It's a phrase I use to this day.

Later, on an assault course, Martin Grace and I had to jump across this big ditch filled with water. Coming up behind us was Tommy, who stopped and stuck his gun in to see how deep it was, but dropped the thing in and started crying. It was totally improvised and a lot funnier than the actual gag they'd got worked out. It was like watching a genius at work.

Tragically Tommy Cooper died in 1984, on stage in a TV variety show that was broadcast live. I was watching that night and saw him come out in front of the curtains and give a funny smile, but it wasn't quite the smile of old. He then sort of sank down and leant backwards and I knew he was dying. They quickly covered him up with the curtain and cut away. Later the news came that he'd had a heart attack. He was a total one-off, and I just get such a kick out of having worked with someone like that.

HISTORICAL EPICS

It was largely my experience with horses and riding that got me my next lot of work, all period pictures. There was a trip up to Yorkshire for *Jane Eyre* to double George C. Scott falling off a rearing horse, and then off to Wales for Roman Polanski's blood-soaked *Macbeth*. Polanski stayed in Portmeirion, the village where they shot *The Prisoner*, and we'd watch dailies in this old theatre. Every week they put an old movie on and this one night it was *Dance of the Vampires* (or *The Fearless Vampire Killers* as it's known in America), the film Polanski made with his wife Sharon Tate. That week the world was watching the trial of Charles Manson, whose followers had brutally murdered Sharon back in 1969. It was strange watching Polanski sitting there in this cinema, a *Playboy* bunny on each arm, watching Sharon on the screen, especially since that morning her picture had been splashed across all the papers. That always affected me.

Years later Harrison Ford asked me to go over to Paris to double him in a few sequences on a picture called *Frantic*, which Polanski was directing. During shooting Polanski kept looking at me. In the end I went over and said, 'Hi Roman. How are you doing?' He said, 'Hi. We've met before haven't we?' I said, 'Yeah, but I bet you can't remember where.' He thought for a bit, but was stumped. '*Macbeth*,' I said. 'Oh my God, I knew I'd seen you somewhere before!' he said, looking a bit taken aback. I guess I'd reminded him of what must have been a very weird time in his life.

I remember my next film, *Mary Queen of Scots*, for more personal reasons because that's when I broke my shoulder. I was doubling the future James Bond Timothy Dalton, galloping down the beach beneath Bamburgh Castle in Northumberland alongside Vanessa Redgrave's double. We had to jump a rowing boat that was on the sand and I had to hit it with my horse and get thrown off. Take one was fine, but on the second take I hit the ground and knew immediately something was

On location in Morocco for Young Winston. *That's Ken Buckle on the right.*

wrong. It is a totally different feeling when you have a serious injury. I saw stars flashing in front of my eyes and had excruciating pain in my shoulder. The doctors at the local hospital said I'd only sprained it, but I felt it was more serious, and I couldn't use it for three months. But the usual macho nonsense kicked in and I carried on working, riding one handed. Finally, 25 years later, after crushing some vertebrae in my back, I went for an X-ray and the doctor said, 'Your shoulder's had a bad break as well hasn't it?' I told him that technically it was never broken, because the hospital didn't put it in plaster and only gave me some mild painkillers, but on this X-ray you could see clearly the cracks. So I did actually break it.

After *Mary Queen of Scots* I got a call from Ken Buckle, who is dead now bless him, but he was my mentor when it came to horses in movies. He was impressed with me on *Macbeth* because we had some dodgy old horses to ride on that, and I proved that I could ride anything. They'd bring them down and I'd knock them into shape. Ken was horse master on this big picture in Morocco called *Young Winston* and wanted me out there. For six months we collected something like 300 horses from small villages all over the place. Most of them were stallions (most Arab countries rarely castrate their horses) and fought like tigers. We also had to build stables. It was a great experience and taught me a lot about organising big location movies.

Logic dictates that on so massive a production the horses have to be found on location. Just try chartering 300 horses from Heathrow to Marrakesh. Once you've

Practicing a horse fall at our stables in Marrakesh, with Tommy Reeves watching in the background.

bought them you have to sort out the best and train them to fall for the camera on cue. It was on *Young Winston* that I learnt to ride falling horses. Ken Buckle taught me; he was the falling horse maestro. In the bad old days on pictures like *Stagecoach*, horses were made to fall using crude apparatus like wires, resulting in many horses being put down. It's just horrendous watching those movies today. They killed no end of them on Errol Flynn's *Charge of the Light Brigade*; you can actually see the horses' necks breaking.

When I came into the business they were still using wires to fall horses, and also toe tappers – that's where you drilled a hole in the toe of the front hoof and attached a cable to it which you pulled upwards as the horse was galloping; this would stop the horse from getting his front legs down and he would do a somersault on his head. Then they also used pits, sloping holes two feet deep, filled with boxes and covered by tarpaulin and dirt, which the horse galloped into, making it lose its footing and fall. These practices were all later outlawed, and rightly so.

The only way to do it now is to actually teach the horse to fall, which creates a lot of work for stuntmen like myself because it can take up to three or four months buying and then training the horses. That's why we always used to go out on all these big horse pictures way ahead of everyone else. It's quite a process teaching a horse to fall. You can't use old horses because they're too set in their ways, you want a young horse that's a bit fiery, doesn't know much, and you then have to get their muscles supple, just like an athlete, before you start the training process.

A cavalry charge in Young Winston. *That's me taking the first bullet, with 300 horses coming up behind me.*

Out of 10 horses, maybe four to six become decent falling horses. Some just don't want to do it, so these horses, because of the intensive schooling they have had, usually become good for the actors to ride.

Directed by Richard Attenborough, *Young Winston* focused on Churchill's early life as a war correspondent. I ended up doubling the star Simon Ward and performed the first horse fall seen in the movie. It's when the British charge into Omdurman only to discover they've been led into a trap. There's 20,000 natives in the wadi instead of the 100 they thought they were going to attack, and the column get slaughtered. Ken Buckle was playing the captain leading from the front with the rest of us cantering behind. But old Ken got carried away and as the bugle blew the advance he hollered, 'CHARGE!' and went flat out into a gallop. We all had to stay up with him, so now it's like the bloody Grand National. Up ahead I saw where I had to fall for the cameras, supposedly in a soft area, but it's like cement, the ground in Morocco in the summer. Anyway I was going so fast, as my horse and I went down I missed the fall bed by 20 feet, and now I was stranded with hundreds of horses roaring down on me out of a huge cloud of dust. My horse got up and galloped away. I just lay there with my eyes squeezed shut (as if that would help) as all these hooves pounded past. Welcome to the art of horse falls, the most underpaid stunt in the business. Thank Christ nobody hit me.

The funniest part of all was that when I'd gone onto the set that morning to prepare the falling area for my stunt, I saw Ken's car with 20 bags of wood shavings tied on the roof and thought, great, plenty of padding. Wood shavings are what we used to use as a falling bed to train the horses on back at the stables. A bed would normally be about two feet thick and 20 feet by 20 feet long, but knowing it would be seen on film if it was that size, I was expecting something smaller and more disguised. Ken presented me with *one* bag of wood shavings, and said that was all he could give me as the other bags were for the other falls later in the day. All my bag of shavings did was colour the ground slightly and presented no protection whatsoever, but hey you're a stuntman, so get on and do it.

Although it was a long hard slog, I loved my time working on *Young Winston.* There I was, a budding stunt co-ordinator learning the ropes on a big action movie from Ken Buckle and some of the best in the business, like Tony Smart and Tommy Reeves. Richard Attenborough was great and took a liking to me. 'Dickie darling', we used to call him, because he called everybody darling. And Morocco in those days was really exotic. I took my white suit out there and looked like Our Man in Marrakesh. It was a relatively undiscovered destination, tourists were only just beginning to arrive; you had all these Swedish girls coming through on desert trips, lounging around the campsites wearing bikinis. Oh my God! I've been back since, on *Four Feathers*, and it's the same beggars, the same music and noise and snake charmers, but the mystique has gone. It's nothing like it was in those days.

The experience and knowledge I picked up on *Young Winston* soon came in handy when it was off to Israel on the western *Billy Two Hats*, with Gregory Peck. Because I had this relationship with Peck going back to *Arabesque*, and I was known as a horseman, they offered me the job of stunt co-ordinator and horse master. I thought, fantastic, I'd always wanted to do a western and I'd never been to Israel before. And Israel then was just emerging as a base for movie production. We built our western town in a place called Herzlia, a holiday resort just north of Tel Aviv. I'll never forget riding the horses around trenches and barbed wire left over from the Six-Day War.

Ted Kotcheff was directing and he had quite a reputation. We called him 'Terrible Ted' because he could be a bit confrontational. I had a big argument with him during the first couple of weeks, but after that he was as good as gold with me, so I really liked old Ted. Years later he had a massive bust-up with Carolco's Andrew Vajna and Mario Kassar on *First Blood* and they never used him again. When you think Ted directed the first Rambo movie, which made Carolco Pictures, it just goes to show that you can be blacklisted in Hollywood. Thankfully

In Billy Two Hats *I played outlaw Harry Sweets Bradley – wanted dead or alive.*
Looks like they didn't take me alive.

I count Mario Kassar and Andy Vajna as two great friends that I have worked for on many blockbuster movies.

I also had a small role in the film as Harry Sweets Bradley, a baddie and one of Peck's gang who in the script is lying naked in bed with a buxom hooker (credited as a 'hennaed whore') when the sheriff (Jack Warden) bursts in and shoots him to bits. To simulate the bullet hits we used detonators attached to condoms filled with fake blood that are stuck on you with the detonator underneath. These detonators kick backwards and easily bruise so you have to wear padding, and thank God they couldn't find any way of hiding the dets and condoms on my naked body, so I was allowed to wear a night-shirt. So the sheriff burst in and I got blown to pieces. Then Ted Kotcheff did some reaction shots of the girl, splashing this fake blood all over her big tits. Ted was just indulging himself I think. But I now knew what henna was! What a great thing film education is.

We also shot down in Ashkalom, a big park in the middle of the country, and part of my job was transporting the horses there. It was an overnight trip so we had to camp out in the middle of the desert. The desert gets really cold at night so I saw these huge bushes and cut holes in them to shelter the horses in and make a fire with what I had cut out. I found out a few days later that the police were called because it was some sort of Remembrance Park and I'd been chopping all these protected bushes to pieces. I didn't know what I was doing. So I was in hiding for a couple of days in case anyone put the finger on me.

Next we moved down to Eilat, staying in the only hotel in town. David Janssen (TV's *The Fugitive*) was there shooting a movie called *Sabra Command* with Gerry Crampton, and David loved a drink. We'd arrive back from work and he'd be on his balcony knocking back the old vodka. Eilat was nothing like it is today; there must be 70 or 80 hotels standing there now. Back then we used to sit at night looking across the gulf towards Aqaba, on the Jordanian side, thinking, wow look at that great big city over there, it looks fantastic, and here we are in tiny Eilat with just one hotel. Years later, filming *Indiana Jones and the Last Crusade* in Jordan, we came back through Aqaba, but this time we were looking across at Eilat thinking, blimey, look how great Eilat looks. We discovered Aqaba was just a little dusty Arab town with lots of street lamps stuck up all over the place, which gave the impression of a big city from a distance.

Some of *Billy Two Hats* was filmed at a place called Moon Valley, which was way up above sea level and housed a large Israeli air force base, and like most high desert it was freezing. Each morning we'd arrive to be greeted by sub-zero conditions, but by lunchtime you couldn't move because of the heat. My wife Jane and I used to ride the horses across the desert to the Valley of the Inscriptions where we were shooting. This was one of the most amazing places I have seen, with graffiti dating back 2000 years carved into the sandstone.

During our drive back to Jerusalem I noticed these Israelis harrowing the roadside. I thought, that's funny, why are they doing that? It was because they returned every morning to look for footprints of any Arab insurgents coming over the border at night. I went back to this region on *Rambo III* and it has totally changed. There used to be this great little restaurant a few kilometres south of Eilat run by a guy who was called the oldest hippie in the world, Rafi Nelson. He was in his 60s and always used to have a couple of good-looking hippie girl travellers working there. You'd go in and he'd be smoking a joint. 'What do you want?' It was always red snapper, or red snapper, or for a change you can have red snapper, maybe a bit of octopus and chips. And they'd literally go out and catch it, bring it back and cook it. It was a really relaxed little place. I've seen it in lots of travel

Doubling Gregory Peck as my horse takes a bullet.

books, Rafi Nelson's near Eilat, just at the bottom of the Valley of Kings. This area is no longer in Israel and the huge hotel, that had since been built next door to where Rafi used to be, was blown up by terrorists a few years ago. It is so sad to see these wonderful places disappearing, caught up in the politics of the world.

Although *Billy Two Hats* did nothing at the box office it was amazing to be on, but tough, up at four every morning and not getting back to the hotel until eight at night. As well as being stunt co-ordinator I doubled every actor on the movie and also found time to do some second unit directing. Looking back now it was a huge task to take on. I'd co-ordinated before but I remember getting off the plane in Israel and thinking, Christ what have I let myself in for, when the sheer enormity of it all suddenly dawned on me. We had to find and buy the horses, train and teach them to fall, build temporary stables, hire local labour, teach actors to ride. My wife Jane was my assistant and we had a great guy working for us called Pampas, who was an Israeli that had lived in Argentina. He was an amazing horseman and because he lived with our horses, at night to while away the time he used to make leather harnesses out of an old piece of raw hide. Some of the articles he made me I still use today. Everything I'd learnt from Ken Buckle on *Young Winston* I put into practice on *Billy Two Hats*. It was a massive deal and wore me out, but it was a good grounding for the bigger movies that were to come.

THE CURSE OF THE GREEN JERSEY

My next batch of pictures also revolved around horses. *11 Harrowhouse* was a comedy heist movie starring James Mason and Candice Bergen, but it's not the plot that's etched into my memory but a series of bizarre accidents involving a character we all had to double that wore a distinctive green jersey. All my mates were there, Reg Harding, Ken Buckle and Frank Hayden, this wonderfully colourful Irishman. Sláinte (pronounced slauncha) we called him, which is Irish for cheers. One day Frank looked a bit the worse for wear. 'I've broken my ribs,' he said to me. 'And I've got to do this stunt where I gallop under a tree and do a back somersault off the horse. Do you want to do it?' Being eager and ambitious (and thinking of the stunt adjustment payment) I said yes. And that's all I remember until I woke up in hospital.

I opened my eyes and there was this great big nurse taking my blood pressure. 'Jesus, what happened?' I looked across and in the next bed was Frank Hayden with his hand in plaster; apparently he'd fallen off another horse later on that day. 'Hello Frank,' I said. 'What are you doing here?' His face erupted in anger. 'You ask me that one more fucking time I'll break your other arm.' I said, 'What's wrong?' He said, 'All fucking night you've been lying there going, "Hello Frank, what are you doing here?" Dozing off a bit and then saying, "Hello Frank, what are you doing here?" Then immediately dozing off again. All bloody night long!' I had concussion and was delirious I suppose.

The first time I did the stunt it was OK, but on the second take when I got up the stunt guys figured I had whacked my head because I kept wandering off into the woods with the crew having to fetch me back. 'Oh, I feel funny,' I was saying. 'I think I've sprained my wrist. Can't think how I did that.' And they said, 'You've just done a horse fall.' I went, 'Oh yes that's right. But I've got a stiff wrist, can't think how I did that.' I was talking bollocks basically because I was concussed. Dickie Graydon took me to hospital where they found as well as the concussion

I'd also busted my arm and broken my knuckle joint off.

Funnily enough it wasn't until years later when I rented *11 Harrowhouse* on video that I saw how I'd actually injured myself. You can see me galloping towards this tree and as I put my hand up, this prop branch that (having been repaired after take one) was rock solid breaks my arm, while at the same time I punch myself in the head, knocking myself out, and then I flip over and land flat on my back, on the falling bed for a change. I had landed *perfectly*, it was my own fist that knocked me out and for years I thought I'd just landed wrongly.

The next morning while I was in hospital the 2nd AD (assistant director) came in and was all flustered saying they had not realised I'd been injured. I thought, oh how considerate. He then said, 'Could we have your costume, as we are waiting to shoot with your replacement.' He grabbed the clothes and shouted over his shoulder, 'Give us a call when you feel better.' It's at times like that when you realise you are pretty much just a number!

The doctors advised me not to ride for a couple of weeks but after two days I was bored and returned to the location, hiding my plaster cast underneath my jacket. Once there I was told that there had been another accident. Reg Harding, who had replaced me while I was in hospital, was dumped on his head and knocked out and now it was Ken Buckle's turn to don the green jersey in a chase sequence outside a stately home. We all had to gallop out on horseback across a gravel courtyard with cars screaming after us. I was right behind Ken, who must have been 15 stone in those days, when I suddenly saw him thrown through the air and bounce along the ground on his head. We all skidded to a halt and ran back. Ken was lying on his back with his head split open and his eye swelling up before us. I thought he was dead. I thought he'd broken his neck. We didn't have ambulances on set in those days so we called Stan the unit driver – 'Stan, Stan, the ambulance man' we used to call him because every day he'd taken this bloody green jersey to hospital with somebody else in it. The doctors knew the wardrobe better than the wardrobe people did. So off Ken went to hospital and somebody else was chosen to ride the green jersey. And this poor guy was shaking in his boots because he'd seen all these people carted off to casualty after wearing it.

Later that afternoon we got word that Ken was fine, he hadn't broken his neck, although doctors needed to pick the gravel out from under his eyelid using tweezers. Then bugger me, a few hours later he discharged himself from hospital and came back to the set. 'You can't ride, Ken,' we told him. 'Have a day off.' Ken is the toughest man you'll ever meet. He has the same philosophy as me, which is, 'The only reason you do not go to work is because you are dead.' (I've seen him in Morocco with his leg split open with pus in it, and he still hobbled into work.) He was a complete mess when I drove him back to the hotel and the girl at reception said, 'Yes Mr Armstrong,' and when Ken walked up she went, 'Yes, Mr *Arrghhh*!' Old Ken looked like the bloody Elephant Man. The poor girl nearly had a heart attack.

I'm sure that green costume was cursed and for years I had a phobia of green. Recently I bought for only the second time in my life a green car. I've only ever had one before and on the first day the bonnet blew up and bent over the windshield. I was given a green Mitsubishi 4x4 to use in Australia for a film and the first time my assistant took it out he backed it into a lamppost. I said, 'Take the bloody thing away, give me any colour you want but not green.' But I'm fighting the phobia. Actually a lot of horse people have this superstition about green. So that was the dreaded green jersey. You've heard of the famous Tour de France yellow jersey, well this was the green jersey of *11 Harrowhouse*. Everybody wants to wear the Tour de France jersey, but nobody wanted to wear this bugger.

Talking about superstitions, I still have one to this day, which is that I always put my left boot on first, and that day I didn't. I remember doing it as a test, and regretting the result! It's a strange superstition, but a lot of stuntmen have it. It's quite prevalent in the horse business as well. What's even more strange is that on the three occasions I've tried to fight it, because I fight all my superstitions, I've broken my arm, my leg and my ribs; very odd. So that is one superstition I still have.

One nice memory from *11 Harrowhouse* was that the man brought over from America as technical advisor for this chase was Yakima Canutt. A legend in his own lifetime, Canutt was a champion rodeo rider before getting into movies as a silent screen actor, but like many actors in those days he did not make the transition to talkies as an actor, which was the stunt world's gain. He ended up as a stunt double for John Wayne and Errol Flynn, and was the first stuntman to realise the need for rigging and designing stunts, achieving iconic status for his work on *Stagecoach*. He later switched to co-ordinating stunts and second unit directing, contributing to epics like *Ben-Hur* and *Spartacus*. Canutt was a trailblazer for people like me, as well as being an inspiration, so I was thrilled to meet and shake hands and talk with this great man.

It was the first and only time I met him. He was in his 80s then and it wasn't long before he died, but I kept looking at him thinking, my God, this guy is one of the legends of movie making. He was so inventive, innovative, clever and technical in the way he broke down stunts and shot them. And he had a larger than life personality. I have an Academy Award for Technical Achievement of which I am truly proud and I am the only stuntman to have a BAFTA, but Yakima is the only stuntman in the world to have been awarded the ultimate accolade of an Oscar for his lifetime achievement and contribution to the world of film. Something that will probably never be repeated.

My expertise as a horseman was put to a real test on my next picture. Tony Richardson, of *Tom Jones* fame and a real firecracker of a director, was making a movie from Dick Francis' first novel *Dead Cert*, and was shooting at Fontwell Park racecourse in Sussex. Lord Oaksey, a very experienced steeplechase jockey who once finished second in the Grand National, was technical adviser. Richardson had tried all sorts of ways to get the jockey's point of view during the race sequences, including using a camera helicopter that scared the horses to death, and a camera car with a crane, which couldn't stay up with the leading pack.

One of the crew had worked with me on the *Black Beauty* TV series when I wore a helmet camera. In the early '70s helmet cameras were mounted on the top of your head and so didn't give any point of view at all, and also created so much leverage on the neck they were extremely dangerous. *Black Beauty*'s director wanted some eye level shots of horses galloping through woods, so my old buddy Bill Weston, through his sky-diving experience, came up with this idea of having a film (video was not around then) camera mounted on the side of your head at eye level. To counteract the weight of the camera we took the engine out of it and put that on the opposite side of the helmet, with a flexi-drive over the top. We formed a company called POV Cameras and used it on *Black Beauty* with terrific results. The guy remembered this and sent for Bill and me.

We arrived on the set of *Dead Cert* at Fontwell racecourse, which I had raced at years earlier riding my father's horses, and met the cameraman Freddie Cooper first. 'What have you got here then?' he asked. I told him. 'If John Wayne hasn't used it, it can't be much good for a horse picture,' he dolefully replied. 'But give it a go anyway.' To hell with you lot, I thought, more determined than ever to do it my way. They brought over a horse for me and off I went for a short ride to check out the horse's suitability to carry me and the camera. I then heard this voice screaming, 'Come over here!' The voice belonged to Tony Richardson. 'No,' I said. 'I'm going for a hack round first, settle the horse down.' Richardson was having none of it. 'I said come over here.' Still not knowing who he was I said, 'Fuck off. I'll tell you when I'm ready.' Knowing racehorses as I did, I could see the horse was a bit fractious and I wanted to settle him down gently because a lot was resting on this. Off I went round the track, finally returning to an exasperated Richardson. 'Now,

*Ready to tackle the Grand National course at Aintree; the first and
only time a head-mounted film camera has gone around there.*

what do you want?' I asked. He turned to Lord Oaksey. 'What do you think? Is
he OK?' Oaksey knew me anyway from my racing days and gave the thumbs up.

I put the camera helmet on and rode down to the start. Richardson was there
getting rather aggressive setting up the other cameras; he obviously had very little
faith in my camera rig or my ability, and told me in no uncertain terms to keep
up with the runners because they weren't going to wait for me or do it again. We
set off and I wove my way through the field, jumping every fence. Richardson
obviously didn't realise I could jump with this camera rig on and said to me at the
end, 'Where were you? What went wrong? I was standing right next to one of the
jumps and you did not go around it.' When I told him I went over the jumps with
the other horses he was astounded and that sort of took the wind out of his sails.

In a state of excitement Bill and I left and drove straight to the labs to get the
film processed because I had such a good feeling about the shots I had achieved.
We waited all night for the film to go through the process baths and when we saw
it we went, wow, this is fantastic. Bill and I sent the precious footage by special
courier back to the set for Richardson to view, and three hours after seeing it
Richardson booked me to ride round the Grand National course at Aintree.

At Aintree I became part of the hierarchy. 'Victor, do you think you could
possibly jump this fence for us?' old Richardson was going. 'Thank you ever so
much.' It is amazing what a bit of success will do. I became the first, and still the
only man ever to gallop round Aintree with a film camera on his head, as opposed
to the lightweight video cameras of today. I even jumped the infamous Bechers
Brook. This camera weighed about 14 pounds and one jockey said, 'Fuck me, if

Dead Cert. *That's me hitting the railings and busting my ribs in the process.*

you fall off, that thing will unscrew your head when you hit the ground.' Because nobody had ridden round the Grand National course with a helmet camera before it caused quite a stir. When the movie reviews came out the headline was: 'Saddle shot saves the day.' *Dead Cert* was a stinker of a movie, but great for my CV.

Going to Aintree was like a Muslim going to Mecca for me. I had such a ball, working with people that I admired, riding great horses and jumping the most famous jumps in the world. Jockeys are very similar to stunt people – although they're always supposed to be in top form, they like to enjoy themselves, I guess to relieve the tension. In the local hotel on Lime Street we staged our own Grand National one night. We took over the bar, tipped chairs and sofas over, and had guys on hands and knees with jockeys on their backs rushing round like maniacs. We had more injuries doing that than we did in the real race. One guy broke his arm, another broke his ribs, and someone else pulled all their back muscles. But it was absolutely hysterical.

I also doubled Michael Williams (Dame Judi Dench's late husband) in the film. In the climactic end sequence Lord Oaksey played a rival rider and we exchange blows, resulting in me flying through the air and landing on some spiked railings. I designed them myself out of rubber hosepipe with balsa wood tips, so they'd collapse easily. 40 foot of real railings were substituted by my dummy ones, but unfortunately I was going so fast I bounced through the breakaway rails and smashed into the real things, breaking a rib and tearing all my knee ligaments. I had to do the stunt again the next morning, stuffed full of painkillers. It's strange, up until then I thought nothing could hurt me, but within the space of about 18 months I broke my arm, broke my ribs and broke my shin. It was a painful lesson to learn that I wasn't invincible after all.

BACK IN BONDAGE

One short cut into the stunt business that I never took was working as a stand-in. As stars luxuriate in their trailer, the job of the stand-in is to literally 'stand-in' for the actor while the lights and camera angles are laboriously worked out. Les Crawford got his break this way before he became Roger Moore's regular stunt double on *The Saint*. When Moore took over as James Bond, Crawford went too. At Pinewood on the set of *Live and Let Die* our hero is tied up with Solitaire, played by Jane Seymour, on a platform hanging precariously over a shark pool. Using a buzz saw in his watch Bond cuts the rope, flips over and swings across to land and confront the villain. Les called off sick on the day of the stunt, complaining of a heavy cold. Guess who was called in as replacement. Having already doubled George Lazenby, I was about to don the shoes of yet another Bond newcomer. But it resulted in a nasty accident, which still plagues me to this day.

Because the platform wasn't braced very well, the weld gave way under my weight as I was doing a full somersault and my feet smashed into the ground, cracking my heels and crushing the pads under them. It was absolute agony but, of course, being a macho stuntman I grinned and bore it and never told anybody. You feel you've failed if you have an accident; it's this strange stupid ego stuntmen have, plus there's the need to keep working. So I stuffed rolls of toilet paper underneath my arches to support my heels, but I was still seeing stars and feeling ill. They fixed the platform and I did the stunt again, with no problems this time, thank God. That night I remember going upstairs to bed on my hands and knees. The next day Les Crawford turned up and Roger Moore said, 'Hello Les, got over the pneumonia then? That was quick.'

Live and Let Die also afforded me the opportunity to work again with Bob Simmons, at closer quarters this time. Simmons was choreographing a vicious knife fight between Bond and baddie Mr Big, played by Yaphet Kotto. It was great watching Bob work. You have people today who say they're fight choreographers but all they do is string a few repetitive moves together. They don't know how to shoot it or how it's all going to edit together. Bob was very insistent on varying the moves and the punches and the angles to shoot them at. I was involved in the rehearsals and saw how he broke a fight down, which I try to do to this day, and I saw the way he co-ordinated it for Roger and Yaphet to step in and do most of it themselves. I learnt an awful lot about fight choreography from Bob.

Although I wasn't on for the whole movie it was a big step forward for a young stuntman to do a Bond. That's why I always tried to give as many people a crack at it as I could when I worked on the Pierce Brosnan 007 films, because I knew it would look good on their resume. The irony was that I'd get far more kudos from doing *Live and Let Die* than I would from say *Billy Two Hats*, and I put tons more work and expertise into *Billy Two Hats*. But that's the business. People don't judge you by what an incredible stunt you've done, but by what movies you've worked on, be it for a day, a week or a month. I did a couple of days on *A Touch of Class* doubling George Segal. 'Wow, you were in *A Touch of Class*,' producers went. 'Gee, we'd love to have you in our movie.' But falling out of a helicopter for *Figures in a Landscape*, because the film flopped, it didn't mean diddly-squat to anyone. Strange, but it's the way the industry still works today.

After Bond I was off to Hamburg for *The Odessa File*, the Frederick Forsyth thriller, which is chiefly remembered these days for the scene in which star Jon Voight is pushed under the wheels of an underground train. This was done in a local tube station with me doubling Voight and jumping onto boxes laid out on the track, and then laying underneath the curve of the platform as the train came roaring by. We used a bit of camera trickery, but it was a real train and so quite nerve-wracking for me. I've never actually seen the sequence but when I tell people about it they go, 'Oh yeah, I remember that,' so it must have been quite effective.

Joe Powell choreographed the stunts on *The Odessa File*. He's one of my heroes and one of the best stuntmen there's ever been. Famously he doubled Sean Connery in *The Man Who Would Be King* when he fell from a collapsing rope bridge into this huge chasm in Morocco. His fall was 80 feet onto a ledge with cardboard boxes as his landing pad; if he missed that it was a few hundred feet into nothingness. All these other stuntmen looked at it and suddenly got terribly ill or received frantic phone calls about going back home. Turning to Joe the producers said, 'Do you want to do it?' And he just said, 'No problem.' By the time they were ready to shoot, the whole edge of this gorge was lined with every tribesman in the vicinity. They had all come to watch this white man commit suicide, so they thought. Cameras rolled, they cut the bridge; Joe whistled down and crashed into the boxes. Getting up he said, 'Was that all right everybody?' Just completely laid back, an amazing guy.

Another tough thriller was *Hennessy*, about an Irish revolutionary, played by Rod Steiger, out to blow up parliament. I was fighting on a roof opposite veteran stuntman Joe Dunne (Joe's son Mathew is now an assistant director I work with a lot in the States) over at Twickenham Studios and we had to crash through a skylight and fall 20 feet onto a pool table. We replaced the pool table with two layers of cardboard boxes, put mattresses on top and covered it all with a carpet, just so the boxes didn't explode and we didn't fall through gaps between the mattresses. Doing a fall with someone else it's important to lock bodies tight together or you'll just smack into each other when you land at different times. And you've got to land as level as you can, not head first otherwise you'll break your neck. So both of us were hugging together like a couple of lovers as we burst through the skylight and WHAM all the air came out of our bodies, we might just as well have landed on the stone floor. That incident always flashes through my mind whenever I build a rig for anybody, so it obviously taught me a lesson.

So what went wrong? The layers of boxes were fine, but putting a carpet over the top, which has no give in it, just made it as hard as an oak table. It's all about lamination. You can poke your finger through a piece of paper, but put several layers of paper together and it gets harder. The same with a wafer thin piece of wood; laminate several together and they become solid. It's basic stuff when you think about it; we didn't think about it hard enough, I guess. But you only make painful mistakes once, and then you remember. And you can still learn. Every day I learn something new, whether it's about on-set diplomacy or how to rig things.

I learnt something years ago from Hal Needham, one of the greatest stuntmen that ever lived. He jumped out of a second floor window and broke both his ankles but still got up and ran off as though nothing had happened in order to finish the shot, that's how tough he was. After that accident he came up with a solution. As with all stunts it's not the falling that hurts, it's the stopping. So the slower you come to a halt the better. Hal showed me this trick of digging a hole and putting in upturned polystyrene cups every foot or so. Then you put a layer of cardboard boxes folded flat over the top of it and replace the earth, and when you jump those cups collapse and it absorbs a lot of your impact without it appearing that you are landing on a pad. I've never forgotten that lesson.

When I was second unit director on *Captain Corelli's Mandolin*, Jim Dowdall, the stunt co-ordinator, came up to me one morning asking, 'I'm going to pick your brains Vic. John [Madden, the director] wants Nic Cage to fall backwards flat on the ground when he's shot. I don't know what the hell to do. The ground's not soft enough and I can't use pads because we will see them.' I explained how to do it with these cups, that Nic could do a pratfall into it and wouldn't hurt himself. Jim tested it and showed John who said, 'That is unbelievable. I would never have thought of that.' So you can still learn, and Hal did it donkey's years before.

CLOSE ENCOUNTERS OF THE KUBRICK KIND

Since inventing the helmet camera that was used to such great effect on *Dead Cert*, Bill Weston and I hadn't had much call to use it. Then no less a figure than Stanley Kubrick wanted to hire our camera and us for *Barry Lyndon*, his costume epic then shooting in Ireland. I'd met Kubrick a couple of years previously, a bizarre encounter to say the least. I got a call to see him at his house near St Albans about co-ordinating *A Clockwork Orange*.

I drove up to these gates and saw a notice: 'Please Shut Gates After Entering.' I pressed this buzzer and a voice said, 'Yes?' 'Hello, Vic Armstrong to see Stanley Kubrick,' I said. 'OK, but when you come in make sure you shut the gates.' 'I will,' I said. 'Don't forget: shut the gates,' reminded the voice. 'Yes I will. I'll shut the gates.' They opened and in I went. I was in the process of shutting the gate when the same disembodied voice boomed, 'Have you shut the gates?' I said, 'I'm shutting them now.' 'OK, come up to the house. Are you sure they're shut?' Exasperated I said, 'Yes, they are shut.' As I drove round the corner there was a big sign – 'Have You Shut The Gates?' And round the next corner – 'Are You Sure You've Shut The Gates?' I got out of the car and when Kubrick opened the door of his house, his first words were: 'Are you sure the gates are shut?' So I had this unbelievable meeting with Kubrick about gates; didn't get the film, though.

In the end the helmet camera wasn't used on *Barry Lyndon*, but I was offered some riding jobs on it, and discovered that Kubrick's obsessiveness was not a one-off deal. He was a complete megalomaniac and sought control over everything. He even wanted all the catering plates and cups and knives and forks made green, so if anybody left anything in the background of the shot it would meld with the landscape. He also went on scouting trips, driving all round southern Ireland with a whole convoy of people just waiting for him to stop and spot a location.

Most amazing of all was the day he walked into the production office in

Ireland and overheard somebody say, 'Oh, it's just another one of those threats.' Kubrick went, 'What threat?' His assistant said, 'We've got people purporting to be the IRA, but it's nothing, it's just another…' Kubrick's face went pale. 'What do you mean another one, we've had them before?!' The assistant tried calming him down. 'We've had a couple in the past, it's nothing.' Kubrick walked out of the office and the next day there was a phone call. 'Stanley here.' The production assistant asked, 'Where are you Stanley? We've been trying to reach you.' 'I'm in Salisbury, England.' He'd moved everything – lock, stock and barrel – overnight to England because he didn't want the IRA blowing him up.

My other Kubrick encounter, of sorts, happened years later when I was making *Tomorrow Never Dies* and waiting for the dailies to arrive one day at the Rank laboratories over at Denham, along with someone who shall be nameless to protect his reputation, and my usual second unit DP (director of photography) Jonathan Taylor. There was another guy in there with us who turned out to be Kubrick's editor and Jonathan Taylor's cousin. We asked what he was waiting for. 'The *Eyes Wide Shut* stuff,' he said. This was Kubrick's first film in over 12 years and there had been massive media hype about it. 'What's it like?' Jonathan asked. 'I daren't tell you,' he said. 'It's looking good but it's so secretive I can't talk about it to anybody, not even my wife.'

As they chatted, Mr Anonymous and I went next door to make coffee. He was being nosy and spotted a film can marked *Eyes Wide Shut.* 'Look, look,' he shouted and started pulling film out. 'Christ,' I said, 'you can't do that.' My foot was jamming the door shut. 'Somebody will catch us.' 'No, no, this is great.' He then tore off about three foot of this negative saying, 'I've always wanted some of Stanley Kubrick's film,' rolled it up, put it in his pocket and closed the can. I said, 'You're going to get us arrested. If Kubrick finds out about this it'll be war between England and St Albans!' Luckily nobody ever did find out about it. Until now, I guess…

FAMILY BUSINESS

There's a lot of luck involved in the movie business. Often it boils down to being in the right place at the right time, although you need the talent to take advantage of the luck when it presents itself. Sometimes the luck or coincidences are so extraordinary that you think fate must have taken a hand in it. Such was the case with my next job. I was visiting Pinewood one day and bumped into a production secretary I knew from *Alfred the Great*. She was doing this TV series in the south of France and wanted me to meet her boss Geoffrey Helman, who said there might be work for me on odd episodes. I gave him a couple of my stunt photographs and the next thing I knew they wanted me to co-ordinate the whole show.

It was *The Zoo Gang*, a sort of geriatric version of *The Persuaders!* with John Mills, Lilli Palmer, Brian Keith and Barry Morse as ex-resistance fighters who solve crimes along the glamorous Cote d'Azur. It was directed by Sid Hayers and my future pal John Hough. I also appeared in every episode as villains, policemen, you name it. It was a fun shoot. The production runner was the son of a noted movie director, who'd used a bit of clout to get him the job. He was absolutely useless, bless him, lovely kid but he wanted to be a rock musician and just smoked dope. I saw the writing on the wall: they were going to fire him.

Now my brother Andy was 16 at the time, great mechanic, loved racing cars and bikes, but was at war with the world and couldn't stick with any job. I thought if I got him out here he could earn a little money and maybe get a new take on life. I phoned home. It was five am in England and my Dad answered. Unbelievably this was the one morning that Andy had got up early. He was driving gravel trucks on a stretch of the M40 motorway being built near Gerrards Cross. 'I'll go and find him,' my Dad said and drove out there, still in his dressing gown, parking near a huge embankment. Scrambling to the top he saw just mud and filth for miles in each direction, except for this one broken-down truck about 100 yards away,

On location in the South of France for TV series The Zoo Gang.

with a guy underneath fixing the back axle. Dad walked over. 'You wouldn't know where I could find an Andy Armstrong, would you?' The guy slid out and it was Andy. He'd broken down right by this road where my Dad had stopped.

Another remarkable coincidence was that the previous week Andy had got a passport for the first time in his life. Was it fate? I wonder. 'Vic's got a job for you,' my Dad said. 'But you've got to be in France today.' Andy dropped tools and walked off. 'What about the truck?' Dad said. 'Fuck it,' said Andy. 'They can bulldoze it in. I don't care.' My sister did his packing and they slung him on the afternoon flight. That evening the crew took Andy out drinking and got him absolutely hammered. Andy was piled into this tiny MG between two infamous ADs of the time, Howard Grigsby and Terry Churcher, to drive back to the hotel and when they got there a comatose Andy rolled out of the door and fell half under the car. It was a narrow one-way street and as they dragged his limp body from beneath the car these local drivers behind them honked their horns and shook their fists, thinking these drunken English had run over a poor Frenchman.

At five o'clock the next morning Andy didn't show, so I went to his hotel room and he was still in the same clothes we left him in, sick as a dog. I dragged him to

My brother Andy in one of the many guises he donned for The Zoo Gang. *He's doubling Sir John Mills here.*

the production office and told him to sit outside and just do whatever they asked. I came back at six that night and he'd been sitting in the same chair just staring into space, absolutely zonked. He eventually got over the hangover and started working and they loved him in the office. I used him as a stunt motorcyclist doubling John Mills. Andy also got friendly with Terry Churcher, who was one of the top assistant directors of his day. At the end of the shoot they decided to drive back to England together and I'll never forget seeing them off from outside the Negresco Hotel in Nice practising their French, or rather the worst 'Franglais' I have ever heard: 'Ooh eh le Auto Route pour Sudbury?'

Back in England Andy had got the film bug and was determined to become an assistant director. He started out by getting a job in the post room at Shepperton Studios. Today he is living in America and is very successful. He has directed and written movies and is also a stunt co-ordinator and stuntman. He's worked on big movies like *Heaven's Gate*, *Eragon*, Tim Burton's *Planet of the Apes*, *StarGate* and *I, Robot* either as assistant director, stunt co-ordinator or second unit director. I'm very proud of what he's achieved, and we work together whenever the chance arises. But that's how he started, just from a little thing like *The Zoo Gang*, and from me seeing a girl I knew at Pinewood and happening to have my stunt contact sheet to hand. Plus the fact that Andy got a passport the week before, otherwise he'd never have made the flight. It's really amazing how fate takes a hand in this business.

SMALL SCREEN STUNTS

ollowing *The Zoo Gang* other television jobs presented themselves, one a national institution, the other a wretched cheap series that almost cost me my life. *Steptoe and Son* had been a hit BBC show since 1962 and despite the numerous big movies I'd already been involved in, it was an amazing thrill to walk onto that famous cluttered junkyard set that I'd watched as a kid. Bill Weston was co-ordinating this particular episode, entitled 'The Seven Steptoerai'. Generally regarded as one of the best instalments, it's the one where Steptoe goes to see the latest Bruce Lee movie and gets his Old Age Pensioner pals to learn karate in order to beat the shit out of some local heavies who are trying to extort money from them.

Besides myself, Bill had brought in all these stunt guys like Billy Horrigan, Paddy Ryan, Marc Boyle, Tony Smart, Tim Condren and Doug Robinson to be made up as OAPs or be the heavies, and we had such a laugh doing it. Years later I showed it to my kids and they just died laughing. I played one of the heavies, and I was supposed to be this real hard-looking guy chewing tobacco, and the kids had never seen me dressed up like that, trying to act, and getting thrown around. It's wonderful to have been a part of something that is British TV history. When you mention *Steptoe and Son* the response you get is, wow, you worked on that!

The same can't be said for *Star Maidens*, a long-forgotten series that almost ended in personal tragedy. It was a science fiction show about aliens on Earth possessing super powers. An OK premise, but not if you haven't got the budget to back it up. These aliens used to talk to their space station with communicators made from Fairy Liquid bottles sprayed gold and stuck together with a bit of glue. God, things were cheap back then. I also did a few episodes of *Space: 1999* and that was the cheapest of the cheap, paid the bare-bones minimum. You'd do a crashing space ship sequence and they'd be shaking the camera and we'd all be rolling about in unison while the props people sprinkled dust on top of you from the ceiling. It's turned out to be a cult show but in those days it was a case of, Christ, there's nothing better, I'll do *Space: 1999* if I'm offered it.

For *Star Maidens* I was hired to double the leading actor, whose alien character looked like a poor George Michael impersonator with blond highlights streaking through his bouffant hair. In this one particular scene he spies a girl (stuntwoman Sadie Eden) in a boat being swept towards a weir and dives in to rescue her. Sounds simple. It wasn't. We filmed at a notorious weir in Cookham on the Thames and because they'd shut nearly all the weir gates, leaving just one gate open, the force of the water pumping through was awe-inspiring. The illusion had to be created of a helpless girl in the boat losing her oars and drifting towards the weir, with me swimming to grab the prow and push the boat away from danger, while in reality I was hanging onto its bow for grim death. The effects team attached an eye-bolt to the back of the boat from which a wire passed through some block and tackle underwater and then off to the side of the river bank, where it was attached to a rope pulled by three burly riggers.

The boat started moving backwards away from the force of the weir, then disaster struck. The eye-bolt came off and the boat shot forwards and straight over the weir with me hanging on the front. Luckily a group of extras reached over, grabbed Sadie's arm and plucked her free as the boat went over the weir, but all I was aware of was this sudden acceleration and dropping and the sound of roaring white water. I hit the bottom, it was about 15 feet deep, and it was like a magnet on my backside. I couldn't move because of the vortex that was being created, everything was spinning around like a washing machine. At times like this hysteria takes over, there's no skill involved, just sheer panic. I kicked and flapped as much as I could. Thank God I had earlier demanded to wear flippers, because they gave me a bit of extra purchase as I desperately kicked towards the surface. The extras saw my hands come out of the water and yanked me out. It was all over in seconds, but it seemed like hours. About 45 minutes later the boat popped up 100 yards away. It had been held all that time in the whirlpool. That could have been me. Needless to say, we didn't try that stunt again.

VIC OF ARABIA

I wake up with my head throbbing, my body in pain. I try moving but my arms and legs are bound to a bed. Two hospital orderlies take off my bed sheet and place it over the body of a woman lying next to me on a stretcher. They leave and in the gloomy light I can see that the sheet has been put over her head – she's dead! I'm in a mortuary! How the hell did I get here?

It began simply enough as I relaxed by a hotel swimming pool in Marrakesh, along with pals Tommy Reeve and Ken Buckle. On the opposite side of the pool was this sexy, westernised Arab girl in a bikini who was with this very elegant Arab gentleman, again dressed in western clothes. They asked what we were doing here. Making *Young Winston*, we said. 'I'm here scouting for a film,' he replied. It was like, oh yeah, I've heard this before. 'What is it?' we asked. 'It's about Mohammad the prophet,' he said. They appeared to have tons of money and were going to shoot it in Arabic and English. The guy was Moustapha Akkad and he promised to keep in touch.

Nothing was heard for a couple of years until Tommy got the call that *Mohammad* was ready to go in Morocco. Along with Ken Buckle he was responsible for organising the horses and I was hauled in to lend a hand. I was to learn an awful lot about how to set up large-scale productions because this was a *huge* movie with thousands of extras and costing $25 million, an almost unheard-of figure in those days. The incredible thing about *Mohammad*, which was later released in the West as *The Message*, was that it was shot as two separate movies, both Arab and English versions. They'd shoot a scene with Anthony Quinn and when that was done change the lighting, bring in a whole new Arabic cast and shoot exactly the same scene, but in Arabic.

Moustapha Akkad was clever on *Mohammad*, he looked at the business and, realising that Americans didn't travel well for these sorts of movies, picked a British

Giving it a bit of the Errol Flynns on Mohammad *in Morocco.*

crew and based the lot of us out of Europe. They say 90% of the US population doesn't have a passport. I'll never forget on *Air America* in Thailand, we had some American crew and after a week one of them came on set thrilled to bits. 'Guys, I've found a Mom and Pops store where we can get hamburgers made. It'll be just like MacDonald's, so we're gonna be OK.' Historically Brits have always worked on movies all over the world and it is what we are known for.

I was in Morocco for months prior to the filming of *Mohammad*, prepping and training the horses at the foot of the Atlas Mountains outside Marrakesh. One day I was training Mars, a particularly unruly horse, to fall. Things went badly wrong and I ended up doing a somersault with the horse on top of me. I will never forget it: there was a crack like a gun going off, and that was my shinbone breaking. I was in absolute agony as I was driven, with Ken Buckle at the wheel hitting every bump in Marrakesh, to this private clinic that the production company had on stand-by for just such an accident. But everyone had left for the weekend so I ended up in the local hospital behind the medina.

You had to see it to believe it. People in corridors on stretchers (a bit like our National Health Service now), with splints on their unwashed feet, and the sheet over me was stiff with crusty blood. I lay on a stretcher as Ken cut my riding boot off and I looked down and saw the step in my shin where the bone had broken. I was in a huge amount of pain but they would not give me any morphine because we had no cash, so Ken pushed the doctor away, loaded up a syringe with morphine and injected me himself. Later in the day as I was being carted down a corridor to the operating theatre I saw a family of swallows nesting in the electrical boxes. The next thing I remember, everything went black.

After the operation they'd put me in the mortuary because there was no bed space anywhere else. It was quite a shock when I woke up to see the dead body of a woman on the stretcher next to me. I felt my leg, hoping they'd fixed it. Fuck, they hadn't, it was only bandages and I'd been expecting a plaster cast. What they did in fact was to put a plate and eight screws through it, bolting it together. Now my arm was aching. I looked to see a needle in my vein but the tube had come out and it was squirting liquid all over me. I was madly plugging this back in when the orderlies came and got me.

The next morning my wife Jane arrived with Moustapha Akkad to pay for the operation and move me to the local maternity home; the only sterile place in Marrakesh with a bed. Six days later I hobbled out on crutches and was told to rest at my hotel. Moustapha was fabulous because he kept me on the payroll; anybody else would have sent me home, but he remained loyal. People like Moustapha Akkad are a special breed. There just aren't people like that around any more, and I was terribly upset when I heard the news in November 2005 that he'd been killed alongside his beloved daughter in Jordan, in a bomb attack on a hotel he was staying in whilst attending a wedding. Moustapha had really hit the big time after *Mohammad* when he produced the hugely popular *Halloween* movies. He really was one of the most wonderful people in the world, who treated Arabs and Jews alike and was a great ambassador for the peace process in the Middle East.

By the second week I was bored out of my head just hobbling around the hotel on my crutches so I visited the stables. When Moustapha got to hear about it he sent a car to take me back to the hotel. 'If I ever catch you down there again I will send you back home,' he said. But I kept going every day and had guys on watch for Moustapha's car. I just had to keep busy. A month later I was riding again with just my heel of the broken leg resting in the stirrup. And 11 weeks to the day after breaking my shin I actually did a horse fall again. I was back in business.

Making a film about Mohammad in the Middle East was always going to be controversial because you're not allowed to portray Mohammad (which we never intended to do); it's the law of the Koran. The timing was lousy too with Spain battling to reclaim the Spanish Sahara, which neighboured Morocco. Incensed by

My first horse fall after breaking my shin 11 weeks earlier. The horse is called Atlas.

our film, the Arab nations had ordered Morocco to halt production, something they'd been reluctant to do, seeing how much income was being pumped into their economy. So the Arabs played their ace, telling Morocco that if they booted us out they'd all help with the fight over the Spanish Sahara. One day we were shooting on a huge set that replicated Mecca when suddenly guys with machine guns arrived. 'Stop filming now,' they said. 'Pack your bags and go back to your hotel.' We were shipped out the very next day.

Without a location the film was doomed. But an unlikely saviour arrived in the shape of Colonel Gaddafi. He used to love stirring it up amongst everybody, Arabs, English and American. And he said, 'Come to Libya and shoot your movie.' At the hotel we stayed at in Tripoli just about every terrorist organisation from the Black September to the IRA were having these conferences which Gaddafi was sponsoring. We even had a cocktail party where Gaddafi came and met everybody on the film. He personally presented all of us with an English translation of the Koran, which I've still got.

Gaddafi's cocktail party had horrendous consequences for one of the Spanish stuntmen on the film, Miguel Pedregosa. A few days after the party he flew to Israel to start work on another film, but having just been in Libya he couldn't use the same passport so had to stop off in Madrid first to pick up a new one. I caught up with Miguel months later and he said, 'My God it was the most terrifying thing that ever happened to me.' After landing in Israel the plane taxied around the runway for ages and when it finally stopped the doors didn't open. A bit strange, he thought. Then all of a sudden soldiers burst in with guns and walked down the aisle straight towards Miguel. Two men sitting behind him stood up and pointed him out. 'This is the man.'

Poor Miguel was frog-marched off the plane, put in a closed room and interrogated about what he was doing in Israel. It was obvious that the Israelis had spies in Libya because they said to Miguel, 'We know exactly what you did. You were at a cocktail party on Sunday night. You were with a guy called Vic Armstrong.' The police even told him what he was drinking, what I was drinking, what time he left the party, what plane he flew to Madrid on, what streets he walked down, where he had lunch with his wife; they knew every single move he'd made. Israel had infiltrated all of Libya, just unbelievable. But you can imagine how Miguel felt when they got him into that room; he was crapping himself. They let him out eventually, but it was touch and go.

The biggest problem in Libya for the Brits was the lack of booze, it being a dry country. I've actually got a certificate that says I'm an alcoholic. The whole crew were given them. We were there for months and the crew were mutinying because we couldn't get anything to drink, so the Libyan authorities finally relented and gave us one bottle of wine per week – just as long as we all signed this piece of paper to say we were certified alcoholics, which placated their non-drinking laws apparently. Strangely, you could buy beer-making kits in the supermarkets.

So of course we started brewing the stuff in our apartments. We used wine bottles and one day one of the bottles exploded, causing a chain reaction – our whole supply blew up. There was beer an inch deep in the apartment and we mopped it up in a mad panic in case the police came in and caught us. But now there was no booze at all. Luckily we'd met some people from ESSO, out there doing the oil pipelines, and they were making a thing called Flash, which was like White Lightning and made of sugar. We tried some of this and Christ it was potent. If you had a hangover every joint in your body ached, it was dreadful. We used to buy this stuff in litre bottles and cut it 50/50 with water.

I was about to embark on a mammoth 600-mile trek to take the unit's 300 horses through the desert in open trucks to where we were going to shoot the climatic battle, and so I made a deal with the ESSO guys for 20 litres of Flash. To test it you tipped some into a spoon and set a match to it, and if it burned nice and blue like meths, that was good, it was pure, but if it burned yellow you didn't touch it because you'd end up going blind. We started loading the horses and equipment into the trucks, along with these big five-litre water bottles. I thought I'd be smart and mark the five-litre bottles filled with Flash, which is a clear liquid, with an X and put them underneath the horses' water containers.

In the desert we ran into a tremendous sandstorm, it was jet-blasting us, and we had to pull up and wait for it to blow through, which took a few hours. Afterwards all the horses' eyes and nostrils were crusted shut with sand so the grooms got this water and started cleaning them up and I nervously watched as layer after layer of plastic cans came off the truck, all the time getting closer to my precious stock of booze. 'OK, that's fine guys,' I said, finally, before it was too late. When we arrived I got all my stuff safely up into my apartment and at two o'clock in the morning people started to knock on the door, 'Vic, can we buy a pint?' I made an absolute killing.

The booze was sorely needed as the luxury apartments Gaddafi had had especially built for us were total nightmares as none of the plumbing worked. When the builders finished they'd simply tipped their cement down the toilet. As for the bath, no water came out because all the fittings were bunged up with cement, too. Much better news arrived one day when I was playing poker. Bill Weston came up to me and said, 'Congratulations.' I went, 'It's not that good a hand.' 'No, no. I thought you'd heard.' He told me there had been a radio message that my son had been born, Bruce. So I flew home straight away to see him. It was a happy ending to a traumatic year.

FACE TO FACE WITH
OLIVER REED AND PETER SELLERS

After the trials and tribulations of *Mohammad* I was back home barely a week before I was off to Austria, training horses and doubling Richard Chamberlain in the saddle for *The Slipper and the Rose*. My first wife Jane and my new son Bruce came along, and it was Bruce's first plane trip of many. Not long after that I did a few days doubling for Richard Harris on *Return of a Man Called Horse*.

Then along came a film called *The Copter Kids*, hardly a blockbuster, but for me a big moment in English stunt history. It was a Children's Film Foundation picture about these kids living on a farm and a nasty motorbike gang rustling their cattle. Marc Boyle and I were playing the two heavies and hoped to supplement our wages by hiring out our own bikes, because we both used to motocross together. 'No,' the director said. 'We've got the world champion motocross rider Dave Bickers supplying the bikes.'

In our first scene we had to round up some cattle on our bikes into a horse truck, then ride inside and drive off. 'I'll go and get your bikes,' Dave Bickers said and we heard these machines screaming flat out, with clouds of smoke coming up through the trees. Basically his way of tuning the engine was just to open it up and blow all the shit out of it. Then out he came, doing a few jumps and it was like, oh my God I'm embarrassed to get on the bike in front of this guy. But he was very sweet about it and I quickly found I'd an affinity with Dave. From our first conversation I realised he was very smart. He might have talked like an old farmer, but he had an amazingly clinical way of analysing things, which I guess is why he won all those championships.

So *Copter Kids*, a tiny little film, was the introduction of Dave Bickers into the film business and today he's renowned all over the world. I started using Dave's talents as a driver and brilliant mechanic because I was being constantly frustrated by the industry's old guard, who seemed resistant to any sort of change. Whenever I wanted something done or built that was to my way of thinking more practical, sensible, safe, a new way of doing it, they said, 'No, can't do that, you can only do it this way,' which was the way they'd been doing it for a hundred years. I got so pissed off with it all that I thought, no, I'm gonna change it and bring my own man in, which was Dave, whether it was making breakaway lances for jousting, or building treadmills, or preparing cars. I'd say to him, this is what I want and he'd do it, or if he couldn't he'd find someone who could.

I had a lot of battles over this for years and trod on a lot of toes from prop people through to special effects because they thought I was taking their jobs. I had to keep saying, 'Guys, he's not instead of you, he's as well as you.' Now everybody uses Dave, he's never stopped working and all those departments that resisted him in the early days are the ones that employ him and made him the millionaire he is.

The stunt industry especially resented my using Dave because he was an unregistered stuntman. I said, 'For Christ's sake – he's the world champion! I don't want somebody who's average at ten things. I want somebody that's fantastic at one thing.' That's the problem today in the British stunt business: we've got all these tests that don't necessarily make a good stuntman, they just mean you're very average at a lot of things. You still need specialist ability to do a job, whether it's riding, swimming, fighting, or driving, you don't want to be Joe Average.

In the days when I started you were brought in because you had one specific skill. Mine was riding, and then it was up to me when I was on a film to learn other disciplines, so that I could earn a living on other types of movies. I taught myself fencing, fighting and high falls. I remember Alf Joint and I built this thing we called 'the blob', it was a great big hessian bag twelve foot square and five foot deep, full of cut-up foam cushions. I'd practice falls into it day in, day out from the roof of my barn. That was before airbags had been invented. So you learn as you go along, but you still have to have a specialist capability to get you the one job that you can do better than anybody else. Then it's up to you to learn the other disciplines.

The next couple of jobs I did were with the great Joe Dunne. *The New Spartans* was an action thriller shot up in Nottingham that despite a good cast, including Oliver Reed, Susan George and Toshiro Mifune, never got finished. Still, it was important for me because it was the first time I ever saw and used an airbag. They brought one over from the States for me to be thrown off this castle and land on. Inexperienced and over exuberant, I launched myself off far too much. The cameraman, my friend Jimmy Devis, saw me disappear from the shot and feared I was going to hit the cement behind him. I actually landed right on the edge of the

The New Spartans. *Luckily there's an airbag underneath me, which I almost missed!*

airbag, bounced off it onto my feet and did a running fall. Eventually they pulled the plug on the film when they ran out of money. The producer used to turn up on a Friday with a bag full of cash and pay everybody out of it, but it got less and less as time went on, until one day he didn't show up at all!

One night we were with Oliver Reed in this hotel and the local rugby club came in. When he'd had a few drinks, Oliver wanted to fight *everybody*. The bar was getting very noisy and boisterous and this small older guy, in his 50s, out with his wife, was getting really wound up. Oliver bumped into their table, knocking some glasses over, and this little guy jumped up and confronted him and his rugby mates. 'I don't like this behaviour in front of my wife,' he said. 'And if you want a fight I'll take you all on.' And these hefty guys all folded up like a bunch of pussycats and cleared off. It was great seeing somebody call their bluff.

Later I heard that Joe Dunne was co-ordinating the stunts on *The Pink Panther Strikes Again* over at Shepperton and wanted a lot of stuntmen for a big fight scene in a gay nightclub. You've never seen anything so funny in all your life as dozens of butch stuntmen dressed up as transvestites, ballroom dancing. It was actually quite surprising the number of stuntmen that wanted to wear dresses. 'Is my lipstick smudged?' they were saying. 'Are my seams straight?' It was absolutely hysterical, like a pantomime. Opened my eyes a bit, I can tell you. As for me, I spent the whole time trying to keep my face away from the camera so no one recognised me.

That was the first time I saw Blake Edwards and Peter Sellers. There was always an aura that came on the set when Sellers arrived, a negative aura for me. As for Blake Edwards, everybody had to leave the set while he walked round and decided what to shoot. It was like, God is here. Nobody was allowed in. Nobody was allowed to talk. With Sellers, if he got bad vibes off somebody or they were looking at him and he didn't like it he'd whisper to his minion, 'Get rid of that guy. I don't like him.' He was also totally paranoid. With some stars, people (and I guess we are all guilty of this) let them get away with this kind of behaviour and pander to them, and it gets worse and worse until they don't know which way is up any more; very odd.

From the mega-millions of the *Pink Panther* films to another comedy series of the more bargain basement variety. *Confessions of a Driving Instructor* was a really cheap film. My old mate Rocky Taylor was doubling Robin Askwith, I was doubling Windsor Davies, and with Rocky driving, we were both in this Rolls Royce which had to crash through a brick wall. The prop department had built a fake wall from plaster, but like they always do, they got carried away with authenticity and it was just like the real bloody thing. When you hit a wall with a car at 60 mph the nose will plough through it, but then you're left with this lump of wall, a solid object, which at speed is like a ten-ton weight, hitting your windshield. And that's exactly what happened, it ripped the windshield straight out and smacked Rocky in the face. Luckily I ducked down in the back. 'I can't see a fucking thing,' he yelled. 'I'm blinded.' But the car was still careering down this road and now heading towards the camera team. 'Go left, left!' I'm screaming. 'Now right, right!!' Finally we stopped and Rocky leapt out wailing, 'I'm fucking blind.' In the end he was fine, but oh my God, I tell you, for nothing little films you get the most drama. You get paid peanuts and nearly get killed.

All stuntmen at times have done things when really we shouldn't have, when your instincts are telling you to back out. But it's such a macho job that, especially when people are expecting the stuntman to say no to something, you think, to hell with it, I'll show them. There's a lot of ego, of not wanting to lose face involved in stunt work. Rocky got smashed up badly on one of those *Death*

Wish movies. He had to jump off a burning building and during the fire test it was decided to make the fire bigger and bigger. So Rocky jumped, and because the fire was so big he had to jump that much faster and harder. He missed the crash boxes and smashed his pelvis. He had to have operations for months.

MRS MICK JAGGER

Trick or Treat was to be the first film from Enigma, David Puttnam's company. Directed by Michael Apted, it was a thriller made on location in Rome, starring one of the then most photographed women on the planet, Bianca Jagger. My friend Vincent Winter was 1st AD and called me asking if I'd like to come on the picture, not as a full time stuntman, but as bodyguard for Ms Jagger, and also perform one stunt on the film. 'Sounds like fun,' I said. It was.

I was due to meet Ms Jagger at Heathrow but the production office phoned to tell me she hadn't made the flight and to go home. This went on for four days. On the fifth day I was told to get on a plane and wait for her in Rome. So I was now in the Hassler hotel, top of the Spanish Steps, in the Presidential suite, fantastic. I was there three days and she didn't turn up. Then the phone went. 'She's arriving at ten o'clock tonight.' I picked her up at the airport and the first thing Bianca said to me as she got in the back of the car was, 'Have you got a piece?' I said, 'Beg your pardon?' She said, 'Have you got a gun?' I went, 'No, of course I haven't got a gun!' She said, 'If I'm being kidnapped we need a gun.' I said, 'I'm not having a gun. By the time I think about using it, it'll be all over.' Then she gave me this duty free bag. 'Don't lose that, there's thirty grand's worth of jewellery in it.' I thought, Jesus Christ. Back at the hotel she started unpacking so I went to bed. One o'clock in the morning, my door burst open. She wanted to go out partying. I don't think we were back at the hotel before four o'clock any morning after that. Bianca was a real night bird. It was unbelievable.

Rome was bubbling in the mid-70s, everybody was in town – Liza Minnelli, Donald Sutherland, Roger Moore – Bianca knew them all and we partied like crazy. Liza Minnelli sometimes stayed the night in our suite and it was funny seeing her again because she used to go out with Desi Arnaz Jr, who'd been in *Billy Two Hats*. They had the room next to mine on that movie and I'd hear them fighting all night long. They had a terribly turbulent relationship.

Bianca refused to go anywhere without me in case she was photographed by the paparazzi, then she could always tell Mick that the guy on her arm was her bodyguard. The problem was you couldn't get her out of bed to go to work the next morning. I'd run her a bath but she was just exhausted. One morning there was a loud bang on the door. I opened it to see just a big hat and a coat saying, 'Hello, you must be Vic. I'm Mick.' Oh my God, it's Mick Jagger! I love the Stones, and was totally star-struck.

For the next four days Bianca didn't go to work but just hung around with Mick. And Mick always included me in the party. One night we went to Jackie O's, which was *the* club in Rome, and when they brought the bill for our meal at the end of the evening Mick went through every item. 'You fucking idiot,' he said, grabbing hold of the waiter. 'You think because I'm a rock star I won't complain and you can top up the bill. You've got three puddings here; I never had a pudding. I'll pay you what you fucking want, but you won't get a tip.' And this poor waiter was going, 'Sorry Mr Jagger, it's a mistake.' He said, 'Fucking mistake, you always expect us to swallow it.' And I thought, good for Mick, he's not going to be conned just because he's a star and embarrassed into it.

I got on really well with Mick. He was a great guy. Years later I was in Mexico City doing *Conan the Destroyer* and there was a party at Grace Jones' apartment. Relaxing in a chair somebody grabbed me from behind. 'Guess who?' I looked up and it was Mick, he'd remembered me. The next day Grace, Mick, my second wife Wendy and I all flew down to a local resort for the weekend. We arranged to meet at the airport but had agreed not to publicly greet Mick because he wanted to remain inconspicuous. Wendy and I were sitting talking when he arrived with a big hat covering his face, and sat down to read his paper quietly in the corner. Nobody recognised him.

Suddenly I was aware of everyone in the airport turning to look at something. Sashaying through the crowd was Grace Jones in this body stocking, you could see every crack and crevice in her body, and slung round her neck was a big feather boa that clashed like hell. With everybody looking at her she walked straight over to Mick. 'Hello Mick darling.' And all these American tourists went, 'Oh gee, look that's Mick Jagger!' For the whole flight these Americans were continually walking past his seat pretending to go to the toilet and coming back to say, 'Yeah honey, that *is* Mick Jagger.' And he was going, 'Oh Jesus, what have you done Grace…'

Years later I did *The World Is Not Enough* with Michael Apted and one day I went up to him on the set and said, 'Do you know this is the second time we've worked together?' He said, 'Really? What was the other one, *Coal Miner's Daughter*?' 'No.' '*Gorky Park*?' 'No.' I left him guessing for a bit before saying, '*Trick or Treat*.' And he went, 'Oh my God, don't say that. I nearly had a nervous breakdown on that movie.' The story was that Bianca found out that *Playboy* had invested money in the film and wanted her to perform a semi-lesbian nude scene. '*Playboy* isn't getting me to go nude for what they're paying me for this movie,' she said. 'I can get 100 grand to do a *Playboy* centrefold.' So it all went rotten, they pulled the plug, and the film never got finished, let alone released. It nearly bankrupted Enigma. But Bianca was very sweet and we got on really well. I had a wonderful time with her.

I had another strange job with a sexy lady a few years later. Vincent Winter was working on *The Stud* in London and called me up again. 'Vic, Joan Collins has thrown a wobbler, she doesn't like the guy that's her masseur, said he's gay, she wants someone more masculine. Would you do it?' 'Sure,' I said, even though I'd never massaged anybody in my life! I turned up, they put me in a white smock, and there was Joan Collins, completely naked. I gave her a massage, and I got stunt money for it; terrific. All my mates were so jealous; they'd have paid just to be in the room watching!

A BRIDGE TOO FAR

This film was a huge stepping-stone for me. I'd just been offered *The Eagle Has Landed* so was in the unenviable position of having to decide between the two. Luckily I chose *A Bridge Too Far*, not realising at the time what a mammoth production it would turn out to be. It was one of the biggest films of its time, costing a massive $25 million. Robert Redford got $1.2 million for just ten days' work! And it had every star you could think of: Sean Connery, Anthony Hopkins, Laurence Olivier, Gene Hackman, Dirk Bogarde, Ryan O'Neal and Michael Caine for starters. In harrowing detail it told of the Allies' calamitous military campaign at Arnhem in Nazi-occupied Holland, code-named Operation Market Garden; Montgomery's bold gamble to end the war in a single co-ordinated thrust.

Alf Joint got me the job. Alf's a very knowledgeable stuntman, a great ideas man. In his prime he was a fabulous double for Richard Burton; he did all the stuff on *Where Eagles Dare*, including the fight on the cable car. In fact they nicknamed the film 'Where Doubles Dare'. And he doubled Lee Remick on *The Omen*, doing the high fall out of the hospital window crashing into the ambulance. He was an amazing stuntman. Alf was up for stunt co-ordinator on *Bridge* and went to see Richard Attenborough, the director, who was desperately worried about the age of the stuntmen because all the soldiers who fought at Arnhem were 19 or 20 years old, young kids basically. Back in the mid-70s there were very few young British stuntmen around and Dickie was going, 'I need *young* stuntmen, we can't make these old men look like these young kids.' So Alf said, 'I work with young people all the time, like Vic Armstrong.' With that Attenborough almost did a back-flip. 'I love Vic, that's exactly the type of person I want.' Of course he remembered me from *Young Winston.* So Alf called my house in a panic. 'You've gotta do this film or I'm in big trouble. The only reason I got the job is because of you.'

On the banks of the Rhine for A Bridge Too Far. *L-R Alf Joint,
Dougie Robinson, me, Paul Weston and Dickey Beer.*

LORD ATTENBOROUGH

**I had the tremendous pleasure of working with Vic Armstrong on
two pictures I directed, *Young Winston* and *A Bridge Too Far*. I also
had the enormous pleasure in presenting him with the Michael
Balcon Award for Outstanding British Contribution to Cinema at
the 2002 BAFTA ceremony. It was an award he richly deserved
because in my mind Vic Armstrong is one of the outstanding
organisers and performers in the film industry.**

So I ended up as stunt co-ordinator with Alf and went off to Holland. Later my
wife Jane and young son Bruce came over and we rented a lovely little house in
Deventer and stayed for six months. It was a gloriously hot summer and Bruce
learnt to walk. It was just an amazing film, with massive action set pieces like the
taking of Nijmegen Bridge by American marines after crossing the Rhine River.
That was recreated 'for real' and it was very dangerous because we used the same
canvas boats as the original attack, and the current was extremely strong. But we

had a lot more chance than the poor guys that actually did it in the war, with no outboard motors. Redford was involved in that and refused a double. All the stars were keen to get stuck into the action.

It was lovely meeting some of the brave old soldiers that fought at Arnhem. Most of the scenes in the film were based on actual events, so if those people were still alive they came out to watch it being shot. Perhaps the most moving were these two guys in a 50-calibre machine gun nest that got a direct hit. One had his hands blown off and the other was blinded. The guy with the missing hands picked his mate up with his bloody stumps, threw him over his shoulder and started running for safety. The blind guy was screaming his head off. 'For Christ's sake shut up,' his mate said. 'But you don't understand,' the blinded soldier protested, 'I'm badly hurt.' It wasn't until later that he discovered his mate's hands had been blown off. Amazing people; I remember them sitting behind the camera with tears running down their faces as this scene was being re-enacted.

Another day my stunt team went for lunch in a café and I noticed a little old man staring at us with mounting fury. I then realised we were all dressed as SS officers and it was obviously invoking terrible memories. If he'd had a gun he'd have shot us all. I mentioned this to the guys and we got up and went back to work. But it did bring home to everyone the realism we were dealing with, and what the Dutch went through.

Another of the really big sequences was the parachute jump that involved 2,500 people in the air. I was doubling Ryan O'Neal, to get a close-up shot of his character landing. My parachute was attached by little hooks onto a huge ring that a crane then lifted up 80 feet in the air – that's a long way when you're just hanging there. I'd then be released, the parachute would fill with air and I'd land safely. That was the idea.

The day of the mass drop was really windy and as I was yanked up on this bloody thing the parachute started flapping about wildly. Suddenly ping, ping, ping, three of these little hooks came loose, then a few minutes later, ping, ping, ping, more came out. Jesus Christ, I thought, any minute the whole thing is going to go. I must have been up there a quarter of an hour waiting for those bloody planes to fly over and everybody else to bail out, while all the time more bloody hooks were popping off, and more slack was building up in my parachute. When it came to the moment they pressed the button and I just went into free fall, but because so many hooks had ripped off I'd only got half the parachute full of air, and it sheered off sideways and backwards. From 80 feet up I must have gone 200 feet sideways. I didn't land in front of the cameras as planned but backwards on a

Going up 80 feet on the stunt rig that almost cost me my life.

road, whacking my head on the ground. Luckily I was wearing an army helmet, but I still saw stars. I got up, happy to be alive. We never bothered setting the shot up again; it was a one-off that didn't work. But it was a stupid thing to do and needless to say that rig was dumped. Only later did I find out that it was illegal in America because it was too dangerous, people got killed using it.

One of my jobs on the film was to hire stuntmen, aware that Attenborough didn't want any of the old timers. It was quite a problem. So I phoned my brother Andy, who at the time was an assistant director on *The New Avengers* TV series, and asked if he'd come across any young stunt guys. 'Yeah,' he said. 'There's this guy from Yorkshire, Roy Alon, he's a complete mad man. We asked him to fall out of this car, and at 25 mph he just pitched himself out on his head, bounced and rolled down the road, got up and said, "Was that all right, chuck? Do you want to go again?"' 'Stick him on the list,' I said. Roy and I worked together on countless movies after that and he became one of the UK's most prolific and successful stuntmen and co-ordinators. It's amazing how many of those young stunt guys that came out to work on *Bridge*, many just starting off, are now stunt co-ordinators in their own right.

I must have used about 100 different stuntmen during that production, but poor old Roy Alon was always the butt of the jokes. In those days we never had specialist stunt padding so made do with judo pads. Sometimes we'd put a wetsuit on underneath the costume for added protection; unfortunately they were bloody hot. 1976 was the warmest summer we'd had for donkey's years and we told Roy to get ready at ten o'clock in the morning for a fall out of a car we were shooting that afternoon. Come midday he was cooking inside this wetsuit and army uniform. Of course we all buggered off for lunch and left him lying on the edge of the bridge. When we came back there were pools of water where his arms were hanging down; sweat was running out of his sleeves. 'Are you all right Roy?' we asked. 'Aye, I grant you I'm hot, but I'm all right.' We never did do the stunt; we were just winding him up.

The film was a logistical nightmare too, just getting people in and out of the location. We also had a huge crew of engineers who kept all the tanks and trucks running. That was funny because just before I went out to Holland I bought a Volkswagen estate car from a guy in a pub for £100, and took it in for a free service from these film engineers. The next day I got this panic call. 'Vic, don't go more than 20 miles away from base in that old thing, it'll break down.' I ignored them and did the whole six months on *Bridge* driving all over the bloody place. After that I took the family back to England, returned to Holland for a month's extra filming, drove to Vienna to work on another picture and then drove back home again. I kept that Volkswagen for another year until my wife was backing out of the garage one day and the suspension went, so that was the end, two years after being told not to go more than 20 miles in it; never had a lot of faith in engineers after that.

I learnt an awful lot working with Alf, especially the importance of rehearsals.

For the scene where the Germans attack the British position on the bridge in assault vehicles we used a big car park and mapped out the whole sequence, what each vehicle was going to do, how it was going to be shot and how each stuntman could be utilised in four or five different parts. All the big set pieces were meticulously planned and the stunt team was coming up with all these great ideas for action sequences. Paul Weston did some really inventive storyboards of a German patrol coming down an alpine pass and being ambushed by the Dutch resistance, until we said to him, 'It's great Paul, but Holland's as flat as a pancake, there's no Alps here.' 'Oh bugger,' he said.

One day in this car park I slipped arse over tit. Looking down I saw these ball bearings, no bigger than grains of sand. They were actually unexpanded polystyrene, but hard as granite and completely round so if you put them on the ground it was just like ice. So I had this idea we'd use them for car spins, because a German Kübelwagen had to come down the bridge and slide sideways. We did a rehearsal and threw handfuls of this stuff on the ground. Marc Boyle was driving and Paul Weston was hanging on the side. The Kübelwagen roared towards us and did an amazing spin, but unfortunately when the ball bearings ran out it gripped hard on the real road surface, jerked sideways and then flipped upside down with these two guys in it, no roll cage or anything. Oh my God they're dead, I thought. Marc stayed inside and Paul got thrown out; unbelievable how it never killed them. We never used the stuff again after that.

Alf Joint bit the bullet on that film too. He was a great high fall man and played a German sniper that got shot and fell off a building. Attenborough yelled action and Alf pitched off the edge of the roof and straight down the wall. Unfortunately he wasn't totally used to the modern technology of airbags which is based on displacement, you land in the middle of the airbag and the air gets displaced through vents, but he landed on the edge so it was like a tube of toothpaste, it squeezed the air all up one end and he had no resistance. He collapsed his lung, chipped his shoulder blade, broke a rib and chipped his hip. But true to his profession he was back with us as soon as he got out of hospital.

As well as being a great learning curve for me, being in charge on *A Bridge Too Far* with Alf lifted me up in the hierarchy of the stunt business. I was now employing all the people that in the past had employed me, and I was also employing possible future employers. I also started my own company, Stunts Incorporated, on that movie, mainly because we were getting fed up of American stunt teams coming over here with hats and T-shirts with their logos on them. The Brits aren't really into that, we're all very retiring and too embarrassed to say how

The original members of Stunts Incorporated: myself, Alf Joint, Paul Weston and Dougie Robinson.

good we are, so I thought, let's give it some panache. After all, the film business is all about salesmanship.

It all started as a T-shirt funnily enough. John Richardson got one made for his special effects crew and when we asked for a few they said, 'No, only special effects people can have these T-shirts.' They all proudly walked on the set wearing them one day and the producer Joe Levine happened to be there and went, 'Jesus Christ, am I paying this many special effects guys?' He suddenly realised there was a 40-strong effects crew, who were basically anonymous until that moment. They never wore those T-shirts again! So we thought, right, we'll get a T-shirt going, but for anyone to have. The design was the British flag with the bridge coming out of it, later replaced by a simple movie camera logo, and they were so sought after because everybody loves stunts – I've even had them stolen off my washing line at night.

We managed to get some great publicity out of it. We gave one to Joe Knatchbull, our location manager, who was Lord Mountbatten's nephew and was at the time going out with the same girl as Prince Charles. Joe went home one weekend and a few weeks later in all the papers was a photograph of Prince Charles wearing our T-shirt playing polo, he put it on in between chukkas to cool down. And everybody went, wow, the stunt Prince. But old Joe Knatchbull was pissed off because he'd given the T-shirt to his girlfriend and she'd given it to Prince Charles, and that's when it came out that she was double dipping a little bit. But it got huge coverage all over the world. We must have made a million T-shirts since then because we used them on every film we did.

So that was the start of Stunts Incorporated. The original formation was Alf Joint, Paul Weston, Dougie Robinson and yours truly. It was a philosophy of sorts, a group of individuals who were the best at what they did. And we employed the best people because you're only as good as the people that work for you. People don't hire Stunts Incorporated as a company to carry out jobs, what they're doing is employing somebody who just happens to be a member. It's merely a badge to sell the person without them having to promote themselves. They see you walk onto the set with Stunts Inc on your chest and they know you're a capable stuntman. It's all about the individuals and not the group itself. I've always striven to keep it that way, and it seems to work.

SUPERMAN

Even if you look back to the 1950s, big expensive international movies had always been made in English studios. In Hollywood's eyes we were white Mexicans, cheap workers, because our rates were so much less than America. But then the first real blockbusters started arriving: after *Star Wars* there was *Superman* and Indiana Jones. It was perfect timing for me, I just happened to be around and hit the jackpot on both of them. *Superman* and *Superman II* were shot almost back-to-back and I was on the production for 11 months. Again it was Alf Joint and myself co-ordinating, having worked so well on *A Bridge Too Far*. We made a good team, complementing each other very well.

Superman was a real eye-opener for me, watching Richard Donner direct. He's a fabulous guy and the driving force behind that movie. The Salkinds produced it and had the rights to the character, but it was Donner who gave the film that big, epic look. He had great vision and he loved Alf, who he'd just made *The Omen* with. Then there was the huge amount of money they pumped into the movie, and the way they went about things. In England film tended to be more of a cottage industry, like an extension of the Playhouse Theatre in Windsor or something. When you're doing an English movie they're whining and whinging over every penny, but on *Superman* it was no expense spared, although the producers did try to pull a fast one when they signed us up. It was only later that we found out they were actually making two movies. Equity eventually got involved and we won the day, we got paid twice.

Besides co-ordinating the stunts, my biggest task on the movie was doubling Superman himself in the flying scenes. Every day I'd be doing some sort of flying, mainly on wires that had to be painted out against a blue or white sky. I'd also have to lie on a body mould that was cast to fit me exactly and positioned at the end of a 15-foot long pole arm that was also painted blue, then the Superman suit

With Christopher Reeve and Wendy at Pinewood for Superman.

was put over me and the pole arm rig. Directly in front of my head was a TV monitor so I could see where I was flying, and make the appropriate moves, say around the buildings of New York, which were superimposed on the background, while below people operated the pole arm to correspond with my movements. To simulate flight they also cleverly had fishing line attached to the tail of Superman's cape to make it float. So I was usually either flying, landing or taking off, all the time hiding the harness underneath my costume; God it was uncomfortable. It really did become a way of life for me after nearly a year on the film.

Christopher Reeve was wonderful to work with, but we used to clash quite often because he wanted to do his own stunts. He was very much in the mould of Tom Cruise and Harrison Ford, stars who get totally involved in the movie. Chris had done very little before *Superman* so Alf and I took him in hand and got his muscles built up by working out every day in the gym, because although he was tall he wasn't well built. Alf was very good at all that because he used to be a physical trainer in the army. But as the film went on Chris wanted to do more and more of the stunts, and we had to stop him doing them because they were just too unsafe for an actor to risk, while stuntmen are 'dispensable'.

The night I took a real battering as Superman.

I remember once I was called back to finish off some bits and pieces on *Superman II* after the main shooting had finished. It was the big fight in Metropolis with the three alien baddies. They throw a manhole cover and it hits Superman in the belly, firing him backward into a car. It was night work at Pinewood and they had a forced perspective street set where the road goes down into nothing – they'd hired midgets to walk about in the distance. I went into the dressing room to get my kiss curl put on when Chris walked by and stopped in the doorway. 'What are you doing?' he asked. I told him about the stunt. 'No, I'm doing it,' he said. 'Chris, you can do whatever you want, but don't stop me earning a living,' I replied. Off he went in a huff.

Next thing I was on this wire device that literally catapulted me backward into the windshield. I also had a metal plate strapped round me beneath my cape, with a big spike sticking out the back. The idea was that this spike would shatter

All I said was, 'Have you got a light?'

the windshield as I hit it. I thought it was a bit low tech, but by this time Dick Donner had been replaced by Dick Lester to finish the movie, there was a new stunt co-ordinator, and I had just come in to do the stunts for Superman. So I was hanging by this cable in front of the car, they'd done all the measurements and simply let me go. Bang, I smacked into the radiator and went somersaulting over the windshield. It really knocked the wind out of me. 'Let's have another go,' they said, raising me up two inches. This time, whack, I hit the top of the windshield and somersaulted over the back of the car, ending up dangling like a conker on a string. So they split the difference and lowered it an inch, pulled me up and let me go and I buried it right in the windshield. It's a nice shot when you see it in the finished movie.

After that General Zod (Terence Stamp), the really tall alien, got hold of me and threw me through the side of a Marlborough truck. It was quite a night; I got beaten up like hell. After getting changed I was leaving for home and Chris Reeve, bless him, came over, gave me a thumbs-up and said, 'Jeez, Vic, you're right, I'm glad I wasn't doing that mate. Thanks a million.'

So Chris and I did clash horns on that movie, but it was purely down to his professionalism: he wanted to do every piece of it himself because as far as he was concerned he *was* Superman, he was a method actor in a certain way. He was a great athlete too and a hell of a good guy, but you just couldn't risk it. And when you see the movie you can't tell it's him or me, which proves there was no need for him to do any of the stunts. People say to me, 'Don't you get bitter when you see the stars getting the accolades for all the stunts you've done?' and I always say absolutely not. I couldn't act to save my life, I'm the worst actor in the world, it terrifies me, but these guys are brilliant at what they do.

For years and years actors refused to admit they had stunt doubles (now and again a few still don't admit to it). It took the likes of Harrison Ford when we did the Indiana Jones films to step up and say, 'I don't do the stunts, Vic Armstrong does the stunts.' And those stars have been fantastic in promoting the stunt business.

HARRISON FORD

I was very happy to acknowledge what Vic contributed to my films as my stunt double. I'd always thought it was obvious to people when it was a stuntman and when it was not. I tried to do as much of the action as I could in order to keep the audience glued into the story, and Vic and Steven accommodated me to the extent that they thought it was safe for the film. But there are many, many places where there was some risky business involved and it was far better to have Vic with all his experience and talent to perform the stunt. But Vic was very generous in allowing me to do perhaps more than had been anticipated.

Most people know stars don't do their own stunts. It's just not viable. Why would you risk a $100 million movie with your star leaping off a building in long shot, when it could be a monkey smoking a pipe for all you could tell from that distance? So it never worried me that most stars said they did their own stunts. I've got the private satisfaction of knowing what I've done. Besides, I couldn't do what they do, and in reality the audience go to see their heroes the stars, not Joe Bloggs the stuntman. We are just a small cog in a huge machine.

When I got my BAFTA award I acknowledged Chris Reeve in my speech and it got a huge round of applause, because there but for the grace of God go all of us. Strangely enough I was in Virginia working when he had his riding accident just 50 miles away, but you couldn't go and see him then because he was too poorly,

Saving Lois Lane. With Wendy about 80 feet above the ground on the backlot at Pinewood.

and I never had the opportunity to see him again. But he was one of the bravest men I ever came across. He was a real fighter.

We did a lot of amazing stuff on *Superman* and experimented all the time; Alf had some great ideas. It was such a massive production that we took up the whole of Pinewood. Superman's ice palace, The Fortress of Solitude, was on the 007 stage and I doubled Chris when he flies out: the first time you see Superman in costume in the movie. That set was so big, with water and icebergs, that we had our own atmosphere in there, little clouds and layers of fog would form that I could fly through. It was an amazing shot. Back then digital work wasn't as advanced as it is now, but some of those sequences in *Superman* have really stood the test of time.

The scene where he saves Lois Lane when she falls out of a helicopter hanging precariously over a skyscraper is I think better than a lot of the stuff they do today. My future second wife Wendy doubled for Margot Kidder, and it was a really tricky stunt because we were still using boxes to break falls. We hadn't perfected the airbag since Alf broke his shoulder blade on *A Bridge Too Far*, we'd steered a bit clear of them, so Wendy did an 80-foot fall into boxes. To get into position was as scary as hell. The helicopter was a full-scale replica and with Wendy perched inside it was lifted by crane up to 80 feet and then hung onto the side of the building, which was a set built on the cement area in front of the 007 stage. Next Wendy clambered into the position Lois Lane was in the film, hanging on for dear life by the seat belt straps. There were no cables: Wendy was holding on purely with her hands and her own strength. Then she let go and manoeuvred herself in mid air to hit the boxes backwards, so as not to break her legs and back by going in vertically. That was a massive fall. Very few stuntmen would have even attempted it.

I did a couple of hair-raising high stunts myself, too. The scene where Superman flies into the courtyard of a prison to deliver Lex Luthor to the authorities was shot on the back-lot of Pinewood at two o'clock in the morning. They'd hired this monster crane to lift me up 240 feet into the air suspended on a wire that would then bring me back to earth. But if somebody so much as hit the side of the crane with a spanner, it vibrated all down the wires like a tuning fork and you'd go, Jesus what was that, what's snapping? 'OK Vic, we're ready,' boomed 1st AD Dave Tomblin's voice and I assumed the Superman position. People don't realise that doing a stunt is part of the film performance, physically and visually. How does this character move? How does he react to a punch? It's all part of the same thing, and that's what you have to understand as a stuntman. So if I was performing a stunt as, say, Superman, I had to be that character, with the same mannerisms as the actor playing him, I couldn't just do my own thing, because that's when a stunt looks like a stunt and stands out like a sore thumb.

So I was up on this wire and they turned the spotlight on me, ready to roll cameras. Laying out in the classic flying position of Superman and looking down, my heart almost stopped beating because there was nothing there, just this chasm of emptiness. Suddenly, I was aware of a car driving along the road at the back of the studio and then the squealing of tyres as it careered into a ditch. This guy had been minding his own business driving back home, seen me spot-lit floating in the sky, cape fluttering in the breeze and gone, 'Bloody hell it's Superman!' and crashed.

In another scene Superman is immobilised by a chunk of Kryptonite tied round his neck, and thrown into a swimming pool in Lex Luthor's lair underneath Grand Central Station. Luckily Luthor's girlfriend releases it and our hero flies out through the roof. I had to double Chris for this, but it couldn't be done in the normal way because the wires that were needed to pull me up through the fake ceiling built at the top of the studio would've cut a hole in the roof (these days that would not be a problem because it could easily be fixed in post with CGI). Alf's idea was to have an upside down set with the ceiling built at ground level over the pit in the floor of the studio, which was eight foot deep. Inside the pit would be placed boxes to cushion my fall from the gantry high above. The whole set was made of wood, except for the small area I was going to burst through. We hoped. It was important to have a solid set except for the bit I was going to dive through, so that the whole thing did not implode as I hit it and ruin the illusion.

While they were constructing all this, the tension was steadily building up until the actual day of the stunt and I went up to the roof of the stage, my heart pounding and my head thinking, what the hell am I doing here? But there I was with Dougie Robinson and Alf holding me upside down by my ankles over a 40-foot drop with this set of a ceiling below me. I got into Superman's flying position ready to go, and somebody was holding two fishing lines that were attached to the corners of my cape so it didn't hang down over my head. The tension was really high, and there was total silence. I heard Dave Tomblin's voice, 'Roll cameras,' and you could hear them all winding up to high speed. I was just waiting, bracing myself to go on his signal. I heard, 'OK, in your own time Vic,' and thought, Oh shit, this is it, and I have to cue myself, which always seems harder. In a really high-pitched squeak I said, 'Now!' The boys let me go and a split second later I woke up in the boxes.

I had to exit the shot through the ceiling piece in the classic flying position of Superman, with one arm extended and toes pointed, but then had to try and fold up as quickly as possible into my landing tuck to avoid injury. With only three feet before I was in the boxes after going through the ceiling, that was tricky: I'd gone in so vertically that I only had time to collapse my arm and tuck my neck, and my knees were touching my shoulders. Alf had taught me that on high falls you should always open your knees when you land, otherwise you smash your nose or take your eyes out because in the impact you just fold up. So the next day all my hamstring muscles were really stretched. But it's on stunts like that one where you pay your dues. That's the moment of truth.

I also did the famous shot where Superman lands in a New York street and spins through the pavement into Lex Luthor's lair. One of the effects boffins had this brainwave where I'd be suspended on piano wires on this mechanism that was wound up like a clock and then released, the theory being that it would start spinning me down through the false roof to land 15 feet below. I looked at this contraption and thought, gee, that doesn't look too clever to me. Anyway, they fitted me into it and hit the button. The thing did unwind, but unfortunately I stayed where I was while the wires twisted round and two seconds later snapped, leaving me to fall the whole way down. I thought I'd broken my heels because I was only wearing these thin little flying boots as Superman. So that idea was scrapped. I can't remember how we did it in the end. Nowadays, of course, they'd just do it digitally.

During the shoot I had suggested a way for Superman to fly realistically, using a helicopter with the pole arm attached beneath it and the camera above me looking down, so that we could fly over real locations safely and give the impression Superman was really flying. This same special effects guy, who shall remain nameless, suggested that we use a glider with the pole arm attached to the front, with me lying on it. I said, 'You must be crazy! Can you imagine what the take-off and landing would be like, with my nose about six inches from the ground? Would you be prepared to lie on it?' And he replied no, because he was scared, he had vertigo. So I replied I wouldn't try and knock out Muhammad Ali or jump off the Eiffel Tower, because I'd be afraid of doing that, and I wouldn't be doing this either! So, another lesson learnt: trust your own judgement.

The destruction of Krypton was one of the film's action highlights and was actually shot over at Shepperton. Besides doubling for Superman and co-ordinating, I was also doing ND ('nondescript', or general) stunt work; in those days you did everything. So I got one of those luminescent suits on to play a doomed inhabitant of Krypton, falling to his death past camera. And I'll never forget this cameraman, after every take he said, 'I didn't see him. Jesus, can't you fall any slower?' I just looked at this guy and there was an embarrassed silence – I think he realised what he'd said. But that's the stupidity of a lot of people, the lack of reality. Half the time because they're looking through a camera or directing they think they can ask for the totally ridiculous and expect you can do it; people think it's a licence to be a complete idiot. Can you fall slower! Well, I think you'll have to have a word with Sir Isaac Newton about that. Some people would ask you to do things that were absolutely stupid, or to do something one way when you knew there was a much better way to do it. They used to drive me mad and that's one of the reasons why I started directing myself.

While at Shepperton I bumped into Marlon Brando a few times. He got a massive pay cheque for playing Superman's father, something like $3 million for a ten-minute appearance. And it was actually true what they said about him, that when he scratched his head it was to look over at what are rather rudely called idiot boards. Great big boards with lines of dialogue on them were stuck up in different parts of the set and he'd look at them and that's how he got those long, thoughtful looks on screen. It was amazing watching him at work. Brando was a very generous, nice person. Of course I was in awe of him, he was an icon.

Superman was also my first movie in America. I went out to New York in July 1977, and it was just a magic time for me. Not so great for the New Yorkers though: we were there during one of the city's biggest ever power failures. Shooting at night on Wall Street outside the building that doubled for the *Daily Planet*, one of our electricians put this plug in the wall for the auxiliary lights and the whole of New York went black. This poor guy was in terror for about three hours thinking that he'd actually fused the entire city, though it was pure coincidence of course. The evening's shoot was eventually cancelled and we got a police escort back to the hotel because all the traffic lights were out. But New York was a fabulous, wild city. When we went out filming, you'd have 500 people at three o'clock in the morning waiting to see Superman. They'd scream and shout as I flew around in my costume suspended on cables from huge cranes.

In New York we did a couple of shoot 'em ups, one on a boat and then a police car chase which was filmed down by the Brooklyn Bridge near some warehouses. Everybody had been warned about what we were doing, except for this one night watchman who came out of his warehouse, because of the summer heat, to sit on a chair and read his newspaper a few moments before we called action. Suddenly screaming past him came all these cars, all machine guns blazing, with baddies in the front car firing back. They nearly knocked him over and he was last seen running for his life in the opposite direction. We wanted to do another take and somebody said, 'For God's sake, make sure that guy's not there this time.' Make sure he wasn't there! I don't think he was in the same state; he probably didn't stop running for two hours. We searched the warehouses, nothing, he'd just disappeared. We scared the life out of him.

So New York was a great adventure and I met a great pal of mine there, George Fisher. One day he said to me, 'Do you want to meet The Man?' I said, 'What man? What are you talking about?' He said, 'Sinatra. He's in town and he's a mate of mine.' So we went round to this restaurant near Broadway. There were a couple of heavies standing outside, one of whom was Gilly, Sinatra's right hand man for many years, who George knew of old. 'You wanna see the boss?' Gilly asked. The restaurant had been shut down just for Sinatra and he was sitting there with a few of his buddies. Then George introduced me. I was in absolute awe, after all this guy was a legend. 'Wanna drink?' he asked. On *Superman* I never drank, in fact I didn't touch a drop for five years, or smoke, I was busy training. 'Jesus,' said Sinatra. 'I never trust a man who doesn't drink.' But we sat there and we chatted and it was like, wow, this is unbelievable, what other business in the world would give you a chance to do this?

Superman turned out to be a great movie, and career changing for me. On top of *A Bridge Too Far*, I suddenly had an impressive resume of big, quality films, plus I was young, ambitious and hard working. I was really off and running.

WINNER TAKES IT ALL

After working on two of the biggest blockbusters of the decade, it was back to bread-and-butter jobs. First was an encounter with one of the most controversial directors in movies, Michael Winner. He was remaking the classic film noir *The Big Sleep* with Robert Mitchum as Philip Marlowe, and wanted me to smash a car into a red London phone box. 'You got permission?' I asked. 'Of course we've got permission, what's the matter with you, just smash into it,' Winner said. 'Tell you what,' I said, 'just to make sure I'm covered, can I see the paperwork that gives us permission to smash it?' Winner got flustered. 'I don't actually mean smash it, just nudge it a bit.' He backed off then, and I did the job and never went back on the film. He's very selfish and he's a bully, in my opinion. If you stand up to him, he backs off. People say Winner's very loyal to certain people, I say it's just because no one else will work with him.

From a veteran in the business I next worked with Ridley Scott, who back then was making the move from the world of commercials, where he was already a legend, to his first feature film: *The Duellists*. I was up in Aviemore in Scotland, with Dickie Graydon and Reg Harding, the usual suspects, playing Cossacks on the retreat from Moscow. God it was cold. Next to our location was a skiing resort and one day Dickie, in full Cossack regalia, rode over and asked some skiers, in a terrible Russian accent, 'Excuse me. Which way is Moscow?' And these skiers said, without batting an eye, 'Well now, if you go down the road there and turn left and then go straight ahead I think that's the way.' And Dickie said, 'Thank you very much,' and rode off into the sunset. To this day those people still think they bumped into a Cossack in Aviemore that was trying to ride back to Moscow; absolutely bizarre.

Today *The Duellists* is a much-admired film and Ridley Scott has forged a reputation for perfectionism. I flew up to Scotland with him and during the flight he went through every detail of the production. He was an incredible guy and you can see how he's succeeded. After directing commercials myself, I can admire his diligence and tolerance in putting up with the patience-trying nonsense you get on a lot of them. I think he's a brilliant contributor to the film and commercial world.

DALLIANCES WITH DISNEY

After *The Duellists* I stayed up north, at Alnwick Castle in Northumberland, for Disney's *The Spaceman and King Arthur*, working as stunt co-ordinator and doubling Jim Dale (best known for the *Carry On* movies of course), who always wanted to do his own stunts. We hired some local students for a battle scene, and one of them, who had been smoking wacky baccy, fell off a parapet and landed on the flagstone-covered ground, but was so stoned he got away with only a chipped elbow and cut head. As he lay spread-eagled on the floor, Jim came up to me and jokingly said, 'It's OK, I got his watch while he was unconscious.' He had a wonderful sardonic humour.

There was another nasty accident when one of the stunt guys fell off a ladder and broke his back. We went to see him in hospital where this poor guy was immobilised and Billy Horrigan, who was a known practical joker, ate all his fruit, except for eight grapes which he carefully placed between each of the patient's toes, then got up and left. Other practical jokes went on, mostly aimed at our 1st AD Vincent Winter. We knew Vince hated heights so arranged to send him up in a camera crane and pretend that it had broken down.

Up went poor gullible Vince all on his own 90 feet in the air when the crane operator started jerking the controls. Vince went white. Then, out of the engine compartment, we set off some black smoke the effects guys had given us and the crane shuddered to a halt. 'What's happened?' Vince yelled. 'Bloody engine's blown up,' we shouted back. 'We can't get you down. Have you got any rope up there Vince? Can you rappel down?' He went, 'No, there's nothing in here. Nothing!' Trying to look concerned, we said, 'Don't worry,' and ran off, coming back with a tiny crash pad that was hurled under the crane arm. 'Line this up Vince, how's that look? Be careful you don't overshoot!' 'I'm not jumping into that!' He was really panicking. We had him up there 15 minutes and the whole crew was in on the joke. In the end we started up the engine and brought him back down. 'You *bastards*,' he said.

I did another Disney picture soon after that, *Watcher in the Woods*, which was to prove highly significant for me. To work with Disney was a big step in those days so I was very lucky to get on the film as stunt co-ordinator. John Hough was directing and he's a wonderful guy. I love his story about how he got his first directing break on *The Avengers*. The director hadn't turned up so Hough, then second unit director, said, 'He's useless anyway. I can do it better and if it's no good I'll pay for it myself.' He directed the episode, it was a success and he never looked back.

The film featured a big motocross sequence that Anthony Squire was meant to direct. I'd worked with Squire on *On Her Majesty's Secret Service* and he was top of his field, but John Hough wanted me to do it. The only problem was that Disney didn't want me. Thankfully Johnny insisted, and I landed my first ever job as second unit director. I brought in Dave Bickers and together we built this racetrack. When news got round that we were doing this sequence suddenly every stuntman in England was a motocross expert. I knew some of them had hardly ridden even a bicycle before, so I decided to hold an open audition.

The challenge was simple. I was going to send out a 12 year-old boy on a motorbike to set the track time and if anyone got within a minute of it then the job was his. This was money for old rope, they thought. But actually only about a dozen showed up. The kid turned out to be Paul Bickers, Dave's son, who was a junior motorcycle champion (he now runs the family business), and he went round so fast that none of the guys got within half his time, so they all went home with their tails between their legs. In the end I gave them all jobs as stunt spectators – at least they had the balls to come down and try. It turned out to be a very good motorcycle chase; there are long lens compressed shots in there and some other unique shots that I had not seen used before but I've seen repeated over and over again since.

Back in those days stuntmen rarely moved over into directing, it just wasn't done, so it was a really significant turning point for me getting that second unit job. Ray Austin, one of Britain's original great stuntmen, was about the only English stunt guy that had made that transition, when he started directing for American television. But it was extremely rare. Ray was something of an icon, but I only worked with him once, when he asked me to help with the tests to find the actress to play Purdey in *The New Avengers*. I choreographed a fight routine for the girls to do and one of them, who was later in *Superman*, Sarah Douglas (whom I had recommended for the audition, having worked with her on *The People that Time Forgot*), kicked me right in the nuts during the rehearsals. Joanna Lumley got the job and she was great. My brother Andy ended up on the series as an AD and named his daughter after her.

I have to say that by the time of *Watcher in the Woods* I was really busting to work behind the camera. I love the creativity of directing. It was getting frustrating describing things to people and them doing it only half right. I wanted to take complete control of the action design and then the execution of it. You have to stand up and be counted sometimes and just go for it, then you're either hung for your mistakes or you're applauded for your successes. Johnny Hough, bless him, had the balls to push for me. And that broke the mould, because every stuntman you meet now has got 'second unit director' on their CV, although 90% of them have never actually done it. They might have stood by a second unit camera and said, 'Why don't you put it over here a bit?' and that's how they qualify as second unit directors; crazy. So everybody is a second unit director now and it's become old hat, but when I made the move it was absolutely revolutionary. People would say, 'If you're the stuntman then who is directing it? You're directing it? Oh.' They were amazed. In America Yakima Canutt and all those great stunt guys had made the leap to directing second unit a lot earlier than us, we were very late doing it in the UK, and I'm proud that I was one of the first to make that transition here.

The '70s of course was before the huge action blockbusters like Indiana Jones, and there wasn't a great deal of need for that much second unit work, there wasn't the emphasis on action that we have today. The kind of second units that I do nowadays are not really second units at all, they're whole units on their own, much more action orientated than normal second units. That's the reason why I always call my crew the action unit.

HIGH ADVENTURE

After *Watcher in the Woods* I went out to Alaska to handle the action on *Bear Island*. The Canadian stunt team out there were really shocked that a stuntman was directing the second unit on such a big movie. It was still practically unheard of. And believe me, *Bear Island* was a *big* movie for its day. And a real challenge. It was an action picture with a great cast, including Donald Sutherland, Christopher Lee, Richard Widmark and Vanessa Redgrave, and I was asked to run a very large action unit. It was a big step up for me. Don Sharp was directing, who'd been a top second unit guy on films like *Those Magnificent Men in Their Flying Machines* and *Puppet on a Chain*. I think he recognised my talents as another second unit director and had total faith in me. I learnt an awful lot from Don. He was a lovely guy.

It was an incident-packed shoot and ultimately a tragic one. We landed in Vancouver and travelled north to Stewart BC, which is right on the edge of Alaska, and worked there right through the winter. For a spectacular chase sequence on a frozen lake we had these hydrocopters built and went up into the mountains to test them out. Don Sharp, Robin Mounsey, Leif Johansson, the pilot John Soutar and I got into a helicopter and landed 7500 feet up, having previously airlifted the hydrocopter up there.

Late in the afternoon we saw this big black patch of nasty weather rolling over the mountains towards us and jumped back in the helicopter to get out. But John couldn't start it; because of the altitude the engine flooded, and the battery went flat. With no power our radio was useless, so we used walkie-talkies to contact base and give them our co-ordinates. By now the storm had hit us and the helicopter was rocking from side to side. Huddled inside we worked out our map reference again, only to find out we'd given the wrong co-ordinates to our rescuers and everyone was searching for us in the wrong place! We were able to pick up the messages from the search plane but couldn't transmit back because the batteries in

Driving one of the hydrocopters for Bear Island. *This was tricky, jumping off a glacier into the sea.*

our walkie-talkies were so low.

Our helicopter was a seven-seater Bell Jet Long Ranger and all five of us sat huddled in the back on blown up life jackets, because your arse goes numb on those little thin seats. It was freezing cold. We thought, Christ, we might be here all day. Then we thought, shit, we might be here all night. In the end we were stranded for four days.

The search plane was at 27,000 feet, right at the apex of the storm – that's how big it was – and eventually managed to pinpoint our distress signal. But they couldn't get skiers to us because we were in a crevasse area and it was too dangerous. We were just going to have to wait it out. We could hear base camp saying, 'They'll be OK, it's a brand new helicopter fully equipped with emergency rations.' But we had nothing, the helicopter was so new they hadn't equipped it yet. Our pilot John had one cupcake, two apples and a sandwich. We split that between us and made it last four days. On the very last day we ran out completely and found a little fishing can with eight pieces of corn inside for bait. With candles we heated and popped this corn and I'll never forget thinking, 'Now, shall I take a big piece or not?' as if a big piece of popcorn's going to make any difference whether you live two minutes longer.

After the first couple of days we seemed to spend most of our time sleeping. I recall waking up once and needing to pee. Outside the snow was 20 feet high all around the helicopter where the wind had created a vortex. I hurried back in and when the door opened the wind and snow blasted inside and woke everyone up. Now we stuntmen have a strange sense of humour and I thought I'd try and cheer everyone up so I said to Leif, our Swedish engineer, 'Good news and bad news Leif: we're going to be OK, but the bad news is we're going to eat you first because you're the fattest.' A bemused Leif replied, 'But that is not good for me because you'd kill me if you eat me.' I said, 'Oh forget it.' So we sat there and sat there, waiting and waiting. Eventually there was a break in the weather and we heard a rescue helicopter coming down the valley to land next to us – this pilot was incredible and would just not give up searching for us. We all clambered inside and took off before the storm closed back in. It was another 12 days before they could retrieve the helicopter, so we'd have been dead if he hadn't gotten us out when he did.

Helicopters were used throughout the shoot to transport men and equipment up to the mountains and John was my pilot. I filmed continuously with John for three months, flying every day. I then finished the action unit and joined the main unit for a stunt sequence, leaving my unit to complete some photographic plates. Horribly, the second day the two helicopters were dropping off the crew when one of them disturbed an empty oil can, hidden in snow, which flew up and ripped off the tail rotor. The machines collided and poor John was decapitated. Johnny Harris, my camera operator, had his head split open. The really shocking thing was that John's wife was on the film as a nurse and still up on the mountain when she heard the whole accident on the radio. It was dreadful.

For the second half of the movie our main base of operations on the film was an old Russian liner and every Saturday night we'd sail into Juneau, the capital of Alaska and a real frontier town with sawdust on the floor. You saw people paying for drinks with gold dust. The boat was also used as a set and for one scene I doubled Donald Sutherland abseiling down from a helicopter and falling into the sea beside it. This was the last shot before our Christmas break, so it was critical we got it.

I'd stipulated that I wanted four lifeboats in the water, but as I prepared to do the stunt we were told that they couldn't be launched because the weather was too rough. That seemed a touch bizarre to me and I hoped that the Russian ship didn't sink in the storm or else we were buggered. The boat had to sail to the leeward side of an island, where the sea was a bit calmer, although it still looked pretty rough to me. The lifeboats were launched and the liner shut off its propellers so I didn't get sucked in by the vortex. I started to rappel out of the helicopter, hoping the quick release would not trigger early because I was 120 feet up. At roughly 70 feet I popped my release and just fell like a dead weight, voom, and hit the ocean. All around me the waves were massive and I watched as the ship slowly drifted away. Suddenly I felt very alone… but then the lifeboats sped towards me.

SIR CHRISTOPHER LEE

I watched as Vic plummeted into the sea, it was the one major stunt I saw him perform, and I remember thinking, God I hope he survives because the water was damn cold, but he did it and did it with aplomb.

They're very brave some of these stuntmen. In the early days they really were taking their lives in their hands, even in films like *Bear Island*. Now of course they have so many built in supports that what looks fearfully dangerous is not as dangerous as you might think.

Vic has done some magnificent things as a stuntman. He's incredibly strong, also extremely intelligent and has a huge sense of humour. And he's very enthusiastic and very easy going. He's also down to earth, you get a straight answer from Vic every time, and I like that.

Later in the same day I had to do closer shots of Donald's character hitting the ocean. He had just finished his close-up, and we went below decks of the Russian ship to wardrobe as I had to get into his costume. 'Come on Vic, get the boots on, let's do this and we can be out of here tonight.' He threw me his right boot but I didn't put it on. As he struggled with his left boot Donald said, 'Come on, let's go!' But I just sat there, waiting. Finally the left boot came off and I put it on, followed by the right boot. I did the stunt and we were out of there just as the sun was going down over the horizon. Sailing back to Juneau, over dinner Donald asked, 'What was that all about with the boots?' So I explained, 'It's an old stuntman's thing, we always put the left boot on first.'

I've kept in touch with Donald over the years and all because of a watch. After *Bear Island* I decided on the spur of the moment to take a short holiday with my wife Jane in LA. Who should I bump into when I arrive at the airport but Donald

Sutherland. We shook hands and hugged. Then he said, 'Stay there,' and dashed off to his car, returning with a small Tiffany's box. Inside was a Rolex watch. 'Look at the back,' he said. It read: 'Vic Armstrong: Left boot first. Donald Sutherland.' He'd remembered. I said, 'Gee, that's great, but what a bit of luck meeting me here.' He said, 'No, last week my wife said not to forget to give the watch to Vic at the airport.' I said, 'But I only decided to come out to LA two days ago.' He went, wow; it totally freaked him out.

I saw Donald again nearly 20 years later on the film *Shadow Conspiracy*. We were shooting in Washington and during lunch one day I pulled my sleeve up and said, 'Look, I've still got it.' The look on his face was priceless when he saw me still wearing that old watch. A few years after that I was dining in London's Ivy restaurant when someone asked, in a mock Cockney accent, 'Excuse me sir, you wouldn't have the time would you?' I looked up and it was Donald.

While we were living in Stewart BC, my three year-old son Bruce came for the Christmas holidays and we went out and cut a Christmas tree down to take back to the motel for Jane to decorate. Three months later I visited the same spot and that Christmas tree was actually 40 foot high, that's how deep the snow was, we'd only snipped the top of it off. There was over 100 foot of snow that winter. It was such a wonderful and exciting place to be.

Bear Island was a great film to work on because I love adventure and the outdoor life. The 29 of us in my action unit lived on this frozen lake in wooden-sided huts that had canvas over the top and just a Billy stove for heat, but it was great. Dave Bickers was there too, and he and I would often go out on snowmobiles. On one trip my drive chain broke so he had to tow me back. We were miles from base camp and I noticed we were going faster and faster all the time. I suddenly realised Dave's chin was out and when his chin's out he's in racing mode. He'd bloody forgotten I was on the back being towed. Hanging on for grim death as we started to really fly along I yelled for him to stop, but he couldn't hear me over the roaring wind. This great big steep slope loomed up and I thought, shit, he's going to get airborne over it. Luckily he slowed up to check what was down there and I rear-ended him because I had no brakes. He said, 'Oh my God, I forgot you were there Vic.' I went, 'I know you bloody did, I thought you were going to kill me!' You have to remember he was a motocross world champion, and those guys have such amazing urges to go *fast*!

Right at the end of the shoot there was another nasty accident, this time involving cameraman Alan Hume. I'd met Alan on *Watcher in the Woods*, he's a great cameraman and went on to photograph Roger Moore's final three Bond

Base camp for the second unit, population 29, was nearly 4000 feet up.

films. We were doing an avalanche sequence and had to blow up some big blocks of ice. I yelled, 'Roll cameras, action.' Boom! All of these ice boulders started roaring down the mountain. One in particular, the size of a Mini car, curved away from its anticipated path and went straight towards Alan, smashed him onto the camera, broke all his cheek bones, his jaw, knocked all his teeth out and crushed his ribs, completely splattered him. He had to have his jaw wired together, but never lost his sense of humour. I saw him a few years later and he had his jaw all wired up, again. 'What the hell have you been doing?' I asked. It transpired that his son was selling his car but had gone to work when someone came round for a test drive. Alan went with this guy, who'd roared down the road too fast, hit a tree and put Alan through the windshield, busting his jaw again; poor old Alan. He was a real gentleman. The crazy thing is he only came in to shoot the sequence because Derek Brown, my DP, had left to shoot main unit on another show and Alan was helping out.

I went from one weather extreme to the other on my next big movie, *Escape to Athena*, shot on the island of Rhodes with an all-star cast led by Roger Moore and Telly Savalas. It was a prisoner of war movie with plenty of action and the director was George Pan Cosmatos, a wonderful, mad Greek guy. He'd interviewed Bob

Simmons first but didn't like him. 'He was trying to tell me how to direct!' Totally paranoid, poor old George. So I played it cool and got the job.

Before going to Greece we'd have these meetings and every idea or concept you gave George he'd say, 'I've seen that a million times, I want something different.' George was always pushing the limit, but he had no common sense. For example, we were going to shoot near the Corinth Canal, which cuts straight through the peninsula outside Athens. There's a railway bridge over the top and George had this idea of a resistance fighter chased by Germans jumping off it into the water below. I asked, 'How far is this fall?' He said about 80 feet. That didn't sound right to me so I did some research and found that it was 350 feet. I called George up and told him it is impossible for a human to fall that far. He said, 'I want this guy to really jump.'

So I started thinking about it, because it's no use saying you can't do something, you have to offer an alternative. That alternative was to do it in three cuts: the real man jumping onto a specially built platform 30 or 40 feet underneath the bridge, a dummy falling a couple of hundred feet or so, and then someone suspended 80 feet above the water on a wire and letting go. 'No. I've seen that a million times, a million times!' There was a pause from George. 'What if we have a boat underneath that he can land on?' I said, 'These are super tankers that go through the canal, they're not going to let you just park it there.' George, however, was thinking more along the lines of the boat not stopping but continuing sailing. 'But then the timing would have to be perfect,' I said, 'because if the stunt guy misses, disaster. Even so, 380 feet is an impossible fall for a human, whether it's into a stack of boxes or water, it's like hitting the ground, it'll kill him.' I carried on arguing and arguing and this was before I'd even started on the movie!

Later at midnight the phone rang. It was George. 'I've solved the problem.' I said, 'What problem?' He said, 'The resistance fighter jumping off the bridge.' Oh God, is he still thinking about that? 'I've solved it. He could be dressed as a German so he'll have a helmet on, he'll be safe.' I said, 'For fuck's sake George, a German helmet's a coal-scuttle. He's not going to land on his head and even if he did it would kill him. And if he hits the water vertical the helmet's going to rip his head off. And the bottom line is that it's an impossible fall anyway!' This went on and on, but I eventually talked him out of it.

Months later we were shooting and George drove us over to Athens to look over some locations. The next thing I knew we were at the Corinth Canal. It was an amazing location. Then the penny dropped, he still had this bug in his brain about this guy jumping off the bridge. 'Well, what do you think?' he said. 'You can't do it,' I said. 'Nobody in their right mind will jump off that bridge. You might get some idiot out of a lunatic asylum and give him enough money to jump, but then you'd be done for manslaughter.' I was really furious, told him to fuck off and stormed back to the car. A few minutes later George sat down next to me, all friendly like a big cuddly bear. 'I wouldn't you know.' I said, 'You wouldn't what?' He said, 'I've phoned my lawyer and they couldn't do me for manslaughter.' I went, 'For Christ's sake!' He'd actually pursued it that far. A wonderful guy, don't get me wrong, I loved him, but oh my God, very trying.

George told me later that on *Escape to Athena* the crew took his beloved black hat and nailed it to the mast of a boat when they finished the film. It really hurt him. The crew hated him so much they nailed his hat to the mast.

For *Athena* I took my usual crew out with me – Martin Grace, Marc Boyle, Dougie Robinson, Roy Alon, Nick Hobbs and Paul Weston. We did some good stuff on it and I think it's a solid action movie. We also had a lot of fun. Nick Hobbs is not the most diplomatic of people. Anthony Valentine was playing a Gestapo officer and was paranoid about his receding hair. He'd only just got to the stage where he could go out without his toupee. Nick Hobbs walked into the hotel one night and went, 'Bugger me, you're Tony Valentine. I didn't recognise you without your hair on.' Nick was a real character. He and the others were always using this swimming pool on the roof of our hotel after they had been for their evening run. And Greece being Greece, they turn the lights off whenever they feel like it. One particular night all the lights suddenly went out; a little while later there was this banging on my door. It was Dougie Robinson. 'Vic, Nick's jumped in the pool.' I said, 'So what, you do it every bloody night.' Dougie said, 'Yeah, but there's no water in there.' Oh shit.

It turned out that they'd drained the pool for some reason, and Nick had broken his arm. We told the producers it was just a bad sprain so I could keep him on the film, otherwise they would have sent him home to save the hotel and living expenses. He was playing one of the frogmen that attack Roger Moore on the beach, so I painted his plaster cast black to match his wetsuit and he did the fight with a broken arm. Thank goodness we had shot the part of the frogmen coming out of the water earlier, otherwise Nick would have had a soggy plaster cast!

For me the action highlight of the movie is a motorcycle chase featuring Elliot Gould and Tony Valentine, which was added at the last minute, and I was asked to direct. My only stipulation was that the dailies weren't to be shown without sound, because I remember seeing *Bullitt* once and the sound broke down, and it just looked like any old car chase. I walked all the back streets in Rhodes to come up with a lot of bike stunts. Marc Boyle was doubling Gould and Paul Weston was doubling Valentine. Dave Bickers built the machines, which were high performance motocross bikes, made up incredibly well to look like German army motorcycles. Dave also did most of the big jumps.

I think that bike chase sequence still stands the test of time. It's been mimicked in a lot of films since. I had to plot it, find the locations, shoot it and edit it, all within two weeks, with no extra equipment. It was a toughie but very satisfying.

The cast on *Athena* was great too. We had a lot of laughs. Telly Savalas I'd first met on *On Her Majesty's Secret Service.* He'd phone you at two in the morning if he was bored and get you down to play poker. He loved being around people and enjoyed beautiful women, chatting up any girl that stood still long enough. And he was very funny. We were doing one scene where the prisoners rappel down a mountain into a monastery. To do their close-ups on the cliff face, the actors had to wear a safety harness underneath their clothes and I told Dougie Robinson to help Savalas put his on. Dougie came back looking quite shocked. 'Telly doesn't wear underwear. I was kneeling down in front of him and said, "Drop your trousers please," and he did and out it plopped, right in my face.' I think he did it for the effect, old Telly.

David Niven was also on the film and was quite wonderful. He'd come and search out the stuntmen's table, sit down and start telling stories about his days in Hollywood. By the end of the evening we'd have 20 people round us listening. Generally the stars love the stuntmen because they're down to earth and a lot more boisterous. I guess we're less intense than actors are, so stars know that they can let their hair down with us. Stuntmen are normally larger than life characters and a very diverse bunch of people, and good fun. God, I've had some wonderfully wild nights around the world with some absolutely crazy people. Things you'd be arrested for in real life.

HAL AND BURT

Back in England I got a call to go out to Egypt where Ian McShane was making a TV movie called *The Curse of King Tut's Tomb*, but there had been a terrible accident. The producers, allegedly for cheapness, had taken no stunt people and when they needed a period vehicle they just grabbed an old car off a taxi rank in Luxor with no brakes; nothing worked on it. Apparently during the shoot the car had to pull up in front of Carter's house, which was on top of a knoll. McShane, who was playing Carter, was inside when the car started rolling backwards down the hill. As the other actors jumped out, he continued struggling with the controls but then, realising the game was up, tried bailing out himself, but got his foot hooked up in the steering wheel and broke his leg in six places when the thing crashed. Cut. Right, pack everybody back to England; the shit's hit the fan. Now they were going back again – having recast with the guy from *Poldark*, Robin Ellis – to do the sequence properly with stunt people and vintage cars.

The producers now decided they needed a stunt person to oversee matters and employed me. I called Dave Bickers and gave him the film's requirements. Together we tracked down a lovely Model T Ford, circa 1915, and a Buick, and we flew with them on a transport plane bound for Cairo. Landing in Egypt we were stuck there for a week because customs wouldn't clear the cars. I kept telling the producers, 'Look guys, the only way you're going to clear this is if you bung 'em a few quid. They don't want the hassle of paperwork, the paper they want has got little numbers written on it, and faces. Just pay them.' And that's what happened. Now it was even more important that these valuable cars got to the location in one piece. Nervous about shipping them down alone, the producers got Dave and I to ferry them to Luxor in two old transporters. It was a great trip. I insisted on travelling behind the trucks in a hired chauffeur-driven Mercedes, just in case they were hijacked, and ten miles out of Luxor this huge rock loomed out of the dust and smashed our sump. So our entry into Luxor was very grand, this Mercedes being towed to our hotel on an old rope behind a truck.

While we were in Luxor we had to shoot a chase sequence, with me driving another bloody motorbike and sidecar. It was all in soft gravel and Dave said, 'Now be careful Vic coming round this corner, don't give it too much throttle because it will slide off with you.' I went, yeah, yeah, why should I listen to a world champion, I know better than he does. Sure enough I came belting around the corner with it open full blast and the thing slid out from under me and smacked straight into a big rock. I flew over the handlebars and split my shins open. And it's so dirty, that Valley of the Kings, with dust and shit everywhere, that I got an infection in my leg and by the middle of the night it had blown up like a balloon. My wife Jane got a bread roll from the hotel kitchen, some salt and boiled water and made a bread poultice, because that's what you do with horses. I slapped this on my leg and by the morning it had sucked all the poison out and I went back to finish the shot. Poor Dave had been up all night rebuilding the front forks of the bike, which were the old girder-style ones and needed an expert touch like only Dave had. A great adventure that one.

While we were in Luxor my great friend Stuart Freeman got married to his fiancée Miriam. At the wedding reception they proudly brought in all the food and one dish was roast goat; basically the whole goat skinned and roasted. My son Bruce who was with us said, at the top of his voice, 'Oh look Dad, we're having dog!' because this thing on the silver platter looked just like a skinned greyhound.

Dave Bickers and I worked together again pretty soon after that, on a Burt Reynolds jewel heist caper movie called *Rough Cut.* It was a chaotic production. Don Siegel, who'd made *Dirty Harry*, was directing and had terrible run-ins with the producer and was fired. When Reynolds heard about it he said, 'The only reason I'm doing this fucking film is because of Siegel. Get him back.' Then Siegel fired the stunt team because he didn't think they were doing a good job and wanted me to take over. Hal Needham was also brought over to direct the second unit.

Hal was the big cheese back then, he'd directed *Smokey and the Bandit, Hooper* and all those stunt movies, and when I met him at Stansted Airport he had gold dripping all over him. He had gold chains, and wore medallions of the movies he'd directed, and had how many millions they'd earned, which was a huge amount, on his belt. As we walked to lunch Hal told me how it was gonna be. 'I don't know if you've worked with Americans much but I like things prepared, I like to shoot fast.' I said, 'Yeah, yeah, sure.' He knew I had a good reputation.

Then I introduced him to Dave. Hal stopped in his tracks. 'Are you *the* Dave

Bickers?' Dave said, 'I don't know about that. I'm Dave Bickers from Coddenham in Suffolk.' And Needham said, 'Did you win the World Championship in Czechoslovakia on a CZ?' Dave went, 'Oh aye, that would have been me.' Needham was on the war film *Bridge at Remagen* in Czechoslovakia when those championships were on, and used to go down and watch. He fancied himself as a motorcyclist too and had recreated the track near to where he was shooting and rode round on it all day. His assistant would wave a flag if the producer ever turned up and he'd quickly nip back to the set. So Dave Bickers was his hero, and this huge American stunt idol was suddenly reacting in awe. 'Oh my God, Mr Bickers, this is incredible.' From that day on I couldn't do a thing wrong with Hal Needham.

The powers that be had looked at *Rough Cut* and realised it had nothing going for it, so wanted to inject a massive action sequence; 'Go to Holland and give us a car chase,' they told Hal. Burt, Hal and I were in a restaurant in Amsterdam when Hal got a call. He came back to the table crestfallen. 'They've cancelled us, said it's too expensive. They reckon the chase will cost $5 million.' 'Bullshit,' I said. 'They're saying that just so you don't shoot it. It can't cost more than two.' Hal said, 'Give us a quick budget then.' Jesus, I thought, I've opened my big mouth now. So I grabbed a couple of beer mats and put down what the stunt guys would cost, the cars, plus hotels and all the rest and it came to about a million and a half. 'That looks about right,' said Hal, rushing back to the phone. And on the strength of those calculations, which were straight off the top of my head – I was just praying they were accurate – Hal got the green light to go ahead with the car chase.

Dave and I picked 20 cars, and Dave hired racing mechanic friends of his, who knew about the essence of speed, to rig them (when you earn a living racing you can't earn anything if you don't get on the starting line). We had two crews working round the clock. Hal couldn't believe how we kept these cars running after smashing them up during the day. We put one of them into the harbour and just fished it out again and carted it back to the garage. Every morning Hal would count these cars as they all drove to work; he was amazed. I also hired a bunch of the best stunt drivers around because I was dealing with Hal Needham, I couldn't mess around, and we just dreamt up this whole car chase from scratch. On the first day one of the car engines blew up and I thought geez, what are we going to do now? No problem for Dave Bickers: he took the spare wheel out and put it on the ground, tipped the car over so it was resting on it with the underneath exposed, pulled the sump off, pulled an oil pump out, stuck another one in, rolled it back onto its wheels, filled it up with oil and away we went. I said to Hal, 'That's why

I employ these guys, they keep us up and running. Anybody else would've towed it back to the garage.' And he said, 'Yeah, this guy's God.'

Hal was great. I like to plan what I'm doing, but Hal would literally just do two takes before yelling, 'OK, move onto the next one!' In the end I went, 'For Christ's sake, you've got to slow down Hal. I don't care who you use in the States but this is getting dangerous now. We're not having a chance to check the safety on anything.' And he said, 'OK kid, I was just waiting for you to tell me when we're going too fast.' He was just testing me out.

Burt was fabulous too. He respected stuntmen and loved them, because he'd been one himself. And he loved Hal. They were great mates and used to live together. Hal only went to stay with Burt for a week and eight years later he was still living there! Burt told me, 'I couldn't get rid of the bastard until he'd earned a few million on *Smokey and the Bandit* and even then he didn't want to leave.' Burt didn't get on well with the producers on *Rough Cut* so enjoyed flying out to Amsterdam to work with us. Amsterdam is a fantastic city. The guys got up to lots of escapades there. We worked hard and played hard. One day Burt came on the set to tell us what a great job we'd done and that he'd organised a wrap party in this private club. It turned out to be a sex club that had closed down for the night just for us. We were all sitting there watching the acts when suddenly this great big gorilla leapt onto the stage. It turned out to be someone in a suit playing with a huge false dick that squirted water over us, especially one guy called Roy Street who'd been heckling the girls. I'll never forget seeing this burly stuntman somersaulting over the seats trying to get out of the way. It was a great night. Burt laid everything on and turned up as well. It wasn't your usual wrap party.

In 1980 when *Rough Cut* was made Burt was one of the biggest stars in the world. Since then he's fallen out of favour, but I've always reckoned that he's been ready for a reappraisal because he's a very good actor. He's one of those stars who like to poke fun at themselves, like he did in *Striptease*, and for me anyone who can do that, like Arnie did in *Twins*, that's the mark of a super actor and a star. I still think there's a lot of value left in old Burt.

LEAPS OF FAITH

Green Ice was another caper movie and starred Ryan O'Neal and Omar Sharif. It did no business at all when it came out but was highly significant for me, and for the stunt business. We shot it in Mexico, over at Las Hadas in Manzanillo, the place where they made 10 with Dudley Moore ogling at Bo Derek on the hot sands. In the film there is a sequence where Ryan O'Neal gets chased into the water by baddies and Anne Archer turns up in a speedboat, throws a rope out to him, he grabs it and is dragged along on his belly, bouncing across the waves. The location they'd chosen was Skeleton Coast, which was miles of just flat sand, boring as hell, and there were really dangerous riptides, so I said, 'We can't shoot there, it's madness.'

I hired a speedboat and went looking for a new site and found this beautiful cove that was like something out of a Bounty advert, just magical. Until we found out its name was Shark Cove, because that's where all the sharks came to mate, which scared the life out of us. We did the shot anyway, with me overseeing it in a helicopter. Suddenly I saw that Ryan was in trouble in the water. I bailed out of the helicopter to put a life jacket on him because the surf was beating the crap out of his body. We got ashore and some long lens photographers took snaps of this and a few days later there were newspaper headlines: 'Vic Armstrong saves Ryan O'Neal.'

The producer was Jack Wiener, whom I worked for on Escape to Athena, a really gruff persona but a fabulous guy. Green Ice featured a daring robbery where the thieves arrive on the roof of a skyscraper in small, one-man hot air balloons, called cloud-hoppers. For their getaway Jack asked me to come up with a device that enabled them to jump off the building and land safely 340 feet below. It had to be small enough to be carried in a cloud hopper, simple enough to be used by anybody without prior technical knowledge or ability – it couldn't be like

An air ram-assisted throw over a rowing boat in Vera Cruz, Mexico on Green Ice.

something out of a James Bond movie or anything outrageous, it had to be simple enough to be made in a backstreet bicycle shop and we needed to film it working practically. Lastly, it must never have been seen in a movie before. 'Oh,' I said. 'That'll take me two or three minutes to think of something Jack. Jesus Christ!'

I got my stunt team together and posed them the questions, to see what they came up with. Most of their ideas were pretty wild, except Terry Walsh, who remembered his sister going to an open day at Chelsea barracks 30 years before, where she did a parachute jump using a mechanism that dropped her 30 feet safely to the ground. I knew someone in the Parachute Regiment over at Aldershot barracks and he told me that it sounded like a fan descender, a piece of specialized equipment that enables a cable-controlled descent. The Royal Air Force used them to simulate parachute landings in hangars without having to jump from a plane. I was shown some and thought, this is a great idea.

Grabbing hold of Dave Bickers I sketched out the bare dimensions of what I wanted him to build for me before jetting off to Mexico for a location recce. First job was to check out the building. Standing on the roof I looked over the edge. It was a hell of a drop, 340 feet. The production manager Colin Brewer was up there with me, on his knees because he was scared of heights. He asked me how much the drop was going to cost. I thought, I've got him now, this is the best time to

Me wearing a dead cat and Ryan holding my son Bruce in Las Hadas, Mexico.

negotiate my price. A thousand sounded a lot, so I said £950. 'What, every time?' he asked. 'Yeah, each time you're risking your life,' I said. 'You're dead right,' he said. 'I wouldn't do it for £9,000. You've got it. But can we go down now?'

Back in England I visited RAF Brize Norton, the base where these things were made originally and which had the best parachutists in the armed forces, the guys who'd taught Prince Charles to parachute. They assigned Keith Teasdale to me, who was a world record holder for high altitude drops, night drops, you name it, and they gave me all the technical data, which matched what I'd sketched pretty much. We changed a lot of the specs, knowing the height and the extra speed we needed and added things like a brake and measuring guide. After testing the fan descender at Cardington in Bedfordshire, we went out to Mexico City to do the final tests and stunt. I made a point of telling the company that I didn't want anybody around when I was doing my test drops, I wanted to do it in my own time and under my own conditions. So it was just Dave and I on the roof.

We set up the equipment and I climbed out into this window-cleaning basket that was swinging like mad and hung over the edge, ready to take the 340 foot leap of faith and let go. 'If you look over in about five minutes,' I said to Dave, 'and you see my hands still on the top of this rig, you'd better reach over with your hammer and bash me on the knuckles because I ain't going otherwise.' I yelled 3, 2, 1, held my breath... and let go. That was the first ever stunt using a fan descender machine. We did three dummy runs and it all worked fabulously. And the rest is history. For the shot in the movie Marc Wolfe was in the camera helicopter following me as I jumped off, coming over the edge with me and dropping 200 feet before peeling away and letting the other four cameras take over. 15 feet from the ground I stopped on a window ledge. Roy Alon then drove up in a truck and I released myself from the cable, jumped onto the roof, slid down the bonnet, into the truck and away. It was all done in one continuous shot.

I ended up doing that stunt ten times, earning £9,500 before eleven o'clock in the morning. Unbelievable. By that time the streets were filled with thousands of people; one sweet old lady came up to me and kissed me. Walking back to the trailer my wife Jane and son Bruce, who was still quite young, navigated their way through the crowd towards me. I was pretty chuffed with myself and said, 'What do you think about that then Bruce?' And he went, 'Yes it's good. Can we have an ice cream at Denny's on the way home Dad?' Kids, they keep your feet on the ground.

That stunt ended up having a big impact on the industry. I thought I'd invented the fan descender for just that one-off job, but we used it again on *Indiana Jones and the Temple of Doom* for the scene outside the Obi-Wan nightclub with Indy and Kate Capshaw's character falling 70 feet through canopies. Then we used it for the movie's climax when Mola Ram drops down and knocks Indy off the hanging bridge. Stuntman Glenn Randall loved this machine so much we gave him one to take back to the States, and of course everybody saw it and they went all around the world. Years later I received a Technical Achievement Academy Award for the fan descender; and it all stemmed from that one conversation with Jack Wiener and talking to Terry Walsh and coming up with that design. But I didn't patent it; I didn't even call it the Armstrong descender, which I should have done.

People are moving on to different pieces of equipment now, but for years the fan descender was a real mainstay, coinciding as it did with the advent of digital wire removal. People became more accepting of using wires as part of a fall because they could remove them in post-production more easily and cheaply. And I reckon it saved a lot of lives and a lot of sleepless nights for stunt people that would otherwise have had to do a really high fall.

It didn't help me though when I had to fall 100 feet off a viaduct into an airbag for the third *Omen* film. My old friend Marc Boyle was co-ordinating the show and asked me to do the stunt. I must admit I stood on top of this viaduct looking down, the airbag like a matchbox beneath me, and thought, what the hell am I

Going, going, gone! Jumping 100 feet off a viaduct for Omen III. *Oh for a fan descender.*

doing here? I've just bought a new Mercedes; I'm never going to get to drive it. By then I was co-ordinating, so I didn't really have to do those kinds of stunts any more, and bizarrely I was also directing myself for the fall, as I was also the action unit director. And with the fan descender you shouldn't really have needed to do high falls like that anyway – it was crazy. But I did it, and it gave me a great sense of achievement. I'm a great believer in self-achievement.

Sometimes you have to confront your demons. I went through the same thing with Carrie-Anne Moss, preparing her for *Mission: Impossible III*, back when Joe Carnahan was going to direct it. She'd been cast along with Scarlett Johansson, though in the end neither ended up doing the movie. Scarlett had never done wirework before and had to jump off a 50-foot building with Tom Cruise. I thought she'd be terrified, but Scarlett was a wonderful girl, no fears, no inhibitions, just jumped off, wow, this is fun. Carrie, who'd done all the *Matrix* movies, was terrified of heights. So it was a huge personal challenge for her.

I took her on top of a 60-foot building and she nearly dented my arm just hanging on walking down the middle of it, not even looking over the edge. I did this with her for half an hour every day, slowly building her up to the time when she'd be dropped in a studio on wires. It was a psychological progression. By the end of the first week she was asking to do the 30-foot practice jump and I said, 'No, you're not ready.' She said, 'I am. I can do it.' I said, 'No.' She said, 'What, are you fucking with my brain?' I said, 'I actually am, yeah. You're going to have to beg me to do it.' 'You bastard,' she said. And I wouldn't let her do it. The next day she said, '*Please* can I?' I said, 'That's better. Yes you can.' And she jumped off on wires, which was a huge leap of faith for her because she was terrified. She was a jelly when she landed, but it was her pushing, not me. And the same thing happened at the end of the second and last week with the 60-foot jump. It's overcoming your personal demons, and that to me is bravery. Anybody that's not frightened of heights is not brave to jump off. I tell you, she was a foot taller when she left that set.

On our last day together she asked me, 'Where'd you get this technique?' I said, 'From animals. I train horses.' You have to kid horses sometimes. I've had horses that won't jump a stick but by the end of the day they're bolting over gates because they enjoy it so much. She said, 'You're not comparing me to an animal are you?' I just grinned and said, 'Well, not really…'

A WEREWOLF IN PICCADILLY

By now as a stuntman I must have driven every vehicle going: trucks, motorbikes, cars, boats, you name it. I'd even learnt to fly aeroplanes in my spare time. Thanks to Alf Joint I could now add a red London double-decker bus to the list. The chance came when I worked alongside him as co-stunt co-ordinator on *An American Werewolf in London.* Alf had got a call out of the blue from director John Landis. 'John who?' Alf said. Years earlier Alf was working on the Clint Eastwood war film *Kelly's Heroes*, when Landis was no more than a gofer. Everybody gave him an awful time except Alf, so Landis always had a soft spot for him. In fact everybody that was rude or dissed him on *Kelly's Heroes* Landis gave the cold shoulder to when he became a director. 'Alf, it's John Landis,' the phone call went. 'Remember that werewolf story I was telling you about on *Kelly's Heroes*? I've got it off the ground. I'm making a movie of it.'

The film featured groundbreaking special effects, but from a stunt point of view the biggest headache was the climax, when the wolf escapes from a porno cinema in London's West End and wreaks havoc in Piccadilly Circus. The police refused to give us permission to shut the area down but said we could briefly stop the traffic, so long as it was at three in the morning on a weekend when it was at its lowest ebb. I knew then that planning was vital to the sequence being a success. Alf was of the same mind: we needed rehearsal, rehearsal and rehearsal. At Brooklands Aerodrome we built a replica of Piccadilly Circus; the whole area was marked out to scale, every road, every curb was represented by bales of hay. It was a big effort because we had twenty-odd stunt people there, all the crew, vehicles, back-up, catering, all for two weeks. The production just saw it as a waste of money, not realising that this kind of rehearsal pays off on the day.

The key vehicle in the sequence is a London double-decker bus, which had to do a 180-degree spin to start off the mayhem. I was the bus driver and whenever I tried to spin the bus it would just slide 10 or 20 degrees and stop, because it was so well balanced. We were sitting there scratching our heads as to how we were going to get this thing to spin when Dave Bickers said to me, 'What help do you need?' Now, the previous day I'd been to get new tyres for my horse truck. The tyre fitter at the shop had a trolley jack under the back end and just pulled the truck sideways, so what I figured we needed were some wheels at 90 degrees to the bus's rear wheels, that could lift the rear end up as I made the manoeuvre. Dave said we needed to invert one of my air rams, that could fire 10-inch fork lift wheels down on cue, but he'd have to cut a hole in the bottom of the bus. 'Do what you want,' I said. 'Just get the rig made.' This is another example of the genius of Dave Bickers.

On the night of the shoot, Dave's team parked up every road with tow trucks and on a given signal just pulled out with their flashing lights to stop any traffic coming through. Every alleyway and doorway had to be policed as well; we couldn't have pedestrians suddenly walking in. It was Alf's idea to have this bus do a 180-degree spin, which was the cue for all the 20 or so other vehicles to swerve and hit and crash bang wallop. Being the bus driver, I was parked down Lower Regent Street, waiting. On 'action' I came belting into Piccadilly Circus. There was a Wimpy burger restaurant on the corner and as I locked up the rear wheels and spun the steering wheel, the front end carried straight on because of the wet road. I thought, Jesus I'm going to make the record books here by going through Wimpy's in a double-decker bus. Just in time, the back end of the bus swung round on Dave's fork lift wheels rig, and started overtaking me – and then it was just hell after that, bedlam, everybody put their pedal to the metal and the wreck was on. Everybody keyed off my bus, Rocky Taylor, Roy Alon, Tony Smart, we were so well rehearsed it was a chain reaction and a superb shot. We had the Dave Bickers team race in with their tow trucks to get rid of the wrecked vehicles, and people with brooms running in sweeping up all the broken glass, so everything looked as though we hadn't been there. Within two and a half minutes of shouting 'Action', normal traffic was allowed back in. The police just couldn't believe how quickly it was done.

The whole thing was repeated the next night to get more coverage, and then we went back to Brooklands and built various shop fronts for close-up stunt shots of people hurtling through them. Now John Landis always likes to be in his own movies and I drove the car that knocked him straight into a travel shop window. I also did a head-on crash with another driver going at 15 miles an hour each, that's a 30 mph impact, a hell of a jolt. And I made the classic mistake of keeping my hands on the steering wheel instead of letting go; you automatically just hold on to the steering wheel to brace yourself. My wrists ached for three weeks after that from the jar through the steering column. Still, it was a very rewarding picture to work on and I loved John Landis, very collaborative and a great guy to work with.

RAIDERS OF THE LOST ARK

While I was out in Mexico on *Green Ice* I kept getting calls to work on this movie called *Raiders of the Lost Ark*, because they said I looked just like the leading man. When I finally got back to England they were just finishing at Elstree, so I did a bit of work on it in the studio. Around that time I was working like a mad man, appearing in some nine movies one week, working days and nights; that's what you do when you're hungry for work. I was absolutely knackered by the end. One was a fire job on Disney's *Dragonslayer*, a full burn. In those days we always used to have in our stunt bag a fire blanket that was made of asbestos, unheard of now. You'd stick it on under your clothes and administer the fire gel. Nowadays they use a special liquid called Zel Gel, which is a fire retardant and a coolant that you slap all over and soak your clothes in and it stops the fire and heat penetrating, so you can do bigger burns. But this was pre-Zel Gel days so we just stuck some racing drivers' Nomex underwear on, a bit of asbestos, a bit of glue, set fire to it and ran around screaming until someone put you out; very basic.

On a full body burn, fear is quite intense. I did another fire job where I was a Spitfire pilot in this cockpit they'd had built. I wore an old flying jacket over the Nomex and thought that would be thick enough. But the trouble with fire jobs is that once the fire has been put out, your clothes are still hot and the heat continues to penetrate, turning your sweat to steam that burns and scalds you. They're horrible things, fire jobs. I hate them. They're very final if they do go wrong.

Back on *Raiders* I still hadn't met its star Harrison Ford, but was cast to double this German guy with a big square jaw. Out on location in Tunisia stunt co-ordinator Peter Diamond was setting up a fight between Indy and this big hulking Nazi brute (played by my old friend Pat Roach) around an aeroplane, and asked me to take over co-ordinating the first unit because he had to run off to do the truck chase. He gave me a storyboard of 30 or 40 pictures. In the meantime they were shooting some other stuff and I hung around watching as Steven Spielberg instructed the second camera operator what angles he wanted to shoot the arrival of a vehicle convoy. This cameraman rehearsed for a while, but didn't like the set-up Spielberg gave him, so he changed it. That's interesting, I thought, he didn't ask or say anything, he just did it. After the shot Spielberg returned to ask how it went and the camera guy said, 'I didn't like your angle so I've changed it.' Spielberg went, 'Have you?' I said to Dave Tomblin, the film's 1st AD, 'Who's that camera operator there telling Steven Spielberg what the angle should be?' Dave said, 'Oh, that's George Lucas.'

By now it was about noon, we hadn't done the fight yet so I decided to get an early lunch. Walking off I heard someone shout, 'Harrison.' I kept walking. 'Harrison, Harrison!' The voice repeated. Then somebody grabbed me by the shoulder and spun me round. It was Spielberg. 'You're not Harrison.' I said, 'I know I'm not Harrison. I'm Vic Armstrong.' Steven said, 'What are you doing here?' I replied, 'I'm a stuntman. I just arrived last night.' 'But you're a fantastic double for Harrison,' Spielberg said, then yelled for Dave Tomblin to come over. 'Dave, this stuntman looks just like Harrison, I thought he *was* Harrison.' Dave said, 'This is the guy we'd first suggested as stunt double for Harrison, but he's been in Mexico, we've only just been able to get him.' 'Fantastic!' roared Steven.

It's amazing really just how closely I resembled Harrison, the way I looked, walked and acted. Even his clothes fit me, except his boots which were a bit too tight, but everything else fitted like a glove. I suppose the time that really sums up how similar we were was when I was walking along and Harrison's kid came up, took hold of my hand and walked along with me – until I started to speak, which made him look up, scream and run off!

In one interview Harrison said, 'Yeah, we look alike. He spent several nights with my wife before she realised.' Funny guy.

HARRISON FORD

Back in those days Vic and I used to look quite a bit alike, so he was extremely useful as a stunt double because the more a stunt double resembles the actor, the closer they can be shot and the more effectively they can be used. But what's really valuable about Vic is his capacity as a filmmaker. Vic is a real storyteller; he knows how to squeeze story to get the most out of it. He brings to movies a terrific imagination and skill with the basics of filmmaking,

Even Harrison's own son sometimes had trouble telling us apart.

knowing where the camera might be put to achieve the most energy and excitement. He's so aware of all the components that are involved in stunts today, the effects department, the prop department, and the actors. Primarily Vic has evolved from a stuntman to a filmmaker, and one of the best.

The next day we shot the fight around the plane. Harrison and Pat Roach squared up to each other and Harrison threw a punch. 'That's great. Moving on,' said Steven. Now as a stunt co-ordinator my job is to make sure that, on film, those punches look like they've connected. I was standing looking right over the lens of the camera and in my opinion it was a miss. Now I was stuck between a rock and a hard place because Steven had called it good, but I thought I'd better say something. 'Excuse me sir, that was actually a miss.' He went, 'Oh, you again.' I said, 'Yeah, sorry, it was a miss.' Steven paused briefly. 'Well, I thought it was a hit.' I said, 'No, I was actually looking over the lens and it was a miss, I think.' Finally Steven said, 'OK, we'll do it again.' After that take was completed Steven, sarcastically almost, turned to me and said, 'How was that?' I went, 'That was good. That was a hit.' And we carried on and created a great fight routine. Three days later we were all watching dailies when the shot that I'd said was a miss came on screen. Steven had printed it. The old heart started to go, but sure enough it was a miss and Steven, who was right in front of me, turned round and said, 'Good call Vic.' I couldn't do much wrong after that, it was great.

The fight concludes with a truckload of Germans arriving on the scene and

Wendy and the Raiders of the Lost Ark *stunt team. L-R Back row, Chuck Waters, Sergio Mioni, Wendy, Rocky Taylor, Billy Horrigan. Front row, Terry Leonard, Peter Diamond and Paul Weston.*

Indy blasting them all to hell. The night before, Steven had talked to Kit West, the special effects chief who ended up getting an Oscar for *Raiders*. 'Kit, I don't like the idea of blood splashing everywhere. I want a sort of mist, a dust feel.' Kit went, 'Umm, OK.' Cut to the next day and sure enough, bang, bang, bang, all the squibs went off and this dust flew into the air. 'That's great Kit. Cut,' said Steven. Then all our eyes started burning like mad and we began sneezing, everybody was in real pain and we couldn't think what the hell was going on until somebody said to Kit, 'What did you use in those squibs?' And he went, 'I was hoping nobody would find out. Steven didn't ask me until late last night and there's nowhere to go shopping in the local town, there's only like two shops and a camel station, so I used Cayenne pepper. It was the only red dust I could find.' And of course we all got these terrible eyes and noses streaming and coughing and sneezing, it was hysterical.

Raiders was shot at a real breakneck pace. I was sitting with Spielberg one day waiting to do a shot with this car and Les Dilley from the art department was diligently dusting it down, making sure it matched exactly the last scene and

Steven yelled, 'For God's sake guys, come on let's get a move on, this is only a B movie, let's go, go, go. Don't worry about the damn dust.' After the problems on *1941* Steven wanted to do *Raiders* purely to prove that he could shoot on schedule, on budget and deliver the goods. When I talked to him about *1941* he said, 'It was never a failure, it actually made money, it just didn't make as much money as my other films had done. But I think I made one mistake with it, I should have made it a musical.'

Tunisia was a tough location, everybody was ill. It was just excruciatingly hot and we had to stop shooting at two o'clock when it reached 120 degrees. You didn't even sweat; all you had was salt on your arms because it evaporated before it hit the air. You'd drive to work in the morning and see Arab people throwing up and getting the shits, and they were the bloody locals! Steven wouldn't eat or drink anything unless he'd physically broken the seal of the bottle himself or opened the can that he was eating from; just because he daren't have time off through illness. We also couldn't understand why the crew was getting so ill, because we all drank bottled Evian water. Until one day somebody followed the guy that collected the empties and saw him filling these Evian bottles straight out of the water truck and putting the lids back on and handing them out. We put a stop to that but people were still ill. And the hotel was bloody awful; you'd have to scrape the meal off the plates.

By now I'd met Harrison and he was great, very down to earth and welcoming, a wonderful guy. We both have the same outlook on life and professionalism. He really is a consummate professional. We worked very closely on all the fights. I'd work them out first before bringing Harrison in, and then choreograph it with him to make sure all the moves and the punches went the way he felt comfortable doing it. Then we'd take it to show Spielberg. And that's how we worked together on the next two Indy movies as well.

Pretty quickly I became known around the industry as a double for Harrison. In *Return of the Jedi* I was tied to a pole as Han Solo and carried by Ewoks through the treetops, because Harrison had a bad back. And before that I did *Blade Runner*. Harrison was busy on another film and the studio desperately needed some pick up shots of him, so they flew over from LA, where the movie was made, and rebuilt some of the sets at Pinewood for me to double Harrison on. They built the bathroom where he finds the fish scales and the whole Chinese market, which was quite a big set. It was funny because I watched the *Blade Runner* dailies of me running through the market and all of a sudden this white unicorn appeared. 'What the heck is that?' I asked the editor. 'Oh that's a film Ridley's thinking of doing.' He was obviously shooting tests for *Legend*, which I subsequently worked on.

In *Raiders* there's that famous scene where Indy meets this hulking great Arab swordsman and simply shoots him dead. Originally there was an elaborate fight sequence planned and a stunt team went up to the coast for two weeks working it out. They really drew the easy ticket – we heard all this talk about fabulous beaches and topless tourists, and there we were stuck down in bloody Nefta with the dysentery mob. When the main crew finished with us they flew up to the coast to join Peter Diamond, who showed Steven the fight routine. Big Terry Richards played the Arab and he swished his sword about and then the fight carried on through the whole of the Casbah.

Steven watched and said, 'Look, I'm going to shoot whatever I can until three o'clock because then I'm getting out of here.' Peter Diamond was dumbstruck: 'You can't do that, it's gonna take four days to film this fight. It's a huge fight and the guys have been rehearsing it for weeks.' Steven said, 'I've got a plane coming at three, I'm out of here, I've got enough, I don't need any more here.' Dave Tomblin butted in, 'For Christ's sake Steven, you've got to do this.' But Steven was standing firm, 'No, I'm out at three.' Tomblin said, 'Well, it's stupid doing this whole routine, you might as well just shoot the guy with a gun.' 'Don't be facetious Dave.' Then Steven paused. 'I'll tell you what, let's try that. Yes, let's try just shooting him.' And the rest is history. It's one of the funniest moments in the movie. And we reprised it on *Temple of Doom* on the cliff top when Indy reaches for the gun – but it's not there.

After working on the plane fight, I went over and joined the second unit, playing a German on the back of the escaping truck in the famous chase sequence, creeping round and trying to kill Indy. I also doubled Harrison quite a bit and just got totally involved with the movie. When the crew wrapped in Tunisia they had a little hiatus and then set up in Hawaii to do the opening scene. I went to Morocco to do some prep on my next film for a week, then I flew out to Kauai and doubled Harrison for the last bit of the giant boulder rolling out of the cave, and some other bits and pieces. Poor Alfred Molina was there too, complaining about the spiders. 'Typical,' he was saying. 'They had to pick me, didn't they, to have tarantulas on me back. I'm scared to death of spiders.'

In the final bit of the opening Indy is chased by Indians, leaps on a vine and falls into a river, climbs aboard a plane, sits in the cockpit and famously comes face to face with a snake. I'd been running all over the jungle, with dust flying off me, when Steven decided it was time for Harrison to take over. I was sent off to stand on the skid of the aeroplane as it took off. Then someone reminded Steven that a camera had already been attached to the wing for close-up shots of Harrison. 'OK, flip that round,' said Steven. 'We'll do some more running with Vic while you go and do some reaction shots of Harrison with the snake. Then we'll set-up again for Vic.'

Harrison got in the plane, leaving the door open so in the shot it looked like he'd just clambered in, and took off. We watched the plane disappear behind a tree and then heard the engine change note. Then we heard a bang! Jesus, they've crashed. We all jumped into boats and roared down the river and sure enough there was the plane buried in the bank, standing on its nose. Harrison and the pilot were sitting next to it, looking disconsolate, but luckily unhurt. What happened was that the open door had affected the aerodynamics and the plane banked and smashed into the ground. What made me sweat was the thought that if I had been standing on the skid at that time I'd have gone straight into the propeller blade and come out like chips. It just shows you how fate lends a hand in life.

After Hawaii it was back out to Morocco to finish pre-production on *The Desert King*, a biopic about Ibn Saud, the founder of the kingdom of Saudi Arabia. The script included a big battle sequence, calling for thousands of men and hundreds of horses and camels, so there was a lot to prepare, but in the end the whole thing was cancelled when the Saudi royal family made it known that they didn't want the film to be made. By that time I was at home for the arrival of my second son: Jane give birth to Scott Munro Armstrong on 12 January 1981. (Three decades on, Scott now works with me as my stunt co-ordinator.)

Meanwhile, *Raiders* was nearing release. Today it's rightly considered a classic, but at the time nobody had any inkling it would turn out like that, to us it was just another movie. It was hot, it was uncomfortable, it was fun but no more fun than any other movie, the same camaraderie, the same people, the same dirty old locations, the same food; nobody knew we were making anything special. That was until I went to Leicester Square in London, to the cast and crew show on a Sunday morning. I'd taken the kids, and when the truck chase was on they stood on their seats shouting, 'Go on Indy!' Suddenly I thought, wow, this is something out of the ordinary. Even to this day the theme music gets your pulse racing. I'm very, very proud to have been part of the trilogy. Like the Bond films it became a family thing. I've got a crew jacket that says on the back:

Indiana Jones, World Tour 1980-1989
England, Tunisia, Macao, Sri Lanka,
Spain, Italy, France, Germany, Jordan, USA
'It's not the years, it's the mileage.'

I think only 18 of those jackets were handed out, because only 18 of us did all three original movies. I also worked on the TV series, *Young Indiana Jones.* So Indy is a very special part of my life.

GEORGE LUCAS

The great thing about Vic when we came over on the first Indy film was he was such a good likeness for Harrison. And Indiana Jones has such an iconic outfit that you could sit on the set and not be able to tell those two guys apart; which was fun, a lot of people were always mistaking Vic for Harrison. It was uncanny actually. So we started out with Vic as Harrison's double; and not only did he look like Harrison but he was also able to learn to move like Harrison. That was fantastic. In time we all came to realize that Vic was also a great stunt co-ordinator and so he became our stunt co-ordinator on the series as well as Harrison's double.

Vic's always very cheerful and very calm on a movie set, he isn't a jump around kind of a guy, or a show off kind of guy; he just does his job. And if a stunt works out spectacularly he smiles, and if it doesn't work out he frowns and says, 'Well, we won't do that one again.' And we did some amazing things on the Indy trilogy. Those movies are built on stunts, and real stunts, there's not much in the way of special effects in those movies, so most of the stunts were real. Vic really was a great addition to our team.

ESCAPE FROM BAGHDAD

Clash *of Loyalties* (aka *The Big Question*, aka *Al-mas' Ala Al-Kubra*) was a strange movie, and an even stranger experience. I got a call to go out to Baghdad for this project that was staffed by an English crew but financed with Iraqi money, because it was about a great Iraqi war hero of the 1920s. I took Roy Street with me. Ironically there was a real war going on at the time between Iraq and Iran, and you couldn't help but notice. Sometimes Iran would send missiles over or you'd spot a jet fighter go screaming past, and then thirty minutes later you'd see these SAM missiles streaking around the sky looking for an aeroplane to hit, but of course it had been and bombed and gone off again. You also saw these kindergarten kids practising marching in school, walking around like little warriors, and then teenagers running around with guns. It was really quite bizarre.

I was supposed to go out there for six weeks but ended up staying three months because the production was totally disorganised, weeks went by without any filming at all. I was supposed to set up this big battle sequence with horses and stuntmen, but I didn't have any stuntmen and I didn't have any horses. So I waited and waited. Go and play tennis, they kept saying. 'Play tennis!' I said. 'It's 120 degrees. It's too bloody hot.'

So we just sat around getting bored in this beautiful great hotel. Luckily, Oliver Reed was in the film and kept us royally entertained. God, he used to get us into so much trouble. One night we were drinking with Ollie in the bar and ended up seeing how many of us could stand on a coffee table. I think we got up to about 12 before this table collapsed. It was just killing time. Then Oliver looked into the restaurant and saw a Texas oil billionaire that he knew. Jumping up, obviously drunk as a skunk, he rushed upstairs to his room and we didn't see him again for 15 minutes. When he came back down he was wearing a western

Clash of Loyalties *was a strange experience, but I got to work with Ollie Reed, and the poster looked nice!*

shirt and cowboy boots and walking John Wayne style into the restaurant to see his buddy. Inside he gave this guy a Texas handshake, as he called it, which basically meant lifting his leg up and smashing his cowboy boot down on the table. Women and other dignitaries surrounded this guy when suddenly cutlery and glass went flying in the air. Ollie then stopped and looked at the guy and it wasn't his buddy at all; it was some Arab with his entourage, deeply offended that this westerner had come stamping on his table and upset everything. The police were called and Ollie was arrested. He didn't go to jail, thank God.

Ollie was great fun and cultivated this hellraising, macho image. He was a tough guy for real and liked to get stuck in during the action scenes of a movie, but he'd never have made a stuntman himself. He wasn't disciplined enough. You've got to do it in cold blood, you've got to be absolutely icy calm and do it when you maybe don't want to, when somebody else says, now do this. You can't perform stunts in the heat of the moment with a couple of pints inside you. A stuntman has to be controlled and calculating. People like Ollie can't do it in cold blood, they can only do it when the blood's up, which is the wrong way around.

On other days we'd saunter down to the swimming pool, bored as hell,

Ollie and the rest of us, and have shoe races in this circular swimming pool. You brought any type of footwear you wanted and put a 50 dinar note inside. Everybody then swam to the middle of the pool, let them go and very gently, so as not to disturb the water, crept back to the edge and climbed out. After that you just sat there drinking champagne, or daiquiris, until one of the shoes touched the edge and whoever's it was took the whole pot. You could earn a lot of money. Those were the sorts of things we did to kill time. The drunker we got, the more ridiculous it got.

Practical jokes, as always, were rife. I'd brought a cassette player along with me and had a tape of a pop song that started with all these sirens going off and machine gun fire and bombs. As a laugh I turned this thing on full blast and put it in the hotel hallway. The unit hairdresser ran out of his room and downstairs in his underpants thinking the Iranians were invading, then everybody started evacuating. I quickly turned it off and threw the tape away in case anyone found out. It was hysterical. Twenty years later I was passing through Heathrow and bumped into the same hairdresser, Mike Lockey, and he mentioned it to me. After all those years he still hadn't forgotten.

During those months in Iraq I did manage to do some work, but not much. In one scene I played an Iraqi pilot flying a bi-plane. There I was, up against the old wind machine with goggles on looking like Biggles and throwing hand bombs over the side. I also did some prepping in a place called Habana, where we were going to do the battles. Driving back to Baghdad the next day all these barrage balloons were up. What the hell's happened here? 'It's nothing, nothing,' our driver said. 'There were no barrage balloons when we left yesterday, has Baghdad been attacked?' I asked. 'No, no, no,' the driver said. 'An Iranian plane came up the Tigris River and we the heroic people shot it down and it crashed on waste ground.' Now I used to watch all this propaganda on the telly, we've shot so many thousand Iranians, 50 tanks destroyed, 20 aircraft; pictures of it all. 'And this thing crashes in Baghdad and there are no pictures of it?' I asked. 'Surely there's something else going on.' But the driver kept insisting his version was correct.

I eventually found out the truth months later, but only after I'd managed to escape. That's right, escape. They wouldn't let me leave the country. Work was building up in England and I told them I had to go. 'No you can't,' they said. 'You can't leave.' I said, 'Just get me an exit visa.' You had to have an exit visa to get out of the country. 'There's no point in having an exit visa,' they told me. 'All the planes are booked.' I said, 'Look, you get me the exit visa and then if there's a seat on the plane I can get on it instantly. If you don't get me an exit visa you're going to have problems with the British crew because we're all going to feel we're being held here.' They must have thought, OK we'll give him an exit visa just to keep him quiet, and then put me on the airport computer so I wouldn't be accepted on any flight, so there was actually no point getting an exit visa. Roy Street and I didn't know this at the time and went to pick ours up.

Walking back to the hotel we passed a taxi rank and there was this great big Ford Galaxy motor car. 'How much to Kuwait?' I said to the driver through an interpreter, 'How much to get me out of here?' He went, '$400.' I said, 'OK, come to the hotel, we'll take off right now.' I was just going to load up and go. He said, 'No, no, we leave at midnight.' I said, 'Why midnight? Why not go now?' He said, 'If we leave at midnight, by the time we get to Basra it will be daylight so the Iranians won't see our headlights and they won't shoot at us.' That makes sense, I thought. I had to give him half the money up front and wondered if he'd ever turn up, but sure enough at midnight he arrived and we slung our luggage in the boot. I left a note for the production that said: 'I'll see you when I see you.' I mean, I'd been there for months and done nothing. I wanted out.

So we set off for Basra. I lay on the back seat trying to sleep while Roy Street sat up front and he's a bit highly strung; all I could hear for the whole journey was, 'Mind that camel!' and, 'Look where you're going you bloody fool!' Just mad, the drivers in Iraq. After 12 hours we got to the Kuwaiti border and the driver pulled up shouting, 'Out you get!' I said, 'What do you mean? We want to get to Kuwait City.' You could see the city in the distance. He said, 'You get another taxi, I can't leave Iraq.' Christ. We picked up our suitcases and stunt bags and headed for the border checkpoint. And I've got this bit of paper, this exit visa; God knows what it said because it was all in Arabic. I handed it to the guard and he looked at it, and then he looked at me and called over his pal. Now my heart really started to pound. Then they called a third guy over and all of them stood looking at this piece of paper, looking at me, looking at Roy. It felt like *Midnight Express*. I thought, Christ, it probably says, 'do not allow to leave' or something. Finally the guard said OK and waved us through. And sure enough on the other side there was another taxi rank and we got into Kuwait and booked the first flight to London.

Sitting on the plane I opened a copy of *Newsweek* magazine and inside there was an article about how these fighter planes had flown from Israel just 20 feet above ground level and blown up a power station in Baghdad, then got out again before anyone could react. And that was what all the barrage balloons were up for. It wasn't an Iranian attack at all, but this amazing under the radar raid. They'd been practising in the Sinai desert for months to destroy this power station where they figured Saddam Hussein was building nuclear weapons. And nobody in Iraq knew anything about it. It was then that I realised how powerful propaganda is. A person only knows what they're told, and that's what propaganda does.

NEVER SAY NEVER AGAIN

I was amazed as anybody when Sean Connery decided to return as James Bond after a 12-year absence. The film was *Never Say Never Again* and I was fortunate enough to work on it. Irvin Kershner directed, and it reunited a lot of the crew behind *Raiders of the Lost Ark*. It was a great movie: South of France, Bahamas, can't be bad.

We started off in the South of France, around Nice and Monte Carlo and I got quickly into the action doubling Sean, with Wendy doubling Kim Basinger, in a scene where Bond rescues Domino on horseback and they're both chased around a castle by Arab baddies. At one point I gallop towards a group of horsemen and burst between two riders, one falling to his right, the other to his left. I burst through, bang, horses flew through the air, but my stirrup caught one of them on the shoulder and it turned my foot completely around, dislocating my ankle. The pain was atrocious. As I rode back, my face ashen white, nearly vomiting in agony because my foot had come out of its socket, I saw a bunch of medics rushing over, but not to me, one of the riders had landed on a wall and broken his back, so that took priority.

By the end of the day my ankle had blown up like a balloon and I couldn't walk, so the boys took me to hospital. The doctors looked at it and I said, 'You can do what you like but don't put a plaster-cast on it because I'm working tomorrow.' The doctor shook his head, 'No, you can't work.' I said, 'Of course I can work, I'm only sitting on a horse, that's all it is for the next few weeks, galloping around the South of France on a horse. I'll be fine.' So they reluctantly just put a bandage on it, even though by now my leg had gone black from the knee to the sole of my foot with all the bruising from torn ligaments. I arrived on the set the next day on crutches and every time I got on the horse the doctor had to pump my ankle full of painkillers.

Doubling Sean as James Bond, with Wendy as Kim Basinger, in Cap d'Antibes, France.

The climax of the chase is when Bond and Domino leap off the castle battlements and falls with the horse into the ocean. We decided to shoot that in Nassau, putting the horse and myself on top of a 40 foot tower inside a box that could be tilted forward, just like the old shows on Coney Island where horses slid out of traps into water tanks. But the difficulty was finding a harbour that was deep enough for the horse not to hit the bottom and close to a ramp exit so it could get out quickly without drowning. Also, close to that deep water you had to have enough solid space to build the platform. Nowhere looked suitable until we found this one place that we thought might work, although the riggers were dubious. In the end they agreed to build the thing and we tested it with rocks that weighed the same as the horse and riders, tilting them out to see where they'd land. I was in a boat watching with Rocky Taylor and the first time we tried it the whole box somersaulted into the sea. 'Look at that,' went Rocky. 'If you was in there you'd be fucking dead now.' I had to agree. 'OK, cancel that,' I said, 'we'll do it somewhere else.'

By now my ankle was much better and I was able to double Sean running through the jungle in the opening sequence where 007 infiltrates a baddies' compound to rescue a girl hostage, played funnily enough by Wendy. I also did the shot of Bond leaping off the roof, dropping and swinging through the shutters of the window, which was fun to do. Inside Bond kills a few of the bad guys, sees the

In action as 007, just prior to jumping off the castle with the horse.

girl tied on the bed, cuts her loose… and she sticks a knife into him. So Wendy is the only person ever to have killed James Bond, even though in the film the whole thing is an exercise to test Bond out.

While in the Bahamas I also did a bit of scuba diving with the shark team and learnt the awful way they train sharks in films. I found it very cruel. People talk about looking after the welfare of other animals in movies but because sharks are killers, or 'just' fish, they don't seem to have any pity for them. The procedure was this: once caught, a rope was put around their tails and they were tied to rocks so they couldn't swim anywhere. In order to breathe sharks must have water passing through their gills, without it they fill up with carbon monoxide and end up dying or getting very dopey. It's like leaving somebody in a car full of fumes and then pulling them out at the last minute when they're on the edge of dying. So the unit had these dopey sharks and two or three divers would just throw them like arrows through this sunken wreck. It was terrible and they killed a lot in the process, poor old things.

I went diving one day with Wendy, who isn't too keen on things in the sea, although she's a great swimmer. Exploring this wreck I looked about and saw two divers carrying a 12-foot shark towards the set to do some rehearsals. I turned round to show Wendy and she wasn't there, just a stream of bubbles, she was about 30 feet above me going like a rocket to the surface. I carried on and stroked

Wendy relaxing between takes with Connery.
She played the kidnap victim who 'kills' Bond in the film's opening.

this tiger shark. What a beautiful creature it was, and quite an experience to meet a real man killer up close.

There were more high falls to do over on Paradise Island. This time my old mate Billy Horrigan, dressed as an Arab, had to be kicked by Connery and fall backward 30 feet into water. He planned to count, one, two, and then turn into the dive, but on jumping off he went, one, two, and wham, hit the water flat on his back. I was with the camera looking down and his face didn't even get wet, he just stopped dead on the surface. He was coughing up blood, having bruised his lungs, and was rushed to hospital. It's amazing if you go flat into water from any height, like 30 feet, what it does to you.

Suddenly Wendy and I got a call to leave Nassau and fly back to London, where we were urgently needed on the first unit in the studio. Glenn Randall, who was on the stunt team, came with us. Glenn hates flying and I started winding him up about the Bermuda Triangle, because we were going to be flying over it. We took off and lo and behold over the Bermuda Triangle something went wrong with the directional instruments in the plane and we had to land in Bermuda. Glenn was now a complete bag of nerves. We arrived during a terrible storm and made a very heavy landing. As we hit the tarmac the overhead lockers burst open, the luggage flew out and duty free bottles were crashing down on people's heads. Glenn was climbing the bloody walls.

We sat around the airport while they tried to fix the plane but it was no good, the flight was cancelled until the next day and we holed up for the night in a hotel. The following morning we got on the plane only to experience another hour's delay. Glenn was sitting next to me with these sleeping tablets and a scotch that he was only going to take when he was absolutely certain we were on our way. More time went by until finally the engines started; great, we're going. The pilot put the hammer down and we began to roar down the runway. A relieved Glenn popped his pills in the scotch and downed it in one. Then suddenly wrrrrrr, the plane stopped halfway down the runway and we came back in. Something had gone wrong *again* and we had to wait another night. Of course by now Glenn's sleeping pills had kicked in and we had to pretty much pick him up and carry him off the plane and back to the hotel.

After glimpsing Sean only briefly on *You Only Live Twice* way back in 1966, *Never Say* was the first time I'd really worked with him, and we went on to make several more pictures together. He was great. If you're a stuntman he's a fabulous guy to double for because he doesn't want to do much at all: he does the acting, you do the stunting, the complete opposite of people like Harrison and Tom Cruise. Sean would much rather go and play golf. But he was very professional and he wanted to know how everything was going to work in the action and fight scenes. Famously he doesn't suffer fools – if you're wasting his time, which is precious to him, the same as anybody, he gets very antsy, but as long as you're professional and he knows you're doing a good job, he's fine. He was good fun to work with.

From England we moved on to Spain, down in Almeria, filming those jet pack machines that take off from a submarine. To simulate them landing we used a crane and had them suspended on wires. Another perilous moment has Bond in an aqua-lung dive into an Arab well from beneath a helicopter. There was no actual well there, just a hole dug in the ground filled with cardboard boxes, with a stone wall built around it. I had to do the jump, which was from about 40 feet. I sat on this trapeze-type seat and a helicopter picked me up and off we went. I wasn't strapped on or anything, because I had to do the jump, and I suddenly realized that we were up 1200 feet with a huge wind blowing and the pilot was flying around trying to keep control.

When we came in to do the run I had to work out when best to topple off

With Wendy leaping into space. The 40ft final drop was accomplished weeks later.
(See picture in the colour section.)

and dive into the well, but I badly mistimed it. Falling, I saw this solid stone wall rushing towards me and knew that if I tucked in I'd smash into it, so I held my position and went head-first straight into the boxes: crash. The second unit director Micky Moore came running over and gave me such a bollocking. 'Don't ever do that again, you could have killed yourself!' I didn't know I was going to get that close; it was only when I was in mid-air that I realized I'd got it wrong. 'Stay there,' Micky said and took a Polaroid of me. 'Keep that in your wallet and next time you think you're going to do anything questionable again, look at that, because that's how close you came to getting killed. I thought you were dead.' He really panicked, the old boy. I don't know where it is now, but there's a picture of me in this last box right next to the wall; if I'd have tucked I'd have gone into it. But it was just one of those things; in stunts timing is everything, and a split-second decision can mean the difference between life and death.

Meantime we'd found a harbour that was perfect for the horse jump shot. I was staying close by and used to look out of my hotel room and it was almost like a hangman's gallows being built, you'd hear the hammering and see this thing getting bigger and bigger and know, Jesus, one day I've got to fall off the top of that with a bloody horse. So the pressure started to build up.

Me as Superman. I worked on the first two movies for 11 months and doubled Christopher Reeve in the flying sequences.

With Ryan O'Neal on location in Mexico for *Green Ice*. He was great fun and we used to spar every day.

Doubling Sean Connery as James Bond in *Never Say Never Again*, falling 40 feet into the sea with a horse, hoping it won't land on top of me!

Myself and Wendy on the streets of Macao shooting Indy's dramatic escape from the Obi-Wan night club, the opening sequence of *Indiana Jones and the Temple of Doom*.

Doubling for Harrison Ford as Indy on the rope bridge that forms the dramatic climax to *Temple of Doom*. This version was built for the key shot of Indy cutting the bridge.

On location in Sri Lanka for *Temple of Doom*. Harrison did his back in riding those elephants and was off for several weeks, so I had to literally step into his shoes.

Ready to go into action as Indy.

Relaxing between takes on *Temple of Doom*. From left to right, my great mate Bronco McLoughlin, Wendy, Harrison and Frank Henson, Mola Ram's stunt double

Wendy, who doubled Lois Lane, on location for *Superman III* with the man himself.

I polished Arnie's riding skills on *Conan the Destroyer*. Every Sunday Arnie, Wendy and I would ride for three hours near Mexico City and picnic on fresh bread, roast chicken and red wine.

With Stallone on *Rambo III*, then the most expensive film ever made. The horse between us is my old friend Huracán that Harrison and I later rode on *The Last Crusade*.

Harrison signed this photo for me. He wrote: 'If you learn to talk I'm in deep trouble.'

Vic —
IF YOU LEARN TO TALK I'm in
DEEP TROUBLE!

Harrison
9-88

When Mel Gibson was in England filming *Hamlet* he visited our house, where Wendy and I taught him to ride on Volador, my Andalucían stallion.

Dear Vic —
Thanks for the most rewarding
experience I've had in films!
All the best,
Mike Starkey

Semper Fidelis, Vic!
Dale Dye
Capt. USMC Ret.

My stunt team on *Starship Troopers*.

I worked on three Bond pictures with Pierce, and I was really disappointed that he wasn't allowed to stay on in the role. He was a great guy and a terrific Bond.

At the Oscar ceremony when I received my Technical Achievement Academy Award.

Jean-Pierre Goy taking a leap of faith on the 1600cc BMW for *Tomorrow Never Dies*.

Filming the climax to the ski chase in *The World Is Not Enough*. It was a fabulous shoot, below Mont Blanc in the French Alps.

The famous boat chase in *The World Is Not Enough* took three weeks to shoot and was a logistical nightmare, but incredibly rewarding.

Action scenes from *Charlie's Angels*. This stunt was filmed outside the California Speedway after the race cars leave the track and hit the regular road, causing a spectacular (pipe ramp) car crash, performed by Tanner Gill.

This sequence was shot in San Pedro when the Thin Man fires a rocket from his Huey helicopter at the three Angels.

This was a lovely spontaneous gesture from Sir Christopher Lee and Andrew Lesnie, the DP on *Lord of the Rings*. They wanted to send me their best wishes and spelt my name with their hands.

Working with Martin Scorsese on *Gangs of New York*. He'd never used a second unit director before but we got on terrifically well. You can see how enthusiastically we are discussing the upcoming scene.

Receiving the BAFTA Michael Balcon Award from Lord Attenborough. A proud moment and a great honour to have it presented by such a tremendous actor/director.

Steven Spielberg takes no prisoners and *War of the Worlds* was no exception, it was tough but working with him again was illuminating. He is a genius filmmaker. This was during the sequence where Tom's character is trying to get to the ferry with his kids to escape the approaching aliens.

Governor Schwarzenegger visits the *War of the Worlds* set.

My dear friend Arnie presents me with the Taurus Lifetime Achievement Award in 2005.

My son Scott with Tom Cruise on the set of *Mission: Impossible III*. This is just after Scott did the spectacular car crash on the Chesapeake Bay Bridge.

Working on *I Am Legend* with Will Smith, who is the most professional actor I've ever met in my life.

A stuntman reunion. From left to right: Gerard Naprous, Tony Smart, me, Jimmy Lodge (my mentor and the man that got me into the stunt business) and George Leech (my father in law).

With Tom Cruise on the set of *Valkyrie*. Tom is amazing and always wants to be in the most integral part of the action. He and Harrison Ford made me re-think how I design action, so that they could perform their own stunts.

Shooting the explosive opening to *Valkyrie* at Victorville, out in the desert between LA and Las Vegas.

In 2003 I was surprised and delighted to be presented with the Big Red Book on *This is Your Life*. It was a memorable evening surrounded by family and friends, and those that couldn't be there sent filmed messages, including George Lucas and Harrison Ford.

My daughter Georgina on set after a scene with Spider-Man himself, Andrew Garfield. Georgina is making the crossover from child actress to stunt girl to fully fledged actress, and carrying on the Team Armstrong theme with the rest of the kids.

Right: My father Bob is the little guy in front surrounded by his brothers and Grandad Andrew in the middle.

Below: Armstrong Action. L-R Scott, myself, and Bruce. It has been a long journey from Scotland to Hollywood via Slough and Windsor.

When the time came we manoeuvred the horse up this tower, which had walls built on the side and around the box so he never saw where he was, and I clambered on the saddle next to Tracey Eddon, who'd taken Wendy's place because she was ill. There were cameras above us, cameras beside us. I heard, 'OK roll cameras,' and my heart rate started picking up. One of my worries was that the horse might go forward and tip over on top of us, breaking our pelvises, so I grabbed a big handful of mane and rein ready to keep his head up as we came out. The cameras wound up to speed, the heart started thumping ever louder as I prepared for this thing to start slipping. Suddenly I heard a voice, 'Cut, cut.' I looked over and the cameraman Paul Beeson was scanning the sun through his Pan glass: 'No, no, the cloud's coming over.' Oh God. We broke for 20 minutes. The horse was taken out. I still had my wetsuit on and was sweating in the trailer. 20 minutes turned into two hours, and then the call came, 'We're going to wrap it for today, we can't do it, the light's gone.' I got changed and went back to the hotel.

It was another two days before the light was right again, then back we went. All of this was of course building up the tension. I walked the horse up, got in the box, climbed on, same thing, roll cameras, they got up to speed and the old heart started pumping. On 'Action' the box was designed to tilt forward, sliding the horse down and these doors at the front were to open to release us into space. But everybody was so highly strung that hearing 'Action', the guy operating the doors panicked and pressed the button too early. The horse had been quite calm until this moment, then suddenly saw where he was and went, whoa, no way José, and backed off completely.

Now, of course, the box wouldn't tilt because all the weight of the horse was in the back. The crew reached over to try and chase him forward but all they did was beat Tracey and myself over the head. In the end everyone manually lifted the box up and as we slid out the horse's last reaction was to try and rear up in a bid to go over backwards, so I held his head forwards as we went down absolutely vertically. Almost immediately Tracey jumped clear while I rode him all the way down, stepping off as we smashed into the water. I deliberately stayed underwater as long as I could because I didn't want the horse trampling on my head, but when I broke the surface he'd already swum ashore. We'd spent two weeks training him so that when he swam under the tower he knew automatically where to get out of the water. So he was fine. His name was Toupee, a lovely horse that I'd ridden for years.

The worse thing about the stunt was as we walked Toupee up the ramp all these holidaymakers watching us started booing and hissing, thinking we were being cruel, when in fact the horse was perfectly safe. We'd done all the precautions, given him endurance training so he had enough energy to swim properly.

Apart from horses there were a lot of car and bike stunts. In the scene where Barbara Carrera gets a snake and throws it into an open-topped car driven by a villain, I had to perform a barrel roll through a wall. We were also lucky to have Mike Runyard handling the motorbike stuff in the South of France, which I co-ordinated. Mike was thrilled to work with Dave Bickers, because years earlier Mike had been an unpaid mechanic for Dave when Dave was in his heyday racing in America with Bud Ekins, who was Steve McQueen's double.

The famous shot in the big chase sequence is when Bond's bike leaps over a car from behind. We did that by fixing a ramp on the back of the car which slowed down so Mike could hit it, jump over and land on the other side. But the art department put so much crap onto this bike, rockets and stuff in a bid to make it look futuristic, that when Mike hit the ground it was so heavy the front wheel just disintegrated. He managed to pull it into a wheelie, and then slowed down until he could actually put the bike down to step off it. The wheel had totally gone. Dave Bickers was up all night rebuilding it for the next day.

While shooting around Antibes I noticed this lovely old boat. I'd just read a book by Errol Flynn called *My Wicked, Wicked Ways* and worked out that this boat was in actual fact the *Sirocco*, Flynn's old yacht. When I asked in the town people said, 'Yeah that's the *Sirocco*.' We used to love to sunbathe on top of it and just imagine the debauchery that had taken place on those very decks. Before I left I got a tiny hook off one of the hatches, just to keep as a piece of movie history.

A lot of controversy surrounds *Never Say Never Again* because it was made outside of the Broccoli family and the official 007 series. There was a lot of politics involved, first it was on, then it was off, and then it was back on again. Later, when I worked on the Pierce Brosnan Bond films, I was never allowed to mention *Never Say*. Barbara Broccoli and Michael G. Wilson always frowned when I spoke about it. 'Don't swear in front of us,' they'd say.

THE RETURN OF INDY

Ever since the huge success of *Raiders of the Lost Ark* there had been talk of a sequel. But this was going to be a lot darker and a more scary ride; hence the title *Indiana Jones and the Temple of Doom*. It was great to be working on another Indy picture because there was such a family feel to them, we were all mates, we relied on each other and we did have a bond of trust.

In the short years since the first Indy movie Spielberg had become something of a phenomenon. Of course he was a big director at the time of *Raiders*, but *E.T.* had just come out and he'd created this company called Amblin which had offices over on the Universal lot, which he proudly took me round on a tour one day. It's funny because during the making of *Raiders* Melissa Mathison, Harrison Ford's wife, was writing *E.T.* and I remember her talking about this little bug from outer space. It sounded really bizarre.

The stunt crew started shooting in Macao, just outside Hong Kong, on Indy's escape from the Obi-Wan nightclub, and the car chase with Short Round (Jonathan Ke Quan), Indy's little assistant, and Willie Scott (Kate Capshaw), Indy's new leading lady. Even by this early stage, relations between Glenn Randall and I were getting a bit frosty. Glenn had been stunt co-ordinator on *Raiders* but this time I'd been officially handed the job and was getting a bit put out by him because he was starting to get heavy handed with me, as though I was the hired help and he was the boss. 'Look,' I said. 'You're here because I'm allowing you to be here because it's a union picture out of England. You don't have any work permits, you don't pay taxes, and I'm officially the stunt co-ordinator.' He said, 'I'm the co-ordinator on this and if I pull out of here Steven and his whole crew are going to pull out of the UK and go back to the States and leave you.' I said, 'Well in that case that's fine, because I ain't happy working with you here.'

So all this was bubbling up in Macao, but I tried to put it behind me and

In the Obi-Wan nightclub for Indiana Jones and the Temple of Doom.

Wendy and myself relaxing after completing the fan descender drop. Stuntman Gareth Milne is in the car.

concentrate on the work. For the jump out of the top window of this nightclub I used fan descenders, and for several days Wendy, who was doubling Kate Capshaw, and myself rehearsed tumbling through canopies on the outside of a real building. That was the first bit of the movie we did and funnily enough the very last shot I did on the film four months later at Elstree studios was from the same sequence, a close-up of me as Indy crashing through the nightclub window to escape the huge runaway gong.

On the day we were preparing to shoot the fall through the canopies on the fan descenders, Paul Beeson the cameraman came up to me and said, 'We will have to cut something off the fan blades, because we need to make you fall faster.' Because of the lights he was using we could not undercrank (speed up the film). 'Whoa!' I said. 'We leave the fan blades alone. They are carefully designed and calculated; I will think of something else.' Together with Dave Bickers we came up with the idea of making the fan spindle thicker, so the wire came off quicker, then at a measured distance the wire came down a slope to the original diameter spindle, thus slowing us down without a jolt. We modified the spindle with camera wedges and gaffer tape. The Mk 2 variable speed fan descender had been born. The design is still in use around the world today, although it now has a more sophisticated spindle and slope set-up!

Trying not to look down – the famous rope bridge. Frank Henson (Mola Ram's double) is behind me.

After finishing in Macao we flew to Singapore, and then onto Sri Lanka for the main location shoot. We landed in Colombo and then drove all the way up to Kandy and into the hills where we did all the stuff with the elephants. The biggest single stunt sequence on the movie was also shot there, when Indy cuts the rope bridge in half. It took thousands of pounds and months to build, and was strong enough for the whole crew to walk across, and God I remember waiting for it to blow because it was a one-off shot, there was no second chance. Of course we didn't do the high falls for real, it was something like 200 feet straight down into a ravine, so the bodies were dummies with mechanical arms and legs flailing about in the air. For the fight on the broken bridge I stood in for Indy and Frank Henson, with his head shaved, doubled the baddie Mola Ram, and we used fan descenders again for some of the more perilous shots of us falling and then hanging on and fighting to the death.

It was funny because Spielberg hates heights and every day he said, 'I'm going to walk across this bridge.' And he'd step onto the edge of it and go, 'Tomorrow, I promise it will be tomorrow.' And the next day he'd take a couple more steps on the bridge. 'No, tomorrow, I'll do it tomorrow.' I don't know if he ever did walk across it, all I can say is that it was as scary as hell.

It was terrific working with Steven again. He has great trust in you and

Working out another fight routine with Harrison.

camaraderie and is such a collaborative filmmaker. I'd suggest something and then he'd have an idea and that's why all those action sequences in the Indy films are so good. Every one of them was storyboarded beforehand, but they went out of the window on the studio floor because he'd say, 'Yeah, looks OK Vic, but could he do *this?*' And I'd go, 'Well he could do, but at the end of that, how about if he went this way and jumped up there?' And suddenly you've got this really spontaneous piece of action. That's why those sequences look so realistic and fresh today because they don't look as though they were rehearsed. Of course each one is meticulously rehearsed, but they've got that spontaneity to them. We all had open minds; we weren't all locked into doing one specific thing.

GEORGE LUCAS

On the Indy pictures Steve usually had a pretty good idea of what he wanted to do, he had his storyboards, so it was usually pretty specific, but then Vic became involved in exactly how that got accomplished. He had to modify things according to what was doable and what was not doable.

Vic has always been very sure of himself and very careful about what he's doing, he's very meticulous. And those are great qualities. No matter what you're doing, whether you're directing

Overseeing an action sequence with Lucas and Spielberg. The legendary 1st AD Dave Tomblin is behind us.

actors, or whether you're directing action, everybody appreciates somebody that's very sure of what's going on and what they're doing. It keeps the whole place calm and moves things along in a good way. It's especially important in terms of doing stunts and things like that, because you don't want things to go wrong and you want somebody who will have thought of everything, and be very conscientious about putting things together. And Vic is extremely good at that.

After Sri Lanka the whole crew flew back to London for studio shooting. By then things were really frosty between Glenn Randall and me and after a week I went into the office and said, 'You're going to have to make a decision guys because I can't work like this, it's either him or me.' Nothing happened until a couple of days later when they said, 'It's all sorted Vic, he's on the plane home now.' In my opinion he just wasn't playing the game and I was fully prepared to up and leave, but they decided to get rid of him. For many years after there was a lot of animosity between us, but we're mates again now and play golf together. It was just a clash of wills and I wasn't about to give in.

Working in the studio was great; it was such a fun movie to be on. I remember

Wendy really was a brilliant double for Kate Capshaw.

it was a baking hot summer and we'd all come to work in shorts. The famous mine car chase was all done in the sound stage and it was built almost like a rollercoaster. One day it was blisteringly hot and Kate Capshaw, who was a lovely, sweet girl, bought ice creams for everyone. 'Quick Vic, quick,' she said, and bundled Short Round's double, Roy Alon, and me into the mine car and rubbed ice cream all over our faces just like a naughty schoolgirl. 'Tell them we're ready,' she said. 'What about the ice cream?' I asked. 'Just tell them we're ready.' So I yelled, 'We're ready up here Steven!' OK, action. We came hurtling down and as we passed the camera we were all eating ice creams. God it was funny, but not for the poor grips who had to run like hell with these two cameras on a dolly to catch up with us, sweating their nuts off only to see us playing jokes. It was like, 'Thanks guys!'

At one point in the chase Kate had to punch a baddie off the back end of the mine car while it was still moving. I was watching from behind the camera, speeding along trying to get it all in line because it was a tricky angle. It was close to lunch and we were still shooting, everyone was sweating and grumpy, but we couldn't get it right, you could see the gap between the punch every time. 'How was that Vic?' they'd ask. 'Missed it,' I'd reply and they'd all growl at me. 'It's not my fault. I'm just saying you missed it. You ain't got it.' The mine car came shooting down again and this time Kate actually hit the man square in the face and

Harrison looks perturbed so I guess he wants to do the stunt himself, and I expect he did!

Steven went, 'Yes, great, now you can't say she missed there Vic.' I went, 'She did.' He went, 'What are you talking about, look, he's got a big fat lip!' I said, 'No, she hit him, but it's crap, it looks awful.' When you throw a film punch it's got to be a massive hit; what Kate did was real but it looked weak because she chickened out half way through when she realised she'd made contact. So everybody growled at me again and Steven said, 'One more time because Vic says that was a miss, missed the guy with the fat lip.' Down it came and Kate threw the punch. 'How was that?' 'Yeah, that was good.' And sure enough, just like that missed punch I called in Tunisia on *Raiders*, when Steven watched the dailies he said, 'Good call Vic, that looks like nothing.'

John Wayne actually invented it – those big haymaker misses look far better on screen than the real thing. And I always say it's the person taking the punch that makes the shot, that makes the punch big. It could be Arnie Schwarzenegger throwing a punch but if the guy on the other end doesn't pop his head it looks like nothing, and yet you could have a wimp throwing a punch and if Arnie pops his head, you go wow, what a big punch. It's the reaction that makes it.

Every Friday at the end of the day we used to have a pound draw. Everybody wrote their name on a £1 note, put it in a dustbin bag which was then shaken, and whoever's pound note was pulled out won the whole lot – it was quite a lot of money. One day Harrison won it. 'For God's sake,' he said. The guy didn't know what to do with it, and we said, 'No, no, a winner's a winner, you keep it, give it to charity or something.' Everyone said goodnight to each other and left. Meanwhile Steven, Harrison and I walked onto the set because I wanted to show them some fight choreography planned for next week. And poor Harrison was walking around really embarrassed with this big dustbin bag crammed full of pound notes. I watched him and saw that he kept putting this bag down somewhere and walking off only for somebody to say, 'Harrison, you forgot your bag.' He tried this three or four times.

We finished the rehearsal and walked to the car park and Harrison started dropping back. Out of the corner of my eye I saw him look around before picking out the tattiest old car, walk over, feel the door, open it, throw the dustbin bag in, shut the door and just carry on as if nothing had happened. I never did hear what became of it. That guy must have sat in his car – he was probably a plasterer or one of the labourers – and said, 'Who's put fucking rubbish in my car?' and it was this dustbin bag full of money. I hope he didn't throw it away without looking in it! But it was a lovely touch from Harrison.

Following that weekend I came to work Monday morning and Harrison wasn't there. He'd been complaining of a bad back for weeks and it had now completely seized up. They'd got an ambulance jet and flown him to the States. The film was facing a crisis. Without their star, the producers were contemplating shutting everything down for two months. I guess I came to the rescue. I put on Indy's gear and they shot on me for several weeks. I did all that stuff of releasing the kids, a lot of the mine car stuff, jumping around the gantry, and the big fight on the rock-crushing conveyor belt, with Pat Roach playing the chief guard. Then, when Harrison came back we just did his close-ups. It really kept the whole film going.

HARRISON FORD

My back problem was caused because we were riding on elephants, and no one had calculated the risk to people unfamiliar with riding them. The position that you have to be in put a huge strain on my back. I ended up with a herniated disc and it became impossible for me to work in that condition, so I took a few weeks off and had an operation to prevent further damage. But thank God for Vic, because of him the production did not need to be shut down. When I returned a great deal had been done on Vic's back, which then needed to be shot on my face to complete the sequences. So he did spare me a great deal of work on that film. He saved us, really.

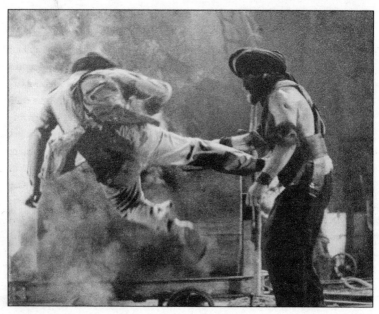

Doubling Harrison in the famous fight against Pat Roach's goliath Indian guard.

Working with Harrison again was wonderful. On the last night of shooting I went over to a local pub to buy the wire riggers a drink, because they'd done such a great job, and suddenly in walked Harrison. He always loved meeting the carpenters and the riggers and was keen to have a drink with the lads. Later on, we both went outside for a breath of fresh air and standing by the back of my car he said, 'You stunt guys are lucky, all the girls fancy you.' I said, 'You are joking, aren't you? You're bloody Harrison Ford!' He said, 'No, nobody ever knows who I am.' I said, 'What a load of nonsense, you're recognized in a heartbeat.' He said, 'I'm not you know. Watch this.' And with that he shouted over at these two young ladies walking into the pub. Both of them stopped and looked, and Harrison pointed to himself and said, 'Indiana Jones, Han Solo, Harrison Ford.' And they went, 'Yeah, right,' and just turned around and carried on walking. 'See, I told you,' he said, 'they don't know me, nobody recognizes me.' Anyway, we closed the pub down that night and ended up having a great booze-up.

Three months later I'd just finished working in Mexico on *Dune* and flew to LA to have a meeting with director Richard Fleischer about doing *Conan the Destroyer*.

I called Harrison and he suggested we meet up for dinner. At the time he lived up near Pickfair and he gave me directions how to get there. I took the car but couldn't remember if he said turn left or right at the T-junction, so I turned right. I drove on a bit further until I saw a boulder blocking the road, which Harrison had told me was the result of an avalanche years before. 'I'm next door to the boulder,' he'd said. I parked and walked into this elegant house and saw a sign on the wall. 'I'm downstairs with the physio, make yourself at home.' I thought, he's having back problems again.

'I'm here,' I shouted. 'Harrison?' No answer. I decided to relax and looked at the view over the Hollywood Hills; fabulous. I walked around for a bit and then sat down. Twenty minutes passed. 'Hello,' I said. 'Anybody there?' Nothing. Now I started to get the feeling that something was wrong, that this was not Harrison's house, because it just didn't look right. I was getting paranoid and having visions of the owner coming out and setting the Dobermans on me because they thought I was an intruder. Having previously walked around the place shouting my head off, I now tip-toed out to the car and raced off down the road. As I went hurtling past the T-junction, sure enough standing outside looking for me was Harrison. I'd gone the wrong way. God knows whose house I'd been in.

Finally I got to Harrison's home and he showed me round. The first thing he did was to take me into one of the bedrooms. Pulling open a drawer he flipped it over and said, 'Look at these dovetails.' He was showing me furniture he'd just made. He was so proud of it. I've always said that's the mark of his professionalism: even the dovetail joints in the back of a drawer that nobody ever sees, he wants them to be absolutely perfect. And that's the kind of attention to detail that he brings to his movies. After a few beers we headed out for dinner. I was looking at the menu when I suddenly realised he'd taken me to a bloody Mexican restaurant. 'Thanks Harrison,' I said. 'Mexican food, just what I need after three months in Mexico City.' He sat there chuckling to himself.

Melissa was also there with us that night and halfway through the meal said, 'Vic, I've wanted to ask you something. The last night of shooting at Elstree on *Temple of Doom*, were you with Harrison?' I thought, oh fuck, I've walked into a family row here. I looked across for some yes or no shake of the head from Harrison, but he was hiding behind a menu, he wouldn't even look at me. 'You know he didn't get in until two o'clock that morning.' 'Yeah,' I said. 'We were in the pub.' She said, 'Well, we were having dinner with very influential people that night. And he just didn't turn up, no phone call, nothing.' I said, 'It's not my fault. You know, you should've done what I do in those situations, just tell them he was working late.' She said, 'I could have done, but it would have been awkward, because it was Steven Spielberg and George Lucas that I was having dinner with. I can't say Harrison's working late with the director and the producer sitting next to me!' He just didn't turn up for dinner; he'd preferred to spend the night boozing with us. Hysterical guy, Harrison.

FANTASY-LAND

One of the most popular fads of the early '80s was for Sword and Sorcery pictures, and I was involved in more than my fair share of them. The first was called *Krull*, directed by Peter Yates, who I knew about of course as the man who made *Bullitt*. I met Peter at a hotel in London along with the film's American producer Ron Silverman, where they explained the story. 'It's set on a strange planet and there are these fire-mares.' I said, 'What's a fire-mare?' They said, 'It gallops faster than the speed of light and sets fire to the ground because it gallops so fast. We want something odd looking.' I suggested Clydesdales, huge horses that I'd worked with before; they're very intelligent, you can teach them to do anything. 'But how do we make them look as though they're galloping faster than light?' they asked. And therein lay the problem. You can't under crank horses to make them go fast like Charlie Chaplin, it looks silly, and you can't slow-mo them either like the Six Million Dollar Man. 'What I would do,' I said finally, 'is shoot them against a blue screen.' They both looked at me as though I was nuts. 'What do you mean, shoot them against a blue screen? You'd have to have a blue screen a mile long.' Not quite, because I'd already visualised in my head using a treadmill in the studio so the horses could gallop on the spot. 'Have you got a treadmill?' they asked. ''Course I haven't, nobody's done it yet, we'll have to invent it and build it.' As the meeting drew to a close the two men still looked unconvinced.

Months later Peter Yates said to me, 'When you left that meeting Ron Silverman turned to me and said, "He's stark, staring mad. Who's going to put a ton-horse on a treadmill?"' So it was very much in the balance whether I got the job or not, but luckily Peter stood up for me and said, 'No, he is a horseman and I think he knows what he's talking about.' They had employed treadmills back in the silent movie era but nobody had used them since, so I didn't invent it, I re-invented it if you like. I got Dave Bickers to build them and it was a huge undertaking. We

Shooting the Clydesdale horses running on a treadmill in the studio. It was an amazing sight.

had wind machines at the front so the horses' manes would blow. In the end they got so used to the treadmill that the moment you turned these wind machines up they just started galloping and when you turned them off they'd stop. I had people walk onto the set and go, 'Oh my God.' When you saw four of these giant horses galloping flat out, just flying, it was quite a sight. And nobody has done anything like it since.

We also took the horses out to film in Italy, to L'Aquila, in the mountains outside Rome, fantastic countryside; it was just like the moon with these great canyons. And amazing weather, with thunderstorms going off 100 feet above your head and lighting bolts flashing about. The Clydesdales were magnificent. My son Bruce had a birthday party and we had nine kids sitting on the back of one of them, and there was still room for more.

So that was *Krull*, it wasn't a big hit but it was a fun movie with a great ensemble of actors, including Alun Armstrong, Bernard Bresslaw and a young Liam Neeson. Robbie Coltrane was in it too and always used to wear odd coloured fluorescent socks, and we'd sit in his dressing room and just laugh and laugh, he's such a character; they were a great bunch. And Peter Yates was fabulous to work with, the ultimate gentleman. I remember location scouting in L'Aquila and we saw these two castles and for me it was no contest, one was an old ruin but had a fantastic

'On Krull *with L-R Ken Marshall, Dicken Ashworth, Greg Powell, Alun Armstrong and Todd Carty.*

backdrop, while the other was just an old ruin. Peter was a great connoisseur of food and he said to me one night, 'Well Victor what do you think, which of those two castles is the one for us?' I said, 'Obviously the first one.' He said, 'What do you mean? I thought the second one.' I went, 'There's no comparison.' He said, 'Really? Do you recall that fabulous meal we had at that restaurant which was not more than ten minutes away from the second castle? I think it's a far, far better castle.' Bless him, he was wonderful. That's what movies should be all about, style and class and elegance.

I was busy working on *Temple of Doom* when I was awoken in the middle of the night by this sexy Italian voice calling me from Mexico. 'Hello, you the Vic Armstrong?' I went, 'Who's this?' 'You the Vic Armstrong, the besta stuntman in da world?' I said, 'I don't know who you are, but call me when you're sober,' and put the phone down. The sexy voice phoned back early the next night. 'Hey, I called you up last night and you ringa the phone off on me.' I said, 'Excuse me, who *is* this?' She said, 'I'm Raffaella de Laurentiis. I'm doing the picture *Dune* and I need you to come out here.' My old friend Jimmy Devis had been directing the second unit but had an awful accident on the set and had broken a few bones, so they needed a replacement. I said, 'I can't, I'm working on Indiana Jones.' 'When you finish Indy?' I said, 'Four weeks, Friday.' She said, 'OK, four weeks Saturday you come out to Mexico.'

Sure enough as soon as I finished shooting Indy I flew out to Mexico, where they'd already been shooting *Dune* for ten months. The production co-ordinator Golda Offenheim, the old goddess of filmmaking, who must have been in her late 60s then, greeted me. 'Vic, wonderful, we've got a party tonight.' I was a bit jet lagged, but put my white suit on and jumped in a taxi. 'So what's this party in aid of?' Golda said, 'It's a wrap party.' I said, 'I've only just arrived!' She said, 'No Victor, we're going to carry on shooting. There's a lot still to be finished.' The party was being held in this beautiful hotel and was in full swing when we arrived. They'd set up a mock bullring and let loose these little bulls and Kit West, the special effects man, who is quite a rotund guy, was pretending to fight them. They're quite vicious these small bulls and Kit couldn't get behind the safety barrier, so they were butting him in the nuts. God, it was funny. Then an hour into the party an attractive woman came up to Golda. 'Ah Raffy, this is Vic.' And she went, 'Uh, so you are the Vic Armstrong.' And that was it, she walked away. But we became, and still are, great friends, and Raffy is one of the most wonderful people I have ever worked for.

Dune was great fun because I just went in and hit the ground running. I looked at all the footage that they needed stuff added to, and went out and shot it over an eight-week period. I did fights with Sting, explosions, stunt falls, parts of sword fights they hadn't finished, a sequence with the giant worms, fire jobs; all sorts. The difficulty was watching the dailies and seeing what the background wall looked like in a scene and then going out and finding it. By then all the sets had been pulled down, so I had to go into the props department to find bits of the set that fitted. It was a lot of work but I thoroughly enjoyed it and got on really well with Raffy and the de Laurentiis gang. It was a huge movie, some of the crew had been there nearly a year and they'd all married Mexican girls and got families.

I'd actually met Dino de Laurentiis a few years before when I worked on *Flash Gordon*, a film I prepped and then left before shooting started because of disagreements with the production manager. I remember going into Dino's office, and it was the classic image of the Hollywood tycoon with a huge desk. I reached over to shake hands, and so did he, and we couldn't actually meet across this desk because he was only a little fella.

RAFFAELLA DE LAURENTIIS

Since we worked on *Dune*, Vic and I have become really good friends through the years, and we've had so many adventures together. He's so talented and makes the work he does so simple. That's the trick with Vic – sometimes you deal with people and everything becomes so complicated, but with Vic he makes it great and exciting but also approaches the work in a way that is simple. And that is a great talent.

I was doing a kid's movie called *The Mommy Market*, it was low budget with a first-time director, and there was an action sequence and I realised that the director had never done any action, so I called Vic and said, 'Can you come and do us a favour?' He jumped on a plane and came and shot a week for us for no money, he did it out of friendship. Those are the things you remember. I cannot say enough good things about Vic. He's a wonderful person.

After *Dune* we went straight into *Conan the Destroyer*, which de Laurentiis was setting up to shoot out in Mexico as well. This was the sequel to *Conan the Barbarian* and Arnold Schwarzenegger was back in the role that first put him on the map. I'd never met Arnie before, though of course I knew all about him. The first time we were introduced he was sitting in make up having his Conan wig put on. He's such a lovely guy, no pretensions at all. Often he'd party with us till two o'clock in the morning, but if you weren't in the gym at five the next day he'd phone you up and go, 'Where are you? I'm waiting for you.' I ended up making several pictures with Arnie, and he really is one of the best.

One of my jobs was to improve Arnie's riding skills, and he really worked hard at it. Every Sunday Wendy, Arnie and I would go to the Parque de Leon, outside Mexico City, ride for three hours and then picnic on red wine, bread and roasted chickens that we'd buy off spits on the side of the road. He really trained hard for that movie. He'd go out running every morning and do his sword work through the streets of Mexico City, and this was at 8,000 feet altitude, then we'd go to the studio and every night we'd go training again. We really pushed him. But Arnie's a lovely guy. At a recent World Stunt Awards he said, 'I wouldn't miss these awards for anything because these are the guys that put me on the map in the movie business, these are the heroes, people like Vic Armstrong.' And that's great for all the stunt industry. He's never forgotten me and we're still mates.

I also really enjoyed working with director Richard Fleischer. 'The fickle finger of Fleischer' they called him because he could be a bit of a terror at times, but he was a legend having made *20,000 Leagues Under the Sea* and *The Vikings*. In fact he signed my application to get me into the Academy of Motion Picture Arts and Sciences. I really got on well with Dick, and ended up doing a couple more movies with him. He was a smashing guy.

Grace Jones was in the film too. I liked Grace very much and I was the first person she called when she came to London a year later to do the Bond film *A View to a Kill*. But she was very hard work. I was responsible for choreographing all the fights, but Grace just had no concept of pulling punches. It was unbelievable. I had to pad up all the stunt guys with much more padding than was normal but she still managed to kick one of them and crack his ribs. I said, 'Grace, we're not doing this for real here. You've got to pull the punches.'

One night, out of the blue, my mother called. 'I think you'd better come back, your Dad's not well.' He was in bed and coughing and very weak. I flew back to London and when I got off the plane the steward said, 'I hope it's not as bad as it seems.' I said, 'What?' He said, 'All you've done is stare out of the window the whole trip. You haven't eaten or anything.' I was absolutely switched off, just thinking of my Dad. I had a gut feeling it was bad. I got home and sadly he died a week later.

Dad was my best friend, teacher and partner. There was not a horse we could not get the better of together, and we had some wild ones because that was all we could afford, other people's rejects. He would be on the ground and I would be on their back, and we turned some bad horses into great horses together. Dad actually rode in his first horse race at 69 years of age and yet he was dead just four years later, such a shame and waste of a wonderful talent. He had shod every gold medal winner in the equestrian Olympics from 1948 in London through to 1964

Dad in the parade ring at Lingfield before his first race.

in Tokyo. Although I was doing well in my career, travelling the world, and he was tremendously proud of me, my only regret is that he didn't live a bit longer to see the real success that I achieved later on.

For obvious reasons I didn't want to go back to Mexico, but I kept getting these phone calls. Raffaella called me personally: 'Vic, you come back or I break your legs. And if you come back, I thena break your legs.' In the end they talked me into returning. And the first person I saw was Terry O'Neill, a weightlifter and a mate of Arnie. Arnie always used to stick his mates in on movies. I noticed that Terry's nose was spread all over his face. 'What happened?' I asked. 'Grace Jones,' Terry replied. She'd smacked him in the nose and totally flattened it.

I'd also brought an old pal to join the movie, Pat Roach. He was a good actor and starting to get a lot of work, culminating in a regular role in TV's *Auf Wiedersehen, Pet.* Arnie used to love watching us spar, but one night I dropped my guard and Pat gave me a black eye. In the office the next day all the girls gathered around me. 'Ooh Vic, what's the matter with your eye?' I told them and they said, 'What a brute, oh, the bastard.' So the next night I was in the gym and Pat said, 'Go on, punch me as hard as you can in the eye.' I said, 'Why's that Pat?' And he said, 'Because I want some of that sympathy you've been getting from those girls all day long.'

So that was *Conan* and the start of my working relationship with Arnie, and we had some wonderful times. Whenever he came to England he'd call me up and we'd do TV interviews together. He taught me a lot about handling interviews. 'I'll talk about you and you talk about me, it's simple.' And it works. He'd say, 'This is Vic Armstrong, he's the best stuntman and action director. Because of his background he knows what stunts need to look like and he'll get the camera and get in there and shoot amongst the action.' And I'd go, 'Maybe, but you can't do that without an actor like Arnie who's a great action actor, he's got guts, he's got timing and he's got rhythm.' That's actually a great way of doing interviews, because you blow each other's trumpets instead of saying, 'I'm a great action man because I've done this and I've done that.' It's not me, me, me, it's him, him, him. It's a really clever way of doing it. He's so shrewd and intelligent, that guy. I've got so much respect for him.

It's amazing looking back on *Conan* because you never knew Arnie was going to turn into the superstar that he did. Not long afterwards we all went over to Italy, Arnie, Dick Fleischer and I, to make *Red Sonja* and we used to spend nights out in Rome. On this one occasion Arnie phoned and said, 'Are you coming out tonight?' I said, 'No, I can't, I've got an early start tomorrow so I've got to crash tonight mate.' And he said, 'I just made this great film, I play this amazing character...' And he told me about some of the action he got to do. 'Sounds great,' I said. 'Go watch it,' he told me. I said, 'I haven't got a VCR in my room.' He said, 'Go into my room.' So I went to Arnie's suite, put this videotape in, sat back and watched what was a rough-cut of *The Terminator*, the first time anyone in Europe had seen it. The next day on the set I went over to Arnie and said, 'Wow, what a movie that was; unbelievable.' And he said, 'Yah, it's going to be good, he's a good director this young guy, Jim Cameron.' And of course *The Terminator* turned Arnie into a superstar.

I worked with Raffaella again just a few years later on *Tai-Pan*. It was shot in Canton and I actually turned down *Aliens* to do it, because I thought I'd never get the chance to go to China again. And of course sod's law I was back there on *Empire of the Sun* not long after. Such is life. I was really excited about doing it because *Tai-Pan* was one of my favourite books, though it ended up being a terrible movie. But whether a film is good or bad, every shot's the most important, every decision you make is the most important. You must never lose sight of that.

At the time Wendy was pregnant, but the baby (her second, following daughter Nina born in 1980) wasn't due for a few weeks. I'd just started prepping the movie, and very often the preparation is the most fun time on a movie – scouting

With Bryan Brown on the set of Tai-Pan *in Canton, China.*

locations, dreaming up crazy ideas and trying to make them work. The tough part is actually sitting down and shooting the damn thing, putting your money where your mouth is. After a few days I had this odd feeling and went into the office. 'I've got to go because my wife's having a baby,' I said. They looked at me. 'We didn't think it was due for two weeks.' But I was adamant that I had to go. Finishing all my meetings, I took a flight from Canton to Hong Kong.

On the plane, I met up with an old friend of mine, Charlie Wang, the head of Salon Films, who took me to the airport for my flight to London. By coincidence it was also my birthday, and Charlie knew all the Cathay Pacific crew and told them, so every time we passed through a time zone the hostesses brought me another bottle of champagne. By the time I got to London I was somewhat inebriated. When I phoned home our lovely groom Jeni told me Wendy was in hospital. They'd been trying to reach me all night in my hotel room and thought I was out partying. I walked into Wendy's room and she was shell shocked to see me,

A proud father with my five day-old baby daughter Georgie.

because she thought I was still in China somewhere. And that was when Georgie was born, on my birthday, two weeks early. I just had this amazing premonition.

Georgie was only five weeks old when Wendy brought her out to China and again the gang was all there: Billy Horrigan, Bronco, Dickey Beer. Wendy used to leave me to baby-sit and I'd put little Georgie wrapped up in a blanket in the middle of the pool table and we'd all play pool around her because it was the one place I could keep an eye on her.

While on *Conan* I kept getting these phone calls about doing a film called *Legend*, a multi-million dollar fairy tale epic directed by Ridley Scott and starring a very young Tom Cruise. I arrived from Mexico City and got a taxi from Heathrow to Pinewood studios for a meeting with Ridley, then a car took me straight back to Heathrow where I met up with Wendy and we flew to Seville in Spain, to start buying white horses to play the unicorns. We'd found five white stallions when the studios started to get on our backs about returning to England to start training them, but we were still searching for a mare. Our last hope was a 10pm appointment in Triana, near Seville, with a local horseman, only the guy wasn't there when we arrived; he was now due at eleven. We headed to a bar and waited. Eleven o'clock passed, twelve, one o'clock, finally at two o'clock in the morning this guy turned up. Of course I'd had a few Cuba Libres by then, and he was drunk; he'd been out partying. In a dimly-lit arena we were finally presented with this stunning Andalucian-Arab mare, a beautiful horse, but it behaved like a thing possessed, snorting and kicking, climbing the walls and breathing fire. Jesus, I thought. But we were so desperate we'd no choice but to buy her.

Strangely enough when we got her home she was the gentlest horse you could ever have in your life. She never, ever behaved that way again. What got into her that night we don't know. We very nearly didn't buy her because we thought she was just too wild, but she ended up an absolute sweetheart, and we called her Triana. Mel Gibson, Sean Connery, Liam Neeson and Denzel Washington all rode her on various films and she was Ken Branagh's horse in *Henry V*, carrying the actor as he delivered his stirring battle speech – 'Cry God for Harry, England and Saint George!' No matter how much experience you have, you can never tell if a horse is going to be that good; you may think you can, but you can't. It really is pot luck. And we were lucky when it came to Triana. We retired her in 1995 after she was diagnosed with a weak heart. She died in her stable in 2002.

Before taking all the horses out of Spain I bumped into a guy I'd used years before on *The Desert King* as a rider and groom. Jordi Casares was young, couldn't speak English, and I liked him a lot but when they pulled the plug on the film he never got his wish to be a stuntman and that was the last I saw of him. Now lo and behold in this bar outside Madrid airport was Jordi. He was just the kind of guy I needed on *Legend* so in my broken Spanish I said, 'Do you want to work for me in England?' 'Si, si, anything for you,' he said, drunk as anything. 'Right then, be at the stables no later than eight in the morning because that's when we're pulling out.' 'Si, si, mañana, ocho, no problemo.' He turned up, bleary-eyed, at seven-thirty with a little overnight bag, feeling like death and we took off. He ended up staying with us for eight months and my Mum even taught him to speak English. Since then Jordi and I have done many, many pictures together and he's now the most famous and successful stuntman, stunt co-ordinator and second unit director out of Spain.

I'll never forget *Legend* for one simple reason. We were shooting at Pinewood and after lunch one day we went into theatre seven to watch the dailies. We came out at 1.15 and there were clouds of smoke everywhere; the whole of the 007 stage was on fire. Jesus. My first thought was the horses, because there was a lot of Styrofoam on the set and when that burns it gives off poisonous cyanide gas. I rushed over to the stables but they were empty – the grooms had seen the smoke and already rescued the horses – but there were cages full of other animals like foxes, and birds, including eagles and pigeons, and we were smashing them open to let them out.

Miraculously, no one was killed. A guard told us that when the last person left for lunch he closed the door and just stood outside the stage and then heard a noise, phufft, and looked in and saw this ball of flame roll along the ground and up round the roof, leaving fire behind as it went. The whole place just went up like you can't believe and was totally destroyed. It had to be rebuilt in time for that year's Bond film, *A View to a Kill*. Amazingly the fire hardly halted production on *Legend*. We hung around for about two days and then did some outdoor shooting while they built another set. Ridley had been the only one smiling when the 007 stage went up, because he was sick to death of the place. I don't think there was one angle on that stage he hadn't shot, so he was quite happy to get the insurance money, build another set and have a new fresh look to his movie.

They say that Ridley is a very visual director and he's indifferent with actors. He's obviously changed over the years, but I'll never forget this one sequence. We had wind machines going full blast, we had unicorns, smoke effects, moonbeams coming down, we had all these pigeons dyed different colours, we had a bear eating honey, we had bees floating around, butterflies and sparrows, we had everything. We were in the studio from seven o'clock in the morning until two, without breaking for lunch, preparing this one shot. When Ridley had everything right he shouted, 'Shoot, for Christ's sake shoot!' And old Bill Westley, the AD, turned around and said, 'What about the max factors then guv?' meaning the actors. And Ridley went, 'Oh fuck. Quick, go and get them.' And Bill rushed out and brought Tom Cruise and Mia Sara on and Ridley went, 'Ah, OK Tom you sit over there and Mia you sit next to him and just talk among yourselves. OK. And action!'

So *Legend* was a fun shoot, but tough. I did everything on it. I was horse and sword master, stunt co-ordinator and stunt double for Tim Curry as the Lord of Darkness. It was a huge amount of work and a bloody long production. Jordi left there speaking fluent English. Tom Cruise was great, too. It was the first time I'd ever met him. To be honest I didn't know who he was, although he'd already done movies like *Risky Business*. He was very nice, but just a kid really. It was a very different Tom Cruise that I met a couple of decades later on *War of the Worlds*, but he did remember one particular shot from *Legend*. It was the final night of shooting and Mia Sara and Tom had to run over a hill and then on another hill that we'd built further up the set we were going to use child doubles, so it looked like the actors were far away.

My young daughter Nina was all set to double Mia and she'd been dressed up all night waiting until finally at five in the morning Bill Westley came up to her and said, 'OK Nina, you can go home now.' She said, 'But you haven't filmed on me.' He said, 'We're not going to do it love.' She stamped her feet. 'But I'm all dressed up. I've got to do it now.' And he went, 'Oh, OK. Ridley, she ain't going to go home until you've shot it.' And Ridley went, 'All right, stop packing up the cameras guys, here we go. And action Tom, action Mia, action Nina.' And she ran up the hill and away and was fine; she was ready to go home. And on *War of the Worlds* Tom came up one day and said to me, 'Hey Vic, do you remember that perspective shot at the end of *Legend*?' He'd remembered it after 20 years.

UP THE AMAZON WITH DE NIRO

The Mission was directed by Roland Joffé, who'd just done *The Killing Fields*, so was hot stuff in Hollywood at the time. It was a really exciting project because we had Robert De Niro and Jeremy Irons, and locations in South America. Looking at it today it has a real adventurous look to it because it *was* a real adventure going out there. In fact it ended up as more of an adventure than I'd bargained for. Sometimes I thought, Jesus, I wonder if we'll ever get out of here alive?

A lot of the film was shot in Colombia in a place called Santa Marta, where we built the actual set of the mission. It was an amazingly rough place with an average of one or two murders a week. And Santa Marta wasn't big; it was just a little town, but so bloodthirsty that we had a police escort to and from work. One morning our convoy was stopped and word filtered back that there was an assassinated body on a bridge; someone had been shot through the head. I think there was either a bit of union strife or a drug feud going on. The next day the same thing happened, somebody from the opposing family had got his head blown off. And the next day there was a third dead body on the bridge.

The film didn't escape the violence either. One of the unit drivers died, a night watchman had his throat cut (he must have seen something at night that he should not have, because the area we were working in was a notorious shipping area for drugs), and a snake bit an Indian woman. There was also a young stunt lad who one day didn't turn up for work. I was told he'd gone to a funeral. 'Whose?' I asked. 'His brother,' was the reply. The police had stopped both men the previous evening to check their papers. Basically the cops just wanted some money off them. So they ran and the police shot at them and killed this lad's brother. A week later the policeman's family got killed. It was that sort of place.

Santa Marta was also where all the marijuana and cocaine was shipped out from. A bunch of us were scouting locations one day on the edge of this vast

Bruce riding with Robert De Niro in Cartagena, Colombia on The Mission.

running river when we heard a crashing sound. We stopped and looked around. There was nothing so we carried on until, crash, crash, this sound got closer. We looked and about 50 yards away was what appeared to be a black Spanish fighting bull just staring at us through the undergrowth. It can't be, we thought. As we stood there it charged us and it really *was* a Spanish fighting bull and you've never seen 12 macho men run so fast in your life. We jumped into our little motor boats and pulled away, just as this bull crashed onto the beach and into the river, snorting and pawing at the water. The story was that the drug smuggler who owned this stretch of land believed that the best guard dogs you could get were these fighting bulls. God, it scared the life out of us. Another time we were shooting some jungle footage when we came across this little clearing with a hut in the middle. Inside, this hut was three inches deep in marijuana dust. It was a big marijuana factory where they made bails of the stuff; amazing.

A lot of the horses used in the film we got from local drug barons. The horse De Niro rode belonged to the biggest drug lord out there. This guy was the original drug baron, the one that started taking mules over the mountains to get the cocaine out. He had a big palace in Cartagena and we went round there on a Sunday morning to have breakfast with him and his family. He had a whole zoo there and a steam train that took you round. And as you went in there were guys with Uzis on the gate. We explained what we wanted and he said, 'OK, you can have it.' I said, 'How much?' He said, 'No, you can have it.' So he gave us all these Spanish horses, all the carriages, all the fighting bulls, anything we wanted. I recall that at the time his brother was on the run because he'd murdered the finance minister and this drug lord had offered to pay the national debt of Columbia if they allowed his brother to return there, but they wouldn't and he went to live in Spain. We also visited his other house in Medellín; this place was 5,000 acres. Unbelievable the money he had. And all from drugs.

We used a lot of locals in the film, too, which was a problem because they were all unemployed and all loved smoking the local weed! By ten o'clock in the morning they were doped out of their brains. And we had to train about 140 of these guys to be mercenaries under the command of De Niro. We really had to knock them into shape and to do that you had to be strict with them. We had these big canoes which were trees hollowed out and I ordered them to get in, but they wouldn't. 'Get in the boat,' I yelled. They were all high by this time. So I got an oar and pushed the lot of them into the water and stopped them as they tried to clamber out onto the dock. 'Get in the boats!'

That night I got called into the office, where this costume designer was crying his eyes out. 'Vic,' said Iain Smith, the producer, 'it has come to my attention that you are deliberately getting the people wet. The colour dyes are running on their costumes.' Typical of movies, they go out and buy special authentic costumes with dye that runs when it gets wet and we're shooting a sequence on a river. 'Jesus Christ, you're absolutely right,' I said. 'We got it wrong didn't we; we got the wrong type of river.' Iain looked puzzled. 'What do you mean wrong kind of river?' I said, 'We've obviously got a wet river, we should have had a dry river, and then the costumes wouldn't get wet.' Ian said, 'Vic, don't be facetious.' I said, 'Costumes get wet, it happens. It's not my fault the dye will run, even if it is authentic. And unless I'm hard on these local guys you ain't gonna get a shot done because they're gonna walk all over us.' I then stormed out of the office. People lose the sense of reality when they're making movies: 'It's a movie, let's be as outrageous and unrealistic as we possibly can because it will be artistic.'

I'll give you another example. The canoes were actually made out of fibreglass, with a skin around them to give an appearance of wood, the theory being that they would be lighter than real dugouts. I thought the best place to test them in conditions that would replicate the turbulent river was out on the ocean, but they kept filling with water and sinking and we'd have to swim ashore; not very wise with sharks around. I couldn't understand it and kept going back to the local boat maker's fibreglass shop and giving them a bollocking. When the canoe sank for the fifth time I went ballistic. 'For Christ's sake can't you make a fibreglass boat that doesn't leak?' And this poor guy explained that every time we left, someone from the art department came in and said, 'It's got to look authentic, so I want axe marks all over it.' So this guy had been taking an axe to the canoe and the cuts he'd made went right through the skin and of course it was leaking water. It's unbelievable that they would worry about that kind of authenticity, when we had already built rough axe marks into the mould, and especially when half the canoe is underwater anyway. Sometimes it's like pulling teeth to get these guys to understand what's needed in a shot; they go, 'Yes... but the aesthetics of the thing, it won't look right.' They just don't have the practical knowledge we have. And so that canoe might have looked authentic but for the purpose it was actually built for, it was useless. That's what drives me loopy. For me it's the most frustrating element of filmmaking.

Cartagena was a beautiful location. I had an apartment that opened out onto this two-mile stretch of beach, and you'd see the most beautiful women in the world strolling past. I had the whole gang there; Billy Horrigan, Miguel Pedregosa, Jordi Casares and Bronco McLoughlin, and we had a wonderful time, it's an absolutely fantastic place. For my birthday Billy Horrigan bought me a little parrot called Wally; he shouldn't have left his mum really but in South America they'll sell you anything on the side of the road. He was such a lovable little chap, but he drove Wendy mad because he thought she was his mum and followed her everywhere squawking and crapping. He just loved being near people and came into restaurants with us and sat at the table, eating your chips and sipping your wine.

Sadly the authorities wouldn't let me bring Wally home, so I gave him to an American woman on the crew who tried to smuggle him out in her handbag, but when she sat down on the plane he started squawking and she was pulled off. In the end I gave him to Eduardo, who owned this bar in the centre of Cartagena that we always went to. And years later I heard that Wally had become the star of this bar, everybody went there just to see him strut around or walk over and start eating someone's meal. It's wonderful that he found such a lovely home.

One night at Eduardo's bar Arthur Dunne, our Irish transport co-ordinator, organized a massive St. Patrick's Day party. The minute you walked in your shirt was ripped off your back, soaked in green dye, and slapped back on you, girls the same, it was a riot. We had green turkey, green potatoes, green beer; everything was injected with this green dye. We got up to some real antics on that film because the gang were all great party makers. Most of the crew stayed at this one hotel, while half a mile up the beach in a much smarter hotel lived the hierarchy, De Niro and Irons. Bronco had organized a weekend party that started after lunch, but come three o'clock De Niro and Irons were a no show. 'Where the hell are they?' he ranted. 'Those bloody arseholes. I'll get them.'

Grabbing a horse he galloped up the beach to this other hotel and rode across the pool area where De Niro and Irons were sitting having a quiet drink under this tropical bar with a thatched roof. 'Hey, you arseholes, are you gonna come and have a drink with the boys or what?' Bobby De Niro looked at Bronco and this horse that had just crapped in the middle of the pool decking and said, 'Yeah we're coming, but have a drink with us first.' So Bronco tied the horse up at the bar, where it commenced to eat the thatch on the roof. De Niro thought it was absolutely hysterical. Anyway they finished their drink and then all got on local horses that were giving rides on the beach and came back together.

De Niro was great and he loved the stunt guys. Jordi and Miguel worked with him most evenings; they'd go up to his hotel room for an hour to talk to him in Spanish, because he wanted to get all the inflections and everything correct. He's a total perfectionist.

We also taught him to ride. One day I saw Bob pat one of the horses and say, 'He's beautiful isn't he?' I said, 'No, I never want to see you pat your horse again.' He said, 'What do you mean?' I said, 'The guy you're playing would have 20 horses like that, it's just a piece of meat to him, with a leg at each corner. I want you to sit up straight on that horse and just be king of everything you survey, just have that arrogance.' And that's what he portrayed. When you first see him in the movie he rides in with some slaves in tow behind his horse; he is sitting up there looking so arrogant and regal, exactly what was needed. I was very proud of him. I worked with De Niro again a few years later on *We're No Angels*. I arrived on the set and watched some shooting and then called out to De Niro as he came strolling by. 'Hello Robert. How are you doing?' He went, 'Yeah, hi,' took another step and then stopped. 'Jesus Christ, it's Vic. What are you doing here?' So that was great seeing him again. Wonderful guy.

There were more antics at our next location, Iguazu Falls, which is an amazing place since it borders Argentina, Paraguay and Brazil. Sometimes we'd say, 'All right, lunch today, where do you want to go, Brazil, Argentina, Paraguay? Let's go to Paraguay and buy a Rolex.' And so we'd go across the border to Paraguay and buy a $5 'Rolex' watch. Paraguay was strange because it was like going to Bavaria. It's obviously where all the Nazis went after the war, because a lot of the houses are like Bavarian chalets and in the jungle you'd see all these blond-haired people walking about speaking Spanish.

My stunt team had now been added to by having one of the world's greatest climbers and his crew join us: Joe Brown, Mo Anthoine and Hamish McInnes. Wendy had worked with them on *Five Days One Summer* with Fred Zinnemann and Sean Connery, and highly recommended them. Joe and the boys were just wonderful, and as full of mischief as my crew, so we got on famously. They did all the scouting of the climbing routes for us, rigged them and doubled the actors on some long shots. They kept us mere mortals safe; we could not have done the amazing climbing sequence without them. Poor Mo died a little while later of a brain tumour; life certainly is strange when you think of the things he had done, from climbing Everest to trekking through Patagonia and everything in between, then the wretched Big C gets him.

While at Iguazu we stayed on the Argentinean side and I fell in love with the country; Buenos Aires is absolutely gorgeous. It wasn't that long after the Falklands War and the crew was told that if anybody talked to us, we should say we were Americans. 'How bright do you think these people are?' we said. 'When we walk into a hotel and hand over our passports, you don't have to be Einstein to work out that we're actually British.' But the Argentinean locals were wonderful. A lot of them were guys who were ex-prisoners of war and they just hugged and kissed us when they saw us, because the only time during the Falklands conflict they felt secure and happy, and were actually looked after and fed properly, was when they were captured. They said they were so well looked after by the British.

At night we'd play practical jokes and games, because our hotel was in the middle of nowhere and there was absolutely nothing else to do. One game we'd play in the evenings was Murder. Everyone got a piece of paper and if yours had a cross on it, that meant you were the murderer. You kept it secret, but you could 'kill' anybody by just catching their eye and winking at them, and then they had 30 seconds to die. We gave out points for the best and most unusual deaths. And people took this incredibly seriously. One night Bobby De Niro and Jeremy Irons joined us for a game in this posh restaurant. We were all trying to guess who the killer was when Jeremy suddenly got up and rushed around the restaurant going, 'Arghh!' All the other diners thought he'd choked on the food, while the waiters panicked because they were terrified they'd just killed this famous actor. Finally he performed an elaborate somersault and landed on the lap of a woman sitting at another table. We all applauded and gave him top marks.

One of the most famous shots in the film is of a priest tied to a cross going over a waterfall in a canoe. Bronco played the part, and was tied up for real and sent down-river. On the very last take I said to the crew, 'We'll say cut very quietly.' So off went Bronco towards this rampaging waterfall and I whispered, 'Cut.' Bronco lay there and started getting agitated and moving his head. 'Keep still Bronco, we're still shooting.' A bit later on he yelled, 'Have you cut yet?' I screamed back, 'Keep quiet Bronco, we're shooting.' And the water was getting rougher and rougher and he was starting to have visions of plummeting to his doom, while we were running down the bank ready to save him at the last minute.

For the final shot of the priest going over the waterfall Madame Tussauds had copies of Bronco made and stuck them on these crosses. They were amazingly lifelike. One night Jordi, Bronco and I had a few drinks and got one of these crosses out of the props department and decided to put it outside Roland Joffé's hotel room. Now these crosses were full size, about eight feet tall and six feet wide. We managed to get it into the elevator and headed for the third floor, except the lift stopped at reception. The doors opened and there were the three of us sheepishly holding this giant cross. The receptionist just looked at us with a glazed expression as the doors shut again. We finally got it up to the third floor, hauled it out of the cramped lift and leaned it against Roland Joffé's door, so when he opened it the thing would fall on top of him. It was a pretty dumb thing to do.

The next morning the hotel staff were in the corridor measuring the cross and measuring the elevator door and scratching their heads because they couldn't get the damn thing back in. How the hell we got it in there to begin with God only knows; we must have been so drunk. In the end they had to saw the cross into pieces. It was bizarre. Down in the lobby the whole crew was in consternation because they couldn't find Roland Joffé. Oh Christ, I thought, what have we done now? Everybody was told to go to work as usual and wait. We drove out, walked the three kilometres through the jungle to the location, and there was a little figure sitting on a rock with bandages round his head and blood dripping down his face – it was Roland Joffé. Oh my God, he's got concussion. Not quite. He'd heard us making so much noise outside his door that night he'd opened it carefully and avoided disaster. To get his own back he'd gone to work ahead of everyone else, daubed himself with fake blood and told his driver to tell everyone that he hadn't been seen. So the joke was on us.

Iguazu was a great location. On Sundays we'd go out trekking round the waterfalls. You could actually walk from Argentina to Brazil right across the top of the falls, some distance from the edge though, because if you got swept away you'd had it. It was an amazing shoot, a real adventure. To scout a route for one shot we rappelled down 150 feet and crawled behind this waterfall. It was incredibly cold, with millions of tons of water hammering down about a foot from your back. If it hit you, you were a goner. What was amazing though were these little birds that blasted through the falling water to nest inside and then blast out again.

A lot of the climbing sequences in the movie were done on an island that rested in the middle of this great waterfall. To get there you had to walk down 300 steps, take a boat across a fast river, and then 300 steps back up. I travelled to Iguazu with my gang two months ahead of the first unit to hunt out the most spectacular climbing routes and then Joe Brown, Mo and Hamish drilled and bolted handholds onto the rocks and camouflaged them with moss. When the main crew arrived we showed them round this island, which was dense jungle with all sorts of weird creatures there, when suddenly we heard this crashing sound. We looked and this great big gorilla came bursting out of the trees. Everybody screamed and scattered in all directions. One big burly rigger just threw his spanner at it and fled. After a few seconds the gorilla stopped and fell arse over tit laughing his head off. It was one of our crew, he'd seen this gorilla suit in Paraguay and rented it, and had been sitting there for two hours absolutely melting inside, and then when he heard us he just put the head on and came crashing through the jungle. It was one of the best gags I've ever seen.

After composing ourselves we continued the trek. The heat was unbearable as I took them round the locations, down 300 steps, across the river, up again, climbing over rocks that were hazardously slippery and slimy. After four hours we got back to the hotel and I was absolutely knackered and wringing wet with sweat. Everybody went to the bar for a cold beer when Bobby De Niro walked in; he'd just arrived at the location from Mardi Gras in Rio de Janeiro. 'Bobby,' said Roland Joffé. 'Vic's going to show you all the places you're going to climb.' 'Oh thanks a lot,' I said, and had to go out and do the whole bloody circuit again with Bob De Niro.

He's terrified of heights, and yet in the film it's actually De Niro climbing most of those cliffs, although we did use a double for some shots. Jeremy Irons did his own climbing too. De Niro psyched himself up into the role he was playing: a tough mercenary who wouldn't have been afraid of heights. He has an amazing power of mind over matter that I really admire.

THE REAL MAFIA

I hadn't worked for the Bond people since doubling Roger Moore on *Live and Let Die* and so was thrilled to get an offer in 1986 to work on *The Living Daylights*, Timothy Dalton's debut as 007. Sadly negotiations stalled and when Michael Cimino, director of *The Deer Hunter*, wanted me for his film *The Sicilian* I accepted. Of course, sod's law, as soon as I said yes to Cimino the Bond people called back and said, OK let's do a deal. But it was too late.

The Sicilian starred Christopher Lambert, a hot star after *Highlander*, and was based on a novel by *Godfather* author Mario Puzo about a Robin Hood-style bandit. I have to say that I found Cimino really quite aggressive. I had a big argument with him after the first couple of days, but then we were fine. He's only directed two more pictures since *The Sicilian*, his career never really recovered from the debacle of *Heaven's Gate*. After that first fight I got on really well with him, although he could be very hard on us. One of the first stunts we did was drive a jeep at speed past this church and Jordi Casares was thrown out onto a marble square. Cimino made us do it 12 or 14 times, but Jordi never complained, he just kept on hitting the marble-covered ground at speed. In the end Cimino (I guess having been testing us) had to concede, 'Fucking hell, this guy's great!' From that day on we could do no wrong.

Later, we shot a scene where Chris Lambert holds up a steam train as it comes out of a tunnel. I actually achieved every schoolboy's dream and got to drive the steam engine. The insurance company would not let the real drivers be on the train as it went through the tunnel, because we were going to blast a fireball inside the tunnel and the train had to race through it. I will never forget the look of trepidation on the driver and engineer's faces as I opened up the steam valves and took off in their beloved engine!

As we were setting it up Cimino approached me. 'Vic, come with me.' We walked about 100 yards into the tunnel and he just sort of stood there, lit a cigarette

My friend and conspirator Christopher Lambert near Palermo, Sicily.

and looked around, so after a few minutes I said, 'Did you want something Mike?' 'Oh, no, no, there's just an asshole out there I don't want to see.' And it was the producer. Cimino wouldn't talk to him so we stayed in this tunnel for half an hour until the producer got bored and left again. It was bizarre.

The Sicilian was a massive production and I don't know quite what happened, because it was one of the greatest scripts ever and yet the end result was horrible. The cast was very good, including Christopher Lambert, Terence Stamp, John Turturro and Joss Ackland. Chris Lambert was sweet; we had so many parties with Chris. And he had the heart of a lion. In one shot he had to ride a horse down a slope, through some sheep, across a ford in the river and out the other side and away at full gallop. We set the shot up. Over the walkie-talkie I said, 'OK Chris, now be careful of those sheep, they might run in front of you, so keep hold of your horse.' 'What sheep?' came the reply. I said, 'The sheep in between you and the river.' A pause. 'What river?' And I suddenly realized he's as blind as a bat, that's why he's got these wonderful starry eyes that people fall in love with, he's absolutely blind, he needs great big thick glasses – he couldn't even see the sheep, let alone the river he was going to gallop through. It was a total blur in front of him. But he came down that slope like a bat out of hell, jumped the sheep, crashed into the river flat out and thundered out the other side. It was more luck than judgement that he got through it, and we were all laughing our heads off. What a wonderful guy.

Because he was the star of the show, the producers wouldn't let Chris drive a car. One day after a riding session with us he said, 'Can I borrow your car?' I told him sure, but to not be long, because we had more work to do with the horses and then would be going home. 'And be careful!' I shouted as he roared off down the road. He was gone for bloody ages and I started to panic. Two hours later he came staggering into the back of the stables, on foot and covered in dirt and blood. 'What the hell have you been doing?' He'd actually got lost coming back but saw the stables in the distance and tried to drive across a field towards them but got bogged down. He got out and started running but fell into a barbed wire fence which he failed to see, shredding his hands all to pieces. 'Whatever you do don't tell Cimino I was driving,' he pleaded with us. 'And I can't see the unit doctor because he'll ask what happened and then tell Cimino.' I took him instead up to my room to dress his wounds. The only antiseptic I had was some booze called Chin Chon El Mono, which is like a very harsh Sambuca. I poured this Chin Chon over his hands and he was climbing the walls screaming because it stung so much. But they healed up really quickly.

Palermo and the whole of Sicily is a beautiful area. While we were there, some big Mafia trials were taking place in Palermo. One weekend we went up to Castellammare del Golfo, which is where the original Mafia don came from before going to America, and where the story is set. During our stay we met the don of dons, Joss Ackland played him in the movie, and this guy was an old man sitting in his chair, just waiting to die. He must have been in his late 90s but when you looked at him you thought, this man was one of the most powerful people in the world, he was the don of dons, Don Masino. I remember he gave me an ashtray as a present.

Don Masino also had two grandchildren. When I first got out there I was told to find stunt jobs for a pair of local lads. 'Hold on a minute,' I said. 'I've got my Spanish stuntmen, English guys, Italian guys are coming over.' They said, 'Look, we'd really like you to do this; these are Don Masino's grandkids.' I said, 'I get the picture.' So these lads came aboard and they were really great, they worked hard and didn't take advantage of their position as grandsons of the Don. One night we all went to Castellammare for a meal and because it's quite a tourist area the restaurant was packed, not a table in sight. 'What were we going to do?' 'No problem,' the two lads said. As soon as the head waiter saw them he waved us over and suddenly there was a table. Of course, we didn't have to pay.

I have very bad memories of my next film, *Million Dollar Mystery*, a revamp of *It's a Mad Mad Mad Mad World* that ended up as a terrible movie. We had a great cast and crew, and it started out as a fun shoot, with locations all over Arizona and around the Grand Canyon. Then tragedy struck when an accident claimed the life of Dar Robinson. Dar was one of the greatest stunt guys that ever lived. He was a high fall specialist and an innovator of stunt equipment. He doubled Steve McQueen jumping off a cliff into the ocean in *Papillon*, he worked on *Rollerball* and *Lethal Weapon* and was the high fall world record holder. He really was one of the best.

It was a relatively simple scene, a motorcycle gang racing along, but Dar wasn't a great motorcyclist and I think the pack was running too fast for him. He just didn't make a corner and went off and crashed. The set's ambulance, unbeknownst to us, had been sent away at lunchtime. We all rushed over there and called for a medi-vac helicopter, while someone else phoned for an ambulance. But because we were in the middle of nowhere in Arizona they're only allowed to dispatch one or the other, so somebody cancelled the helicopter and then somebody cancelled the ambulance, so in fact nobody was coming. When they eventually discovered the mistake the helicopter set off, but Dar had really lacerated his liver and broken his arms, legs and ribs after hitting some rocks. He died three or four times, but had his heart restarted by our insert car driver John Carpenter and other crewmembers giving him CPR. He finally died in hospital. That was terrible, but it was an accident, he didn't make a corner and there but for the grace of God.

I've worked on a few films where people have been killed, or died from various causes and it's always the same: everything shuts down, you re-group and basically the dollar speaks and the production starts up again, it's really bizarre. But it's not the same afterwards, there's a cloud hanging over the film. I've seen it too many times. On *Starship Troopers* three of the camera crew got killed on the way back from Thanksgiving weekend when a guy driving another car had a heart attack, careered across the road and hit them. It's really horrible but it happens. If you do enough movies you're going to see that.

Years later when I was doing *Blade: Trinity* in Canada I had to travel down to LA for a meeting about *Mission: Impossible III*. Flying back to Vancouver wearing my World Stunt Awards jacket, the kid sitting next to me asked, 'Are you connected with the World Stunt Awards?' I said, 'Yeah, I'm on the committee.' He went, 'Are you a stuntman?' I said, 'Used to be.' This kid said, 'Well you might remember my Dad, Dar Robinson.' And this was Shawn Robinson, his son, and a stunt rigger now. He was just a tiny kid when his Dad died and I remember him crying his eyes out. So I get a terrible taste in my mouth when I think back on *Million Dollar Mystery*. It was all for nothing. Years later, I had Shawn work for me as a stuntman on the opening sequence of *Valkyrie*. He is a really good hand, and as totally dependable and inventive as his Dad.

STEVE, SLY AND KEN

Empire of the Sun is a semi-autobiographical account from the J.G. Ballard novel about a young English boy (played superbly by Christian Bale) learning to grow up in a Japanese internment camp in Shanghai during World War II. I really thought it was the one that would get Steven Spielberg his Oscar, because it was the world from the viewpoint of a kid, and that's exactly what Spielberg is; that's how he looks at life, through a kid's eyes.

It was a big production and we started off in China. Shanghai was amazing. I'd read *My Wicked, Wicked Ways*, Errol Flynn's book, which was great; he lived in Shanghai through the halcyon days, when it was a den of debauchery, before communism took over. To work there was fantastic. There were no stunt people per se in China that we could use back then, so we ended up hiring and training 50 local students for the street riot sequence when the Japanese invade and the kid loses touch with his Mum and Dad. These students were all bi-lingual. I deliberately picked English course students from the university so they could understand the concept of what we were doing. By putting them in amongst the 2,500 extras that were crowding in the square, crushing our actors, we had this cocoon of real Chinese people around to explain to the crowd what was happening, but at the same time acting their hearts out as though they were a mob. It worked absolutely brilliantly. They also played the people in the rickshaws that got shot; these kids were just fabulous, and with our training performed like seasoned stunt people. But I quickly realised how corrupt China was in those days. My local stuntmen were supposedly getting paid $40 a day, plus overtime; these kids were only receiving $5 a day with no overtime, but they weren't even getting that. My interpreter, a lovely lad, complained to the production: 'Look, we've been here for three weeks, we're supposed to get $5 a day and we've had nothing.' And the next day these officials came on the set and

My daughter Nina appearing with the young Christian Bale in Empire of the Sun.

took him away, we never saw him again.

We got on so well with these 50 students that at the end of the shoot they took Wendy and I, and my English stunt team Wayne Michaels and Dickey Beer, out to dinner at a real Chinese restaurant as a special treat. I felt like a black man in Alabama in the '50s walking into a whites-only restaurant, because as we entered all the diners literally stopped eating and looked us up and down, almost in disgust to see us coming into their place. Our students were much more internationally orientated so totally ignored this and sat us down and made a real fuss of us, but these diners could hardly adjust to white people eating in their restaurant. Remember this was before Shanghai and China had really opened up to western tourists. I'll never forget some of the dishes; a bowl of clear oily broth with wrinkled up chicken claws in it, another with a skinned snake floating in the centre, crushed turtles, the most hideous things ever, but we had to eat them first and then everybody dived in. It was a wonderful night; all our Chinese stunt girls got up and sang. It was a moment that you couldn't buy, the result of a really close relationship.

After China the production moved to Spain, where the whole prison camp and the Japanese runway were built. Wendy appeared in the film – she's the woman hanging out laundry in that iconic shot when a P51 aeroplane suddenly appears over the washing line and screams over her head – and my daughter Nina had a little scene too. One day I went to work and Steven was shouting, 'Where's Nina? We need a little girl to play marbles with Christian.' They sent a production car dashing down to the beach where I thought Wendy and Nina would be, and brought them back to the set. I coached Nina with her dialogue, and like a kid she was totally cool about it, no nerves. (She was later invited to present the bouquet to the Queen at the royal premiere in London, which was a great honour and a memorable night.) A few years ago when I went to Greece on *Captain Corelli's Mandolin* I met Christian Bale again, now a full-grown man, and he saw Wendy and immediately said, 'Hey, Wendy, how's Nina? Still playing marbles?'

Back home I got a call from a line producer in Ireland to do another picture for Michael Cimino, called *Michael Collins*. The producer said, 'Cimino told me that you're the first person I've got to contact to make sure you're available.' I went, 'OK, fine, I'll do it,' and told him what my fee was. 'I'll get back to you,' he said. A few weeks later Buzz Feitshans of Carolco Pictures called. 'Hey Vic, we're doing *Rambo III* in Israel, love you to do it.' I said, 'Shit, I've already agreed to do this film with Cimino. I don't think I can get out of it. Cimino's relying on me.' About two weeks went by and I'd heard nothing back from this line producer on *Michael Collins* so in the end I phoned him, only to be told that my fee was too much. 'Why don't you come to my London office Vic and we'll see what we can work out.' I said, 'Whoa, that's the deal, that's what I get.' He said, 'We can't afford that.' I put the phone down, incensed. If they had no intention of paying me, at least they could have called and said so. As I was storming round the kitchen looking for something to punch, the phone rang. I picked it up, 'YES! WHAT?' 'Hey… it's Buzz again, are you *sure* you can't get out of the Cimino picture?' I said, 'Do you know what, I think I can wriggle out of it.' Isn't fate an amazing thing?

A week later I was in the departure lounge of Heathrow airport about to fly out to Israel for *Rambo* when I thought, I'd better just call this arsehole on the Cimino picture to tell him I'm not doing it. 'Are you coming in for a meeting?' he said. 'I'm not coming in. I don't know if you can hear it in the background, but they're just calling my flight. I'm off to Tel Aviv to do *Rambo III*.' This guy's attitude changed completely. 'Look, we can do a deal.' I said, 'I'm not a car salesman. I told you what the deal was and you said no, so that's it, I'm out.' I could hear this guy's voice cracking on the other end of the line. 'What the hell am I going to tell Cimino? He's going to blow a fuse.' I said, 'First thing I'd do is buy him a new fuse, and then tell him what you like mate, because I'm out of here.' And I put the phone down. In the end Cimino never made the film anyway.

Rambo III was the most expensive film made up to that date, costing in excess of $60 million. We started shooting down in the Dead Sea at night, for a sequence where helicopters attack a small convoy. I had Jordi getting blown up and being flipped upside down into the side of a jeep; it was a huge shoot 'em up. We finished in under a week, but the film was dropping behind schedule already. It had been far too ambitious to expect to shoot all that stuff at night, and the director Russell Mulcahy was fired, unfairly in my opinion, and Peter MacDonald took over. I think Mulcahy was treated quite badly. He was a lovely, sweet man, very artistic; he'd made *Highlander* of course. He got set up and shot down in flames. That was a total assassination as far as I'm concerned.

We did some great action on *Rambo III*. Wendy was with me and must have played about 20 different parts, from women to Afghan rebels. One of the most famous sequences in the film is the Buzkashi game that Rambo plays, which involves grabbing and carrying a dead goat whilst on horseback. During the filming of that scene we'd play polo at lunch time. Sly, like the rest of us, would have a quick bite to eat while the grooms changed the saddles of the horses, rolled the Buzkashi pitch dead flat and watered it and then we'd all come out and play polo. Sly was in his polo phase at the time. We taught Sly to ride really well on that film; you see Rambo in the Buzkashi game bend down and pick that dead goat up off the ground at full gallop, and Sly did it for real. He was so thrilled when he did it.

Sly's got a great sense of humour, too. We were filming the sequence where he rescues his boss the Colonel from a Russian jail. He drops through the roof and lands, hides round the corner, a guard comes by and Sly does a big high kick and almost takes his head off. The stunt guy doubling the guard was probably five foot ten and as Sly lined up the kick – and he's very athletic, can kick way above his head – he started joking, 'Jesus Christ Vic, couldn't you get a bigger stunt guy?' As the cameras started to roll and Sly ducked down behind his pillar I swapped stuntmen, and brought in big Terry Richards who was about six foot four (he played the swordsman in the iconic sequence in *Raiders*). 'Shh, don't say anything,' I whispered to the crew. 'And... action!' Sly watched the guard's shadow, and when it hit a certain mark he stepped out, went to kick him... and stopped dead. His eyes went up and up and up to Terry's head. By now Sly's neck was craning backwards. 'What the fuck!?' There was deathly silence; then Sly started laughing. He thought it was a brilliant ruse.

My young son Scott came out on location for *Rambo*, in fact all the kids came out with their nanny. (I was like King Farouk with my entourage: I had the nanny, my Mum, four kids, Wendy and myself, so when we went out to dinner we needed three taxis!) All the weapons we were using on the film fascinated Scott and I introduced him to Sly, who's really lovely with kids. 'Here's my Rambo knife,' he said to Scott, who watched with his eyes wide open as Sly made slashing movements with it in the air. Then Sly got out his Uzi machine gun and let Scott fire it. Later on he stood posing for photographs with him. Scott was only ten at the time and mightily impressed. That night he said to me, 'That Syl...' It wasn't Sly, it was Syl for Sylvester, now they were mates, you see. 'That Syl's a good guy isn't he Dad? If I ever had any trouble at school he'd be the guy to call, wouldn't he?' I joked, 'Sure, he'll come round with that knife and that old Uzi and soon sort them out.'

A few days later Scott left to return to school, and a week after he arrived back home I got a call. 'Dad, those photographs with me and Syl, can I have one now?' I said, 'Why, what's the matter mate?' There was a bit of a pause. He said, 'Well, I've told them at school that me and Syl hung out over there, and he let me fire his Uzi and they're going, "Yeah yeah, get out of here."' So I sent the pictures back to England, which soon made the doubters shut up.

When they were growing up, my kids normally came out to visit me wherever I was filming in the world. We had a nanny for the younger ones with us all the time, and my Mum or friends would bring Bruce and Scott out for us, and brought their schoolbooks too. Their school back in England was only too happy to accommodate us; we'd explain the situation to them and they were fine about it. Nowadays, of course, you're not allowed to take your kids out of school for extended periods of time, which to me is just stupid, because I've always thought that travel is the best education you could have.

One Sunday I went with Sly out to this big desert area where we were going to shoot the final battle. Sly had a lot to say about that movie, his input on *Rambo III* was enormous. 'I want 250 horses there,' he said. 'And 250 horses over there.' He was just getting into his stride when I said, 'Whoa, let's stop there Sly. Firstly, I can't get 500 horses in Israel; they just don't have them. We'd have to get them from the Arab countries surrounding us and that's just not going to work. And this ground, there's only about an inch of sand, underneath it's all black rock, you can't fall horses or men on this stuff.' 'Shit,' he said. 'That's no good, what do you suggest? Where can we get a lot of horses?' I said, 'Well, Spain, Morocco, the States.' He went, 'Tell you what, let's go to the States, tell them in the office when you get back.' I walked into the production office and Buzz was there. 'How'd the location scout go? Is the battle gonna look good?' I went, 'Yeah, it's going to be a

Stallone rides into action on Rambo III. *He was an incredibly dedicated man. He was down to 3% body fat training every night after work, and yet still would play polo and clown with the stunt guys.*

good battle Buzz, but we're going to shoot it in America.' He went, 'What!?' I said, 'That's what Sly wants to do.' 'Like hell, where is he?' Buzz went dashing off and came back 45 minutes later. 'Yeah, you're right, we'll shoot it in America.'

We decided to go to Yuma, Arizona. But it was going to take a while to organize and set up this big sequence, so what were we going to do in the meantime? 'I'll tell you what,' said Sly. 'You know the stick fight?' – our opening sequence had Rambo fight some big bruiser in a warehouse, that we were going to shoot down by the docks in Tel Aviv – 'I've always wanted to shoot in Thailand,' Sly carried on. 'Let's go there.' So literally the next day Sly and I were on a plane straight to Thailand and we started scouting for locations for the stick fight. I invented and devised the fight sequence literally on the spot and then we added all the monastery stuff in there too, to make the whole move to Thailand worthwhile. I was very happy to be shooting there because it's one of my favourite places in the world.

After that we moved to Arizona for the battle climax. The logistics were massive: 5,000 people and 500 horses in the field. I used civil war re-enactment groups, guys who in real life varied from brain surgeons to mechanics, and they were fabulous. Every night the commandant would come over and I'd say, 'OK, I want 125 on that hill, 25 on that hill, 275 on that hill and 75 over here, ready to go at seven o'clock.' And sure enough in the morning there they were. They treated the whole thing like one big exercise, camping out, having their bonfires, cooking their beans and doing their own make up, just brilliant.

My main concern was that with helicopters flying about and massive explosions going off, this was going to be dangerous. Tommy Fisher was the special effects guy. He got an Oscar for *Titanic*, and is one of the greatest in the business (he's also my golfing partner and one of my closest friends). He does go in for big explosions, which is what we needed, but when you've got horses and 5,000 people spread around the desert in big master shots, you're worried that somebody might be off their mark and get blown up. We did not have one mishap with the special effects, but at the end of the first day six people had been taken to hospital with broken ribs and ruptured spleens after falling off horses. I said, 'We should have a meeting about all these injuries.' And the commandant of the re-enactment groups went, 'Yeah it's fantastic, we've never had so few.' 'Jesus Christ,' I said. 'Any injury is a worry to me.' And he said, 'Normally we have a lot more than this!' Those re-enactors had the reins in their teeth, they were firing their guns and galloping hell for leather just like John Wayne, they were really living it. It was great.

On big crowd numbers I tend to use flags or flares to cue the action. It's a fairly fail-safe system, which I prefer to using radios, because even if we had enough radios for everyone, they sometimes don't work, or people don't listen to them, or they never stop talking into them. For this battle sequence I had a white flare for stand by, a green flare for action, and then I just kept blazing red flares into the sky so they knew it was a cut. Everyone could see the signals from anywhere on the battlefield.

One day, I fired the flares and everything went off perfectly on cue. A little later there was total panic: one of the armoured personnel carriers, called a Ferret, was on fire. Now these flares were special S.O.S. safety flares designed to burn out 200 feet above the ground. But this one flare stayed alight and just happened to fall through the little hatch in the vehicle's turret and set fire to the bloody thing, unbelievable. You could try to do that a thousand times and the flare wouldn't even hit the ground alight, let alone go through a turret hatch not more than two feet across!

After the megabudget of *Rambo III* it was a real change to work on a film that had hardly any money at all. That's what I love about the business, I enjoy doing low budget movies as much, if not more, than I do the ones with millions of dollars. The film was Kenneth Branagh's *Henry V*, and they wanted me to train all the actors to ride, run the second unit and stage the battle of Agincourt, quite a feat with a tiny budget. I met Branagh and we talked about the battle. 'I see this like Kurosawa,' I said. 'Like *Seven Samurai*.' Branagh's face lit up. 'That's exactly how I've visualized it.' He was really excited, so we bonded from that moment on.

KENNETH BRANAGH

Henry V **was the first film I ever directed and Vic was one of a key group of people who helped me out with what was obviously a scary endeavour. Meeting Vic I remember being struck immediately by the fact that he was not, for somebody who already had a really significant career, full of himself. And additionally, which I was very grateful for, there was no sense of being patronized or any sort of sense that somehow one shouldn't be doing this. I think he rather took to the slightly mad, youthful energy of the whole project. He paid us all the courtesy of giving us a level of professional respect, which was very encouraging; it gave you confidence.**

Even though I'd agreed to do the movie, the backers hadn't green-lit it yet, but I insisted the producers needed to find cash from somewhere so I could start training the cast, because hardly any of them could ride. The thing with English actors is that they're not terribly physical. Out of the whole cast only Brian Blessed could actually ride a horse, as he owned his own stables. We had some wonderful actors on that film: Richard Briers, Emma Thompson, Ian Holm, Judi Dench and her husband Michael Williams, the guy I doubled on *Dead Cert*, falling onto the railings (which he remembered well). All of them came up to my house for horse riding lessons, Ken Branagh included. The film was actually green-lit in my kitchen – one morning Ken and the producers were all having breakfast when the phone went; the producer took it, turned round and gave us all a thumbs up. 'We've got the money.'

Unfortunately the time I was training the cast was just after the actor Roy Kinnear had tragically fallen off a horse and later died on *The Return of the Musketeers*. These actors were all great friends of Roy and were understandably a little nervous. So I used my horse Triana, who was so responsive, and could teach anybody to ride. I was very proud of all the actors when I saw the finished result on the set, especially Ken. During the sequence at Harfleur he is at the top of a ramp with explosions and fire lighting the whole set behind him as he rears Triana, delivers the famous 'Cry God for Harry, England and Saint George!' speech and then gallops down the ramp and away. That would have been trying

Ken Branagh in Henry V *on my beloved horse Triana.*

for a stuntman to do, even without the dialogue!

It's a hell of a good movie *Henry V*, even though we had hardly any money. I shot all of the battle of Agincourt in a week on a field at the front of Shepperton Studios, which had a reservoir on one side, a housing estate on the other and trees down the end. We put up tons of smoke and long-lensed the whole thing (as per Kurosawa). We had about 100 extras and I gave them five different sword routines each, even the guys in the background who just had sticks painted silver because we couldn't afford swords for them. It was a really good battle, I'm very proud of it, although I did get through four cameramen. I worked them quite hard. This was in November, and it was freezing cold. You can't shoot before nine in the morning and you've got to wrap by four in the afternoon because of the low light, so I pushed and pushed. I love to do a lot of set-ups in the day and we really cranked the set-ups out on that... and four cameramen left, they'd leave for the night and then not turn up the next day, so the production would have to send a replacement down.

On the very last day we were shooting like mad because I *had* to finish, we'd no money left. It was getting late and the cameraman, complaining that the light had gone, showed me his meter with nothing registering on it. 'OK,' I said. 'There's just one more shot.' He said, 'How can we? The meter's off the clock, there's no light anywhere.' I said, 'There is up there.' He looked up, and you could see the lights of Heathrow Airport creating this glow in the sky. The cameraman looked at me, dumbfounded. 'I want to do the arrow firing shot now,' I said. 'When the volley of arrows fly through the air into the French cavalry.' I had it all ready to go, we shot it and if you watch the film, those flying arrows are being lit by Heathrow Airport. It really was a race to get that whole battle sequence done, but very satisfying.

Even today people remember the long tracking shot at the end of the battle, with the horse and soldier carcasses strewn around the field and Branagh finding the boy, played by Christian Bale, and carrying out his dead body. We did things on that sequence that I'd never done before. I got one of my stunt horses, photographed him in every position lying down and then sent the pictures to Shepperton, where they made a series of Styrofoam models that were turned into vacuum moulds. You can knock a thousand of those out an hour; the most expensive part of the process was that some poor sod had to paint each one a different colour. So in that shot all the dead horses were in fact vacuum moulds, just half a horse, and it looked much better than the stuffed dummies they usually used in movies. They looked so real my own horses wouldn't go near them; they were scared to death of them. And we did the same with all the dead soldiers. It's about half a mile that shot, and we rigged up some loud speakers so everything was done to the music. It was amazingly moving, and so inspirational and innovative of Ken to dream it up.

KENNETH BRANAGH

When it came to the battle itself, Vic was very clear about what was possible and what wasn't, what was efficient to do, what was a good angle for a shot, or whatever. He was very generous with that, without ever framing it in any terms of criticizing. One has worked with people who do that sort of intake of breath, 'Oh Christ I can't believe what he's asked for,' and Vic never had that. And that was terribly important to me because it meant you could share ideas with him early, you didn't have to walk round either a delicate ego or a slightly 'been there, done that' personality, and that was ever so helpful for a first time film maker. It was also clear then that Vic had an eye for shots beyond what were purely stunt shots. He had an eye and an interest in how the story was being told, and an interest in more than just his department. It didn't surprise me when he later moved into direction.

Above all, what struck me as we went along was the fact that Vic still seemed to enjoy enormously what he did, the excitement of working in film and the sense of it being almost first time each time. He seemed to take from and share your enthusiasm. I enjoyed enormously working with Vic and he made a significant contribution to the film.

I'm still very proud of that film and Ken was great. He had a huge reputation as an actor, the press talked about him as Laurence Olivier's heir almost, but this was his first movie as a director, so the pressure was enormous. But on set he was totally calm, totally organized, knew exactly what he wanted. When I was working on *Mission: Impossible III* years later, Ken was originally going to play the villain and we hadn't seen each other since *Henry V*. We gave each other a huge bear hug and he asked how the horses were. Nice bloke.

THE LAST CRUSADER

It had been five years since the last Indiana Jones movie and I was thrilled when the call came through that the gang of Spielberg, Ford and Lucas were all getting back together again for *Indiana Jones and the Last Crusade*. I'd given up doing stunts years before, but came out of retirement especially for this film – how could I refuse? From the script I knew what had to be done, and that it was going to be tough, so I went to the gym for three months to tone up, because it was always shirt off with Harrison. Although I've done bits and pieces of stunt work since, *Last Crusade* was the last major movie I worked on as a stuntman proper.

I went out to Almeria in Spain weeks before the main unit got started, to set up and shoot the now famous tank chase. It was Micky Moore, the second unit director, and myself; we got the horses and worked out what the gags were going to be. There was supposed to be no press because the actors and Steven weren't there yet, but in the Spanish equivalent of *Hello* magazine there were telephoto pictures of me talking to Micky and the caption read: 'This is Harrison Ford talking with Steven Spielberg.' It was so funny; they weren't even in the country.

The stunt I'm most proud of in that film is when I leap off the horse and land on top of the moving tank. I used the same horse that I'd taken out to Israel for *Rambo III* and that Stallone rode, he was called Huracán (Spanish for Hurricane) and was a good old film horse. But there was a lot of training involved, like getting him comfortable galloping next to the tank and then running straight when I stood up on the saddle for the jump. We also had to bulldoze into the side of a hill to create a slightly raised path for the horse to run along. The problem was that I couldn't get too close to the edge of the path in case it gave way, as the horse would slip down into that narrow space between the tank and the wall and get crushed. But then if he was too far away, I couldn't make the leap across, which was going to be about 18 feet laterally. And if he ducked away at the last minute, I was going to

The now famous leap onto the tank. I nearly missed the damn thing.

end up thrown into that gap. It was quite a tricky stunt. In the end I put rocks on the ground to keep the horse in a central position.

To help with the leap, I had a flexible steel strap made that had the pegs I would use as stirrups mounted on it, way up by the horse's shoulder blades, to lift my feet up onto as I made the move to jump. The strap went right around the horse's girth and the theory was that it would negate any movement which would absorb my push from the horse, which otherwise would be a bit like trying to push off a squishy sofa rather than a solid table. As I rode and got the rhythm of the gallop, just at the last second I brought my feet up onto the pegs and jumped. The first time I did it I completely mistimed the jump, and barely made it across to collapse in a heap on the tank. The second time it worked perfectly, I hit the horse's stride just right and leapt as he was on an upward step, which helped propel me the 18 feet to belly flop on the back of the tank. Although it winded me a little, I did not feel a thing. I guess the adrenaline was up!

It was lucky I did that stunt early on, because a few weeks later I had a rather nasty accident. We were doing the sequence where I was on top of the tank fighting a German baddie, played by Simon Crane, and a truck full of enemy soldiers pulls up alongside. Cut to inside the tank and Sean Connery as Indy's Dad fires a cannon and blows the whole thing up. Because the truck was going to flip upside down, we couldn't put real people in the back, we had the same animated dummies that fell off the bridge in *Temple of Doom*, so when the truck exploded they'd shoot up in the air with their arms and legs flailing. Dickey Beer was driving the truck, with an air cannon that was going to flip it over at the same time as a huge fireball was released. Simon and I were on the tank, ready. OK, action. We started fighting,

Back in the saddle as Indy one last time.

the truck blew up next to us and flipped over perfectly on cue and we all skidded to a halt. Cut. Then it was madness.

Fire was splattered everywhere from the fire gel in the truck, and one of the cameras was on fire. A crew hand rushed over to put it out, and fell over and broke his arm. Meanwhile Dickey Beer lay upside down in the burning truck and needed help fast. Simon and I jumped off the back of the tank but I caught my toe – it slipped behind the bumper bar and my heel locked beneath the tank while my whole weight fell forwards onto my knee, which bent my leg completely the opposite way, ripping all the ligaments in and around my knee. I collapsed off the tank. I couldn't move and was throwing up with the pain – my knee was shot. They wanted to fly me home and get it operated on, but I said, 'No, I still have to finish the movie in my stunt co-ordinator role as well.' Luckily it was all riding for the next few weeks, so Jordi Casares took over for a while; he did some of the bit with Indy hanging on the side of the tank and getting dragged along and crushed against the wall. So I was fortunate to have got that big jump out of the way early, and also the stunt where I gallop and pick up a rock that Indy shoves into the gun barrel of the tank, which then blows up. There was some great stuff on that show.

When Harrison and Steven arrived in Almeria the main unit started shooting. I remember setting up the shot where Indy first steals that horse. He gets up on a rock and as this Arab rider comes by jumps off onto him; it's the classic cowboy

Even action heroes need their sleep. I call it power napping!

and Indian gag. I was standing on this big rock about 18 feet above, looking at the ground and telling them where to put the sand down when I became aware of somebody next to me. 'Put a bit over there Vic, because that's where I'm going to land.' I looked and it was Harrison. I humoured him along and then got up into position on the rock. 'Put a bit more sand there,' I said. 'And I'll jump when the horse is here.' And Harrison said, 'I'm doing this Vic.' I said, 'No, no, no Harrison you're not, I'm doing this. This is dangerous: you could break your ankle landing; the horse could head butt you on the way down; you could put your knee through your face when you land; or the horse could rear up and fall on you. No, I'm doing this Harrison.' He said, 'I can do it, I can do it.' I said, 'I know you can do it Harrison, but come over here.'

I took him behind the rock. 'Harrison, you're costing me an arm and a leg here buddy.' He said, 'What do you mean?' I said, 'You're doing quite well out of this film I presume, but we get bonuses for extra stunt work and if you keep doing all the stunts I'm not making any extra.' And he said, 'Oh my God, I'm sorry Vic. Man, I'm sorry. Next time I'm so ignorant kick me in the ass will you?' He was truly mortified that he was taking food from my table, as it were. I'd only said it to stop him, in a diplomatic way, from doing the stunt because I did think it was too dangerous. Not that he couldn't have done it, he could have; it was just not worth the risk. Look at the movie and I jump off the rock, knock the horse down, punch out the Arab, put my leg across the horse, it stands up underneath me and I gallop off kicking somebody on the way out. It was technically very difficult, but it was so funny blackmailing Harrison into not doing it.

Another day Harrison said to me, 'Vic, your stunt guys are a really great bunch, how about you and me giving them a little party?' I said, 'Yeah they'd love that, we always love a party.' 'Great. Don't worry about organising it, I'll get my assistant to do all that.' I said, 'Fabulous, thank you.' He paused for a bit. 'Would you mind if we invite Steven to the party?' 'Of course not.' He said, 'How about Sean and a couple of the actors?' 'Absolutely.' Anyway this carried on, and more and more people got invites. He had these little invitations made up that read: 'Vic Armstrong and Harrison Ford invite you to drink and food Saturday.' He even put my name first. It ended up that the whole bloody film crew were coming, nearly 200 people, and I was thinking, Jesus this is going to cost us a fortune. But not to worry, we had a great time; everyone partied until four in the morning.

Back to work on Monday I saw Harrison and said, 'I tell you what Harrison, you'd better let me have my half of that bill for the party so I can start thinking about paying it off.' He went, 'Party? What party would that be?' I said, 'Saturday, the party.' 'I don't remember a party.' 'Yeah, the party you and I gave.' He said, 'No, you're hallucinating, we didn't have a party.' And the penny suddenly dropped, he wanted to give a party but didn't want it to look as though Harrison Ford the big superstar was throwing a party for everybody, it was Vic Armstrong and the stunt guys and Harrison throwing the party. He wouldn't let me pay, and refused to acknowledge there had ever been a party. It was really sweet of him.

HARRISON FORD

Vic's contribution to the Indiana Jones movies was extremely valuable. The action scenes are fundamental to the character of Indiana Jones, and without having the success of the character's physical nature he would have lost a great deal. Vic's intelligence and skill in creating the action sequences for Indiana Jones was a remarkable contribution.

Happily because of our relationship and our understanding of each other we were able to work closely together. Steven would leave Vic and I to come up with the choreography for a fight scene, we'd show it to him and he'd either make suggestions or take it on board.

We had a really great time making those movies and I still value Vic's friendship.

Working out some fight choreography. I'm on the tank tracks next to George Lucas.

Around this time Harrison had gotten into tennis, and was so pissed off because his wife Melissa had bought him this posh new ceramic tennis racket, which cost something like $400, while the rest of us were playing with normal rackets. 'I told her not to buy this,' he complained. 'Now when I walk out on the court everybody will think I can play the bloody game.' He was only learning like the rest of us. Wendy and the kids came to watch and afterwards Nina said to me, 'While you were playing Daddy, Steven asked if I wanted to be in the movie and I said, I'll have to ask my Dad. He said I could either play a small part here in Spain or play the girl that presents Hitler with the bouquet.' Wendy and I decided she could play the girl with the bouquet at the book burning, because that was shooting in England where we could control it and get the time off school.

So Nina walked over to Harrison and Sean to hand out ice creams and then walked over to Spielberg. 'Here's your ice cream Steven, and by the way I think I'll play the part of the girl in England.' By this time there was quite a crowd of people around who hadn't been privy to the earlier conversation, no doubt thinking, 'What!? This little kid is telling Steven Spielberg she'll appear in his movie!' And Steven said, 'All right Nina, no problem.' And sure enough he gave her the part. Wendy was her chaperone and they sent a limo to pick her up and had a trailer for her. It was lovely.

As Indy in the Venice boat chase. This shot was filmed at the rather less glamorous EMI studios Elstree. Wendy is driving.

We went all over the place on that movie, Venice, Jordan, Germany, the US, and there was a hell of a lot of stunts and action, a huge amount of choreography involved working it all out. It was one of the biggest movies I ever worked on, no question. It was huge, logistically. Apart from the tank battle there was the motorbike chase, which we did in the States, and the Venice boat chase, which was actually mostly shot at the London docks where we later did the jet boat stuff on *The World Is Not Enough.* Wendy doubled Alison Doody on that, while I doubled for Indy. There was also the terrific opening train sequence that we shot out in Colorado with young River Phoenix.

We also went to Green River, Utah, for the scenes of young Indy in all those caves. The unit drove up there from the airport in one coach while the stunt crew had their own, and we bought Jack Daniels and coke and lots of other booze for the trip and it was an absolute riot. It was just a rolling party. We even ended up trying to lasso the driver as we arrived. One of the guys was so out of it we found him walking down the centre of the road mumbling, 'I'm walking back to LA, I don't like this place.' LA was three days' drive away! Everybody was talking about this coach trip, and at the end of the shoot, driving to the airport to fly out, the other coach was empty because everybody was on ours waiting for the party to start. So we deliberately did nothing and sat there like monks. But when we got on the plane we started to party again, and the poor stewardess was trying to give her safety talk with all of us interrupting and imitating her. Thank God she was an American stewardess with a sense of humour – normally they can be monsters. In the end she said, 'If we do crash, put your head between your knees and kiss your asses goodbye. Have a good flight.' And that was it, she just walked off laughing. She came back later with the booze trolley, which she just left in the aisle for us, and everybody was grabbing great handfuls of miniatures. They were supposed to sell them to you, but this girl knew she was onto a loser with us. It was great.

Sometimes, stunt guys just need to let off steam. With this job there's a lot of pressure: you can see people get injured or killed, go through divorces; it's not just a one-off holiday, you're actually doing it as a business, 365 days a year. You've got to enjoy it, otherwise it ain't worth doing.

It was very collaborative working with Steven, it always is. He trusted me and trusted my judgement and my recommendations. It's great when you get that repartee with a director, that collaboration, it's just brilliant. What impressed me most about Steven on that movie was when he first came out to Spain and we dashed around location-scouting and prepping for the following week's shoot. At the time he was working on three films: planning the next one, editing the last one, and shooting this one, Indy. He was on the phone, writing notes, you name it. We finished this particular location scout and got to the point where the tank goes over the cliff and Steve asked, 'Vic, do you think we could have Indy hanging on a vine underneath the cliff's overhang? We see him slowly dropping and then cut to the top to Sean standing there, and we see the plant at his feet getting pulled down into the ground as though Indy's hanging onto its roots.' I said, 'I guess we can. But where the hell did that idea come from?' And it was while we were driving near some riverbeds which had flooded, the banks were cut away and you could see roots sticking out through them. He'd got the inspiration from that. And this is while he's working on three movies at the same time; what an amazing brain he has, so inventive.

While everyone was working on the picture, we all knew it was going to be the end of the Indiana Jones trilogy (as it was then). I'm so proud of those three movies. You only have to hear the theme music and it's like, yes! When I was doing *Blade: Trinity*, the Indy DVD box set came out and all my crew told me, 'These are the movies that made me decide I wanted to be in the film business. My Dad took me to see them when I was a kid.' Along with the Bonds, they are the movies I'm most proud to have been associated with. Bond and Indy are two amazing franchises, and they've changed the history and shape of cinema. I'm very, very proud to have contributed what I did to all of those films. It was a labour of love, and I absolutely adored it.

GEORGE LUCAS

It was a pleasure to work with Vic on the Indiana Jones pictures because he's so easy to get along with, and understated. He's a very calm person to be around, and in those kinds of areas of stunts and danger it's nice to have somebody who doesn't get excited, or nervous, or create problems. He's always thinking about other people, while at the same time he's very talented at what he does and he gets things done without getting people all upset.

He's also very down to earth and laid back. I'd call Vic a mild man, like Clark Kent, very mild mannered, but under that he's Superman. And he's also very honourable. The best thing that I can say about anybody is that they're true to their word, and Vic is and always has been.

At the wrap party of *Last Crusade* there was a feeling of sadness that this was the last Indy movie, but it's like that at the end of every movie, it's always emotional because you're saying goodbye to a family you've had for six months. But you all end up working together again on different movies, sometimes movies that never get finished. And that's just what happened straight after *Last Crusade*, when Micky Moore asked me to work on this chase movie in Miami called *Arrive Alive*. It was supposedly a comedy. Well the studio backing it, Paramount, thought it was a comedy. The whole thing started off with a killer whale in the Miami marina leaping up and biting the head off a woman. This was supposed to be a comedy? And it starred Willem Dafoe, not known for his comedic acting.

Anyway I went to meet the director Jeremiah Chechik, who seemed totally uninterested as I ran through my resume until I got to *Henry V*. 'Oh my God. You did *Henry V*.' He started doing back-flips almost, he was so excited. *Henry V* basically got me that show, because he thought it was the greatest film ever made. So we prepared the movie in LA and then all flew over to Miami to start shooting. Jeremiah was a lovely guy, and we bought a bunch of old cars for this big chase around Miami, plus we had an airboat that smashed through one of the casinos. But the studio was pretty unimpressed with the dailies and we kept getting these negative reports back from them saying it wasn't funny enough.

They even wanted to sack Dafoe and get Martin Short instead. After about three weeks of shooting we knew it was going down the tubes, but still carried on and hired a thousand extras for the scene at the marina with the killer whale. Then one day we broke for lunch, and nobody ever came back; they'd pulled the plug and that was it. Three months of preparation down the toilet. But that happens sometimes in movies.

TOTAL RECALL

Paul Verhoeven had an amazing reputation as a fiery director. I remember asking him how he got started. 'I was doing films in Holland like *Soldier of Orange* and *Turkish Delight*,' he said, 'and I wanted to break into movies in America, so my agent was trying to get me a script and then I got this thing called *RoboCop*. I said to my wife, "This is a heap of shit, I can't go over and do this," and my wife said, "Look, Paul, just take it, go over there and do the best you can, at least it'll get you to America."' So he took her advice and it turned out to be quite a hit. The next thing he got was *Total Recall*, a science fiction actioner with Arnold Schwarzenegger, filmed out in Mexico City at the massive Churubusco Studio.

At the beginning of the movie Paul was adamant that he didn't want a second unit because he'd had three second units on *RoboCop*, fired each one in succession and ended up shooting it all himself. But the producers insisted he had a second unit on *Total Recall*, headed by myself. So now I was on a real hiding to nothing because I was being forced upon him. I'd had to beg and borrow a little monitor and the first thing he gave me, my first shot on the movie, I'll never forget, was Arnie on the building site at the beginning and it was a close-up of the drill tip hitting the cement. That's all it was. By the end of the shoot, five months later, I had four cameras, a huge tent, four monitors; the works. Paul absolutely adored what I did. After the film wrapped he told me I'd done 1200 set-ups that were in the movie. I did an amazing amount of shooting, all the fight sequences. I was working full-blown.

Verhoeven's a real character. I remember on the first day I got all the stunt crew together and we were picking guys to play the baddies, and he was standing in front of them going, 'OK what I want, ya, is when you get shot, bang, you go "Arghh!!"' He was throwing himself all over the place, and this set was made out of volcanic rock, which was razor sharp, and he was just bouncing off it and falling about. All the stunt guys were going, Jesus Christ, if the director's doing that, with no protective pads on, just a short-sleeved shirt, what's he going to expect *us* to do when we shoot?

We did have a few clashes and disagreements though. All directors try to push you to do things their way, which may not be the best or safest way in your opinion. I first met Verhoeven in Amsterdam at Schipol airport; I flew in for the meeting and then flew out again. We went through the script from beginning to end and we went through the notes I'd made about all the action in it. I built up a good repartee with him. We got to the part where the two women, Rachel Ticotin and Sharon Stone, have a fight outside an elevator and I said, 'This is one chance Paul where we can do a really good fight between women, where they actually land punches instead of pulling their hair and tearing their blouses and all that old nonsense.' And he went, 'Ya, ya, that's good.' You could see his eyes light up; he liked the idea of that. I knew we couldn't hide pads under the skimpy costumes the actresses were wearing, so decided instead to pad the walls of the set and have very high compression padding under the carpet, so you could hit the floor and bounce around. I worked out a really good fight routine, but the key to it was having one actress and one stunt person at a time, unless it was a special shot where you saw both girl's faces and they weren't doing anything really physical. There were some throws and other stuff where you could easily break an arm if you didn't know what you were doing, if you did a Grace Jones and went crazy.

On this particular shot one of the girls had to throw the other one over her back and Paul insisted that both actresses did it. 'No,' I said. 'It's got to be a stunt girl whichever way around you want it, but one stunt girl, one actress.' But he kept on insisting and insisting. 'No, in my opinion it would be much better...' And at the end of it he looked at me and said, 'Basically what you're telling me is I'm a fucking idiot.' I said, 'Now, that's a catchy phrase you've used there Paul, not that I'd use it myself.' And he fell about laughing.

Sharon Stone was funny. We all thought that Rachel Ticotin was going to be the big star, she was a fabulous actress, looked gorgeous and yet she went nowhere. Sharon Stone you couldn't drag into the gym, she just didn't want to train, didn't want to do anything, yet she became a superstar in *Basic Instinct*. Wendy was doubling Rachel and Donna Evans doubled Sharon and did all the kicks and everything else really, we mainly shot Sharon for close-ups. Though I must say she looked dynamite in those close-ups!

Back at that meeting in Schipol I had mentioned to Paul how we were going to shoot the sequence where Arnie and Rachel are getting sucked out onto the

With the gorgeous Sharon Stone, who went on to become a big star after Total Recall.

Martian surface. I broke it all down. Now you have to remember this was in the days when wire removal was a problem, and very expensive to do digitally. In the first part, where they're getting pulled along the ground, we'd drag them by wires. Then when they're hanging on for dear life and flapping about in the wind, we'd fly them by wires on hip harnesses, shooting them from the waist upwards. And finally for the wider shots we'd build a vertical set and put the camera on its side, so when they let go it looks like they're literally flying into space. This way the body language would be correct and you could not sense that they were on wires, because the pick points were not where you would expect them to be. 'Ya, ya,' said Verhoeven.

Months later on the set I heard this loud commotion on the other stage. 'Go and see Paul Verhoeven,' an assistant said. 'He's having a screaming fit.' I went over and he was raging. 'The fucking wires, I see the fucking wires Vic! You said this would work, it's not fucking working!' I said, 'I know Paul, but you're only supposed to shoot them from the waist upwards. Once we have them fully suspended from the ground we go to a vertical set, don't you remember?' He said, 'Ya, ya.' There was a pause. 'What do you mean a vertical set?' I said, 'What I meant was we build the set on end.' 'OK, tell the fucking producers that.' So I told them and they said, 'We can't afford that.' I said, 'Guys, at all the production meetings this is what I said we'd do.' In the end they gave in because the only way

To Vick
thanks for the food when I have me
it made me look good ☺
your friend   Arnold Schwarzenegger

In the gym rehearsing Arnie for the scene when the station depressurises. Joel Kramer is on the left.

you could shoot it was with a vertical set. And it's one of the most memorable parts of the movie, audiences were wondering, 'How the hell did they do that?! It looks as if they were levitating!' And it was a trick I learnt from Alf Joint; they did those sorts of things on old movies like *The Thief of Baghdad* back in silent movie days. But people don't use techniques like that nowadays.

I hadn't worked with Arnie since *Red Sonja*, so it was lovely meeting him again. Since then he'd made it really big, but he hadn't changed at all. Some little TV show came over to interview me and they wanted some shots of Arnie too. He stood there talking to them and really laying it down thick about how great I was and then when he finished he turned to me and said, 'That's what you told me to say wasn't it Vic?' He was just brilliant. We had such fun on that movie, and some of the best parties I've ever been to. And Arnie was the instigator. The wrap party was fantastic. Arnie bought everybody water pistols; everybody had a stack of them on their table, a recipe for disaster. We had the dinner and Paul Verhoeven stood up and was very complimentary about my second unit and me. And then the party got wilder and wilder. By the end you had people running round with big water pistols full of vodka, shooting it in people's faces, and red wine being sprayed everywhere, it was absolute mayhem, just a blast. And that was Arnie.

I'm very proud of *Total Recall*, I think it's a terrific movie. I had a great crew with me – Simon Crane, Graeme Crowther, Jordi Casares, Gabor Piroch and Bronco McLoughlin were my key stunt players, joined by Leon Delaney, Billy Lucas and a host of others. I actually used 11 different nationalities in my stunt crew; I like to pick the best from everywhere I can. I used Simon Crane on *Indiana Jones and the Last Crusade* doubling a bald German – I paid him to shave his head – and then used him to double Michael Ironside on *Total Recall*. He's had an amazing career since then. I first met Simon on *The Living Daylights*, when I shot some of the tests to find the new James Bond. The producers wanted a love scene and a fight scene, and I went up and did the fight scenes for them. I got two stunt guys in: Doug Robinson and Simon Crane. I remember saying to the producer Barbara Broccoli, 'This guy Simon is really good, and he really fights well.' Simon was then working as a stuntman and I later got him his first co-ordinating job, on the *Young Indiana Jones* TV series. He went on from there to co-ordinate a Bond film and today he's one of the top guys in the movie stunt business. I'm competing with him for work now, which is brilliant.

Simon doubled for Ironside in the fight in the elevator, where he has his arms cut off and falls to his death. We built the elevator in the studio and had Simon suspended on wires. Just before the moment when he is supposedly having his arms cut off, Simon had to do a somersault off the elevator and end up hanging onto it. He landed awkwardly – the wires ended up over his hands instead of beneath them as his full body weight landed, and they cut into his hands, slicing through to the bone. He was out of action for a couple of days.

That wasn't the first time Simon had been injured, actually. Years earlier on *Rambo III* Simon had broken his collarbone doing a fall off the roof of a truck in an ambush sequence. He went to hospital and I gave strict instructions that they must not keep him in overnight. He came back to the hotel and the next day I said, 'Right Simon, put on a Mujahideen costume.' He said, 'Vic, I can't work!' and I said, 'Trust me, just put the costume on and walk around with water for the stunt guys.' A little while later one of the production crew asked me, 'How's your stuntman that's in hospital?' I said, 'He's not in hospital, he only broke a collarbone and he's got another one of those on the other side of his body. He's back working. Look, that's him over there.' The guy looked at Simon in his costume and said, 'Wow, that's amazing, I thought he was off the show.' That was my whole reason for getting Simon back to work – otherwise the economists would have sent him home, to save the wages, per diem and hotel expenses. In fact Simon was back full time in two weeks. The production did view me as a bit of an ogre and a slave driver, but I was doing it to safeguard Simon's job. And it worked.

Years after *Total Recall* I got invited to Oxford University to speak to their film society. They hung posters up and did a show reel for me, and I had the biggest audience they'd ever had, bigger even than Warren Beatty, who was there the month before. A lot of people there were saying quite aggressively, 'Don't you feel you're corrupting young people and creating violence by showing violence in movies?' I had to sort of defend myself. One girl in particular was remonstrating about the blood and gore and gratuitous violence, but by the end came up to me and was totally excited and inquisitive asking all sorts of 'how did you do that?' questions, including, 'How did you cut his arms off in *Total Recall*?' She'd totally changed and was actually fascinated by the whole process, violence and all. It was a great night. They had to call time five times and finally throw everybody out, but they were still asking me questions as we were filing through the door.

Total Recall was a big, big movie and a great show to work on. Wendy was there with the girls and a Nanny, and my Mum flew over to Mexico with the other kids to visit. One morning she was waiting outside the hotel when Arnie came out, looked at her and asked, 'You with the crew?' She said, 'Yes, Vic Armstrong's my son.' Arnie smiled. 'Oh gee, you're Vic's Mum, come on we've got to get some photographs!' And he stood there and posed with them; made the kids' day.

It was a hard slog too, really gruelling. I ended up shooting six days a week. And they were literally pulling down the sets around me. Paul's not a fast worker; he'll just keep on shooting until he's done, so you were always running out of time because construction needed the set. So as I was going around shooting, it was like termites tearing the sets down behind me. You had to make sure you got all your shots because that was it, there was no going back.

I handled a lot of the night sequences and all the stuff in the subway train. Our producer Buzz Feitshans was great. I started a ritual back on *Temple of Doom* that when I finished night work, I'd come back and have a glass of wine with my breakfast. Remember it's the end of your day and you're actually trying to get to sleep when it's daylight. It's very difficult to black out your room in a hotel and there's noise and everything else, so a glass of wine helps you go to sleep. I told Buzz about this and he said, 'OK, call round the office I'll have something for you.' So when we finished night shooting I'd take my crew into his office and on his desk were bottles of rum, wine, whatever we wanted, and my crew, who were mostly Americans, couldn't believe it. 'This producer does this for you?!' I said, 'Yeah, we go way, way back.'

I'll never forget my last day on the movie. I was shooting nights in the city set. The main crew had some more day shooting to do, and then *Total Recall* was in the can. I wrapped and drove back to my hotel; the next morning I was off to Thailand to start work on *Air America*. I went inside my room and suddenly the door banged shut behind me, and there was Paul Verhoeven, his beautiful assistant Lynn Ehrensperger, Simon Crane, all the stunt guys and the actors, they all piled into my room and had ordered this huge breakfast and champagne. It was a total surprise from Paul and the gang; they'd all got up at five in the morning when I finished work to say goodbye in style. It was a lovely gesture.

I later worked with Paul again on *Starship Troopers*, but before that, around 1994, he was going to make another picture with Arnold called *Crusade*, a massive epic. By then Paul was a great buddy of mine and had total faith in me, so I was going to shoot all the sequences out on location in Morocco and he was going to shoot the studio work. During meetings Verhoeven expressed a desire to have 600 horses on the production. I went, 'Jesus! 600 horses, you have no idea how much room they take up. It's a huge undertaking: you have grooms, one to every two horses, you have the saddles, blacksmiths, tents, catering, living accommodation, the water, it's a massive, massive commitment. You're going to get people dying. With that amount of people and horses, somebody's going to die, you know that. It's going to be like a small city.' He said, 'Oh my God. Do you mean that?' I said, 'More than likely, somebody's going to get kicked, or trodden on, or have a heart attack. That's just what happens when you get that amount of people together for six months.' He said, 'How many horses do you think we should have?' I said 300 would be more than enough, and he seemed to be OK with that. A couple of weeks later one of his assistants called. 'Paul's been thinking about what you said about the horses, but he wants to go back to using 800.' He'd added another 200. 'Whatever guys,' I said. 'It's your money.'

I had started work on the film, researching the period, when after a week Paul phoned me up. 'Vic, I think you should be the first to know that we're going to pull the plug on this. The budget is going north of $120 million. It's so expensive it's not on.' I said, 'Shit. What a bummer.' It would have been an amazing film. It was going to be typical Verhoeven, loads of great sex and violence. There was one brilliant sequence where Arnie escorts this girl, who fancies him like mad because of his body, and they get captured by a band of vagabonds. Arnie is whacked over the head and the whole screen goes black. When he wakes up we the audience see through his eyes a jackal snarling and snapping in his face. The camera pulls back and back and Arnie has been trussed up and stuck inside a dead donkey with his head sticking out of its arsehole. Surrounding the carcass is a pack of jackals. Eventually he bursts out, chases the jackals away and then hunts after the girl. Just great stuff, it's a shame we never made it.

More's the pity, I had actually turned down *Braveheart* to do *Crusade*, and so ended up doing neither. I was very disappointed, because my Scottish Armstrong ancestors were up in the Borders region, actively fighting the English during the time of William Wallace. Even before that, they say the reason the Romans built Hadrian's Wall was to keep the Armstrongs out of England!

TROUBLE IN THAILAND

I was still on *Total Recall* in Mexico when I got the call about *Air America* and was asked if I could get to LA to meet the director Roger Spottiswoode. I flew up for a weekend and we talked about the movie and he said, 'I thought looking at your credits you were a much older guy. At least you could have sprayed your hair grey!' Then, as I was about to leave he said, 'Excuse me Vic, I want to ask you about one of your crewmembers.' 'Oh fuck,' I thought. He said, 'We've got an actor that's been recommended for this film, but I've heard some strange things about him, what do you know?' And he mentioned this guy's name; he was playing one of the smaller roles on *Total Recall* and he was an absolute pain in the arse, useless, a complete jerk-off. I went, 'Uh-uh.' And he went, 'Hmmm.' And that was it, I left. Suffice to say, that guy did not get cast.

There were more problems to follow on *Air America*. The movie starred Mel Gibson and Robert Downey Jr, and was about pilots recruited into a covert and corrupt CIA airlift organisation operating in Laos during the Vietnam war. I'd never worked with Mel before but I'd met him, and got on really well. In all my dealings with him he's never been anything other than a really nice bloke. When Mel was in England filming *Hamlet*, he came to the house and we taught him to ride; well, Wendy did most of the teaching. It was quite funny because he was hurting his balls when he was riding, so Wendy had to go out and buy him a jockstrap. She told the woman in the sports shop, 'You're never going to believe it, but I'm buying this for Mel Gibson.' The woman immediately said, 'Oooh, can we have it when he's finished with it?' Even a few years later in LA when he asked me to do *Braveheart*, Mel was still joking abut it, the cheeky bastard: 'Your jockstraps weren't big enough for me Vic, I had to send your wife out to buy me new ones.'

At the time of *Air America* his wife was expecting, and Mel had her flown over to have the baby in Thailand. She stayed in Chiang Mai while the rest of us were filming up country in Mae Hong Son, so Mel had a Huey helicopter to fly him back to see her. And it was always an open invitation: 'Vic,' he'd say, 'if you or any of the boys want to come back, you're welcome to jump in.'

Before I got out to Thailand I had calls about Mel's regular stunt double, Mic Rodgers, who wanted to work alongside me as co-ordinator. I told them no way. During my career whenever I was on a show I'd always give somebody a unit to co-ordinate, so later in life they can go onto a job and say, I was one of the co-ordinators on *Total Recall* or *Henry V* or whatever. But this guy, I just didn't like the way he was saying that he wanted to be co-ordinator. That was my job, and I was directing the second unit. 'He's more than welcome to work on the movie,' I said, 'but no co-ordinating credit, end of story.'

I got out to Thailand with my crew and started organising everything. Then I got a call that Mic Rodgers was coming out. Great, OK. He arrived on a Saturday and we met in the hotel that night. 'Hi Mic, how are you doing?' 'Yeah, fine,' he said bluntly. He's not the most personable person. 'Welcome aboard,' I continued. 'Come and meet the gang, we're all going out to eat.' He said, 'I'm going to meet Mel tonight. I've got a few things to discuss.' I said, 'OK. Big deal. As if I give a damn. I'll be out of here tomorrow if that's what they want.' So Mic went off to meet Mel and come Monday I said, 'Where's Mic? Is he coming out today?' They said, 'No, he's on the plane. He left last night.' Mel had obviously told him, no, Vic doesn't want it and that's the way it is. I'd said he was welcome to stay on and double Mel, but he'd left. Anyway, Mic went on to good things; he stayed with Mel and started directing second units.

Robert Downey Jr was terrific. He had a minder with him and a trainer, and trained every day. He was off the drugs and straight, and was such a sweet lad. He and I actually nearly died together on that picture. We were in Chiang Mai and I'd shot a sequence in which Downey's character is drunk and they tie him to a rope under a helicopter and Mel swings him over the rooftops, past monasteries and stuff. Dickey Beer was doubling for Downey. To get the close-up shots we needed of Downey hanging on this rope, we got a Huey helicopter and built a scaffolding cage out the side, with a little seat in it for Downey. The camera was in the Huey looking out, not seeing the scaffolding that's all around Downey; just looking at him holding this rope.

I was sitting in the front watching a monitor, and Dave Paris was our pilot. He was trying to do a flat spin but this helicopter kept juddering, it just wouldn't come round. 'That's really strange,' he said. 'Let's try it the other way.' It did it again.

Simon Crane, Mel Gibson, me and Robert Downey Jr. Air America was a fun show to work on.

'OK, let's try it back the other way.' Occasionally I'd take my eyes off the monitor and look out of the windshield to see how things were. I looked up this time and all I could see were rooftops coming straight at us. We were in a vertical dive and pulled away with inches to spare... Everybody at the airfield was watching as we disappeared below the rooftops of the houses, just waiting for the plume of smoke to come up. Inside I held my breath as the helicopter tipped downwards, skimmed over the tops of the houses, and came back up.

I've been in situations like this before with a pilot when there's almost been a fatal accident, you just let them calm down in their own time. Dave parked the helicopter, shut the engine down and walked off down the tarmac, getting his head into gear. My camera team piled out as white as ghosts. Robert Downey just said, 'What's going on Vic?' He was completely oblivious to it all, bless him. 'It's fine Bob,' I said. 'Just a little malfunction.' Dave Paris returned, having cooled down. 'What the hell was that?' I asked. 'We had what is called a rotor stall, Vic.' 'What do you mean a rotor stall?' I said. You imagine that if the rotor stalls then it stops stone dead. In this case it was still spinning but not getting any air lifting over the blade; the only way to get more air flow over it was to dive the chopper and get more speed, but we weren't very high up, only 80 feet. Luckily Dave knew instantly what the problem was, slung the nose down, dropped and got just enough speed to pull us out in time. 'Jesus,' I said. 'I thought we were going to hit those telegraph wires across the houses.' But Dave was actually aiming for the wires, because being a military helicopter the Huey had a cheese cutter on the front that could cut through them. 'I was just worried about hitting the roofs,' he said. So was I! But this is why we have professionals flying for us: Dave knew instantly what to do to get us out of trouble.

Interestingly, when I was still in Mexico City on *Total Recall*, just after signing up to do *Air America*, I was telling everybody that I had this terrible feeling that I was going to die in a helicopter. During that time there had been a number of recent helicopter crashes on films. Four people died on a Chuck Norris film in the Philippines. Marc Wolfe, who was our aerial co-ordinator for the helicopters in Thailand, had an accident in Greece that killed a Canadian stuntman who tried to jump out of the crashing helicopter. There'd been a crash in LA, and of course the infamous accident on *The Twilight Zone* movie when Vic Morrow and two child actors were killed by a helicopter crashing onto them. So there were all these accidents with helicopters happening. As someone once said, I had a bad feeling about this. Out one night with the boys on *Total Recall*, walking to our favourite restaurant in the Zona Rosa, we passed this cafe and one of the waiters cried, 'Hey Vic, Vic Morrow, come here.' I looked and it was one of the stuntmen that I'd used as an actor on *Dune* years before. He was obviously between jobs. But I thought, God, this has to be an omen, he's calling me Vic Morrow! And so when I was in that helicopter in Thailand plummeting to the ground, I really thought I'd had it.

Later in the shoot we changed locations from Chiang Mai to Mae Hong Son, right up in the north, and flew up there in these C-123s, which were like little Hercules transport planes with jet assists on their wing tips. I arrived first, along with Roger Spottiswoode, to start prepping. I also wanted to get one of the good rooms at the hotel. When we went to the airport to pick up the rest of the guys, their plane was on the edge of the runway, tilted on one side; it had crash-landed. These Thai pilots would not use any reverse thrust; they just came in and stood on the brakes, and being a short runway this plane skidded along and burnt through its tyres. One of them blew and the plane skidded to the side of the runway. Because the C-123 is a cargo plane there are no windows, so the guys inside just heard this huge bang as they landed and the screeching of the tyres as the brakes locked up. Suddenly the whole plane filled up with blue smoke, it got sucked in through the wheel arches, and they thought they were on fire. We had two parachute experts amongst the crew and one of them was putting his parachute on and preparing to jump out, with the plane at ground level! Anyway it finally came to a halt, the door opened and they all piled out.

Amidst all the accidents we managed to have some fun on *Air America*, it was one of the craziest shows I've been on. On Saturday nights we'd all dress up as the Blues Brothers, and one particular weekend we wanted to throw a big stunt party. We rented this little tourist bungalow that had a swimming pool, which was the only pool within about 300 miles, and the special effects guys said they'd do fireworks for us. It was a great night, except that the firework display consisted of just dynamite, that's the only 'fireworks' the effects crew had, so these *huge* explosions were going off. We were right on the Burmese border and the whole population of Mae Hong Son must have thought they were being invaded by Burmese terrorists. We actually cracked the swimming pool too because of the concussion of the explosions; it cost a fortune to get it mended.

We always used to eat in this one restaurant in Mae Hong Son. And I was pissed off because we were their best customers – ours was always the fun table, many a night Mel Gibson turned up on his motorbike just to hang out with us – but the waiters always stuck us at the back and gave other punters the prime tables. I said to the head waiter one day, through my interpreter, 'Why do all these other punters get the best tables with the balcony on the roadside to see all the pretty girls walking by, and we're stuck in the back?' The guy pointed up, and all the other tables had ceiling fans. Our table didn't. Then I realised: without fail every night somebody from our group would end up dancing on the table. That's why they gave us a table without a ceiling fan – the restaurant was worried about us getting decapitated! They were thinking of our welfare, bless 'em.

During filming I got the chance to see parts of Thailand you'd never usually see; we'd just get in a Huey and fly around. I remember giving one of my stuntmen, Graeme Crowther, a unit to co-ordinate, sending him down to this little one-horse town called Mae Sariang. After a couple of days he started whinging and whining: 'It's lonely down here Vic.' I did feel a little bit sorry for him so I said, 'Let's take a care package down for him.' We went out and bought a Blues Brothers' hat, a pair of dark glasses, a bottle of vodka, a bottle of freshly squeezed orange juice, some condoms, *Playboy* magazine and porno tapes, and stuffed it all in a box and tied one of the drogue parachutes to it. We got a bloody great C-123 and flew all the way down to this god-forsaken little place and came in at about 100 feet across their airfield. They were shooting at the time. We could hear them on the radio saying, 'Go away, we're shooting!' 'To hell with it,' I said. 'We're coming in.'

I had the Blues Brothers' music playing on their waveband; it was like *Apocalypse Now* except instead of Wagner it was Jake and Elwood blasting out from every radio on the set. We strapped ourselves in and opened up the back of the plane

Yes, it does take this many people to make a movie.

and threw this package out, then hit the afterburners and just took off and flew back without saying anything. And this package floated down on its parachute and landed in the middle of the airfield. They drove over there, wondering what the hell it was, picked it up and saw that it had Graeme Crowther's name written all over it. They opened it up and all this stuff fell out... I hope they saw the funny side of it all. You can go stir crazy sometimes, but *Air America* was one of those films you could do that kind of stuff on, it was just great.

I guess it's that kind of sense of humour that sets stuntmen apart from the rest of the human race. We've always had a reputation for it. We do have these wild moments. And if you don't, then you haven't really got the right temperament to be a stuntman. Although it's all calculated and worked out, you still have to have that edge to you to do the job that we do. Otherwise it would be so boring, it would be like going to a regular job, and that's not what we want to do. We are different from normal people. You could be hanging around a set for days, but then you've got to be ready at a moment's notice to be at 100%, full bore capacity to do what you're paid to do. It's a different kind of job and a lot of people can't take it. And there's the living in hotels and being away from your family; you have a lot of sacrifices and if you can't have those wild moments, then it's not worth doing.

FUTURE WARS

Over the years I've worked with some of the best directors in the business, and I rank Jim Cameron right up there amongst them. He asked me to co-ordinate and handle second unit on *Terminator 2*, but I was busy and couldn't do it. I'd just begun prepping an action movie called *Universal Soldier* when I got another call from Cameron, who'd just wrapped on *Terminator 2* but needed me to shoot this big opening future war battle sequence. Bloody typical, a film that was massively expensive only had four nights left to get this sequence in the can. Christ, I thought.

We filmed at an old steel works they were knocking down, just outside of LA in Fontana, where they'd shot the original *Terminator*. I drove down there and had meetings with Jim in his little motor home filled with videos and he was showing me bits and pieces he wanted to recreate. 'I watched the first *Terminator* last night,' he said suddenly. 'And you know, if I had to make that film now, I just couldn't do it.'

Jim also wanted some background plates shot for later use in f/x scenes featuring the future war, as he was going to put in these huge Hunter Killer robots above the actors. Trouble was, for the opening sequence we had the actors all going right to left on screen, but for the other scenes they had to be going left to right. My idea was to shoot the opening sequence and the background plates simultaneously because we only had four nights, not much time to get it done. 'But they'll all be going the wrong way Vic,' Jim argued. 'Yeah,' I replied. 'But all you do is flop the plates and have them go the other way.' Jim said, 'Good idea, let's do that.' So I started work and did a hell of a lot of shooting. I had guys with Steadicam cameras strapped to them running through the action, and as they looked like futuristic weapons, nobody even realised they were in the shot because I put them in the background.

That first night we finished at five in the morning and sent off the dailies. I guess Cameron is like Spielberg: he watches every inch of them. He was editing the film at the time; that's the only reason he didn't shoot these scenes himself, he just didn't have the time. I was preparing for the next night's shoot when I got these frantic calls from my assistants. 'Oh my God, Jim Cameron's going mad. All the dailies are wrong. They're crap, it doesn't work.' 'What are you talking about?' I said. The crew were shitting themselves; they were all terrified of Cameron and siding with him. 'Yeah, Jim's on his way. He's going to take over.' He arrived and got out of his car, steam coming out of his ears.

'All the fucking things are the wrong way round,' he yelled. 'They're all going in the wrong direction.' I tried calming him down. 'Whoa, whoa, don't fucking shout at me like that. The reason they're the wrong way is because we said we were going to shoot both sequences together and you were going to flop the plates.' And he went, 'Oh. We did, didn't we, you're absolutely right. Yeah. Oh shit. It's great then, fantastic. See ya.' And he got in his car and drove off. The whole crew was now going, 'Oh yeah, well of course we knew that.' I said, 'You bunch of arseholes, you were all ready to have me hung, drawn and quartered, you bunch of wimps.' They were all hiding when Cameron got out of his car. Like most directors, as soon as you meet them head on they're great. Jim realised what I was doing was correct and that was it. I don't think he liked being shouted at in front of his crew, but I think that's the way you have to treat directors sometimes. It's like a bad horse, if it attacks you then you attack him back, and one of you is going to back down.

I met Jim years later on *Shadow Conspiracy* when he came out to meet for lunch with his wife Linda Hamilton, who was in the cast. We all went out together and had a great time. We were laughing and joking and I said to him, 'You are an arsehole to work with.' And he said, 'I know I am. I can't help it when I'm shooting.' The problem is he's a total perfectionist and therefore an arsehole when he's working, because of that perfectionism. Socially though he's great fun. But directors are very, very selfish; they've got to be to get what they want. And I still think to this day that Jim Cameron is one of the greatest action directors there's ever been.

After *Terminator 2* I went back to start work on *Universal Soldier*, a project I'd been on for quite a while. Mario Kassar and Andy Vajna, who ran Carolco and are great friends of mine, called me up and said that they wanted me to do this big picture. It was about two soldiers who killed each other in Vietnam that are reanimated and genetically engineered to form part of an elite fighting force; but one of them goes mad. I met the director Andrew Davis in the lounge of Heathrow airport and we talked over the script. Then I went over to the States and started prepping. Then it all went rotten. The script went through rewrite after rewrite, and started to become a political movie rather than an action adventure movie, and suddenly Andrew Davis was out of the window, gone.

At one point I was in with a very strong chance of directing it, but they were going to try one other guy first, Roland Emmerich, and he got the job. Emmerich had done a little sci-fi movie called *Moon 44* with Malcolm McDowell, which he said he'd made for about $2.5 million, but I figured that it cost a lot more than that. Anyway they all watched it and thought, wow, if he can do this for $2.5 million and we give him $25 million to do *Universal Soldier* it's going to look like $100 million! I think the budget ended up around $32 million.

His partner Dean Devlin was around, too. He was a writer then and I got on very well with him. We'd discuss storylines and ideas and they'd appear in the script. Of course Emmerich and Devlin went on to huge things with *StarGate* and *Independence Day*, although they've gone their separate ways since.

I devised a lot of the action on *Universal Soldier*. We knew we had this huge truck that acted as a laboratory for these futuristic warriors, so I came up with an elaborate chase involving the truck, and picked all the locations around the Grand Canyon. I also shot the opening sequence on the dam. I ended up shooting a huge amount of action on that movie. And Jean-Claude Van Damme and Dolph Lundgren were great. I shot and devised all the fights involving them. Admittedly they're not the greatest actors in the world, but Emmerich played it right, played them both as terminator robot-type characters and it suited their ability, let's say.

After the huge success of *Universal Soldier*, Sony wanted me to direct a picture for them. I had various meetings with executives and they kept sending me scripts. One film that I didn't get to direct, when it happened a few years later, was *Universal Soldier: The Return*. Mic Rogers, my old 'mate' from *Air America*, who hadn't done a fraction of what I'd done, got a break and landed that job. In hindsight it was just as well I didn't direct the sequel, because it didn't turn out well and was a flop at the box office, but at the time I was deeply pissed off.

Little did I know that my own directing break was just around the corner.

DIRECTOR'S CHAIR

While I was gearing up for *Universal Soldier*, George Lucas and his producer Rick McCallum had been calling me to go to Spain to do a week's shoot on his *Young Indiana Jones Chronicles* TV series. 'Absolutely,' I said and caught a plane with only one thing in mind, to prove to George that I could direct, and then maybe he might give me my own episode; that's the only reason I did it.

George had bought some footage from the Jane Fonda/Gregory Peck film *The Old Gringo* because only about 12 people saw it; the film did no business at all. The sequence he wanted to use in this particular episode was where Mexican bandit Zapata attacks a fortress, using a train to ram the gates. George had this footage on laser disc, came down to where I was prepping *Universal Soldier* and for three hours a day we'd sit together and re-edit the sequence with big gaps in the action where they were going to splice in young Indy. So, when they started shooting George said, 'Get Vic, he's the man to do it because he's been with me on the editing.'

I got time off *Universal Soldier* and flew to Spain to meet Rick McCallum. We went over the storyboards that night and at five the next morning I got up and started shooting. I shot for seven consecutive days. After the third day all the electricians turned it in, because I was working till about eleven at night. I worked them so hard, with so many set-ups, they left and we got new electricians in. Rick said, 'We'll get Spaniards in, let 'em go.'

Lucas gave me a clean brief to do whatever I wanted. I love *Lawrence of Arabia* so I had some spectacular high wide shots of horses galloping up through canyons, tiny figures on the horizon. I was having a great time shooting. I had Sean Patrick Flanery with me who played young Indy, I did all the explosions in the town, horse falls and fights, it was great; I had freedom to do the lot. Towards the end of the shoot Rick came up to me and said, 'Vic, I was talking to George last night and he asked if you would like to direct an episode. Spielberg was supposed to be doing it but he's not got the time, so would you like to do his episode?' I said, 'You'll have to give me two or three seconds to think about this; of course I bloody would.' George had obviously seen my footage and loved it, and that's how I got to direct an episode of *Young Indiana Jones.* And that was the only reason I went out there, to prove to George Lucas that I could direct, that I wasn't just about action, that I could direct actors and dramatic scenes, and it paid off. I was thrilled to bits that my plan had worked.

My contract for *Young Indiana Jones* was great. Rick McCallum faxed over this letter and I had to tick one of the boxes, either a) I hate you and George Lucas and don't want anything to do with this project or b) Yes I will direct the episode, please send me a script immediately. To me that sums up the humour and the irreverence that these guys have, because all they want to do is shoot movies, the rest is bullshit, and this is how you do your deals, it's the equivalent of a handshake in the old days. George just loves films and has no interest in the trappings of fame. I mean, he still walks around in his old trainers. I remember when he came down to Lantana Studios in Los Angeles when I was on *Universal Soldier*, to do the *Young Indy* editing job. He owned a post-production facility nearby so we arranged to meet there. He turned up two hours late. 'I went the wrong way,' he said. 'I've never been here before.' That really amazed me; he owned the whole damn corporation and had never even been there.

An up-and-coming writer by the name of Frank Darabont had written my episode, entitled 'Austria, March 1917'. It was full of political intrigue and involved Europe's attempt to persuade Austria to join their alliance against Germany. During one of our meetings we were discussing casting and Frank said, 'I don't know what we can afford, but I'll tell you who I'd ideally like.' I said, 'Before you say anything Frank, there's one person I think I can get who will be perfect for Count Czernin, the Foreign Minister for Austria, and that's Christopher Lee.' And Frank said excitedly, 'Oh my God, that's who I was going to say! I visualised Christopher Lee as Czernin when I wrote it. My God, if you do get him, could I have his autograph?' Chris agreed to play the part and he was fantastic. He's the easiest actor to direct in the world, he was so prepared. And he brought me a cigar every day. A true gentleman.

SIR CHRISTOPHER LEE

I remember we shot that episode in the Czech Republic and I played the Foreign Minister of Austria, a very dodgy character. I

heard that it was George Lucas's favourite episode of the whole series, which may have helped me get the *Star Wars* job later on. And Vic directed me, and directed me very well. He is one of the greatest ever stuntmen, a top second unit director, a top stunt co-ordinator, and also a director in his own right. He's had a great career and deserves it.

I saw Frank Darabont a few years ago when he did a rewrite on *Mission: Impossible III*, and of course he's now become a big time director and writer after *The Green Mile* and *The Shawshank Redemption*. We started talking about *Young Indy*, and I mentioned him asking for Christopher Lee's autograph, but he now said he couldn't remember doing that. I bit my tongue and didn't say anything. It's quite funny how people change. I also recall while directing that *Young Indiana Jones* episode Steven Spielberg coming out to see me, and being so excited that Christopher Lee was in it. He told me Christopher Lee was his favourite actor in the world. He just loved him.

When I got the Indy script I flew out to Czechoslovakia. Everything was on a tight schedule; you only had 12 days to shoot it. As executive producer George stayed in LA, Rick McCallum was my producer on the ground and he drove the whole thing along, and was fantastic, totally supportive and one of the greatest guys you could ever meet. As for George, he just left me totally alone, as long as it all came in within the budget and the time. I remember for one scene I wanted young Indy to wear the trademark Indiana Jones hat. I called George to ask permission because in all the episodes I'd watched he never wore it. 'Vic, it's your call, whatever you want. It's your episode.' So I had total freedom. George was just so easy to work with, and I'll be forever grateful to him for his confidence to let me just go off and do my episode. I have to say George loved the way I worked, because I shoot very fast and I shoot a lot. George still says that I hold the record for the whole of the Indiana Jones series of 72 set-ups in one day. He'd brag to everybody, 'My friend Vic, he shot 72 set-ups and you're never going to get anywhere near that.'

It's strange but my approach to directing proper was no different than my approach to directing second unit, neither was directing actors any different to directing action, because all you're doing is telling the same story. Indeed I found it much easier because you're making decisions for yourself, you're not trying to second guess somebody else, so it's actually much tougher doing second unit. The actors had total confidence in me. I talked to them, I rehearsed them, I could visualise all the angles, and I had a great cameraman in David Tattersall and kept the camera moving. There were no storyboards, I simply dreamt up the shots from the written word on a page. I felt totally at ease directing. I just found it a total relief and such freedom.

I made sure though to cast good, solid actors. In one sequence there was no dialogue at all spoken. After this big meeting, the Emperor of Austria must decide whether to switch sides and go with the Allies; it's a big moment for his character. He wanders into his room alone and stares out into the night sky. A hand comes into shot, it's his wife, played by Jennifer Ehle, a fabulous actress, and he looks at her and kisses her hand and you can see just in body movement that he's made up his mind to sign a new pact with the Allies. When George Lucas saw that scene he said it was a fantastic piece of storytelling, you could see the whole emotion in visuals alone. But that's about trusting your actors.

When I finished the episode, which came in on time and on budget, George worked on it for two weeks assembling a rough-cut. I then went up to his Skywalker Ranch to watch it. It was like, whoa, this is it. I've hit the big time. I sat with the editor and watched the episode, noticing that George had left out a few things. Disappointed, I announced that it was my intention to do my own cut. 'That's why I'm here. Just let me do my cut and show it to George.' And that's what I did, changing a few things around. Two days later I was sitting in the theatre with George Lucas ready to watch it, and my heart was thumping like mad. Shit, what have I done – I prayed he would like my cut! When it came to this one bit where I'd radically changed the edit, George looked at me and said, 'Actually that's very good, I like that better, well done.' Thank goodness, I thought, there is a God up there.

GEORGE LUCAS

Over the years I'd gotten to know Vic very well and I thought he had a lot of talent. He was very successful as a stunt co-ordinator on the Indy movies so we used to give him little second unit assignments to do. I also knew that he had proved himself to be an excellent second unit director on other movies, so when we started the *Young Indiana Jones* TV series I let him direct an episode. The great thing about television is that it's a great place to be able to bring up people who are untried. I just had a lot of confidence that he would be a good director. He always worked well with the actors, he's very easy to get along with, and he's very sure of

himself, and those are qualities that you want in a director. So I figured I'd give him a shot. Mostly it was just because we were friends and I thought he deserved it.

I think part of the reason that Vic hasn't gone on to do more directing is that he's such a good second unit director that everybody wants him for that. I think that he's in such demand on the action side of things that people don't automatically think of him as a dialogue guy, but he is, he's very good at it. His *Young Indy* episode contained very little action or stunts, just actors and dramatic situations, and he proved what a capable director he is. Vic is very talented in lots of different ways and took to directing very well. He did a great job with *Young Indy*.

It was thanks to George and my *Young Indy* episode that I landed my first feature film as director, although I'd flirted twice before with movie directing, receiving no credit on both occasions. Jack Wiener, who I did *Escape to Athena* and *Green Ice* with, had produced a movie called *F/X*, which had been a big hit, and was in Toronto shooting the sequel, but was having trouble with the director, Richard Franklin. I was all set to go over there to film a big shoot 'em up for the second unit when at three o'clock in the morning Jack called again. 'Vic, we've got a lot of problems here. I think the director may leave so we may want you to take over the movie.' I went, 'Oh, OK, terrific. Thank you very much.' I went back to sleep, or tried to get back to sleep, and then caught my flight, all the time wondering what kind of a hornet's nest I was going to walk into when I got out there.

If you're a member of the Director's Guild of America you have to meet the director if he's been fired or you're replacing him. I wasn't at all sure what kind of reception I was going to get from him but when we met he said, 'Thank goodness you could come, because I've got to go right now.' He had some kind of personal problems going on, but I think there was also a lot of stuff happening behind the scenes that I didn't know about. 'That's fine,' I said. 'But it's still your movie. I'm just finishing it off for you. Anything you particularly want me to do?' He gave me a few pointers about what he'd dearly like to have happen in the sequences I was going to shoot, then left the next day and I took over. Three weeks later I finished the film and the following night we were having the wrap party, and the director turned up. It was really quite bizarre, it was like, OK we've used you, that's fine, now go away again. To this day I don't know what the politics of it all were and I didn't particularly want to know, it was just a case of shoot it, do the best you can and get out.

Not long after that I got to exercise my directing muscles on another movie. It was called *Double Impact* and starred Jean-Claude Van Damme as twin brothers, separated when young, getting together as adults to avenge their father's murder by gangsters. Back then, I'd never heard of Jean-Claude Van Damme. (This was before I did *Universal Soldier* with him.) I went to have my hair cut and told this girl I was flying out to make a film with Van Damme and she cut a great lump out of my head. 'Oh my God!' she screamed. 'You've heard of him then,' I said. 'Heard of him, he's a sex symbol, he's fantastic.' Van Damme hadn't broken into the big time yet, he'd only really done video movies, but when I met him in LA he came over as a very charismatic guy. We had dinner in the restaurant at the Bel Age Hotel and he was talking about his role. 'In this scene I jump up and kapow!' Suddenly he knocked a waitress over. 'Oh excuse me madam.' He carried on and knocked into someone else. 'Oh excuse me sir.' He was acting out his fight scenes, doing the splits, everything. It was quite hysterical.

I'd been hired to direct the second unit, be stunt co-ordinator and also play Van Damme's father in the movie. I arrived in Hong Kong to start prepping and called my brother Andy to come out and be my 1st AD. I have to admit that I had reservations about the director Sheldon Lettich right from the start – nice guy, but not massively experienced as a director. As filming continued, it's fair to say that I began to have more and more input, though Lettich remained the credited director of the film.

Because of this increased input, I couldn't play the part of the father as well. 'Look, my brother's coming out, let him play the part; he looks like me only a bit smaller.' Perfect, they said. When Andy arrived I told him, 'Things have changed Andy, you're now Jean-Claude's father,' which was a bit of a surprise for him, but he played the role, very well actually. He gets massacred at the beginning, that's when the two kids get split up. It's a really gruesome shoot 'em up and it was quite funny directing my own brother getting blown to pieces.

My happiest memory of the movie is that at the end of the shoot, Richard Kline, the wonderful DP, introduced me to Phil Gersh, the legendary agent who had handled Hollywood's elite actors for decades. Phil kindly agreed to represent me, and I was a first for him, because he used to represent people like Humphrey Bogart, and here I was asking him to represent a stuntman. He did a wonderful job for me, and pushed my career along. Eventually, when Phil retired, he handed me on to his son David, who is now my great friend and agent still.

Ironically, despite its somewhat troubled production, *Double Impact* became a

My brother Andy getting a fiery kick from Dolph Lundgren on my first movie as a director, Joshua Tree.

huge success. It's a big action film and if you look at Jean-Claude's performance I think it's the best he's ever given. Producer Moshe Diamant had promised me a movie of my own to direct, and true to his word, tried to arrange for me to make a picture with Dolph Lundgren, but Dolph's agent wanted to know what I'd done before. 'Well, George Lucas recommends me,' I said, having just done the *Young Indy* episode. 'Get George Lucas to give us a call then,' they said. I phoned Lucas's office and Rick McCallum was there. 'Look Vic,' he said, 'George doesn't phone anyone, let alone agents, but he'll take the call if they call him.' Which was incredibly gracious of him. I told Dolph's agent to check me out with George Lucas if they wanted. So it was on the strength of *Young Indy* that I got *Joshua Tree.*

I was really excited about getting my first real directing job on a movie, even if it was a 'crash and burn' film. I put some original chases and action in it though, and overall it was a good experience. Dolph Lundgren, bless him, he's a great guy but not the most accomplished actor in the world. In the film he plays a trucker who escapes from prison and takes a female cop hostage as he seeks revenge on those who framed him for murder. I did have some great supporting actors too, including George Segal, who was lovely, and Geoffrey Lewis.

Although I don't think the story holds up, *Joshua Tree* is a good, solid action film and did reasonably well. But the producers really screwed me on post-production and I didn't have the time to finish the film off the way I wanted. They just thought, right, we've got a great movie, it's going to go straight to video anyway,

With Dolph and the beautiful Kristian Alfonso on Joshua Tree.

so we'll do it as cheap as we can, everything that we spend is coming out of our profits. So I was a bit angry about that, but you live and learn. You really don't have any control over your movie; you finish your edit and then they cut it their way after you've gone. Very, very few directors have final cut. Maybe I regret now not fighting for the movie more, but I had another project coming up, and I just got so beaten down by the arguments. Incredibly, *Joshua Tree* (which has also been released as *Army of One*) has become quite a cult movie over the years, and I still get letters every week from the fan club.

After *Joshua Tree* I was offered a lot of scripts, but nothing came of any of them. I was offered the Tarzan film *Greystoke 2*, signed a contract and everything, turning down second unit on *The Fugitive* as a result, pissing off Harrison Ford a bit. But pre-production dragged on and on and in the end it never got made, turning instead many years later into a straight to video piece of junk with Casper Van Dien. After that, I've been reluctant to sit around twiddling my thumbs waiting for directing jobs and in the process missing out on big second unit movie work.

Sometimes producers hire me as insurance should the director not work out on a film. One example was *Johnny Mnemonic*. The director was Robert Longo, an artist from New York. The film was based on a novel by cult sci-fi writer William Gibson, who I met. I read the script and thought, oh my God I'd love to direct this. This is fantastic. But instead I was hired just to be there in case Longo wasn't cutting it, and then I'd have to take over as director. I shot a huge amount of the film as second unit director and came up with sequences as usual. Robert was a lovely fella, but again inexperienced as a director, though he got through it and it all worked out. But I didn't get to direct it, which I was bitterly disappointed about because it was a hell of a good script, though the film itself didn't turn out as well as it should have.

Johnny Mnemonic was played by Keanu Reeves, who may be a big star, but can be a bit of a one-note actor in my opinion. While *Johnny Mnemonic* was in production *Speed* had just been released, which was another film I was on the list to direct. David Gersh, my friend and agent, called me and said, 'Vic, I'm in a terrible position. Jan de Bont is a personal friend of mine, as you are, and the studio want me to recommend one or other of you.' Jan de Bont had more technical credits as a cameraman, so they went with him and the rest is history. *Speed* was a fantastic script. One of the reasons the film works so well is because at the editing stage, I reckon they did what they did with the shark in *Jaws*: they cut around Keanu Reeves. If you'd seen more of the shark in *Jaws* it would have been a disaster, and they did that with Keanu in *Speed*. That's what they should have done in *Johnny Mnemonic*.

Maybe I didn't get the director's chair again because *Joshua Tree* was dismissed as a crash and burn film, and didn't get any kind of critical attention. But I'd dearly love to finish my career just directing. It's much more satisfying, much more enjoyable and much less stressful than second unit. When you're the director you turn up on the set and you say, do this and do that, and everybody does it, it's quite funny. People are looking for a leader on set, they want somebody to say, you go there, and you do this; all they want is to be told what to do. A director's life is 80% of the time just answering questions. That's mostly all you do, and once a crew realise you have confidence in yourself and you know what you're doing, they'll follow you anywhere.

But still, you're always learning. 40 years in the business and I'm still learning by the minute. It's amazing. I learnt a lot from Spielberg on *War of the Worlds*; particularly how very diplomatic a director has to be. He was doing a scene with Tom Cruise and wanted him to change hands. I would have come straight out and said to Tom, 'Don't do it with your left hand, do it with your right hand.' But Steve said, 'That's great Tom, great, but maybe, I wonder what it would be like…' He ummed and aahed a bit and then Tom said, 'Would you like me to do it with the left hand Steven?' 'That's a good idea Tom, yeah, do it with your left hand.' So he'd got him to change hands. If I'd have done it my way Tom might've said, 'No, it only works with the right because I'm facing this way and this is what motivates me.' It's very clever the way 'actor's directors' work with actors.

ARNIE'S LAST STAND

Despite no main unit directing jobs coming my way, I was soon as busy as ever when it came to second unit and co-ordinating work. I got a call from an old mate, Brian Cook: 'What are you doing?' 'Nothing,' I said. 'Oh God, we've got problems here, you've got to come on down.' So I agreed and negotiated a deal and started work on *Last Action Hero*, a massively expensive movie with Arnold Schwarzenegger. It was lovely seeing Arnie again, but this was the first time I'd worked with John McTiernan, who was one of the top directors back then – he'd done *Die Hard* and *The Hunt for Red October*. He was a really sharp cookie, a very intelligent man, and I was very impressed with him. We were shooting nights down in south central LA, doing a whole ton of pick-up shots and just gelling the whole movie together.

I only worked on the picture for a couple of weeks, and after we wrapped Arnie invited me down to cigar night at his restaurant in Santa Monica. Monday was always cigar night. Everyone who was anyone in Hollywood was there, heavy on the schnapps and the cigars, including Danny DeVito. A year before DeVito had asked me to do his film *Hoffa*, but I ended up not doing it and handing it over to my brother. So Danny was sitting there, a big cigar in his mouth. 'You know Arnie, this Vic Armstrong, he never does movies, all he does is he gets them and then hands them off to his lookalikes.'

The first time I met Danny was about *Hoffa*. I went to his offices at Warner Bros. and couldn't believe how small he was in person. We sat down and he started talking about the film, but kept changing the subject. 'Look at this, this is dangerous.' On the floor was a small electric ride-in Batmobile car. He'd played the Penguin in one of the Batman films of course. 'This could cause an accident.' 'Why's that?' I asked. 'Well look, there's no floor in it. You sit in there, the kids press this and if they put their feet down, they can get dragged underneath.' I said,

'Oh, it's the kids' is it? I thought it was yours.' He stopped in his tracks and looked at me aghast… and then broke out laughing. We got on like a house on fire after that. He's a great guy, with a marvellous sense of humour.

At this cigar night Arnie was sat next to me and said, 'What are you doing next week?' 'Nothing,' I said. 'I'm going home in a few days.' 'Good,' said Arnie. 'We've got these new restaurants, Planet Hollywood, and we're opening one in London. Get Wendy and come to the opening night.' 'Thanks, that'll be great.' 'Call my assistant in the morning.' I said, 'Absolutely.' I woke up at 8.30, splitting headache. I shut my eyes and woke up again at 9.30. My head was still dying. Oh fuck, I'll get my head cleared first, then call the office. Ten o'clock the phone rang. 'Hey, you forehead,' went this voice. 'Oh, hi Arnie.' 'I have to do your secretarial work for you. You haven't called my assistant.' He was so sharp; he'd drunk as much as I had, yet was compos mentis and giving me a rollicking for not calling his secretary.

So he gave me all the details and the following Saturday Wendy and myself went up to London for the opening of Planet Hollywood, and it was fantastic. The crowds outside were amazing, you couldn't get near the place; people were up lampposts so they could get a look. All the stars were there, Stallone, Bruce Willis, who did a short gig playing harmonica, and Van Damme. Arnie sat us at his private table, and it was a truly memorable evening, especially the moment when I was walking to the bar and Arnie grabbed me, 'Hey, Vic I've got a friend of yours here…' – and before I knew it he'd gone and I was face to face with Michael Winner! He'd gone up to Arnie, and Arnie didn't want to chew the fat with him, so he literally turned him in his tracks and plonked him in front of me. 'Here you are Vic, here's a countryman of yours, have a chat,' and whoosh, he'd gone.

Last Action Hero was my last movie with Arnie, although we've remained friends ever since. I have such respect for him as a person and for what he's achieved in the movie business. If he puts his mind to anything, he accomplishes it. He's since gone into politics of course, so I'm sure that if they ever changed the law and he wanted to run for President, he'd get elected. Brilliant guy Arnie, I love him dearly.

ARNOLD SCHWARZENEGGER

Vic is truly one of the most extraordinary stunt co-ordinators in the business, and that's why I loved working with him on several movies. No one does better action sequences than Vic. Some stunt co-ordinators are good with explosion scenes, some are good with car chases or gun battles. But Vic is a master of them all. He is hungry and determined, and it shows in his work.

After *Last Action Hero* I was asked by Mike Nichols to do *Wolf*, and shot a lot of test footage of wolf transformations, got on really well with him. Then a pal of mine, Steve Kesten, was doing an action picture called *Rainbow Warrior* with Steven Seagal. As a favour I agreed to do it, pissing off Sony because now I couldn't do *Wolf*. They were going to shoot all over Alaska, and I flew up there on a private jet with Seagal looking for locations. Suddenly the film was put in turnaround and I was paid off. They eventually made it under the title *On Deadly Ground*, a terrible movie.

Back home a producer called Robert Shapiro talked me into working on a new version of *Black Beauty* starring Sean Bean. During production I got into a big argument with the production designer, the legendary John Box, who'd done *Lawrence of Arabia*, *Oliver!*, you name it. Don't get me wrong, I had the utmost respect for him, but he was a bit aloof. One day we were discussing the birthing sequence of Black Beauty which was to be the opening of the movie, and Box, having found a great location, said, 'We will shoot this in Sussex.' I said, 'What about the foal?' He said, 'We'll take the foal down there.' I said, 'How are you going to do that? Once it's born it can't travel for two weeks, and by then it's not a foal any more.' Box was having none of it. 'I want to see it take its first steps in beautiful countryside.' I said, 'That's getting arty farty.' 'What do you mean?' he blasted angrily. I said, 'You have to be practical.'

The producers had also brought this horse trainer over from the States, and I asked him how he proposed to do the birth sequence. 'We'll get a foal and fold it up and have it coming out of a prosthetic rear end of a mare.' I said, 'What are you talking about? You can't fold up a foal once it's been born, and who's going to give you their baby horse to play around with? That's bullshit, you're talking out of the back of your head.' Box and this trainer looked at each other. 'How would you do it then?' I said, 'We get black mares that are about to foal, put them in my stables at home and just watch them, and wait for signs that they are going to give birth.'

So we found a trio of black pregnant mares, who were due to give birth within three weeks, decorated three of my stables to look identical and placed a video camera in each. I then hired two guys from the BBC who did wildlife documentaries, people who had the patience to film a caterpillar turning into a butterfly, to just sit and watch. These fellas lived in a trailer in my truck park for three weeks, watching the surveillance video cameras 24/7 for any sign of the birth starting. We also had a film camera set up to go in the saddle room. I was enjoying a rum and coke one Sunday night when one of the BBC boys ran in. 'It's on. It's on.' I jumped out of my chair and rushed into the stable, but the foal was already

Trying to act in Black Beauty. *I don't think that hat helps. Where is Harrison when I need him?*

half out, we'd missed it. A week later the same thing happened. 'It's on Vic,' but this time she was just going into labour. By now the director had arrived, and was banging on the stable door. 'Shhh,' I whispered. 'Don't come in.' It was right at the moment of birth. It pissed her off a bit until she saw the footage.

Suddenly we had a problem. In the story little Black Beauty has a white mark on its forehead, but when I pulled the afterbirth away I saw this foal was totally black. We stopped the cameras as I grabbed the make up we had standing by for just this scenario, and put a white smudge on his forehead, then carried on filming. The magic of movies. And it's a beautiful scene. This little foal is just like Bambi trying to stand up, its legs are going all over the place; there's no way you can fake that. What you're seeing is Disney for real. That foal thought I was its mum for days afterwards, it would snuggle up to me because I was the first thing it saw. After John Box and the production saw what a success the scene was, I got on with them very well. Once Box saw what I did and respected me, he was an absolute gentleman, but it's funny how you have to fight for your ground in this business.

Black Beauty turned out to be a lovely film. My kids, Scott, Nina and Georgina, who played Merrylegs' young owner, were all in it and they just adored it. I had a small role too, as a nasty horse master who whips poor old Black Beauty. It was fun, but it was also a hard shoot; animal movies are always horrendously difficult to make.

A TOUCH OF THE ERROL FLYNNS

A round this time I was preparing to start Paul Verhoeven's medieval epic *Crusade*, when it was suddenly cancelled. The next day I got a call to work on *Rob Roy* with Liam Neeson. The director was Michael Caton-Jones, who later told me how he got the job: 'MGM asked me to do the next Bond, but I didn't want to do a Bond so they said, "What would you like to do then?" I said, "*Rob Roy*. I know Liam Neeson's *desperate* to do it." They said, "Really, Liam Neeson? Yeah, we could make that fly, let's do that!" So I drove straight home, tracked down Liam, who's a mate of mine, and said, "Liam, before you say anything you can't turn me down because I've told them you're doing this. You've got to do *Rob Roy* for me, it's a great part, and it's perfect for you." And Liam went, "Oh, all right then."' And that's how the movie came about. Amazing.

Caton-Jones' idea for *Rob Roy* was to basically make a Scottish western, which is exactly what it was. And coincidently enough, it was written by Alan Sharp, who had written that western I did in Israel, *Billy Two Hats*. I think it's a great movie. It didn't make a huge amount of money box office-wise, but like *Henry V* it was highly critically acclaimed and it's one that you're proud to have on your resume. I had a good second unit on that film and we shot some terrific footage. Everyone remembers the climactic sword fight, for instance. It also had an excellent cast. Liam was fabulous. He's a great mate of mine and a really genuine person, one of the few people in the business who hasn't changed since the first day I met him (back on *Krull*); he's exactly the same sweet, generous, kind-hearted man, and a great actor. I bump into him all over the world in airports or on film sets and we sit and have a drink and a chat, and on *Gangs of New York* we used to go out most nights. Just a lovely man.

Tim Roth was the funniest. He was playing the film's baddie, and I have to be honest I didn't know him from a hole in the ground, although Caton-Jones raved about him. I taught a lot of the actors to ride before location shooting in Scotland, and Tim turned up one day at our stables in a leather jacket, leather trousers and biker boots, smoking a cigarette. Oh my God, I thought, I've got to teach this guy to ride. Maybe if I put handlebars on the horse it might work. I brought out Triana, who'd taught so many other actors to ride, put him on and started showing him what to do. Obviously like anybody he took a little while to get really used to riding, but he had so much fun that before we knew it he was down at the stables all day, every day. He was just hooked, and picked up all the basics in about three days.

He was a natural horseman, so we had him doing everything within a matter of weeks. He loved it, but the first time we were riding around in Scotland Tim pulled up this horse a bit too sharp and it reared up. 'Jesus, what was that?' he said. 'Relax,' I replied. 'It's fine. Just relax your hands and give him his head.' Then he thought about it and said, 'Well, actually that felt quite good!' From then on, every time he galloped onto the set he skidded to a halt and reared the damn horse like The Lone Ranger – it scared the life out of me. But you couldn't tell him off because he was having so much fun. And it was great for his character as well; he looked so flamboyant on his horse.

Jessica Lange was fabulous, too. Her teenaged daughter was working at the stables on location and she had to be there on time otherwise Jessica would tell her off; a really down to earth woman. She'd be laughing and joking with us and the assistant would say, 'We're ready for you Miss Lange,' and she'd go off and do the rape sequence, come back out again and carry on with the story she was telling. A consummate actress. But there was one incident: Roger Deakins was the cameraman but after the first few weeks I was aware that something was not quite right because they kept shooting test footage with Jessica. One day I was driving back to the hotel with Roger and he said, 'I think I'd better go to my room and pack.' I said, 'What do you mean?' He said, 'I've just shot my bolt. We've had this thing with Jessica saying she's got lines on her face and looks older than she should, so I turned to her and said, "Jessica, you're not 25 any more, I can't make you look 25, my dear." There was a stony silence and an icy look in her eyes that told me I'd overstepped the mark.' Sure enough, he was on the plane home the next day and they brought in Karl Walter Lindenlaub. So poor old Roger left over that, but he's since gone on and won two BAFTAs.

For the last month on *Rob Roy* I was spending every weekend flying to Malta, prepping *Cutthroat Island* for the director Renny Harlin. Late on Saturday night after shooting I'd drive to Glasgow airport and jump on a plane, scout locations

Matthew Modine and Geena Davis, the stars of Cutthroat Island.

all day on Sunday then get the last flight out of Malta to Scotland, drive all night and get back about six in the morning and go straight to work again on *Rob Roy*. It was exhausting, but I didn't want to turn down Renny Harlin, who at the time was a really hot director after *Die Hard 2* and *Cliffhanger*. And *Cutthroat Island* was a big, big movie. It starred Geena Davis, Renny's then-wife, who was a wonderful, sweet woman. She wanted to do a lot of the stunts herself, and she's got all the guts in the world. There's one scene where co-star Matthew Modine is hanging on a rope and she has to jump off a clifftop and catch his outstretched hands. Stuntman Claudio Pacifico performed the actual leap, but for the close-ups we had Geena on a fan descender 150 feet up. She had to step out over rocks and hang in space, drop and grab the hand of Matthew Modine's character. She was terrified, but did the shot and acted her heart out, and that is the sign of true courage.

I really got on well with Renny and Geena. At one of their parties one night Geena offered me a flaming blow job! It consisted of blowing out a flaming concoction, and drinking it with your hands held behind your back. She truly had a wicked sense of humour. People forget how big they were back in the mid-'90s. One day Renny showed me this magazine that ranked them as one of the three most powerful couples in Hollywood. When the film came out Renny paid me tribute and was very generous.

RENNY HARLIN

I met Vic Armstrong in the early '90s, as I was looking for the best possible stunt co-ordinator for a very complex film. For *Cutthroat*

Island we needed horse stunts, and choreographed sword fighting sequences, regular fist fights, huge falls, high wire work, and water sequences. Vic was calm and always on top of his departments. He brought horses from Hungary, sword masters from Italy, and ocean experts from Australia. With his bear-like demeanour, and good humour, I felt that Vic was the solid rock that I could always count on. He mapped out everything very carefully, and what's most important, he made it safe for everyone. We had amazing times together on several continents. Besides the shoot, we had some great dinners, and took over some fun bars in the course of our travels. I would do it again with Vic any time.

It's a shame that *Cutthroat Island* just didn't click with audiences, but we did some good action in it. Bruce, my son, was on that one and dislocated his knee; one of the horses spun him round, scared the life out of me. A year later Renny asked me to do *The Long Kiss Goodnight*, but I reluctantly turned it down in favour of *Starship Troopers*. I had earlier read the script, which was great, but I thought there was *too* much action, and I think you can get sick of action if they overload it. Eventually they did trim it down a bit and it was a good movie. While working on *Troopers* I was in my trailer one night parked in Sony Studios when there was a loud knocking on the door. I opened it and it was Renny and Geena. 'We've been meaning to visit and share some vodka with you.' They loved their vodka. They came in and had a shot of vodka each and then went off, and the following weekend I was invited to stay at their new house outside Santa Barbara. They really were a lovely couple; I think they'd forgiven me for not doing their movie.

Besides Malta, a lot of *Cutthroat Island*, like the jungle scenes and the sea-faring stuff, was shot in Thailand. I was working for producer Mario Kassar again. Mario's a wonderful guy, the great thing about him is he gives you $100 million or whatever, you spend your money and he doesn't bug the director or keep showing up on the set; the perfect producer.

While in Malta I heard Oliver Reed had been cast and was coming over. I hadn't seen Oliver since those escapades we got up to in Iraq. He arrived, came on the set and watched us shooting. He'd had a couple of drinks but he was holding it together. The next night, Saturday night, we had this great big party and everybody was having flaming blow jobs from Geena Davis. Ollie inevitably turned up and sat in a corner. When I saw the vodka bottle coming out I went, oh heck, we might have some trouble here. Sure enough a little while later I looked over and he had his shirt off, he was a big barrel-chested man, and was stomping about. Now I knew he was getting drunk, because he got aggressive when he drank. Renny was looking over and said, 'God, I'd better go over and have a chat with Ollie before he gets totally hammered.' 'Good idea,' I said.

So Renny went over and sat down with Ollie and they started talking… and you could see Renny's face drop and a look of abject horror take over. I couldn't decipher what they were saying, but I could see Ollie gesticulating wildly and pretending to have a wank. Suddenly he got up and staggered away, leaving a bewildered Renny to come back over to me. 'Oh my God,' he said. 'I don't know what to do, he's got to go, he's got to go.' I said, 'Why?' Renny said, 'He's playing Geena's uncle in the movie and she goes to him for help, but he's rewritten the whole scene.' Ollie had described the new scene to Renny like this: 'So she comes into the den I'm in. I'm in there with all these old whores, and she comes and sits down. I say, "What do you want, bitch." And I'm jerking off at the time, and she says, "I want your help." And I spunk all over her hair. And I say, "All right you bitch, I'll fucking help you."' Renny was shaking his head. 'This is my wife he's talking about Vic.' By now Ollie had collapsed, got up again, and staggered off into the night. 'I've got to get rid of him,' said Renny. 'We can't have this in the movie, Jesus.'

Sunday morning I woke up and walked down to the hotel breakfast room and there was Ollie, all dressed up and packed and on his way out. 'Fucking arseholes. I'm outta here.' And he was gone. And that was the last time I ever saw Ollie, bless him. But it was so typical of him, and perfect.

BUG HUNT

I was in Thailand working on *Cutthroat Island* and the phone rang at four in the morning: 'George Cosmatos here.' Oh my God, I thought, because after his antics on *Escape to Athena* I swore I'd never do another movie with him. But before I put the receiver down I realised I'd agreed to work with him again. Oh shit, I'd better tell the wife.

Since *Athena* George had had a huge hit directing *Rambo: First Blood Part II* and had just finished *Tombstone*, it was the films in between that weren't so clever. So it was with some reluctance that I flew out to Richmond, Virginia to make *Shadow Conspiracy*. It wasn't the best script and in the end the film just didn't gel. George was just as mad yet wonderful as ever. He used to call everyone a fucking idiot, he was renowned for it, but he was the sweetest, most generous person you could meet – he was always taking me out to dinner and insisting on paying for everything. But once again, when he was shooting he became a monster and we had fights all the time. He'd ask for the most ridiculous things.

For the shoot 'em up climax he wanted this guy diving through a screen, but it was made out of rubber. I said, 'George, he's going to bounce off it. You're going to need to put cuts in it or make a paper one.' He said, 'I don't want a paper screen, I've seen that a million times.' We started shooting and it became comical, the actor couldn't rip through it, he was going boing, boing. It was horrendous and I must have said something, because that night after we wrapped George came over to me with a sullen expression on his face. 'Why you insult me in front of everybody?' he said. 'What do you mean, insult you in front of everybody?' 'You called me a fucking idiot,' he said. 'Well if I did I apologise, but you *were* being a fucking idiot by shooting that.' 'I know,' he said. 'But you shouldn't say it in front of everybody.'

It was a nightmare shooting that movie. George hated everybody. 'He's a fucking spy you know,' he suddenly said one day. 'The production man, he's a fucking spy.' 'Who's he a spy for?' I asked. 'For the studio, they're out to get me.' He was totally paranoid, but a lovely man. *Shadow Conspiracy* turned out to be his last film, and he died in 2005. There's a special place in my heart for George.

I was still on the east coast of America when I got a call from Micky Moore, one of the greatest action unit directors of all time. He'd been offered a movie called *The Phantom* but had recently suffered a heart murmur so wanted me to do it for him. It was a comic book-style movie about an action hero played by Billy Zane, who was great, a nice guy. I went out to Thailand again to shoot it, and bizarrely I had the same room in the same hotel that I had on *Cutthroat Island.* We were down right where the tsunami ended up hitting years later, a lovely area, very non-touristy in those days, and we had a hell of a time. In one scene Billy had to do a transfer from a horse onto a bi-plane, and in another sequence a truck goes across a rope bridge, which snaps and twists over and a kid ends up hanging out. We pulled off some great action on that movie.

One of the producers was Alan Ladd Jr, the son of the famous film star. He's been very supportive of me over the years, and actually offered me a movie to direct after *The Phantom.* Called *With Wings As Eagles*, it was set during the Second World War and had a huge budget. Arnold Schwarzenegger was set to star as an SS officer who gets sickened by the conflict when his whole family is killed in a bombing raid, and he ends up helping all these American prisoners of war to escape across the Alps. It was a really good script by Randall Wallace, who'd written *Braveheart.* We never made it in the end, which was a shame.

While I was still in Thailand shooting *The Phantom*, Paul Verhoeven got in touch and wanted me to do this futuristic picture called *Starship Troopers.* I was really keen to work with Paul again because our collaboration on *Total Recall* had been fantastic and I think he's a brilliant director. It was a huge project and I believe it's one of the best visual effects films ever made. Based on a 1959 novel by cult sci-fi writer Robert A. Heinlein, it tells of a future war between Earth and millions of rampaging giant arachnids. Cue lots of scenes of swarming bugs slicing open soldiers with their pincer mouths and impaling them on their razor-sharp legs. Some scenes were straight out of *Zulu*, like when all the bugs come over the horizon to attack an isolated fort, smash over the wall and slash people to bits. Amusingly the first guy that gets his head slashed off is my nephew, Jessie Johnson.

Knowing that we were going to have lots of scenes of monsters chopping people up, I'd got a guy called Casey Pieretti on my crew, an amputee with only one leg. When he was younger he was pushing a car that had broken down and some drunk ran into the back of him, crushing his leg. He got a prosthetic leg, but was still very physical: he learnt to rollerblade one-legged, and had now decided to be a stuntman, so I told him, 'Absolutely, go for it Casey, you are just what we need.' In one sequence a soldier gets bitten by a bug, is thrown up in the air and his leg comes off, so Casey designed his own specialised prosthetic leg that could be released from a pin – the effect was really bloodthirsty.

In a shot like that, we obviously didn't have the whole monster, that was put in later by visual effects, so the sections picking up soldiers, and shaking them like a terrier with a rat, were mechanical props. That was one of the most difficult jobs on the film, matching the live action stuff with the effects. Paul and myself really worked hard to make sure the bugs fitted into the landscape, fitted with the people, that the action matched the bugs. There were all these live elements in every single shot, there was never just a visual effects shot, everything had interaction. For example when a bug hit the ground you'd see footprints and dust coming up. All of this had to be sorted out in advance. You'd literally have to measure the size of the bug, 30 feet high and 15 foot across, while you were setting the shot up, and then everybody had to work around that frame so they didn't pass through the invisible bug that the effects guys were going to put in later. It was a really intricate shoot.

Our first location was Casper, Wyoming, a place called Hell's Half Acre, and while I was there one day it hailed and snowed and the whole place froze up, so I've boasted ever since that I've actually seen hell freeze over. It was the most amazing location, up in the high desert. After Wyoming I moved to South Dakota. We drove there, right through Deadwood Gulch, where the Deadwood stage came through, fantastic place, real old bandit country. While I was shooting in South Dakota, Paul was shooting in Wyoming, then when we finished our respective shoots we all changed places again and I went up and finished what he was doing in Wyoming, while he finished off what I'd started in Dakota. To do that you really had to appreciate each other's way of working, and I had to understand what Paul was trying to achieve in the movie. Later on he presented me with the film's release poster and wrote on it – 'You weren't my second unit director, you were my co-director.' He is an amazingly big-hearted and generous guy.

It was a big, big shoot; logistically it was incredible. We shot the longest film explosion ever, three quarters of a mile, for the scene when the jet fighters come in and bomb the bugs and the flames burst towards you. The special effects supervisor was John Richardson, who I'd known for years, we did *A Bridge Too Far* together, amongst many other movies. We did that explosion in a valley in South Dakota and spent about a week putting in tons of dynamite and thousands of gallons of petrol. I had five cameras out there, side angles and forward facing; I

On the set of Starship Troopers *in Wyoming, with Michael Ironside.*

was standing behind my main camera on a hill in front of the advancing explosion and I'll never forget seeing that thing set off, bang, bang, bang, getting bigger and bigger all the time heading towards us... I thought, shit, are we far enough back here, because this is some fireball coming! You could feel the oxygen getting sucked out of the air around you. And sure enough it finished where they said it would, but my God there was a wall of heat that came at us.

I guess they could've done that shot with CGI, but I still don't think they've cracked fire in visual effects realistically. It always looks like it's stuck on to me. I think that attention to detail, and that attention to actual physical work, is what makes *Starship Troopers* so good.

We all worked really, really hard on that movie. The responsibility on me was huge, because it was such a hectic schedule that the stuff I was shooting in Dakota they'd never have a chance to do again, so they trusted me to go out there and shoot the storyboards. I had about six volumes of storyboards, six inches thick, that had every single scene in them. On that movie you couldn't just go and shoot from the hip, it had to be specific: the effects guys had to know what we were shooting, because they were planning and preparing stuff knowing I was shooting footage that would match into it, and fit the budget. Phil Tippett was the main SFX guy, a real genius who'd made his name on *RoboCop* and other films. I went up to San Francisco and spent a few days at his effects studio looking at the bugs and discussing what techniques we would use to shoot them. It was only a work

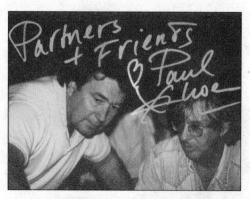

With Paul Verhoeven; a real character and a great friend.

in progress then, still developing, because they were buying computers to do things that had never been done before.

Although everything was planned in advance, the film still had a feel of spontaneity to it and Casper Van Dien, who played the lead, believed in it totally. He was terrific. We came back and finished the movie at Sony Studios, which is my favourite studio in LA (it's very much like Pinewood); it used to be the old MGM studio in Culver City. One scene we shot there was when this escape pod crashes into a cavern. We were using all this silica dust on the set and I couldn't wear a mask because I was shouting instructions all the time, and because of that I've got a scar on my lung today. Right at the end of shooting I got really ill, I had a temperature of 105. It was this shit on my chest. Years later on *War of the Worlds* I became ill again and the doctor who x-rayed me said, 'You've got a nasty scar on your lung. It's nothing serious at the moment but I'd like you to check it out when you come back next time.' The things you do for the movie business.

Starship Troopers wasn't as big a hit as I thought it was going to be. It was probably Paul's dash of excess blood and gore that blocked out a certain audience. But it's a classic today, people love it. It's a film I'm very proud to have worked on. I don't think you'd ever work on a more involved visual effects movie than that. It was a phenomenal shoot. The rehearsals, the planning and the plotting, and the set building, the stuff that had to be thought up in advance, it was mind-boggling.

And it was a real labour of love working with Paul Verhoeven. I adore the guy. Yes he's tough and he doesn't take prisoners, but he's honest, he doesn't bullshit you. He tells you the truth. He's a great guy, Paul.

TOMORROW NEVER DIES

One day out of the blue Roger Spottiswoode, who I'd done *Air America* with, called: 'Hey Vic, how are you?' I said, 'I'm great Roger, how are you doing?' He said, 'Well, I have to apologise to you.' 'What do you mean?' He said, 'I've just taken your movie.' I said, 'Really?' 'Yes. I'm doing the next Bond film, *Tomorrow Never Dies*, and they told me that if I didn't do it, then you were the next one on the list. Do you hate me forever Vic?' 'Oh my God... But no, of course not,' I said. 'Then would you consider doing my second unit?' Of course I agreed.

I hadn't been associated with the official Bond series since *Live and Let Die*, although I'd come close a couple of times. I was offered *The Living Daylights* and worked on the screen tests to find Roger Moore's replacement as Bond. Then they called me in to do *GoldenEye*. I met the director Martin Campbell and was asked who I'd have as my stunt co-ordinator. 'Well, I like to oversee all of that myself,' I said. 'It's what I've grown up doing and I'm good at it. So I like to be the stunt co-ordinator, but I'll also be the action unit director.' That didn't sit too well with Campbell, who instead went with another second unit director, and brought in other people, including Simon Crane, to handle stunts.

To be honest we had a few production problems on *Tomorrow Never Dies*, but I think we made a good movie, I think it's one of the best Bonds in recent years. More bang for your bucks. It was a huge project and Roger Spottiswoode was very demanding, but I really liked him. The first thing I did was the pre-credits sequence. It's always a tough job coming up with an opening sequence on a Bond. We all put our heads together and thought, what shall we do? I know, let's have Bond infiltrating a big arms deal in the Khyber Pass. Originally we had all sorts of ways of getting Bond in there. My idea was to have him jump out of a plane at fairly low altitude and below radar wearing a flying bat suit, which has these wings that connect the arms and legs and can slow your speed down, so he'd be

Shooting the action-packed opening of Tomorrow Never Dies *in Peyresourde in the French Pyrenees.*

basically paragliding. Skis would then extend out of his boots and he'd perform a ski jump landing onto a really steep mountainside, and that's how he got to the arms deal. I worked out how to shoot it with no visual effects. In the end though it was dropped.

When we first came up with the arms deal idea, the producers wanted to know exactly what was going to happen. 'Tell you what,' I said, 'let's give them the biggest shoot 'em up of all time, let's give Bond a jet fighter on the ground that he can use like a big handgun and shoot the crap out of everything.' We found this amazing location in the French Pyrenees, and when we turned up to shoot, we had beautiful bright sunshine. But we wanted the cold oppressive look of an Afghan winter, so we could only shoot first thing in the morning until 9am and then again in the late afternoon after 4pm. So for the whole day the special effects guys would be laying explosives and we'd rehearse the action, and then as soon as the sun was over the horizon it was, OK guys here we go, and we'd shoot the crap out of it, blowing things up. We were there for two weeks and used nine cameras on most of the big set-ups. Plus we had a ski slope across the valley and had to stop all the tourists skiing, who otherwise would have been in the background. There were also avalanche people going out to check surrounding ski slopes in case our explosions caused an avalanche up the mountain. It was a nightmare. But I thought it was a terrific opening scene.

The main thrust of the pre-credits sequence is that Bond has to hijack a jet fighter. But because the runway we were using was so steep and narrow, the high speed jets could not land, so we actually dismantled the jets, took them up there, and then rebuilt them. Another problem was that while these jets were able to taxi around the runway, they couldn't take off either and we needed footage of Bond escaping in one. We solved that by arranging for real jets to approach our runway at something like 160 mph and touch the ground literally for a split second, before roaring off again. I filmed the shots of the planes at very high speed, so that we could slow them down in post-production to look like they were moving at take-off speed. In the editing we just used the moment of the plane taking off. This manoeuvre was very dangerous for the pilots, and it was also bloody dangerous for us standing at the end of the runway with the camera. When you see these things coming at you from half a mile away you suddenly realise how fast 160 mph is, especially when they roar over your head at about ten feet. And if the pilot doesn't lift up in time or doesn't get enough speed, we're all goners. It was worth it, though, because the footage turned out really well.

Originally most of the film was going to be shot in Vietnam, so I had a great scouting trip to Hanoi and Ho Chi Minh City, and found some fantastic locations. There were all sorts of things we were going to do out there. But on the day my crew and myself were at Heathrow airport ready to fly to Ho Chi Minh City to start work, we were told our visas had been withdrawn. I guess in the end the Vietnamese government had decided that they didn't want a decadent western film crew in their country. So what were we going to do now? I didn't want to go back to the studio, because we were all ready to go. 'Tell you what,' I said to the guys, 'let's go to Bangkok. My great friend Santa Pestonji, who I have done nine films with in Thailand, runs a film facility company and he'll sort something out for us.' So I literally made one phone call to Santa, caught a flight to Bangkok and within six hours of getting off the plane I'd found a perfect rooftop to film the scenes of Bond being shot at on his motorbike by an enemy helicopter, while he's supposedly being chased through the streets of Saigon.

In the film Bond escapes from the villain's headquarters with Chinese agent Wai Lin, played by Michelle Yeoh, and makes a fast getaway through the streets on a motorbike. We chose a 1600cc BMW, a big heavy thing, which was totally the wrong bike physically to use for what we wanted to do, like riding across rooftops and jumping over things. But visually it was the perfect bike, because it drives me mad in movies when somebody steals a bike and it just happens to be a motocross bike perfect for all the stunts they're going to do. I knew I had to get somebody good to ride this bike, someone safe, because safety is always the number one concern (it is only a movie after all), but especially since my wife Wendy was doubling for Michelle. Plus, I hate bikes because so many accidents happen with them. I called my brother Andy and he recommended Jean-Pierre Goy, who used to work for Rémy Julienne, a great French car stunt co-ordinator who had worked on many Bonds. Other people were recommended to me as well, and after weeks of deliberation I still hadn't got anybody, but I really needed to make a decision because it was getting close to shooting.

I arrived home from the location scout in Bangkok, turned on the TV and it just so happened that there was a programme on about stunts, featuring Jean-Pierre Goy on his motorcycle riding up and over the handrail of this 180 foot bridge, rather like the one in *A Bridge Too Far*. This is an omen, I thought, so I phoned him in France. He came over the next morning and we just hit it off. He was fantastic; we could not have done half the stuff in that sequence without him. Amazingly Jean-Pierre had never ridden a motorcycle until he was 16. He was a show jumper until he got bored with that, sold his pony and bought a motorcycle, and within four years he was world's trial champion. For her part, Wendy was fabulous, and completely trusted Jean-Pierre when she was climbing around the bike and facing backwards and he was doing wheelies with her sitting on the handlebars.

The highlight of the bike chase is when Bond jumps over a helicopter. That was done for real, although there were no blades on the chopper and it was suspended on a hydraulic lift. But it was still a hell of a thing to do. For that shot we built a Vietnamese street set in the UK, near St Albans, and rehearsed for about five weeks at massive cost. I have to say that the Bond producers Barbara Broccoli and Michael G. Wilson were fantastic; they gave me everything I asked for. Jean-Pierre had the unenviable task of performing the stunt. He had to reach a speed of 62 mph in 5.8 seconds, hit a wooden ramp, crash through a balcony in a five storey building, clear a street of 45 feet and drop 12 feet onto a roof opposite cushioned with a 20 foot mountain of cardboard boxes. In all we used 10,000 boxes, all specially made, and when it rained we had to wrap them in plastic; what a nightmare. But you have to do these things to make it safe. As an added precaution, the front of the building that Jean-Pierre was landing on top of had to be a breakaway, in case he came up short and hit it. So it was a huge undertaking, time-consuming and expensive, but preferable to doing it as a visual effect, or using a cable, because you can put your hand on your heart and say, yeah, he really jumped that helicopter. And I

Wendy doubles Michelle Yeoh in the famous motorbike chase, with Jean-Pierre Goy.

think that's a great bike chase, I'm very proud of it. After coming to prominence in *Tomorrow Never Dies*, Jean-Pierre has gone on to great things: he has a contract with BMW, and is still in demand for movies; he rode the 'Batpod' bike for that big chase sequence in *The Dark Knight* for example, winning a Taurus Award. Again it was fate that Andy recommended him, and set him off on a whole new career.

This was the first of three Bond films I was to make with Pierce Brosnan, and he was great. He used to say that he loved working with the action unit and wished they'd made the whole movie. When I started working with Pierce I explained to him, like I do with everybody I work with, that the secret to all these types of movies is seeing the actor in the midst of the action. For the motorcycle chase I picked certain spots where it was going to work best for Pierce to be on the bike. They actually flew Pierce out to Thailand just so I could use him in a few shots. While he was down there they also took him near the 'James Bond Island' where they made *The Man with the Golden Gun* for a beach scene, but basically he came out just for my unit to work with him.

One particular place where we shot a portion of the bike chase I nicknamed smelly alley. On my walk around with the camera crew before shooting, they asked why it was called smelly alley and I said, 'You'll see.' There was a warehouse there that tanned hides, so you had all these green, rancid, rotting slabs of meat and it *stunk*. That's where we did the firework truck exploding. And we put Pierce into all of that. But we had to walk up smelly alley to get to lunch. God, it was disgusting. And imagine the heat; it was 120 degrees out there. I had some new shoes Nike had given me, and one day when we were working on a roof it was so hot the soles melted off them. Sometimes it was like working in a pizza oven. But for me it's essential to get out there on location and get stuck in. When I'm dreaming up action sequences like the bike chase I'm totally influenced by the environment, where it takes place. The only way I can devise all these things is to actually go and see the location itself. For me that's very inspirational. I can walk into a set or a location and look at it and begin to visualize stuff; things start gelling. As Rick Carter, Steven Spielberg's fantastic production designer, said to me years later on *War of the Worlds*, 'The location has to speak to you.' It's like writing a story; you get creative. I can suddenly visualize the whole sequence, the size of it, the length of it, the violence of it.

Bond's other mode of transport in *Tomorrow Never Dies* is a remote-controlled BMW car that's chased around a multi-storey car park in Hamburg. It was another big action set piece that we analysed and worked out bloody well. That whole sequence came about when the crew was being driven by coach to Stansted Airport, to look at where Q first reveals the BMW to Bond. I was sitting next to Roger Spottiswoode and together we were dreaming up what the hell we were going to do in this car park chase. Literally within 15 minutes we had the whole routine mapped out, stuff like when Bond fires a rocket off the top of his car. I'd always loved the Sam Peckinpah effect of somebody blasted with a shotgun and getting jerked back against a wall and I said to Roger, 'Let's do that with a car, but this time Bond's got the shotgun, which is basically the rocket on top of the roof rack, and it hits the car that's coming towards him and that gets snatched back.' We also devised the leap off the car park roof at the end. And as a little present to BMW I tossed in their logo on the car bonnet that comes up as a wire cutter.

I wrote this all down and when we arrived I went up to Barbara Broccoli (who'd been following us in another car) and said, 'Barbara, we've sorted out the car park chase.' 'OK great; let's hear it.' I went through the whole sequence of Bond driving and smashing up cars on seven floors of this car park and she just stood there with her mouth agape. 'You're mad Vic. How long do you think that's going to take, and how can we do it?' I said, 'It's not that bad.' She said, 'But it's seven floors! We can't do it.' I said, 'No, we can do it all on one floor, all we need is an entry and an exit, and we can just revamp the cars and use a colour scheme to differentiate each floor, it's not a big deal.' Barbara looked at me with her lovely half-smile, half-disapproving look, sighed and said, 'OK, go ahead.'

L-R, Terry Madden (my 1st AD), Pierce, Gerry Gavigan (1st AD main unit) and myself in Bangkok.

All we needed now was someone to lend us their car park, and let us cause havoc inside it. We searched and searched and finally Brent Cross shopping centre in north London said yes. But we did have a little accident. During shooting one of the cars that Bond's rocket hits was on fire. It was a good old blaze, so I let it continue until I saw black smoke rolling along the roof and then said, 'Better cut now I think guys...' The Health and Safety fire department took over but they couldn't get their water pump started. Oh my God, I thought. Dave Bickers was with me and I said, 'I think we'd better get out of here. This black smoke is not looking too good.' As we went out, we passed the firemen trying to start their pump and old Dave, in his own inimitable style went, 'I've got one of those old Coventry engines at home. Don't touch that carburettor. Now put your hand over here, turn the choke off and now pull it twice, and then give it one big pull.' And the thing started. He knew exactly how to do it, and thank God they then managed to put the fire out. It made headlines in the local paper, but Brent Cross, far from being angry, loved it because of the publicity: people were flocking to the place.

For the chase Bond is in the back seat manoeuvring the car by remote control using his mobile phone, so we couldn't have a driver visible. A special car was designed for someone to lie down on the floor beneath the back of the front seat, with an extended steering wheel and three video monitors from lipstick cameras, one on each side mirror and one in the rear view mirror, so he had a three dimensional view of what he was looking at. The worst thing was that the driver, who was laying flat on his back covered with black cloth watching the monitors, was actually getting motion sickness.

The climax to the chase is when the BMW, controlled by Bond from a safe distance, is pursued onto the roof of the car park, filmed in Hamburg, plunges off and smashes into a shop front seven floors below. To get the aerial shots I used a flying cam, which is a remote controlled mini helicopter built round a camera, and had that over the roof and racing at the window and then slowing down at the last second, which you couldn't do with a real helicopter. For the car itself crashing into the shop front the special effects supervisor Chris Corbould and Dave Bickers had this great truck with what looked like a missile launcher on it, onto which you mounted the car to be fired, you could jack it up and point it at any angle. They put the BMW on a cannon, pointed it at this shop window, 3, 2, 1, kapow, and just blasted it in there; it's a great shot, it worked very well. It was a real shop too, and they were quite happy to let us demolish their front. Money gets you most things, and Bond is the golden key. A lot of people say no to film companies and authorities put barriers in your way, but if it's a Bond film they suddenly change their tune and go, 'Will Pierce Brosnan be here, will the girls be here?' It's amazing – the power of the Bond trademark.

A DOUBLE DOSE OF CONNERY

So *Tomorrow Never Dies* was a hell of a shoot and a great team effort, but amazingly I almost didn't do it. At the same time I was offered *The Avengers*. I read the script and it was excellent. They'd captured the flavour of the '60s TV show really well and the cast was especially interesting, Ralph Fiennes as the irrepressible John Steed, Uma Thurman as Emma Peel and Sean Connery playing a mad scientist out to control the world's weather. At the time my negotiations with Eon Productions for the Bond picture weren't going particularly well. I guess I was more expensive than the people they'd had before. So I was seriously considering doing *The Avengers*, but in the end everything was resolved with the Bond people and I did *Tomorrow Never Dies*.

Curiously while I was still on the Bond I got a call from Warner Bros., who wanted me to do a bit of work on *The Avengers*. The studio had looked at the movie and realised it was missing action, so somebody had dreamt up this brand new sequence. I literally finished the Bond film on the Friday and on the Monday started work on *The Avengers*. The main unit was wrapping in Windsor Great Park as I met with the director Jeremiah Chechik and discussed what they wanted. It was a chase between Mrs Peel's E-Type Jaguar and a swarm of mechanical bees controlled by these pair of baddies, played by Eddie Izzard and Shaun Ryder, the singer from the Happy Mondays band. Shaun was a funny bloke, smashed out of his brains every morning, couldn't drive either and he was supposed to be the getaway driver, which made things difficult. Both great guys, though.

So we planned this chase. A lot of the aerial shots and explosions were done over at Rissington, which is a disused airfield in Gloucester, the rest was at High Wycombe amidst beautiful countryside. Then I got a call from Jeremiah. 'What lens did you use on all that stuff with the Jaguar?' I told him. 'Well it looks a bit funny Vic. It's good, it's interesting, but it makes the picture look really squishy, you know, a funny shape.' Fuck. We'd been using the wrong film equipment; we'd shot the whole thing with Anamorphic lenses and they'd used spherical lenses, so when Chechik projected our stuff it was all squeezed up, the Jag looked like a bloody Volkswagen Beetle. Presumption is the mother of all fuck-ups. I'd presumed that the camera rental company would send us the same equipment as the main unit, who'd wrapped the weekend before. They hadn't.

Everybody was mortified, but it was just one of those things. In the end we had to re-stage and shoot the entire sequence again in just half a day. Talk about shooting from the hip and thinking on your feet! But it was actually a fun shoot and when the film came out one of the critics said the best performance came from the bees. *The Avengers* got a real roasting from the press and was a big flop at the box office; the original script that I'd read had been changed so much that it ended up not making a lot of sense.

Not long afterwards I was working again with Connery on *Entrapment* and we were all invited to a preview screening of *The Avengers*. We sat there and watched it and when the lights came up Sean turned to me and asked, 'What do you think of it?' I thought for a moment. 'Interesting,' I diplomatically said. 'It's a heap of shite,' said Sean.

Entrapment was intended to be a follow up of sorts to *The Rock*, Sean's recent big action hit. The director was Antoine Fuqua. I got on really well with him and we dreamt up some really huge action sequences, like a big helicopter chase through Hong Kong, just massive stuff. But the script started to evolve and change into more of a romantic caper movie than an action blockbuster. Antoine had come on the project because he wanted to be a big action movie director, and subsequently was at loggerheads with the producers and also Rhonda Tollefson, a partner in Connery's film production company Fountainbridge (named after the district of Edinburgh where he grew up). Naturally I was stuck in the middle, Antoine wanted me to invent stuff and the producers gave me bollockings for coming up with all this big action. This went on for several weeks; it got really ugly, until I got a call one Saturday night from an AD. 'Antoine left this morning. I went to the airport with him to say goodbye. He's really upset but he said he couldn't take any more, it's just not going to be his bag, it's not what he signed on for.' So Antoine left and they hired Jon Amiel, who's a very eloquent man, and the movie totally changed: now it was a love story with Catherine Zeta-Jones.

For the climax where Catherine and Sean rob a bank at the top of a skyscraper, we needed a suitably dramatic building. I remembered that on *Tomorrow Never Dies* we visited Kuala Lumpur in Malaysia, with the intention of using the famous

Behind the camera on the Sean Connery thriller Entrapment. *Camera operator Peter Field is on the left.*

Petronas Twin Towers as the headquarters of the baddie Elliot Carver. But the Petronas people said it was the wrong portrayal for their building, it couldn't be seen as the villain's HQ. MI6 yes, but not the baddies. So we flew to Hong Kong, and driving from the airport I saw all these buildings with scaffolding round them, covered in netting to stop things falling off, but on the netting they'd put these giant advertising banners. That's when I came up with the idea of having Carver's face draped down the side of the building and Bond and Wai Lin jump off the roof on ropes and rip their way down.

Now on *Entrapment* I went back to my idea of doing some kind of high fall on the Petronas Twin Towers. I revamped it a little bit by having them hanging, then dropping and finally swinging on Christmas lights underneath this huge walkway that connects both towers. But we discovered we couldn't shoot the Petronas, because you can't light it at night. It's 1500 feet high, you can't get enough lights in the world to fire up there. So they built a 140-foot segment of the towers in the 007 stage at Pinewood and we shot around that; it was Wendy doubling Catherine Zeta-Jones. I think it was an amazing achievement and one heck of a sequence. It's become quite iconic; a lot of people have copied that sequence, but that all came from a disused Bond idea that I had and then revamped.

It was also nice working with Sean again; we keep bumping into each other, and I see him on the odd golf course. Unlike Ford and Cruise, Connery doesn't get involved in the stunts, nor should he. Instead we used this guy called Gabe Cronnelly, who looks exactly like Sean. There's a scene in *Entrapment* where Catherine Zeta-Jones is performing the sexy dance move sequence with the laser lights while Sean's talking to her underneath, except Connery wasn't even there. We also used Gabe on *Indiana Jones and the Last Crusade* for all the action on the tank, the plane crashing into the shepherds' hut and a lot of the other stuff.

The other big stunt on *Entrapment* was the opening jump off a New York skyscraper, using a fan descender. I went to New York to look for a suitable building and because Frank Sinatra, old blue eyes, had died, they turned the Empire State Building blue as a tribute to him. While I was there I shot all the background plates for the shots of the thief hanging on the outside of the building and breaking in, which were shot at the studio against a translight. It was months later that I went back to New York to shoot the stunt itself. I had found this amazing building, 101 Park Avenue, which had five sides, and each side offered a different backdrop or angle. Luckily the weather matched exactly the plates I had shot months earlier. It had taken months to get permission from city officials because we had to shut down Park Avenue. Mark Mottram performed the stunt, which started with a 40-foot free fall into an airbag, which would later be edited with a fan descender shot of a dummy falling 150 feet and stopping outside a window. Mark could not see the airbag beneath him, he was just looking out onto Park Avenue about 400 feet below him. Mark said it was scary as hell because although he knew the bag was there (sitting on a platform we'd built sticking out from a section of flat roof about four floors below) it still felt like he was jumping into Park Avenue.

In between the two Connery movies I did a small action picture called *Black Dog* starring Patrick Swayze and Meatloaf for Raffaella de Laurentiis, who I hadn't worked with for a few years. I had just finished Bond and was going to take a couple of months off; we had booked a chalet in Zermatt for Christmas. I went into my gym one evening and when I came out Wendy said Raffy had called, and would call back in 30 minutes. Well, two minutes later she phoned again, so I knew it was desperate. She said I had to fly out to North Carolina immediately to put a crew together and shoot a truck chase; the crew that was already there was being fired. Oh God, I thought. This is fun. After agreeing to do the film I went to bed, then at two in the morning the phone rang and it was an assistant from the film. 'We're just ringing up to know if it's OK to send a fax through, we don't want to wake the house up with a fax ringing.' I said, 'It's a silent fax, and you've just woken the whole house up by phoning me.' He said, 'Oh my God, I've just done that haven't I. I'm sorry, I'm sorry.'

I flew to Atlanta to view the film already shot, then on to Wilmington, North Carolina. I was picked up at the airport and remember thinking, I wonder what hotel they're going to put me in, obviously they wouldn't put me in the same hotel as the 20 stuntmen and stunt director they've just sacked. I walked into the lobby and out of the corner of my eye I saw this gaggle of people having a meeting. I recognised that they were all stuntmen. Oh Jeez. So I turned my collar up and sneaked up to reception and whispered, 'My name's Armstrong, Vic Armstrong. You have a room for me.' And this woman roared, 'Oh Mr Armstrong, I've been expecting you!' As she said that I sensed all these heads turning round. Of course they all started coming over and when I got to my room every two minutes one of them would ring me up: 'I'll be willing to stay on.' In the end I kept a couple of them, but essentially hired a new stunt team.

It was on *Black Dog* that we had a terrible accident. During the chase a truck crashes and explodes. We had a safety meeting prior to the explosion and everybody was standing around this truck, then we all went to our relative places to start prepping for the shot, and literally 45 seconds later there was this huge explosion. Without warning the truck had blown up. There'd been a malfunction on a special effect and five gallons of fuel just went up. One of the riggers, Donk, who I'd worked a lot with over the years, got terribly burnt, and a local lad was also horrendously injured. They were right next to this bag of petrol when it exploded.

THE WORLD IS NOT ENOUGH

I'd had such a great time working on *Tomorrow Never Dies* that I always hoped they'd use me again on the next Bond film, and when Barbara Broccoli called me up about doing the action unit, I asked who the director was. They hadn't got one. I said, 'What if you get one who doesn't want me?' And Barbara said, 'Oh no, you're part of it,' which was wonderful of her. Michael Apted finally came on board and he's a lovely man, I really got on well with him, wonderful dry sense of humour. Simon Crane came on as stunt co-ordinator and we had a good relationship, I think it worked very well.

The first big set piece on *The World Is Not Enough* was the pre-credits boat chase on the river Thames. When they proposed this chase I must say my heart sank because I thought, my God, the logistics of it all, but I had my regular team with me: Terry Madden, my AD, Jonathan Taylor, my cameraman, and Kenny Atherfold, my grip, and here was a chance to do something really special.

All the script said was that Bond's boat leaves the MI6 building chasing a female assassin in her boat, that they had to finish at the Millennium Dome, plus a hot air balloon had to be involved. That was the brief. First of all we had to decide what boat Bond should use. Simon had this idea of modifying these jet boats from New Zealand that he'd seen in a magazine, and they turned out to be absolutely perfect. Then we started plotting the chase, and Simon and I would meet every Sunday and go up and down the Thames looking around and getting ideas. Chris Livett of Livett Launches was our guide for anything on the Thames. He is a Waterman to the Queen, and his family has worked and owned companies on the river since 1710. Chris was amazing, and knew everybody and everything there was to know about the Thames; we could not have done it without him.

Overall it was a huge project, with 60 boats on the payroll. One day when we were shooting the chase, I was cruising up the Thames, past the Houses of

Filming the boat chase on the Thames. MPs in the nearby Houses of Parliament complained we were making too much noise.

Parliament, and I just looked behind me and this whole armada was sailing up. There were wardrobe boats, special effects boats, food boats, make up boats, everyone had different boats that could whip in and out, because you couldn't keep going back to a base. It was phenomenal. We also had to employ people to keep the crowds at bay. When news broke that we were filming along the river, hordes of sightseers turned up every day. In the end I said, 'Don't worry, let them in, they can hang around, see what we're doing, take pictures.' And once we did that all the pressure was off and nobody was trying to sneak photographs.

Maria Grazia Cucinotta (from *Il Postino*), who played the female assassin, was absolutely gorgeous and such fun to work with. She was so trusting when we set her off down the Thames driving the boat at high speed, with a stuntman crouched at her feet out of shot ready to leap in and take over if things got out of control.

Of course when Pierce Brosnan turned up, the crowds got bigger and wilder. We shot for two days with Pierce, put him in the jet boat and he did quite a bit of driving himself. At one point we were filming right in front of the Houses of Parliament. I was in the lead camera boat and Pierce had to swerve across and shoot under Westminster Bridge, but he got muddled because of some water in his eyes and went the wrong side of one of the pillars. From my camera position it looked like he'd crashed and hit the bridge. My heart almost stopped and I was

With the gorgeous Maria Grazia Cucinotta.

waiting for the explosion... Everything was OK, but he scared the life out of me. Pierce could really drive that boat though, and was having a great time. The shots like the ones he did for real on the river, not against blue screen in a studio, are what make a movie for me.

We got a lot of complaints from the politicians in the Houses of Parliament that we were making too much noise, what with boats racing up and down and gunfire, until the then Home Secretary Jack Straw told them, 'Come on guys, there's an awful lot of money being generated by all this, the film, and the publicity London will get from it.' After that they were fine.

On his second and last day with us Pierce had to fly out to Spain, so wanted to finish early that afternoon. 'Look Pierce,' I said. 'If we work on through the scheduled lunch break I can get you out of here, and I'll tell you what, I'll buy you lunch because that means we've wrapped this whole location.' 'Sounds good to me,' he said. So we shot like mad outside the Millennium Dome, finished, and then six of us jumped into the Sunseeker boat (the one the assassin drives in the movie) and Chris Livett just opened the throttle, stood this big thing on its arse and we went, voom, flat out down the Thames. Now usually on the Thames you can't go over ten knots… we were doing 35 knots, screaming down the river, banking around the corners and roaring past police launches, but the officers just waved at us – the power of Bond (and Chris Livett). We then pulled up outside this very fancy restaurant near Tower Bridge and had a great liquid lunch. Three hours later we were all still there – so much for finishing early.

Plotting out the boat chase I thought it would be great to shoot and see all the iconic tourist sights and beauty shots on the Thames, and then get off as quickly as possible into the Docklands area, where things were more controllable. So after Bond goes under Tower Bridge, he turns right up a little narrow chute that in reality was a dead end – though the audience wouldn't know that – which brought him out into the Docklands. We shot at the Victoria docks, near London City Airport. That's where we blew up all those boats. I recall this guy turned up on the set one day from some environmental agency. 'Who's he?' I asked. 'Oh, he's fish preservation,' I was told. He had sonic boom speakers to put in the water, to scare all the fish away from where we were shooting, because explosions underwater can kill fish. So we explained everything to him, where the explosions were going to be. 'OK, fine,' he said. Next morning we turned up and this guy was at the completely wrong end of the dock. 'For Christ's sake!' And it was a four-hour set-up to get all this shit in place. 'This is where we're shooting,' I said. 'This end, you have to bring all your stuff down here, but I don't know if we can wait.' He said, 'Don't worry, my equipment doesn't really work anyway.' So we just carried on, but technically he had to be around to scare the fish away.

Before each take we also had to phone the airport. We could see the end of the runway from where we were shooting and the planes took off almost over our heads. So we had to time all our takes in between the landing and taking off of aeroplanes. All the tourists flying into London must have thought they'd got into a war zone, with these great fireballs blowing up beside their plane.

I have to say the jet boats were phenomenal, and because they only needed a few inches of water and could literally skim over the surface, I came up with a sequence where Bond vaults out of the river and hits London's streets. I made it so Bond is able to manoeuvre the boat through back alleys and the like because of a burst water main. That idea was ultimately scrapped, but instead we had him smashing through a fish market and a restaurant; it was just to add variety to the chase and it worked very well.

I must mention here Sarah Donohue, who doubled for Maria Grazia Cucinotta.

Travelling up the Thames in style with Maria at the controls.

She and Simon Crane went off and they rehearsed all those boat manoeuvres, how tight they could turn, all that stuff. Sarah was an amazingly gutsy girl and a brilliant race boat driver. She actually nearly died a couple of years later in Italy doing power boat racing. One engine came off and her boat crashed and went under, and she was trapped inside. She was clinically dead for a couple of minutes. But she's back racing again now.

Overall the boat chase took about three weeks to do, which was fantastic because the potential for going over schedule on a thing like that was massive, but it worked out brilliantly, and it's still one of my favourite action sequences, it's so unique. And the whole thing was done for real, the only CGI in it was the torpedoes that Bond fires, because the authorities wouldn't let us put actual torpedoes in the water, but the rest was real. We did some amazing stuff on it. Someone came up with the idea of doing a barrel roll, turning the boat 360 degrees in mid-air. I said, 'Wow, yes, if we can do it.' As usual Dave Bickers came up with the solution, of outfitting the rear of the boat with two jets – one pointing upward, one downward – and firing both simultaneously as the craft ramped out of the water. They tested it and it worked perfectly and Gary Powell, give him his due, went out and performed the stunt on the Thames, which was a hell of a dangerous thing to do. If he'd got his timing a split-second wrong it would have had terrible consequences.

The boat chase was originally three or four times longer than what ended up on screen. Obviously sequences like that always start out longer and get chopped down at the editing stage, as they try to reduce the running time in order to get other parts of the movie in. But this is where you've got to dig your heels in and fight for the bits you want, and then the arguments start. On the boat chase the editor, who was a lovely man, actually wanted to take out the barrel roll. 'No fucking way,' I said. He said, 'You don't understand Vic, you might like it, but you are too close to it, having shot it.' 'But it's great, it's unique!' I argued. And thank goodness they left it in.

PIERCE BROSNAN

That boat chase was a fantastic sequence, one of the highlights of my time doing the Bond films. And Vic was a top man, he saw that I could equip myself, saw that I could handle the jet boat and let me do it. That's when it gets down to trust and confidence between the stunt guy and the actor, and Vic has a sixth sense about people's abilities. You have to have that intuition when you're dealing with such big action sequences and stunts.

So I had the boat all to myself, there was no interference from anybody; Vic just let the cameras roll. Of course, there was the possibility of things going wrong. I was strapped in with two oxygen tanks and scuba gear either side of me, because if I did flip the boat at 30 mph it was going to be a hard impact. But I remember Vic's beaming face on the camera boat as we would do certain passes and takes. The House of Lords got pissed off with us and complained bitterly that we were assaulting their ears. But who cares, it was such a great stunt sequence to be part of.

Then we went out to the ski resort of Chamonix, below Mont Blanc in the French Alps, to shoot the scene where Bond is terrorised by parahawks, propeller-driven Russian army snowmobiles that could fly through the air using a paraglider chute to stay airborne. With Bond you're always trying to come up with original vehicles. Simon Crane and myself searched everywhere for something that could both fly and move along fast on the snow. In the end we customised snowmobiles and I think they come over very effectively. In any action sequence the main concern is to vary things, to keep the viewer enthralled in what's going on. Before you get bored with these things in the air, let's land them on the ground, they unhook their parachutes and away we go on a different kind of chase.

There's a lovely moment where Bond suckers one of these machines over the edge of a cliff; a several thousand foot drop. Bond thinks he's triumphed until he sees a second parachute open and the chase is back on. My idea was to have a black parachute with a red hammer and sickle on it; a homage to the scene in

The flying parahawks in Chamonix.

The Spy Who Loved Me when Bond's parachute opens to reveal the Union Jack. It would've been great, and I think that was the right moment for a laugh. But for some reason or other the producers didn't go for it; pity.

We did a lot of intricate stuff in that sequence and working in snow always presents problems. But it was a fabulous location, just awe-inspiring. I got such a kick out of being there. But it was dangerous too. While we were there, a huge avalanche wiped out three chalets that had been in the region for 100 years, and families were killed, it was horrendous.

Probably the film's biggest set piece was the helicopter attack on a caviar factory owned by Robbie Coltrane's character Zukovsky. I think that was the largest outdoor set ever constructed at Pinewood. We extended the water tank and had a 300-foot tower crane on which we suspended a full-size helicopter. That crane was so big I could actually see it from my bedroom window 22 miles away. The helicopter had no rotors, but the chainsaw blades dangling underneath were real, and operated by someone from special effects. The idea to use these chainsaw blades came from back in the *GoldenEye* days. Michael G. Wilson had seen them in a documentary somewhere; they're normally used in America to trim back tall trees where they might interfere with power cables. So the producers had wanted to use this idea for years.

Production designer Peter Lamont and his team built this amazing set with factory buildings, huts and wooden walkways and there were explosions galore.

Everything was going fine but I soon realised that we needed some upward shots of real helicopters swooping around, not just the mock-up hanging on the crane. 'We can't Vic,' the producers said. 'We can't fly real helicopters at the studio; also we can't fly them at night.' But I was insistent, and they're very good Barbara and Michael, they listen and they think. 'So what do you suggest?' they asked. I wanted to take a few roofs and huts over to Aldershot, where we could fly at night because it's an army training ground, and Peter Lamont, who's fantastic, said, 'No, when we've finished here let's take *everything* down there.'

Amazingly they re-built about two thirds of that set over at Aldershot on stilts and walkways so I could drive underneath and shoot helicopters coming over the top and swirling round, and when you look at the sequence today that's what gives it such a terrific sense of realism. Marc Wolfe, my helicopter pilot and friend for many years, did some amazing flying with these great chainsaws hanging 20 feet beneath the chopper. He had to land it on a specially designed platform with a slot cut out, which he had to position the saws in as he landed. I've got to say, once again, the Bond producers did what I asked of them. They're brilliant like that, the Bond people. They really look after you and make you feel like you're part of the firm.

It was also my idea to have Bond's BMW Z8 cut in half by one of the chainsaw-packing helicopters. I set the gag up where Bond runs and escapes and gets his key out to start his car by remote control. I wanted everyone to think, here we go, it's another Brent Cross car park chase. Bond gets in the car, shoots one of the helicopters out of the sky with a stinger missile and then sees these blades behind him and dives out just in time as the car is sliced in two. I thought that would be a nice little throwaway gag. And for me that's what the essence of Bond is, you've got to keep throwing those little funnies in.

VIC'S ANGELS

I had a decision to make: stay at home and make a movie at nearby Pinewood Studios, or go to LA and work with Cameron Diaz, Drew Barrymore and Lucy Liu on *Charlie's Angels*. I remember seeing Barbara Broccoli and saying, 'What a choice.' And she went, 'You're joking aren't you?' Even though she thought the script was terrible. 'Well, what can you do,' I said. But actually it turned into a good little movie and was a big hit. A guy called McG was the director. He'd never made a feature before, he'd only done commercials and pop videos, and he was all over the place, very, very enthusiastic but didn't really follow the plot that much. He wanted me to give him all the action that I could, so I was very involved with the dreaming up of the action sequences.

Like the TV series, the film opened with little scenes introducing the girls' characters, and I shot all of those bits, like Lucy Liu doing some show jumping; she was actually a good rider and did most of that herself. Cameron Diaz was seen passing her driving test. We had a car designed with a steering wheel on the left hand side where she sat, but it was actually a right hand drive car, we dropped the steering wheel down and the stunt driver was sitting next to her as though he was the driving instructor. And this car was up on two wheels, skidding and doing 180 spins, and Cameron was laughing her head off, she's got so much guts. I sent her to Rick Seaman's stunt driving school out in the Mojave Desert with my brother Andy, who called me that night: 'Jesus Christ Vic, she's unbelievable that girl, she was going 45 mph backwards changing lanes!' You know how difficult it is to drive a car backwards, but you imagine doing it flat out in a rigged car and not losing it. She's brilliant. I called her Lead Boot from then on.

All three girls were fabulous, and not long after I was in Rome working with Cameron Diaz on *Gangs of New York*. I had an original film poster of *Charlie's Angels* and approached her on the set with it. 'Cameron, could you sign this for me?' She looked at it and said, 'Where did you get this old poster? Haven't you got one of the special chrome ones? I'll get you a chrome one, and I'll get the other girls to sign it as well.' A couple of weeks later after finishing on *Gangs* she returned to the States and sure enough posted back this beautiful chrome poster that she'd got both the other girls to sign with the message – 'You made the angels fly' which was lovely.

Andy also worked on *Charlie's Angels*, and devised the helicopter chase at the end. A lot of the actors' close-ups and action was shot using a helicopter up against a green screen in the studio. Then I went down to San Pedro and hung the same chopper on a rig to do all the external shots with a real background. We were tipping it over on its side one day to simulate it crashing and suddenly there was all this dripping fluid. What the hell is that? Somebody went over to check and discovered there was 75 gallons of fuel still inside the tanks. And this was the same helicopter they'd had in the studio for a week shooting Lucy Liu hanging off it, and Drew Barrymore fighting inside. They'd had this on the studio stage. Just unbelievable.

Shooting around California I had a wonderful blast of nostalgia. My Dad and I always used to watch *Bonanza*, *Wagon Train* and *Gunsmoke* together; we loved those old TV westerns. And on *Charlie's Angels* I actually worked on the same hillside in the area that a lot of those shows were made. I recognised this place that I'd watched as a kid with my Dad; it was a lovely private moment.

So from a poor script I think McG, Andy and I actually made a pretty good movie. But I had a lot of heated conversations with McG and everybody else concerned with the film over the amount of Chinese martial arts action they wanted. They had a whole bunch of Chinese martial arts experts and it was going to be just like *The Matrix*. The studio's thinking was, well, if that was successful let's put all that stuff in our movie too. But this was going to be even bigger than *The Matrix* in its wirework and martial arts. All that's fine in moderation but this was just over the top, and too expensive and unnecessary, so I drastically cut down the martial arts content to just a few scenes. And before the film was released one of the Sony bosses, Gary Martin, called me. 'I just want to thank you Vic. Everything you said was absolutely right about cutting down the martial arts stuff, because we have more than enough and I think we've now got a decent movie here. I really do. So thank you for doing it.'

I came home on a Saturday from *Charlie's Angels*, played golf on the Sunday, and five o'clock Monday morning flew out to Kefalonia in Greece to work on *Captain Corelli's Mandolin*. I met John Madden the director, hot after *Shakespeare in Love*, who'd never had a second unit director before, so we talked about how we were going to work together, and how to do the action. Then we started shooting. I was out with Terry Madden, my AD, on the second day, looking over a landscape. Terry had been there ahead of me prepping things with my DP Peter Field while I was finishing *Charlie's Angels*. He said, 'Now, the Germans are going to come over this hill.' I said, 'Germans? What Germans?' He said, 'Vic, have you read the script?' I went, 'No, Wendy's reading it. I was going to read it tonight.' Terry said, 'Well, it's the Germans attacking the Italians.' I said, 'Oh, is it really?' From then on in my life, whenever there is any confusion I say, 'Just tell me, are the Germans in this?'

The novel was a massive bestseller but I don't think the film quite worked, although it's a beautifully shot movie. Kefalonia is a lovely island, not a traffic light anywhere, absolutely gorgeous and unspoiled. It's where the original story was set. I worked on the film for quite a few weeks and also shot all of Christian Bale's scenes (he played a resistance fighter) because they were getting behind schedule. Then I had to leave to meet Martin Scorsese in Rome, as he wanted me for *Gangs of New York*. By now John Madden was so confident in what I was giving him that he desperately wanted me to stay, to advise him on how to shoot a brutal scene in which all these Italians and Greeks are machine-gunned to death by the Germans. I explained that he didn't need bullet hits on everyone, just on every third person standing at the front, the rest just had to fall down. That was more than enough. Half the time you don't see blood hits – unless it's a specific thing in a movie, they're a waste of space. On all of *Mission: Impossible III* we didn't have one blood hit. A, because it helps the ratings, B, it speeds things up, and C, in certain situations you don't miss it.

So I explained all this but still they wanted me to stay on. 'I can't, I've got to meet Scorsese.' That involved flying back home and getting another flight. 'Tell you what,' they said, 'if you stay on, we'll charter a plane and fly you direct to Rome from here.' I thought, wow, this is the big time, this is living. So I set up the massacre sequence and afterwards a car took me to my hotel, I got ready, then it drove me straight to the airport where this big twin-engine plane was sat on the runway, with a stewardess and two pilots who asked, 'Just let us know when you'd like to take off.' I said, 'Let's go now.' It was a big 20-seater and I was the only passenger. 'Would you like a cocktail sir?' this beautiful stewardess asked. By the time I got to Rome I didn't want the flight to end.

At the Cinecittà studios I had a couple of days of meetings with Scorsese and came back to England. Then the film's backers Miramax called: I wasn't needed until much later in the shoot, in the meantime Harvey Weinstein wanted me to go out to Morocco on *The Four Feathers*, directed by Shekhar Kapur, who'd just made the acclaimed *Elizabeth*. They wanted me to shoot all these large-scale battle scenes between the English forces and the Mardi's army of natives. I had 200 horses, 80 camels, 1500 foot warriors and the film's star Heath Ledger, who was terrific.

Jordi Casares was now a stunt co-ordinator and was running the stunt department. We started working with Heath on his riding and he was a real athlete. I thought he was going to be the next Harrison Ford. In one scene we even had him vaulting onto a horse at full gallop. The Mardi's army has massacred a group of British soldiers and taken their uniforms, in order to get close enough to the main British force and spring a surprise attack. Heath's character is on horseback amongst them trying to warn his buddies, but he's too late and his horse gets shot away from under him. He sees another loose horse galloping amidst the 200 others thundering down, runs, grabs hold of the saddle and does a pony express mount. We taught him to do that and he did it fantastically well. In fact the first time he tried it he leapt so much that he didn't land on the horse but went right over the other side of it. The adrenaline was really up. A few years later I was in Australia and read an interview with Heath where he said, 'On *Four Feathers* I had this action director called Vic Armstrong and he was great, he taught me to ride and vault onto a horse. It was fantastic.' He was so proud of that moment.

It was an incredibly tough picture to work on, especially with all the dust. If you think you've got nearly 2000 living things in the desert and you know that they're peeing and crapping everywhere, camels and horses and people. Every time they charged this big cloud of dust would just swamp you. You'd have to wrap big bandanas round your head and your eyes and wait for the dust to settle, then you had to carry on and get ready for the next take. But that dust is literally full of crap that's dried and is now floating around. Everybody had a bad chest, God it was awful. Plus it was Ramadan, and the extras weren't allowed to eat or drink during daylight because they were Muslims. It was 120 degrees and we had to hide our water bottles from them and secretly have a quick drink or munch on our sandwiches so they couldn't see us.

All in all it was a funny project to work on because Shekhar Kapur didn't have a total grasp, I don't think, of the battles. Mind you they let me do it all, so that was fine. Otherwise he was a sweet man. It was also great working with Jordi Casares in his role as stunt co-ordinator, having been this young fella that had started off with me way back in the day. Together I think we pulled off some terrific battle scenes. There are some huge shots in there. Working with DP Jimmy Devis (my

Spectacular high shot of a battle scene from The Four Feathers. *A post-production mixture of over 16,000 horses, camels and The Mardi Army.*

great friend who I'd first met years before on *Ryan's Daughter* in Ireland) I did a big high shot of all the soldiers forming a square and you see 20,000 people attacking it. I used the 200 horses and 80 camels, plus the 1500 people on foot, and did ten different shots of everybody charging with a locked-off camera. But what I did was one time I'd have the camels at the front, the next time the people, and the next time the horses out front, so when you look down you see this massive advancing mob, all in one shot and all in different formations, and you see it's not replication. It was actually multiple takes put together, but you can't see the join, and it's a spectacular shot.

MARTY AND HARVEY

I decided to stay on in Morocco after *The Four Feathers* and enjoyed a short holiday there with Wendy. Then I got a call from Harvey Weinstein; they needed me urgently on *Gangs of New York*. We arrived back home just in time for Christmas and there was a stack of video cassettes waiting for me, all black and white Soviet silent films, movies like Sergei Eisenstein's *October* and *Battleship Potemkin*. There was a note with them from Martin Scorsese's office saying, we want you to look at these movies for stylistic reasons. Oh God, I'd better watch them then. I'd better do my homework. And I'd be sitting in the lounge and the kids would come in. 'Hey Dad, what are you watching?' They'd look at the screen with all this heavy Russian stuff going on and say, 'See you then Dad, bye.'

But it was a good job I watched them because I'd be working with Scorsese on a scene and he'd suddenly say something like, 'Remember on *Battleship Potemkin* with the big crane shot at the Odessa steps?' Or, 'There was a shot on *October* when he goes into the kitchen...' You've really got to do your homework with Marty. In the end we came up with our own terminology: a Russian angle, or a Dutch/ Russian angle. When you look at all those Eisenstein movies, instead of having a close-up of somebody where you see the background, they'd shoot almost looking up the actor's nostrils, and this was what Marty and I called a Russian angle. A Dutch angle is famous in the business for when you tilt the camera like they did in *The Third Man*. So we'd be working together and Marty would go, 'Let's have a Russian angle here Vic,' or a Dutch/Russian angle, it just became film speak between us. No one else knew what the hell we were talking about.

Marty was a terrific guy. He'd never used a second unit director before in his life and wasn't sure how it was going to work. 'How do we do this?' he asked. I explained what my function was, started off working with him on a few things, and pretty soon he gained enough confidence to allow me to go out and start shooting bits and pieces on my own. The battle between the gangs was probably the biggest set piece I worked on. I auditioned 300 guys for that, and brought in wrestlers and fighters and English stuntmen. I planned that whole battle sequence and worked with Marty shooting it. Then he left to carry on with studio interiors while I mopped up all the assorted bits of carnage, like ripping people's faces open and breaking kneecaps. I used lots of amputees and put false legs on them; we did shots of people being hit with clubs and you see their leg crack inwards. Somebody else falls under a horse and cart and gets his legs cut off. I used a double amputee for that; real bloodthirsty stuff.

Meanwhile poor old Marty was having a tough time because he was over schedule, which was why I was there, and getting grief from above. I'd often go and see him with a cassette of what I'd been shooting. 'How are you doing Marty?' He'd grumble and moan. 'Watch this,' I'd say. 'It'll cheer you up.' And I'd play all the gory shots and he loved it. 'What are you doing now Marty?' I'd say. 'I've got a half-hour set-up to do.' You could see by his expression that he wasn't looking forward to it. 'Come down on my set then Marty and watch us, we're going to chop this guy's legs off.' So he'd come over and stay with us for a bit and had a great time.

The cast on that movie was terrific. Daniel Day-Lewis was terrifying. He was 100% in character for the whole duration of the shoot. We clashed horns a couple of times, because on set when you talked to him you weren't talking to Daniel Day-Lewis the actor, you were talking to his character, Bill the Butcher. It was as if he'd slit you open with his knife, no problem; scary stuff. But a great guy in reality, a very quiet, sweet man.

And then we had the gorgeous Cameron Diaz. It was lovely seeing her again after *Charlie's Angels*. I shot a lot of her scenes because they were desperately trying to finish with her as she'd gone over schedule by weeks and weeks and was due on another movie. I shot the whole sequence where Cameron escapes, tries to get on a boat and ends up being mugged and then killing her assailant. I also shot Marty Scorsese himself. The scene outside Barnum and Bailey's when it's on fire, we had Marty running through the shot; he loves acting. So I actually directed Martin Scorsese. Albeit just, 'Action! Cut!'

Leonardo DiCaprio was a lovely guy, but very intense. He obviously took his lead from Daniel Day-Lewis. But you can't help but get that professionalism and enthusiasm and dedication to a movie when it's a Scorsese picture, it really is an exceptional experience. For me *Gangs of New York* was a labour of love. I was originally scheduled to work on it for six weeks but ended up staying almost 12 weeks. I was going to work on *The Scorpion King*, had meetings and everything in LA, and then *Gangs* went on and on and I couldn't leave it. The producer Mike Hausman said to me, 'You can't go Vic, Marty just doesn't want you to go.' I said, 'It's OK, I understand.' He said, 'You're going to thank me one day. I'll be the guy that saved you from *The Scorpion King*.' Mind you, how bad can it be, I was living close to the Spanish Steps in Rome, working five or six days a week, dinner in wonderful restaurants, it was all very pleasant.

Working with Marty was an education. I learnt an enormous amount. There's a little incident in the film where an elephant runs amok. There was no elephant in reality, it was put in later by visual effects, but you had the crowd running and chasing it, and the interaction of it knocking stuff over and crushing things. I had to pace out the distances and explain to Marty how you do all that, because he'd never worked with effect shots before, he was a different kind of filmmaker. So it was an absolutely wonderful exchange of ideas, but a great learning curve for me.

I was also the new boy; they'd been shooting for four months by the time I arrived, although I knew a lot of the crew. Nor did I have my usual second unit; they'd spent all the money, so my team was literally cobbled together. We had a local boy doing the video playback; my AD was a 3rd AD on the main unit who they'd promoted; things like that. I also worked and became close friends with two wonderful DPs: one was Florian, the son of Marty's DP on the film Michael Ballhaus, who has since gone on to lighting his own big shows, and Marco Pontecorvo, who has also blossomed into a fantastic main unit DP. It was actually guerrilla filmmaking. It seems strange to say you're doing guerrilla filmmaking with a guy like Martin Scorsese, but it was a whole different way of working: it wasn't calculated, or mechanical, or mercenary, and you felt as if you were doing something artistic. It was a really interesting way of going about things. I had so much fun.

Marty's knowledge of film was really quite scary. One day I was doing a shot where someone was attacked and thrown through a window. We dug the floorboards out to get my Russian angles, so we're looking up as this guy's kicked in the head, and Marty said, 'You remember Vic, you did a shot a bit like this on *Henry V*.' And he explained it in minute detail. 'Did I?' 'Yes,' he said, and proceeded to tell me the angles, everything. Plus he knew I'd shot it, rather than Ken Branagh. I couldn't even remember it. He's got such a mind for movies; just phenomenal.

Another day I asked why he liked using a lot of top shots, looking downwards with the camera. 'Well I'll tell you,' he said. 'When I was a kid I was always a bit weak, I couldn't go out in the street because somebody would punch me in the nose. I didn't go out of my house much, you know. So I'd be on the third floor fire escape and I'd see all of life going on below. So I always look at life from above.' So that's why Scorsese uses so many top shots in his movies.

Gangs was a wonderful shoot and I think we made a great movie. I remember when I was working on that, I received the Academy Award for the fan descender. When I arrived in LA there was a bottle of Kristal champagne for me from Marty. He still sends a card every Christmas, and he's just a lovely, genuine person. I loved working with him.

MARTIN SCORSESE

Vic Armstrong is, of course, a legend in the film world, in the tradition of the great Yakima Canutt. I had an extraordinary experience working with Vic as second unit director on *Gangs of New York*. We worked closely together on the battle scenes, and in order to give him an idea of what I needed I screened a few silent Soviet films by Eisenstein, Dovzhenko and Pudovkin – there were scenes and shots in these pictures that served as specific reference points for us. Vic immediately understood what I was going for and how to achieve it. He has an innate sense of the vocabulary of cinema, and a comprehensive knowledge of film technique going back to the silent era. He truly knows the dynamics of film language – the control of movement within the frame, in the foreground and background, and movement of the frame itself. Vic is a true filmmaker, and he was invaluable on *Gangs of New York*. I had a great time working with him, and I could never have made it without him.

After *Gangs* I did some more films for Harvey Weinstein over the next few years. *Kate & Leopold* starred Hugh Jackman and Meg Ryan. One sequence involved Hugh borrowing a white horse from a hansom cab and chasing a mugger through Central Park. Weinstein was on the set yelling, 'Don't do a damn thing with that chase until you get Vic Armstrong out here.' So I flew in and met with the director James Mangold, who was very nice. 'Harvey thinks you're really the bee's knees,' he said. 'So this is the chase, what can you do?' I knew lots of people in New York so we got a crew together really quickly.

At that time New York was ultra busy: *Stuart Little* was shooting, *Spider-Man* was shooting, and there were at least two other film crews around. It got so bad that it was decided that each film company had to be at least two blocks apart from each other. You had to be really careful in the morning when you turned up for breakfast, because you could walk off to find your crew and discover you were on totally the wrong film. That happened several times, it was really quite bizarre.

After I sorted out this horse chase I stayed on for some more work that they had, like Hugh Jackman hanging off a bridge, and we also did a fan descender drop. We ended up shooting all over the city. I always love going to New York, I think it's one of the greatest cities in the world, after Rome. And I saw the Radio Man. He's a real character in New York, and he's called Radio Man because he has a radio hanging on a bit of string round his neck. He's like an old bum and rides round on a bicycle with all his stuff in it. But he's a total film buff. If you're lost in the morning and wandering around and you see him, you can say, 'Where's so and so shooting?' and he'll give you their call time, the street they're on, and what sort of stuff they're doing that morning. And if you give him your name he'll tell you what your call time was. He's an amazing character. Lots of people have stuck him in their films in little guest spots. You can be driving into New York and there is what looks like a bum on the side of the road, who will suddenly turn round and say, 'Hey Vic, how are you doing dude, are you working on so and so's film?' That's the Radio Man.

I've got to say that Hugh Jackman was fantastic. This was not long after the first *X-Men* film, and his star was still on the rise. He was certainly new to me. But after returning home I went straight up to Pinewood and saw Barbara Broccoli. 'Look,' I said, 'I know Pierce has got one or two more Bonds in him, but I've seen the next James Bond after Pierce, Hugh Jackman, he's fantastic. He's got all the right characteristics, he's Australian like George Lazenby, so he qualifies, and Australians have a great dry sense of humour that's very British. Plus he's a good-looking guy, great character and great fun to work with. I think he's just magnificent.'

To give you an idea of what he's like: during the horse chase in *Kate & Leopold* there's a bit where Hugh corners this mugger, takes his stirrup off and swings it round on the end of the stirrup leather, threatening the mugger, who drops the bag he's stolen and runs off. Hugh is very athletic, but he wasn't a good horseman so we doubled him galloping in and skidding to a halt. As the stunt rider went to grab the stirrup leather, I saw it slip off the saddle. Before I could leap forward, I saw out of the corner of my eye this other body dive below camera and on his hands and knees grab the stirrup leather and hold it up for the stuntman to reach down, pick it up and carry on with the shot. I looked and it was Hugh Jackman. He's a real team player; that really stood out in my mind.

When Pierce Brosnan was eventually replaced as James Bond, Hugh did end up being a close candidate for the role, but his career had advanced too much. He'd done more *X-Men* and had proved himself to be a bigger star than somebody that needed to do Bond; it wouldn't have been a good career move. But back in those days he would have made a terrific 007.

The Great Raid was Harvey Weinstein again. He was producing *Cold Mountain*, which I was going to do; I had meetings with Anthony Minghella, who wanted me on it. But I started, excuse the pun, to get cold feet about it. Then Harvey called: 'I've got this other picture in Australia, it's called *The Great Raid*, and you've got to do that one as well.' I said, 'OK, Harvey, if you talk to them and fix the schedules.' But film companies never co-operate with each other, so they couldn't get the schedules worked out. Being selfish I said I wanted to do the film in Australia, because I'd never been and I was desperate to work there.

The story was a good one, too. It was set during the close of the Second World War when General MacArthur triumphantly returned in force to the Philippines to defeat the Japanese, and sent in American Rangers to rescue prisoners in the north facing execution. I was working with a great friend of mine called Chris Anderson, an Australian stuntman who'd lost his leg in a horrendous boating accident. He was with a crew filming these ocean racers when suddenly one came right over the top of them, hit their boat and sliced it in half, ploughing everybody into the water. Eventually the safety boat arrived and dragged them all on board, but Chris had been hit in the crutch and smashed his pelvis, his hip and his thigh. He'd also severed the artery so there was blood spraying everywhere, and they were 20 miles offshore. Quickly they slung him in a speedboat and raced him at 60 mph for the shore, bouncing over these waves, and then rushed him into hospital. He died a couple of times due to loss of blood, and in the end they had to amputate his leg, because gangrene set in. He's a great guy and he put a terrific crew together for me out in Australia, one of the best I've ever worked with.

After shooting for several weeks though, I felt I wanted to come back home. The director didn't really want a second unit, and it wasn't a fun atmosphere. Then I got this call at four in the morning from Harvey, 'Vic, I'm perturbed.' I went, 'Oh yeah, what's going on?' Harvey said, 'I've just seen a rough-cut of the movie, it's called *The Great Raid*, but there's no fucking raid in it! You've got to give me a raid.' So I was forbidden to leave by Harvey Weinstein. I ended up choreographing and shooting this big action set piece, with lots of tanks blowing up. We did a heck of a lot of great stuff, and some of those Aussie stunt guys did the best and most realistic fire jobs I have ever seen. They were amazing.

While I was out there I played a lot of golf. One day I was on this tee and a bunch of Japanese guys were walking ahead of me towards the next green. I played my shot, and it bounced off the head of this kangaroo that was lying down. You could hear it go 'clunk' as it hit its skull and the kangaroo jumped up, shook his head, looked around and stared really menacingly at the Japanese who were walking by; it was nothing to do with them, but they got the blame for my stray golf ball. There are so many of these kangaroos just roaming around the place, and it led to a tragic incident. We cast the American Rangers and prisoners from local guys who lived in the area where we were working. One night they were coming back from shooting in a minibus. One guy had arrived on the set with his own motorbike, so was riding back home on it and overtook the minibus. As he passed them, 100 yards down the road a bloody kangaroo jumped out and knocked him off his bike and into the path of a car that was coming the other way. The car hit him and took his head off; just dreadful. A lot of the extras were in shock. Alas, it's just one of those awful things that sometimes happen on movies, and in life.

DIE ANOTHER DAY

When I read the script for the new James Bond movie I thought, wow, this is a good one, and was excited to see that we were going to go to Cuba, because I love my rum and coke and a good cigar, and had always wanted to go there. Other locations included Korea and Japan. On my previous Bonds the most exotic place I went to was Bangkok, which I'd been to lots of times. So I thought, Cuba, Korea, Japan, this is great, now we're talking. In the end I never went further than Aldershot and Pinewood Studios. Korea turned into Aldershot army range, and Japan went bye-byes altogether. Actually I did go to Iceland, to be fair, but that didn't even feature in the original story.

The film starts in North Korea, where Bond has to assassinate an arms dealer who lives in a secret base that's surrounded by land mines and bombs. The problem was how people were supposed to get in and out. So we came up with the idea of using one-man hovercraft, which would float over the mines. Special effects supervisor Chris Corbould set up a workshop and we had a production line to build these hovercraft. My two sons Bruce and Scott were part of the crew building and keeping the machines running. We ended up with about 16 of these things. Of course we then needed people to drive them.

Down in Southampton there's a huge hovercraft museum and the owners said to me, 'This is a great guy, he races hovercraft. You don't need stuntmen, him and his mates, they're terrific.' I said, 'OK, let's see them.' We were on the beach, the tide was out, and I pointed to a post some way off. 'Go to where that marker is, go round it, come back, turn in front of us and then speed off again. I just want to see the manoeuvrability.' This guy went roaring off and went all over the place. 'Where the hell are you going? I told you where to go.' He said, 'Oh, I didn't know what you meant.' I turned to the museum guys. 'He might be able to drive a hovercraft but he's useless to take direction.' And that's what happens when you

Another explosive Bond pre-credit sequence.

get non-stunt people in, they're all individuals and do their own thing, they don't realize the importance of where they have to be at a certain time. What's going into the lens is what matters. You can be doing great stunts over there out of frame, but if you are not going to be seen, you're just a danger and a waste of time.

That's when I made the decision: right, we're going to have a school of hovercraft driving. I set it up over at the location where we were going to shoot the sequence, Aldershot army range. It's quite funny because I looked at all these photographs from North Korea, and it does look just like Aldershot. But God, it was lashing with rain, there was mud, it was freezing cold, and these stunt guys were roaring all over the place, crashing into trees backwards, and smashing into each other. It was great fun watching them driving these things and they were having a hoot. One time Roy Alon fell out and I think Tony Smart drove right over him, or vice versa, but the great thing about hovercraft is you can do that, it's fine, because it's just compressed air going over you.

Eventually they all got the hang of it and they were absolutely fantastic, as accurate as they come. Then we returned to the backlot at Pinewood to shoot Bond arriving at the base in a helicopter. The art department had built this huge set of the villain's headquarters and I said, 'Look, you've got this great big set, so we might as well blow it up. As he goes, Bond shouldn't leave it standing.' So we shot a lot of mayhem there.

That pre-credits sequence was a big number, but nothing quite matched the ice car chase. In the script the main baddie Gustav Graves, played by Toby Stephens, has this palace made of ice built in the middle of a frozen lake. So we had people searching the world for frozen lakes. Originally there was going to be an ice yacht race in the film that we were going to shoot in North America, up by the Great

Lakes. There's an area there where it gets really cold, but the Rocky Mountains act as a barrier so you get a relatively small snowfall. That's why ice yacht racing is really big over there, and some of these yachts reach 90 mph. I flew to the Great Lakes via New York to meet the guy who builds these yachts, to get the moulds and the plans from him. This was just after 9/11, so while I was in New York I visited Ground Zero. It wasn't for morbid reasons, you just had to go and see this thing that was a turning point for the world. It was still smouldering. You could smell it, and there was dust everywhere. If anybody stood still long enough they'd get covered in a veneer of ash. And all these pictures of lost loved ones were still pinned on all the fences and wires. It's wrong to say it was a tourist attraction, but it was like a pilgrimage.

In the end we ditched the ice yacht chase and turned the sequence into two cars battling it out on the frozen lake. The producers said to me, 'What do we need if we do an ice chase with cars?' I said, 'They've got to be four-wheel drive, otherwise they'll be too slow and spin everywhere, even with studs on the tyres.' I'd done ice racing in Canada; that's two-wheel drive and it was just a lot of power, like motorcycle speedway, they're just going round the corners in power slides, but you've got no control really. So I said, 'You've got to make them four-wheel drive.' They went, 'OK.' A week later they came back to me. 'Vic, we've just had a costing on this, it's over a million pounds just to make them four-wheel drive.' And I went, 'If you want the ice chase, we've got to have it.' They said, 'OK.' Two days later they came back. 'Are you *sure* you need it?' I went, 'Yes, if you want an ice chase of any sort, we need four-wheel drive.' And give them their due they gave Chris Corbould the go-ahead, and he set up a whole production line at Pinewood pulling all the engines out of the Aston Martins and the Jaguars and putting in short V8s and then big Ford Explorer front axles. Corbould and his team had to re-jig and design the whole thing. To get those cars all balanced and running like they did was absolutely phenomenal.

Then we had to find the right location. I planned to shoot it where we were going to do the ice yacht racing, but that was a bit drab visually. Next we went up to this frozen lake in Anchorage, Alaska and that worked much better. I was about to OK this location when somebody came back from Iceland with photographs of icebergs floating in open water. 'That's great,' I said. 'But will that freeze over?' Because Iceland is not as cold as, say, Greenland, and you do get shitty weather there. Sure enough when we did a recce it was torrential rain. It was pouring down. This glacier is the biggest in Europe, near Höfn, where the ice breaks off and falls into this lake, and then the lake seeps out into the sea. There's a man-made barrier

The ice car chase is one of my proudest achievements as an action director.

stopping the icebergs going out into the ocean, so they just float around in this massive lagoon that's a couple of kilometres across. Now all we had to do was pray for cold weather.

Three weeks before we were set to go out there, it hadn't frozen properly, not enough for cars to drive on. We needed the ice to be at least ten inches thick for safety reasons. Finally we heard it was starting to freeze over, the ice had reached nine inches. 'Yeah, let's go for it,' I said. Just before leaving I attended that year's BAFTA film awards. I was collecting the Michael Balcon Award for Outstanding British Contribution to Cinema. It was a fantastic, memorable night for me, and such a great honour. I got home at three in the morning and then at five a car arrived to take me to Luton airport where I caught a 7.50 chartered jet to Reykjavik. As I arrived at the check-in all the gang were there, cheering and clapping. We caught another flight down to Höfn and the next morning I visited the lake, which was bathed in glorious sunshine, like a Mediterranean summer's day. We also had ten inches of ice; it was perfect. But my driver said to me, 'Don't get excited, this is just one day, the sunshine will be gone tomorrow.'

Safety was our prime concern. We had these ice expert guys looking after us and they were brilliant. Every morning after I picked where we were going to shoot that day, they'd go out with their drills and cut down to check the depth of the ice before giving us the all clear. Everybody had to be clocked onto the lake and clocked off, it was very strict. You couldn't have more than five people standing together and every vehicle had to be at least 30 feet apart. And we all had special survival suits on underneath our clothes, which gave you probably another minute of survival time in the water, because it was so cold. Although quite honestly if you

With the crew responsible for making that sequence a reality.

fell in, you'd be dead. It was very scary working on the ice because it was like a trampoline, you could feel it bouncing as the cars went along.

We were also safety conscious about the cars. We thought about having airbags that would keep them afloat should the ice break, but they became unworkable because something big enough to float the car was too big to get inside. George Cottle was doubling the Korean baddie Zao in an open-top Jaguar, so he was OK, he could just leap out of the car if there was trouble. It was Ray De-Haan in the Aston who was in more danger, so he always kept his window open for emergency exits. We also made a conscious decision not to use seat belts; that at least would give the drivers a few more seconds to get out of the car in case of an accident. After all, we were in the middle of nowhere, you weren't going to hit another car; the only thing to hit in the whole area was an iceberg. So, no seat belts.

As we were prepping the sequence I thought, what are we going to do that's exciting on a big open lake, where do you get your drama from? In the end I had the two cars fitted out with much the same type of equipment and had both opponents pretty equally matched, so they had to outwit each other. It was like two fencers duelling: if one makes the slightest mistake, the other will go in for the kill. I wanted to make it big and lavish, using wide shots, moving shots, to show the vistas and the ice, because it was the most incredible place to see a car chase taking place. The end result looked like a ballet on ice with cars, and it is a sequence I am extremely proud of. And we had brilliant weather for 13 straight days. Every morning my driver would say, 'I've never seen this, I'm 60 years old and never ever in my living memory has it been like this for more than four days. I don't know who you've been paying off.' We were so lucky. One day we did shut down early because the ice suddenly started melting, and we found we were standing in three inches of water. The safety people called us off, but then it froze up again overnight and we were OK.

After finishing the car chase I took a small crew up the glacier to shoot the scenes where Bond escapes from the ice palace in a dragster, which was an idea developed from the dumped ice yacht sequence. So Bond races in this thing across the lake, being chased by a giant laser blast slicing through the ice and ends up hanging over the precipice of a glacier – cue one of the worst sequences in Bond history, when he paraglides on a giant wave. That was absolute garbage, appalling CGI nonsense. I think if you lose the trust of the audience, then you're screwed. I'm a great believer in CGI, I think there's a place for it in the stunt business, but used correctly. Everybody keeps saying to me, 'Why did you do that bit with the wave?' And I say, 'It was nothing to do with me! It was the director's choice.'

To get onto this glacier we had to fly by helicopter through cloud because it was so high. We were shooting up there for four days, and when I got back to base camp to check that all the equipment from the car chase was packed up, you couldn't walk out on the lake. The day I left the temperature rose and the ice started melting, then the clouds came over and it pissed with rain. We were so lucky. 13 days of brilliant sunshine and the day we moved out it got shitty. But it's true to say that for my whole career I've been exceptionally lucky with the weather when I have been shooting.

Before heading home, I insisted that the whole crew had a night stopover in Reykjavik. I'd heard it was the party capital of the world, and my crew is known to like the odd party. Barbara and Michael, being the sweethearts they are, said OK; they knew what was going on. While I was in Höfn, Sharon Mansfield, my script supervisor, and I edited the footage we had in the evenings, put music on it and titles like 'Thanks to the crew', and converted it to NTSC, which is a system that would play on the plane. The next morning as we took off on our chartered plane and the champagne corks popped, I cued the stewardesses, a bunch of screens dropped down and the whole crew saw the complete car chase. A massive cheer went up. They loved it.

Back at Pinewood, they'd built this huge ice palace set, but were only going to use it for a two-day shoot of a party. So I said, 'Guys, let us wreck it, it'll give us a good ending to the car chase.' So that's how we came up with the idea that Bond and Zao would race off the ice lake and roar into the building, and we'd have an indoor car chase. The only bit of the outdoor chase that wasn't filmed in Iceland was when Bond's Aston Martin flips over to evade a missile, because we couldn't have a two-ton car landing on its roof on ten inches of ice, it would have been far too dangerous. So I went back to Rissington airbase, remembering it from *The Avengers*, and Peter Lamont and his art department constructed a series of iceberg cut outs, some one-dimensional, others three-dimensional, ranging in size from five foot to 30 foot high. We sprayed the ground blue and white, and then firemen covered it all with water, and you couldn't tell the difference from the real thing. The beauty of Rissington is that there is nothing on the horizon, you can see to infinity; exactly what we needed so that you could see nothing past the icebergs we put on our horizon.

I'm so proud of that sequence. I think it was pretty wacky and different and unusual. Of all the stuff I've done over the years that was the best car chase. I had a fantastic crew on it; everybody was the best you could ever have. And George Cottle and Ray De-Haan were incredible with their driving, so accurate. We only had one mishap. In Iceland, Ray just over-cooked a four-wheel slide on one take, and hit an iceberg that spun him round and whammed him into another iceberg that just totalled the Aston Martin. I said, 'Don't worry Ray, it was a bigger disaster when the *Titanic* hit it.' His eyes were going round like pinball machines. So I gave him a couple of days off. There was hardly a scratch on the iceberg, but the Aston was absolutely mangled. (Just as well we had more than one of them!) It really was one of the best shoots I've ever done. Michael G. Wilson came out with his son for a rare visit and they really enjoyed it.

For the other big duel in the film, this time using rapiers in the hands of Bond and Gustav Graves, I turned to the ultimate sword master, Bob Anderson. When I started in the business, Peter Diamond was the top swordsman, and Bob Anderson was his right hand man. Then Bob left and went to Canada to coach their Olympic team. He really was a world-class swordsman. While we were doing *Entrapment* we went to a screening of *Zorro* because Catherine Zeta-Jones was in it, and I was so impressed with the sword fencing. So when this sequence came up in the Bond film I said, 'We've *got* to get Bob Anderson for this.' Although he was in his 80s he still had great vision and so much originality. Bob came in and rehearsed and rehearsed with the actors and got some great fencing doubles in, and I think he came up with a memorable sequence. He choreographed it all; I can't take any credit. But I take credit for getting Bob Anderson on the film. And that's what stunt

Meeting the Queen at the Royal premiere of Die Another Day.

co-ordinating is about, it's getting the right people in, and giving them the right equipment, time and space to do their job.

Whenever a Bond opens the premiere is always a lavish affair, but for *Die Another Day* the producers really pushed the boat out, because it was celebrating 40 years of the franchise. This time the premiere was held at the Royal Albert Hall in London, which had never before been used as a cinema. They kitted it all out at an unbelievable cost. It was also a Royal premiere and I was introduced to Her Majesty the Queen, which was a very proud moment. I've got that photograph on my study wall. I think there must have been 2,000 people invited, and afterwards there was a marvellous party. It was a fantastic night. Truly nobody does it better than Bond.

MICHAEL G. WILSON and BARBARA BROCCOLI

Vic Armstrong is one of the most exceptional personalities working in the film industry today. He has worked with Eon Productions on many of our films from *Chitty Chitty Bang Bang* through to *Die Another Day* and has been responsible for many spectacular action sequences in the James Bond films.

For decades Vic has been in demand by movie-makers as one of cinema's top stuntmen, stunt designer and arranger and, most recently, as second unit director on many action movies. He is renowned for having an excellent relationship with actors, as well as contributing remarkable story-telling skills to any scene.

Vic's first appearance in a James Bond film was as one of the 'Ninja' stuntmen in *You Only Live Twice*, but we most value his

contribution to our films in the pre-title sequences for *Tomorrow Never Dies* and the stunning River Thames boat chase in *The World Is Not Enough*, as well as the visually superb action sequence of the car chase on ice, filmed under difficult conditions in Iceland for *Die Another Day*. He has helped to push the boundaries of action filmmaking and we were thrilled when he received BAFTA's 'Michael Balcon Award for Outstanding British Contribution to Cinema' in 2002 – the 40th anniversary of the James Bond films.

The only sad note for me was that *Die Another Die* turned out to be Pierce's swan song as James Bond. I never thought for a second that it would be his last. I always thought he had another two left in him. He'd really grown into the role. I was very disappointed that Pierce wasn't allowed to stay on, because I liked him both as an actor and as a man, and we got on so well. He really was a brilliant Bond.

PIERCE BROSNAN

Vic was a great guy to work with on the Bond films and a legendary stuntman. He's somebody who when he walks onto the set fills you with the greatest of confidence. There's a fantastic sense of humour about him, too, he knows how to have a great time and do hard, good work. But most of all, he knows what makes a great action sequence, and where to put the camera so you get bigger bangs for your bucks. Vic has all those attributes. He's the man.

CRUISE MISSILE

For a while I'd been hearing rumours about the trauma of shooting this movie in Prague called *The League of Extraordinary Gentlemen*, based on a comic strip about Victorian literary heroes battling evil forces. A lot of my mates were working on it, and I heard all these horror stories that they were going over schedule and over budget, not getting things done, it was awful. Worse, I was told the relationship between the director Steve Norrington, who'd directed the first *Blade* movie, and the star Sean Connery was far from good. They'd clashed terribly, and I'd heard that Connery was personally asking for me.

Before agreeing to come over, Terry Needham, an old mate of mine, said, 'Vic, when you come out and do the action unit on this movie, you may end up doing the first unit, because Norrington may resign when he hears you're coming.' Norrington had also allegedly been clashing with the producers.

So I turned up and they showed me round and then they said, 'Well, you'd better go and meet Norrington.' And actually he was as quiet as a lamb and very polite with me; I had no problems. He explained what he needed doing, then the producers told me what they wanted doing, and how long I had to do it. I shot for several weeks out there and did a lot of good stuff: the tank crashing through the Bank of England, the car chase through Venice, the Mr Hyde creature throwing doors around, and sword fights with Dorian Gray and Mina the vampire girl. Plus I worked a lot with the actors, because Norrington would do half a sequence and then go off and do something else, so I'd have to finish it. It was bloody cold as well. We never had studios, we worked in old buildings and old warehouses, and they were actually colder inside than it was outside. It was dreadful. But God, that was a calamitous production.

After that it was over to Vancouver, to work on the opening sequence of *Blade: Trinity*, a big motorbike chase. It was a fun shoot and I met David Goyer, a really

With Scarlett Johansson, when she was up for a role in Mission: Impossible III.

nice fella; he'd written the original *Blade* movie and also *Batman Begins*, but this was his first film as director. After I left I heard that things turned a bit ugly, there was a personality clash between Wesley Snipes and David and the two were constantly at loggerheads. I was asked to go back and act as a sort of go-between, but I didn't fancy that very much. I was pleased to be out of it.

While I was still in Vancouver I got a call from an old mate called Kevin De La Noy, who was a producer on *Mission: Impossible III.* He wanted me to meet the director Joe Carnahan and Paula Wagner, Tom Cruise's partner in his film company. I was really excited about joining the *Mission: Impossible* team and started prepping the movie and working through the script after I finished *Blade.* Frank Darabont was also brought in as a writer, and we all contributed ideas.

It was decided to base the production in Berlin, and use a place called Krampnitz as the location for one of the action sequences, a big helicopter attack involving explosions and blowing buildings over. Krampnitz was an old military camp that the Russians abandoned when the Berlin wall came down; right on the eastern border past Checkpoint Charlie. Since then it had deteriorated and was just a

Scarlett performing some stunt tests. She was great. No fear at all.

bunch of ruins really. Another set piece involved Cruise and Scarlett Johansson leaping off a building. Scarlett was lovely, a gutsy, fun person. I wanted to adopt her, but her mother wouldn't let me. She's very similar to Cameron Diaz in that the whole place lights up when she walks into the room.

Another location we were going to use was Ghana. Roy Alon was going to be my point man and run things there, including training a whole bunch of local people to play mercenary soldiers who shoot at Cruise as he's being chased across rooftops. We both flew out to Ghana one weekend and Roy turned up with his safari suit on. He was so excited about doing the movie. But when I arrived back in London I heard it was all over, the studio had pulled the plug. What the politics of it all were I still don't know. Literally between getting off the plane and getting in the car to go home, the whole thing was canned. I had to ring Roy and tell him, 'You know all that stuff we're doing in Ghana, it's history.' He was bitterly disappointed, as everybody was. Millions went down the toilet because of it.

So I went back home and Wendy and the kids needed a holiday so I thought, let's all go to LA and have a break. We'd only been there two days when I got a call from Steven Spielberg's office about my coming to work on *War of the Worlds.* It's funny how fate deals its hands: that was a film I had been desperate to be involved

My philosophy on life (well, maybe), on location for War of the Worlds.

with because it sounded like an epic, and I always like to be involved in big movies that are successful. Plus it was working with Steven Spielberg again, and I thought I had a great relationship with him. Then I'd heard Simon Crane had got the gig and I was really pissed off. But negotiations fell through with Simon and luckily I was in the States, and literally within days I was on location back east in New York. Man, we hit the ground running on that film, it was great.

I hadn't worked with Steven for almost 20 years, so even though it was my fifth film with him, there was an element of my being the new boy in his crew, of checking me out to see if I could still hack it. And in the end I shot a good deal of stuff, including parts of the scene where Tom Cruise's daughter in the film, Dakota Fanning, runs down to a river and sees hundreds of bodies. She needs a pee, runs through some bushes and comes out by this river. A bunch of dead bodies float by and she runs back to Dad. Steven knew exactly what he wanted for that scene, it had to be the most beautiful day and the water had to be sparkling. 'I must have sparkling water,' he said. 'I must have sparkling water.' The weather was shitty for most of the shoot, but amazingly the day we shot that scene we got brilliant sunshine from dawn to dusk. My luck with weather came through again.

We also found a place with bull rushes, so we had all this flock blowing in the air. It worked so well.

My unit shot the bodies, and we had about 20 dummies made up at great expense, but they never looked right to me. They'd float too deep in the water so you couldn't see them, and they never looked like humans, strangely enough. I'd already decided to use about ten stunt guys and throw them in the river to simulate the dead. My son Scott was one of them. 'But nobody can go in the water, it's too cold!' people said. I said, 'Of course they can go in the water. I've swum Glacier Bay in Alaska, in the ice. It's cold, but if you've got a drysuit on you're OK for a while.' We set up a heated tent that they could go into to keep hypothermia away after coming out of the water, and these guys were much better than the dummies because you could actually control them, you could get them to float close to the camera or float them away. So we had 20 dummies and 10 real bodies, and we filmed the scene five or six times and then multiplied them. We did lose a couple of dummies, so I would think some poor home owner down the river got the shock of their lives seeing a dead body turn up at the end of their garden. That scene was a big moment in the film, much discussed by critics who compared it to the horrific images we saw on TV from the Rwanda war, and we shot it in just one day.

Working with Spielberg again was illuminating because after nearly two decades people change. I don't think he enjoys life as much as he did in the early '80s. Maybe it's because there's more pressure on him now due to his phenomenal success. I remember that we had more laughs and jokes in the old days than we did this time around. There's just so much pressure on him and so much attention, and in the old days there wasn't. That's always going to affect someone. But he was great on *War of the Worlds*, absolutely focused. He's got such an eye; he's a genius filmmaker. And he really inspired me to push on in the stuff I've been directing, to say there are no boundaries in film.

Spielberg had a brilliant crew working with him on *War of the Worlds*. Janusz Kaminski was his cameraman. He is (and I say this with great affection and my tongue in my cheek) completely mad, but one of the best cameramen I've ever seen in my life. At first I thought he was certifiable, and a really rude and horrible man, but after about three weeks I realised, wow, this guy is amazing, and now we're the greatest of mates. You only think he's nuts because he's so good at his job. He's so talented that he can light a set in minutes and then he gets bored and so starts fiddling around and doing crazy things. He's a real extrovert. I used to meet him at dailies at five o'clock in the morning when I was shooting, but he was so conscientious and did that every day for the entire shoot. We'd discuss things

The Governor visits the set, and two modern movie icons meet.

and he was a great help and supporter.

On a film Steven takes no prisoners and so *War of the Worlds* was tough to work on, but I thought the end product was excellent. That opening sequence in New Jersey, my God that was gruelling; it was cold and icy, it rained, and it was the breaking-in period for everybody. It was also probably the biggest sequence on the film, when the alien machine bursts out of the ground and everybody's running and getting blown through shop windows. We split that up and did some back at Universal Studios in LA months later, close-ups of cars crashing through shop fronts, things like that. It was a heck of a sequence to co-ordinate.

There was also the scene of the car ferry flipping over. That boat was completely CGI but the passengers falling off into the water were all 100% real, because I didn't want to start replicating people. So I had ramps built and platforms that people could jump off in all different positions and falls, hitting the water in different areas. Then the effects crew took all those individual people and made them the passengers on the CGI boat, so everyone is doing something real and something different. The visual effects guys did a great job on that. We also had huge jerk cables that snatched people out of the water for the shots with the mechanical arms of the alien tripods. They snatch at survivors in the water and pull them up; again those people were real. In fact the first one grabbed out of the

With my son Scott and daughter Nina on the War of the Worlds *set in Bayonne, New Jersey.*

water was my son Scott; he flew about 30 feet into the air.

Actually, most of the Armstrong family worked on *War of the Worlds*: Wendy, Bruce, Scott and Nina. In the scene where the American forces fight the aliens in open ground, Scott was behind the wheel of a Humvee that was on fire, and had to race over a hill towards Tom Cruise. The two became quite good mates, and Scott and I worked with Tom on his next project, the resurrected *Mission: Impossible III.*

I'd only just finished *War of the Worlds* when Paula Wagner called to tell me that *Mission: Impossible* was back on again, this time with a new script, a new cast and a new director in J.J. Abrams, the co-creator of hit TV series *Lost.* This being his first feature film, Abrams had never had a second unit before and wanted to direct everything himself, as you do when you're starting off, so I could see that potentially being a problem. But he was pretty positive about what he wanted, so we worked out the style of the movie and started prepping it and breaking it down.

Knowing Tom Cruise as I did so soon after working with him, watching him handle stunts and action, I came up with a radical approach to *Mission: Impossible III*, and that was to design every single stunt for Tom Cruise to do himself – not his stunt double, but Tom Cruise. And that's what we did, for the whole movie, and this was a blockbuster packed with action. Really there's no difference between rigging a stunt for a stuntman to do and rigging it for a huge superstar like Tom

Cruise, provided the actor has the ability: the safety aspect is paramount for both individuals. Although you do design stunts differently when it's going to be the actor, as you want every camera angle to look at the actor's face to prove to the audience he's really doing it, while normally with a stuntman you're trying to cheat and hide his face. It was quite an interesting proposition, to set up all the stunts for Cruise to perform.

I knew Tom was great with heights, so we had him jump off an 80 foot building on a decelerator. That took balls, because nothing kicks in for 60 feet; you're basically freefalling until the last few feet, when it slows down and eventually stops. In the studio he performed 100-foot swings across a giant green screen and then released himself and dropped onto an airbag. There's also a scene where Ethan Hunt, Cruise's character, parachutes off a skyscraper and gets hooked up on a lamp post in the street below, hanging upside down over a busy road. A big horn blasts and he turns round to come face-to-face with a massive articulated lorry coming straight at him with its lights blazing. He releases himself and drops onto the road as the lorry goes into a jackknife and skids over the top of him. And we had Tom Cruise doing that, a massive semi-truck and trailer going over the top of him. I laid under it for some of the tests, and so can appreciate the sheer nerve required.

The problem today is that we're so used to seeing spectacular stunts accomplished using CGI that on *Mission: Impossible III* people didn't realize the sheer extent of what Tom did, because they assumed it was digital. But we can put our hands on our hearts and say, he did it. Unfortunately in the movie you can't actually see that it's Tom under that truck, it could be a double, but he did it. I watched him do it!

Another stunt that took great guts was shot at the Vatican in Rome. Tom runs at this wall, and fires a hook onto the top of it that's got a wire attached to his chest, with an electric pulley that enables him to run horizontally upwards. With Tom safely on top we changed locations to Caserta just outside Rome, where we built our own 75-foot high wall. Lying on his back at the top, Tom then just rolls off and does a freefall, face first, with a wire now hooked to his back, stopping an inch from the ground. It was my little homage to the first film.

That was actually the first stunt we shot. Now to have Tom Cruise dropping from 75 feet and stopping just inches from the ground, right at the beginning of the production, it was a bit, 'Uh-oh, this could be the end of my career...' In the end we did it five or six times, and in the take we nailed, that's in the film, Tom's chest just touches the ground and a little puff of dust comes up. Tom had to have the balls to hold that action all the way down and not go 'Arggh!' at the last second. Then he gets up and runs off, all in one shot. He's got some heart I can tell you. He's a big-hearted fella.

I also knew that Tom was a great driver, so I set up a sequence where he could do a bit of stunt driving. We shut down a freeway in LA and had 400 cars all driving at 30 mph so that Tom's car could cut through them; it was hugely complicated to co-ordinate. We didn't have any rehearsal time with Tom because he was shooting with the main unit right up until I needed to shoot him, so we rehearsed with the stunt drivers and I came up with this idea of sticking duct tape on the backs of the cars (out of shot), an arrow pointing that way, an arrow pointing this way, to show the route to take through all these cars. You couldn't say to the driver, 'Turn left at the red car, then right at the white one,' because there were loads of red cars and loads of white ones. When Tom arrived we ran him through it once and he said, 'I'm OK, let's do it.' I said, 'Oh God, OK, let him loose. Roll cameras.' The insert camera car had a clean run down the inside and we just followed him. He led the way and went screaming through and it was just absolutely brilliant.

Tom really is a superb driver, and just before *M:I:III* was released I did a little promo thing with him for the children's channel Nickelodeon. His office asked me to come up with something that he could do for the kid audience that would tie in with the movie, and show that Tom was doing his own stunts. But also get across to kids that no matter what work you do, you have to prepare and be committed. 'All right, I'll have a think about it,' I said. A couple of days later Tom was about to call me to talk over what I'd got rigged for him. I'd been thinking about recreating the jump off the roof when Wendy said, 'You keep saying what a good driver Tom is, why don't you do a driving sequence?' I said, 'You're absolutely dead right, he's one of the best drivers I've ever seen.' And suddenly a little light went on in my head. Let's put Tom in a specially prepared stunt car with a little kid, we can have a competition where he picks some kid out of the audience; how lucky is that kid gonna be sitting next to Tom Cruise in a speeding getaway car.

Tom called 20 minutes later and I sat explaining this. 'We'll have you in a stunt car, you'll have a fire suit on, the whole works, and the kid will be sitting next to you. We'll have lipstick cameras all over the car so we can see you, plus cameras outside covering all the action and I'll choreograph a car chase where you'll do 180s, throw spins, 360s, and out-manoeuvre the baddies.' He listened to all this and just said, 'Fantastic!' I carried on, 'Then at the end Tom, as the *pièce de résistance*, we'll have you do a pipe ramp.' A pipe ramp is a device that we use to flip cars over onto their roof. 'Could I?' he said. 'Could I do a pipe ramp?' I said,

'Yeah, you do the stunt, why not. We're going to set it up safe for the stunt guy; we'll set it up for you.' 'Oh my God,' he said. I could hear the excitement on the other end of the phone. He was on for about half an hour and he was just buzzing.

I contacted Rick Seaman, who I'd first met on *Million Dollar Mystery* years before, and now rigs my brother Andy's cars in the States. Rick runs a stunt driving school (the one I'd sent Cameron Diaz to for *Charlie's Angels*), so he's got these cars with big motors in them, you can throw them around, you can smoke the tires, and they're all roll caged. We found a suitable location in San Pedro and I shot there for a day with doubles. Andy came in to 'play' the lead baddie driver. Then Tom arrived, and I explained that we had the pipe ramp stunt all set up. Tom immediately said, 'I want to do the pipe ramp today.' 'What? Really? OK.' We put the helmet and fireproof clothing on him and took him out there. I had the car all set up and Andy at the controls. 'Do you want to see Andy do a pipe ramp to get the idea of what's going to happen Tom?' I asked. Typically he answered, 'No, let's do it!' That morning I'd told everybody and Andy, 'Be prepared to do the pipe ramp Andy, but you won't be doing it because I know Tom – he's going to come in and say, "I can do that."' And when Tom walked on the set and said, 'Let's go,' the whole crew looked at me as if to say, you read that one right. I just knew that's how Tom would behave. So we set him up and told him to put his foot flat on the floor when he took off; because of the distance he was travelling we knew exactly what speed he was going to hit that ramp at. I had four cameras outside and three cameras in the car. And he hit it, bang, perfect, flew through the air and skidded along on the roof.

The next day Tom came down again and I talked him through the whole car chase sequence. I had five cameras in the car (along with the kid, who'd not been there for the pipe ramp), four other cameras set up around this parking lot and we had Tom sliding around doing 180s, reverse spins, bursting through a wooden warehouse door, the lot, chasing Andy and some other stunt drivers. Tom and Andy agreed they would be going at between 35 and 50 mph on the very narrow route through the warehouse. Only afterwards did Andy admit it was tough to keep up with Tom, and at times they were doing over 75 mph! Andy said he kept thinking, 'Please, please don't spin out Tom, because I don't want to be the guy who not only embarrasses his brother Vic, but also smashes into the back of the most expensive star in the world and knocks him through a wall!' We had a blast though because I knew what a hell of a driver Tom was; I had supreme confidence in him.

Tom absolutely loved doing his own stunts, totally adored it. And we got on really well. On the last day of shooting *Mission* in Shanghai he called me up. 'Vic, I

Up on the roof in Shanghai at the end of shooting on Mission: Impossible III.
L-R: J.J. Abrams, me, Nina, Tom, Wendy and Scott.

want a photo with you and the Armstrong stunt team.' Because Wendy was there, along with Scott and Nina. He also knows the rest of the family, too. I said all right, but he kept calling and calling. In the end I wrapped the action unit in Pudong and shot across Shanghai with Wendy and the kids to where the main unit was filming. We walked into a room and could hear them shooting on the roof above. And then we heard, 'Cut, and that's a wrap folks. That's the end of the movie.' Unbelievable timing. We walked out onto the roof and Tom went, 'Hey, there you are, come on over here and let's have that picture taken.' Fantastic guy.

We did some great action on *Mission: Impossible III*. I reckon it's the best of the lot. I don't think the first two *M:I* films match it for realism. That train climax in the first film with the helicopter in the channel tunnel killed me, just stupid CGI again. And the second one was just John Woo doing more John Woo stuff, which as great as John Woo is, we've all seen a dozen times before. I think we made the action on number three harder and more exciting. One example was the helicopter chase; that was incredible. Originally it was going to be shot by the first unit. That was the thing with J.J. Abrams, he was dashing from his unit to my unit, and I was just sitting around waiting to do something. Within a week or two, however, he quite sensibly could see the amount of work that had to be done, and that I wasn't an idiot and was capable of delivering good stuff.

So I went down to Palm Springs to shoot this helicopter sequence. We had two helicopters and a camera ship flying amidst these huge wind turbines, in and out, under the blades, over them, round them, through them, and at night with all the lights on. I shot for two weeks down there and it was a bit nerve wracking because of my conviction that I'm going to see the end of my days in a helicopter. You'd be sitting in the cockpit looking at the windmill blades swooping down on you, and then these helicopters tearing through the air and peeling off at the last minute, and then look behind to see another big windmill blade hurtle down. Terrifying. Anyway, once we'd done it, J.J. Abrams realized that he was never going to be able to do the whole movie himself, so loosened up and let me shoot and direct stuff, and he was one of the nicest directors I've ever worked with. He has such a huge IQ; he's a sharp man and a great guy. We had such a good time.

Probably the biggest sequence was a terrorist attack on a bridge, which was going to be shot in Chesapeake Bay. We scouted this bridge, but in the end couldn't shoot on it because it was 100 foot above water, it was three miles long and it was going to be hurricane season. It just wasn't practical to shut it down. So we built a replica bridge outside LA, which was just an earth mound tarmaced along the top, with plastic rails and a plastic superstructure put on it. My son Scott did one of the best cannon turnovers I've ever seen on it. The problem was that this 'bridge' was 22 foot wide and supposedly 100 foot in the air, so he had to keep this Range Rover from smashing through the rails. In the scene, the car is hit by a rocket from an airplane, you see a big fireball go off as it slides sideways and then flips over. Scott had two buttons to hit; the explosive one to simulate the rocket, and then the one to flip the car, while at the same time keeping the vehicle within this 22-foot wide bridge.

He carried out a test, as we do, in a parking lot, and did about four somersaults that would have sent him crashing off the side of the bridge. So he calculated just how far he could let it slide before he fired his cannon, and you're talking millimetres. We had seven cameras on this one shot, plus a helicopter camera, and he came down and fired it absolutely on the money because it went and spun and then spiralled on its arse before flipping over. I sent the videotape to Tom, he was on the main unit set, and I could hear the shrieks from where I was, it looked so fantastic. Everybody rushed over to have their photographs taken with Scott next to this wrecked Range Rover. Hell of a stunt.

Tom did an amazing stunt on that bridge sequence, a violent snatch back. Amidst all the gunfire he's in this car trying to retrieve his gun when there's a

Tom Cruise, about to be blown sideways on Mission: Impossible III.

rocket fired towards him. Tom crawls out just in time and tries to run clear as the rocket slams into the car and there's a huge explosion that blows him sideways through the air, smacking him hard into another parked vehicle. Everybody thought that must be digital, but no, he actually did it. In fact we had to shoot it five times to get it right. The way he hit the side of that car was like, wham, and every one of the stuntmen watching went, 'Wow, that's the sort of shot I'd like on my show reel.' The marketing people obviously liked it too: they ended up using it as the final shot of the trailer.

I also worked with Philip Seymour Hoffman on that sequence and he's a bit of a fiery character. It always makes a difference when as a second unit director you get an actor on the set, instead of the doubles. Shooting is usually much more difficult because they're saying things like, 'Why would I fall that way?' And I'd say, 'You've just been shot, you're going to hit the ground.' They say, 'Yes, but I'd probably fall over on my left arm instead of my right arm...' You get into all kinds of these ridiculous conversations and end up saying, 'Well thank you for your opinion. Now please do what I just told you – please!!' Sometimes you might listen to their ideas of course, but there are all sorts of extra pressures when it comes to stars, you've got hair and make up, and people start tweaking their costume, all sorts of nonsensical things come in that slow you down. It's not always more productive having the star on the set, but it's worth it in the long run because it's what makes the sequence real.

In this one shot with Philip Seymour Hoffman I had a big Huey helicopter hovering near him, I had my Steadicam, Tom's photo double was there, and Philip had to run away from the vehicle he's just been broken free from and step up onto the skid of the helicopter, but I wouldn't let him get in because the helicopter was just hovering and it was too dangerous. I did a couple of takes and said, 'It's great Philip, but as you're approaching the helicopter could you just look over your shoulder, because when the first unit get here they're going to want a shot of you from Tom's point of view. So if you could turn so we can see your face, you'll be eyeball to eyeball with Tom.' And Philip turned to me and said, 'No.' I went, 'Oh.' He said, 'No, I wouldn't look round then. I wouldn't look round for you and I wouldn't look round for J.J. if he was here. I just wouldn't look round at that moment.' So I said, 'OK. It's a wrap guys.'

I didn't say anything else to him, and just walked away. 'Knock it on the head guys, let's go home.' Because it was bloody hot, really uncomfortable, and I didn't want to be out there if he didn't want to be out there. I'm only there to shoot him and make him look great in an action sequence in the movie. As I was walking off the bridge Philip came running up behind me, grabbed hold of my arm and spun me round yelling, 'Don't walk away from me.' I said, 'I'll walk away from whomever I like, and don't you dare talk to me like that.' Now we were face to face. Everybody on the crew went quiet and started looking at their shoes. He said, 'We were discussing the scene.' I said, 'No, we've discussed it, you're not going to look around, you've made that very clear. I've already got a shot with you not looking around, so we're getting out of here. I don't want to be out in this heat all day long.' He said, 'Well, let's discuss it.' I said, 'We've just discussed it over there. You told me your answer.' He said, 'Well I suppose I could look around like this as I get onto the helicopter…' You could see the olive branch coming out. I said, 'Yep, that would be good. That would be lovely. Let's do that then.' We set the cameras up, he looked over and that's the shot in the movie.

Afterwards Philip came over to thank me and was very friendly, so all credit to him, to have the balls to be able to do that. He could have just gone home. And I've got to say he was a total gentleman from that day onwards. It was a bit like when you

With my pal Arnie at the World Stunt Awards. He's such a lovely guy, no pretensions at all.

have a fight at school with somebody and you then become great mates. Whether he was testing me out or what, I don't know. But he was fantastic from then on. After the World Stunt Awards when I got my Taurus Award he said, 'Hey Vic, I saw you on the award show, that was fantastic. There looked to be a lot of love out there with you and all your gang and Arnold, and everybody. Congratulations.' And I thought that took a big heart after we'd had that big old fight. I was also the first to congratulate him when he won his Oscar for *Capote*. He is a brilliant actor.

The climactic fight between Philip and Tom Cruise that we shot turned out really well. Again I designed this fight to be done for real with Tom, always figuring I'd use a double for Philip, but because Tom was doing it, Philip wanted to get in there. We had them in this Chinese pharmacy place with glass partitions, and they were knocking seven sacks of shit out of each other, crashing through a glass door, smashing into a table and rolling onto the floor. We had a padded floor and a breakaway top, but it was toffee glass and that can still hurt. After the take Philip jumped to his feet, his eyes wide open. 'Did I actually do that? I've never done anything like that before! Wow. How was it, was that OK?' And I said, 'That was fantastic.' So everything you see in that fight was Philip and Tom going at it hell for leather. And Philip was brilliant. He sweated bullets and really went up in my estimation.

ROY

In recent years we've lost so many great stuntmen, including Peter Diamond, Alf Joint and Marc Boyle. But when Roy Alon died in 2006 it was a big shock. He was only in his mid-60s. He started with me way back on *A Bridge Too Far*, when my brother told me about this mad man from up north who fell out of a car, landed on his head, got up and said, 'Do you want me to do it again, chuck?' I knew Roy a long time and we'd worked together on so many films: *Superman*, *Green Ice*, where we made modern stunt history with the first fan descender drop, *Temple of Doom*, where he was the Thuggee that Short Round walks on to get in the mine car, and the Bonds. He was one of the new breed of stuntmen that came after me that really went out and did major stunts, not just talked about them.

He was a practical joker too, and we used to love hanging around together. In the '90s Roy was stunt co-ordinator on the TV cop series *A Touch of Frost* starring David Jason, and used to call me and say, 'Vic, I've got a little driving job, do you want to come up?' Although I'd retired from doing physical stunts I was always happy to come back just for Roy. Once I went up and drove an eight-wheel gravel truck, with Roy in a car doubling David Jason. We came round a bend and skidded head on and literally stopped just six inches apart. It was great. For another shot I had to drive the truck and stop right in front of the camera. As I was skidding to a stop, I saw one leg of the cameraman Jamie Harcourt move away from the tripod, getting ready to run. But give him his due, he held it right to the end. I stopped maybe five feet from the lens, but it's pretty ominous seeing a great big eight-wheeler charge at you, especially when you are looking through a long lens that foreshortens everything.

Another show Roy worked on was *Coronation Street*, one of the longest running soaps on British TV. And one of the big regrets of my career is that I never got to appear on the show. Roy always jokingly said, 'Your career's not complete Vic until you've done *Coronation Street*. But don't worry, I'm going to get you on it.'

Roy, in the white turban, working on Never Say Never Again.

That was his main aim. He called me once about a job on the soap but I couldn't do it, I was working on *Mission: Impossible III.* I was absolutely choked. I actually thought about coming home from *Mission: Impossible* just for the day to do it, and then fly back again. But I couldn't get the time off. So I never did *Coronation Street,* that was going to be it, I was going to have the T-shirt and everything. Now Roy has died I guess it will never happen.

Roy died of a massive heart attack. He suffered a minor stroke and was taken to hospital, but even lying ill in bed he kept taking the oxygen mask off to talk, and putting it back on again. Then at six o'clock in the evening his heart went. Yet he didn't smoke, and he didn't drink. He worked under stress a lot, but I don't think that's what killed him. Either way, it was the end of an era when Roy died. He was a real tough stuntman, and an innovative guy. I really miss him.

LAST MAN ALIVE

I was going to take the summer of 2006 off when I got a call from my agent David Gersh. A director called Francis Lawrence wanted me out in New York to work on *I Am Legend* with Will Smith. It was too good an opportunity to pass up, as I love New York and I'd always wanted to work with Will. So the next thing I knew I was out there. Wendy worked on the movie as well, she was the vampire creature trainer, and Nina and Scott were part of the team, too. Team Armstrong.

The film wasn't without its trials and tribulations, though. When I first talked to Francis I asked where he was going to shoot. 'We're going to do it all in New York,' he said. 'Shut the place down.' That's just a huge undertaking. Ridley Scott was originally going to do the film years before with Arnie, and his idea was to shoot a few plates in New York and then go to Bratislava, or somewhere in one of these cheap countries, and shoot it all in the digital world. So I arrived and started casting all the creatures, and met Will Smith, who is the most professional actor I've ever met in my life, just unbelievable.

My brother Andy worked with Will Smith on *I, Robot*. They were shooting one night when there was some malfunction on the camera and everyone had to hang around for an hour or two. 'I'm sorry Will,' Andy said. 'Do you mind waiting for a bit?' And Will said, 'Hey man, I don't care, this is what I'm paid to do.' I told Will this story during a meeting one day and he said, 'Absolutely right, it's what we're paid to do. When I was a little kid my Dad was a refrigerator repair man. I used to go out with him and we'd have to go down to the cellars in these old places and you'd have to move the fridge and behind them you'd find a dead rat or other even more revolting things. So listen, what movies pay me, I can do this all day long, so don't worry about me.' Wonderful man, Will, fabulous attitude; and this is one of the most successful actors of all time.

The only guy that's comparable to Will Smith is Chow Yun-Fat, an absolute legend. I did a big shoot 'em up with him on *Shanghai*, the first one he's done since *The Replacement Killers*. And he was wonderful, he'd turn up whenever his call time was, sit on the set all day long, stand-in during lighting set-ups if you needed him to, he'd go to lunch with the crew, come back when the crew came back, and stay on the set till you said wrap. 'It's amazing that you do this Yun-Fat,' I told him one day. And he went, 'It's what I'm paid to do. In Hong Kong this is what we do.' And Will Smith was that same type of character, when you called him he was there, and he stayed until you didn't need him.

I Am Legend was a big action movie. I did the car racing around New York, and that was a huge deal because we had to shut down ten blocks in Manhattan, down near Fifth Avenue, Seventh Avenue, into Central Park. We could only shoot at weekends, and then only from when the light was first up in the morning, and we had to wrap by ten am. I'd be on the set at three o'clock in the morning getting things organised. We had 350 production assistants, led by my 1st AD Chris Surgent, all with orange hats and orange flags so that we could recognise them from the crowds, and we'd send them to every doorway, every alleyway, every crossing, basically to keep everybody out of the immediate vicinity, both for picture reasons and safety. We were doing 70 mph with a Shelby Mustang and a camera car, and you didn't want a pizza delivery boy rushing across the road and becoming a hood ornament.

One night we filmed a big sequence underneath the Brooklyn Bridge. This was much later in the shoot, during winter. It was incredibly cold and we had something like a 1200-strong crowd there. In the scene they're all rushing and pushing the gates trying to get through, and this helicopter takes off and crashes. We had a big delay and the crowd were waiting around a long time. It was well below zero, two o'clock in the morning, and people were freezing and getting tired. Then Will Smith suddenly jumped up and got hold of the God mike, which is a microphone that assistant directors use, connected to loud speakers all over the set so people can hear instructions, and he started rapping, doing this amazing concert underneath the bridge. The whole crowd were clapping and singing along, it was brilliant. He lifted everybody's hearts and warmed everybody up. Even at the crew party after we wrapped, he came on and did a fantastic 15-minute set. Wendy was standing right down the front and said, 'My God, you'd pay a fortune to be front row at a Will Smith concert.'

While I was in New York, George Lucas called about Indy 4. I had a few meetings about it, but ultimately I was heartbroken when they changed their strategy and went in a different direction. It's one of my disappointments, because

L-R Stefan Zürcher, Daniel Craig, producer Bill Carraro and me in Switzerland for The Golden Compass.

I've always had a good personal and professional relationship with them, but I'm still thrilled to have done the original trilogy.

While that was going on I was asked to do *The Golden Compass*. Actually they'd already shot the movie and edited it, but realised it was a bit bland and flat, so I got this call to help inject some energy into it. I met one of the producers, Deborah Forte, who told me they needed a sequence with Daniel Craig in the North Pole, so I had to go up to northern Sweden to check out locations. I was dubious I'd ever find one up there, because if you're shooting an action sequence with the lead actor, you need a huge infrastructure to support it all and I didn't think northern Sweden would have it.

So I suggested Switzerland. I knew a place that was perfect, where we shot some of *On Her Majesty's Secret Service*, up on top of the Jungfrau mountain range at the back of the Eiger, at about 11,000 feet on this huge glacier that's dead flat, so it looks like the North Pole. I also knew great people out there like Stefan Zürcher, who was one of the stunt skiers from *Secret Service* and now runs a production company. So after scouting northern Sweden and not finding what I wanted, I went out to Switzerland and came up with a sequence for that location, and set the whole thing up there. Stefan built a base camp and everybody would arrive in the morning by helicopter and was given a number and a harness: everybody was roped on at all times. It was a truly stunning location and we shot the whole thing in five days, it was so well organised.

The sequence I'd devised had Daniel Craig trapped and shot at by these baddies, and sliding down the rock face. I'd never worked with Daniel before and he was great, very easy to work with, I loved directing him. He later said it was the most fun he'd had on the whole shoot, and it was a terrific little sequence, one of the moments in the movie where you go, wow, that's real; and you need some realism in those types of films that are just so full of CGI work. Don't get me wrong, I love CGI, it's a great instrument to use, for example on falls you can hide airbags, you can hide the rig the guys are falling into. In the old days you had to frame all that out, now you see the guys falling, the rig is simply erased, and the guys carry on falling into infinity, it's brilliant. So it's a fabulous tool, just so long as you don't use it to create your characters or your story, then it becomes a cartoon for me.

CHINA SYNDROME

eturning from Switzerland I shot all the battles and the polar bear stuff for *Golden Compass* at Shepperton Studios. Wendy was the stunt co-ordinator for the London studio shoot, and she taught Eva Green to fly on wires, which she was terrified of at first, but Wendy soon built her confidence up. My youngest daughter Georgina was a flying witch as well. Then I had to cut short my work on the film, because Rob Cohen wanted me to handle all the action on the third *Mummy* movie. So I literally finished one night on *Golden Compass* and flew straight to China to meet everyone for a recce. I have to say *The Mummy: Tomb of the Dragon Emperor* was one of the nicest working environments I've ever had in my life. Rob Cohen was fantastic, he's a great storyteller and we had a very close collaboration. I learnt an awful lot from him, from his planning and his vision. It's amazing that after all these years you can still learn stuff. He was wonderfully level-tempered. I'd heard stories about him being fiery and a tearaway, but I never saw him lose his cool once. His karma was fantastic. The most generous person I've ever worked with.

One day during lunch I was talking about various things, and told my story about how Donald Sutherland had given me my Rolex 30 years ago, and how special it was because it had 'Tiffany & Co' on the watch face. Rob suddenly took his watch off and showed it to me – it also had 'Tiffany & Co' on it! He said that in 30 years I was the first person he had ever met that had the same watch. In all that time I hadn't met anyone with the same watch either, so we became the 'brothers by watch'.

All round it was a great movie to work on. Jet Li was wonderful, very quiet, very respectful, no fuss, just gets on and does his job. And it was delightful working with Michelle Yeoh again. She's a gorgeous, lovely lady and hadn't changed at all since we made the Bond movie together. Brendan Fraser was great, too, but he's a very intense guy. He's such a slapstick comedy actor that I was surprised how

With Rob Cohen on the set of The Mummy: Tomb of the Dragon Emperor *in Montreal, Canada.*

intense he was. I didn't shoot that much with him though, just a few fights and training him up.

Again it was very much a family affair. My son Scott worked on the film doubling Luke Ford and Wendy was there, too. In fact Wendy and I did a little cameo at the end in the ballroom dancing sequence. It was quite funny because that tux I'm wearing was Brendan Fraser's. It didn't fit him any more so they gave it to me – and it fit perfectly.

I finished *Mummy 3*, had a lovely family Christmas and then Wendy and I went over to LA where I met up with Steve Harding, an old mate of mine from when he was a runner on *Billy Two Hats*. He told me he'd just had a meeting with Tom Cruise's people about *Valkyrie*, which they'd shot in Berlin under Bryan Singer's direction. I'd heard horror stories about the film. Singer can apparently sometimes be a hard taskmaster, and a lot of people I knew who worked on *Valkyrie* had a really torrid time. Anyway, I thought the film was finished but Steve said, 'Oh no. You see, Tom Cruise's character Stauffenberg, who's the guy who tried to kill Hitler with the bomb in the bunker, plays the whole film with one arm missing, three fingers on one hand blown off and a patch over his eye, but they haven't explained how he got those injuries.' So they wanted to recreate the battle of El

Tom Cruise and me, along with James Armstrong my nephew and stunt co-ordinator in Victorville.

Alamein, with Cruise part of a convoy of German tanks that gets attacked by British planes. It was my job to set the thing up.

The location was Victorville, which is halfway between Los Angeles and Las Vegas. I met Bryan Singer, who was absolutely delightful to me, despite those horror stories I'd heard. I mapped out the whole sequence, the convoy, what bombs would go off, how many we'd have, and where Tom Cruise would be for the final big explosion. We had a simulated 500-pound bomb go off in close proximity to Tom and the other actors – we didn't double them, it was really good stuff. The only stipulation was they wanted Tom in a Kübelwagen which flips over on its side at the end, and then you cut to him lying on the ground and there's blood seeping out, so that's the back-story told.

It was a great shoot that took us about a week, and we had a blast, in more ways than one. It was 112 degrees; when it's that hot you don't sweat, salt just appears on your body. We had aeroplanes flying over and explosions. It went like clockwork. Tom was great as usual, and Katie Holmes was there too; both of them stayed in their trailer overnight in the desert. I also had my nephew James Armstrong as my stunt co-ordinator, and he did a brilliant job. I didn't have my usual crew of old stuntmen, these were all young guys, including Shawn Robinson, Dar Robinson's son, the lad I'd met on the plane a few years before, who'd been a little kid when his Dad got killed on *Million Dollar Mystery*. So it was wonderful to be able to use Shawn, who's now a fully credited stuntman and a wonderful guy. It's strange, because most of the kids I used on *Valkyrie* were second-generation stuntmen, sons of old mates of mine.

While I was on *Valkyrie*, Harvey Weinstein was on the blower to me about spicing up his new movie *Shanghai* with a bit of action. I like Harvey, he's very much a throwback to the old style of producer. He's got great guts and focus,

What a thrill it was to work with the great Chow Yun-Fat.

he doesn't drink, he just lives and dreams his movies; a frustrated director, loves action, that's why he gets on so well with Tarantino. We get along because he knows I won't go over schedule, I won't waste money, and I'll give him big bangs for his bucks and put the action where it should be.

On *Shanghai*, which we shot at studios in Thailand, I took all the storyboards and re-designed the shots, and I put stars John Cusack and Gong Li into the action sequences, so now each of the action bits had a reason to be there, rather than be just action for action's sake. I did a lovely scene with Gong Li, a really bloodthirsty shoot 'em up outside a hotel, very Brian de Palma-esque. Harvey was over the moon with it. And there was a great assassination sequence with Chow Yun-Fat in a casino. I also rewrote the Japanese invasion of Shanghai, which I'd been through once before on *Empire of the Sun*, and I came up with what I think is a very exciting and visual sequence.

SUPERHEROES

Back home I didn't have much time to put my feet up before director Phillip Noyce called. He was making a movie called *Salt*, about a CIA agent accused of being a Russian spy. Originally it was going to star Tom Cruise, but he'd pulled out and Angelina Jolie was taking over. Funnily enough, they didn't have to change the script too much.

I met Angelina in Los Angeles and we chatted about the film, and what style of fighting we were going to use for the action sequences. I thought we'd do Muay Thai, which is a Thai martial art/boxing type of thing where you use your knees, your head, elbows, just about everything – it's a very violent form of fighting which I love. There are a couple of wonderful films that feature it, *Ong-Bak* and *Ong-Bak 2* starring Tony Jaa, and the fights and action are stunning. What I love most about them is they're Thai-made films, and so don't have the technology that we have, they don't have the CG effects, so what you see is very much what people can physically do. It's wonderful and much more realistic, which is why they've been such a success. So I brought in a stunt team that I work with all the time in Thailand, led by my friend Mr Seng, and we started working out the fights and training Angelina in the Muay Thai style; she was well into it, she was loving it.

We shot in Washington D.C. and New York, and one of the biggest scenes I did was in a very tall apartment block where Angelina comes out onto a window ledge and crawls around the building. Angelina's wonderful I have to say, she's got nerves of steel, is not fazed by height at all and very trusting in everything you ask her to do.

ANGELINA JOLIE

When Vic Armstrong says, 'Go out that window,' and you're 30 floors up, you think, 'Yes sir.' And you step out on the ledge. When you've made it back and completed a good stunt, he smiles at you

and you feel on top of the world. So I thank Vic for all he's done for film, stunts, and actors and for sending me out the window! Be warned, whenever Vic says 'I've got an idea,' something dangerous is about to happen. That's why we love him.

While we were shooting *Salt* there was massive press attention surrounding Angelina, but she knows what she's doing, she's nobody's fool, and is a very sweet girl and a really hard worker. Brad Pitt was also around, the first time I'd met him; they're actually a very nice and normal family, and Angelina's a dedicated mother.

About halfway through the shoot Angelina wanted Simon Crane to come on the movie as well, to give her any advice she felt she might want; they've been buddies ever since working together on the first *Tomb Raider*. I didn't think it would be right for both of us to work on the movie at once so I decided to leave. I loved working with Angie though – she will forever be my #1 action actress and human being, and we keep in touch to this day.

Simon had been due to come to England to do some reshoots on *The Wolfman*, so instead I took over on that while he finished the last half of *Salt*. I watched the rough cut of *Wolfman* several times and thought it needed a lot of work doing to it. Then I had meetings with the director and the studio and they told me what they wanted reshooting. It was primarily the climactic fight, though I did lots of other bits and pieces, like the Wolfman running all over London, and through the forest at night. For the big fight they'd shot the werewolves standing up like humans, and they just looked like men in furry suits, it just didn't work. So we had them quadrupeding, as we say, where they run along on all fours. Because you can't run at speed in that configuration, we used wires to assist: with wires taking off 35% of your weight, you can cover the width of a room in one bound. So we did a really good fight, although in all honesty I don't think the film was ever salvageable.

After *The Wolfman* I was offered *Knight and Day*, starring my old friend Tom Cruise. The script was full of action and humour and really appeared to have everything going for it. Unfortunately 20th Century Fox did not want to do my standard deal, and sadly I had to decline the offer. Tom Cruise did call me at home to ask why I would not be doing the show, and when I told him it was Fox's dealings he appeared to understand. Funnily enough when we were rehearsing the film I ended up doing instead, *The Green Hornet*, Tom's co-star Cameron Diaz, who of course is an old friend of my brother Andy's and mine from *Charlie's Angels* days, was rehearsing in the same location for *Knight and Day*. She came rushing across

With Scott and brother Andy shooting an exhilarating car chase for The Green Hornet.

to say hi, so we put her in one of our stunt cars and she amazed and mesmerised the guys with her fantastic driving skills. On *Charlie's Angels* our nickname for Cameron was Lead Boot, and she did not disappoint us. She even said to Andy, 'When I get a quiet time, I want to come and work for you guys as a stunt girl.'

The Green Hornet was a big-screen version of the classic '60s TV show, and I had a wonderful time doing it. I came away very impressed by the star Seth Rogen, a very intelligent man. The director was Michel Gondry, who had no idea of physical action; I think the most violent thing he's ever done is sharpen a pencil. He's very artistic, and very nice on a personal level, so I got to have a lot of input into the action stuff.

What I always do when I start a movie is talk to the producer, the director and the stars, and then I work out what we want in the action sequences. On *Green Hornet* the big set piece for me was a car chase at night around the streets of LA. When you conceive and then put together a sequence like this it all sounds great, but people don't take into account that when you're doing a car chase you have speed involved, so therefore you're covering a lot of distance, and to see it at night you have to light it all, which is immensely expensive. You also have to shut down roads, which you usually can't start using until 12 o'clock at night, and then you

My brother Andy's come a long way from The Zoo Gang. *I'm incredibly proud of him.*

have to be off by 5 am when the morning rush starts. I avoided all this by deciding to shoot the whole freeway chase sequence (apart from a few shots using the on-ramp and off-ramp of a real freeway) on the roof of an enormous abandoned mall in Hawthorne, just south of LAX airport. We made the rooftop into a freeway with all the signs and road dividers, and it worked like a dream.

I've always tried to look at an action sequence from the audience's point of view, and imagine what they're going to experience when they're sitting in the cinema watching it. And sometimes it's more fun imagining and working out sequences than actually doing them. Often it's an anti-climax when you come round to shooting. I love the preparation of movies more than anything.

So I sat down and planned this car chase, and Andy is fantastic when it comes to this kind of thing, because he's got great ideas and we bounce concepts off each other. We plotted a whole bunch of car crashes, with each crash different than the last, because we like to be original. I think I used about 30 drivers every night for three or four weeks, and did a major crash every single night. The first smash-up was Andy, he wanted to do a crash, so I had him do a cannon roll where he comes down the road, spins the car and it flips and rolls about four times. I was a bundle of nerves watching him doing it. Then the next night was my son Scott smashing through the front of a bus in a flaming pick-up truck. That was an amazing stunt. Scott is driving the lead baddie's pick-up when it gets shot, bursts into flames, goes hurtling down the road, hits a bus head-on and goes out through the roof and spins into the street on fire. It was a huge impact; he doing something like 60 mph, so inwardly I was really nervous again. And then the following night was my nephew James's turn; we put a cannon in the back of his car and when it exploded the whole thing somersaulted, so that was nerve wracking too. I was a complete bag of nerves all the time on that shoot, not that I could show it of course.

That whole sequence really was a family affair, with Andy as the co-ordinator on the main unit, Scott as the co-ordinator on my unit, and then Wendy came to work on it, and my daughters Nina and Georgina, and James and Jessie my nephews – there were eight Armstrongs working on it. Some might say this is nepotism, but I disagree. In this day and age you don't get apprenticeships any more, nobody learns the trade from the ground up. My kids have grown up on movie sets, they've seen what we do, they've seen the planning, they're with me when I'm scouting locations, so they understand what I'm looking for, and how to achieve it. I find it odd that if a son or daughter takes over the family business, be it a butcher's shop, a factory, whatever, that's fine, but whenever that happens in show business, it's called nepotism.

I'd almost finished *Green Hornet* when I got a call out of the blue from Ken Branagh. 'Look Vic,' he said, 'I'm doing *Thor* in America, do you think you'll be able to fit it in?' Having had such a good time working closely with Ken on *Henry V*, I almost bit his hand off to say yes. I met all the Marvel people and explained that I would be finishing *Green Hornet*, which would overlap slightly, but Andy could leave *Green Hornet* early to start the prep for *Thor*, and they were fine with that. I was also introduced to the one and only Stan Lee, which was fun, to meet such a comic book legend. He's an amazing character and a lovely guy.

Ken Branagh could be thought an odd choice to direct *Thor*, knowing his classically trained background, but I think he brought a lot of class to the film, and stopped it from getting too cartoonish. It was wonderful working with him again after so long and the two of us were actually a great combination: he looked after the dramatic elements while I dealt with the action. Ken gave me total free rein and we did some big sequences down in Santa Fe, New Mexico at a western town they'd used for the Russell Crowe film *3:10 to Yuma*. We turned it into a modern town, which is where Thor first arrives when he comes down from Asgard. We did some huge explosions, and generally blew the crap out of the place.

During the Santa Fe shoot I did an amazing shot with Natalie Portman, for which she will forever be a hero in my estimation. The shot involved Natalie being inside a

Team Armstrong on Thor *in Sante Fe. L-R Andy Armstrong, James Armstrong, Jesse Johnson (my sister's son), me, Bruce Armstrong and Scott Armstrong.*

4 X 4 racing through the desert, and she had to open the sunroof, climb up and look out. We shot it from a helicopter, and before we started I explained to Natalie that it would be noisy, scary and dangerous, and dust would be blasting at her, because for technical reasons to get the shot I had to use prime (not zoom) lenses, which needed the helicopter to be within 15 feet of her. I would initially start at 1200 feet, and dive down to 15 feet, and the inertia of the chopper stopping with all that speed built up was exhilarating to say the least. All she said was, 'What do you mean dangerous? Terminal?' I said, 'Yes, but if the chopper does crash we go down together, because I'm in there shooting it.' She then just said 'OK.' I did about seven takes at dusk, so pressure was on to get the shot in a limited time, and on every take little Natalie came out through the roof of the 4 X 4, acting her heart out with a huge grin as if she was just relaxing on a tropical beach. She really has *cojones*.

When you're working on an all-out fantasy like *Thor* it's a tough choice between rooting it in some kind of reality, or just letting fly. Always your first thought is to base things in reality. For example, I did a bit of work on the Nicolas Cage film *Season of the Witch* in Louisiana, and there's a scene where this witch picks up Cage by the throat and throws him 30 feet across the room through some bookcases. It was during pre-production, and Andy was shooting 'Real Viz' which is like a moving storyboard, a fully edited together video of the action scene, with real people doing real action, which is far more useful than the usual 'Pre Viz', that's basically a cartoon made on the computer of suggested shots for a sequence. Andy had prepared the snatch rig to

With Nic Cage on Season of the Witch *in Shreveport, Louisiana.*

have Nic fly backwards, hit the ground and slide into the wall. While it was a big hit, I said, 'That looks a bit tame Andy.' He said, 'Well, I'm just trying to make it realistic. In the story we're not trying to kill him.' I smiled. 'Forget realistic. Some witch picking him up by the neck and throwing him and stabbing him with her wings? Forget realism, whatever looks most spectacular, that's what we'll go for.' And we did. So you have to marry one with the other. Your basic first thoughts are to go for realism, and for what would actually happen and what motivates it, but then you go into the storyline and you say, that's not very spectacular, let's do it this way.

And that's pretty much been my approach on *The Amazing Spider-Man*. Yes, the film is based on a comic book, but the character Peter Parker supposedly lives in the real world, so you have to give it some kind of reality. Of course, it's crazy thinking he can swing on spider's webs, but it's like Indiana Jones, Superman, or James Bond: it's just taking that truth and stretching it enough for the genre that you're working within. Like the poster tagline for *Superman* said: 'You'll believe a man can fly,' and that's what you want to do, you want to believe the extraordinary can happen, but you want to see it happen in a realistic way.

I saw some of the previous Spider-Man movies and I must admit I didn't particularly enjoy them. They looked ridiculous at times, and so much of it relied on CGI. So when Michael Grillo, who'd been our line producer on *Green Hornet*, brought me on board I was delighted to hear that everyone wanted to get away from CG as much as possible and reinvent the way Spider-Man moved. In the last few years there's been a definite resurgence in doing things for real, and that's why I think my brother Andy and myself were brought onto the new Spider-Man movie, because we always try and go for realism first, that's what we do, we're not people that rely on computers to do our job. However, we were smart enough in the early days to realise that computers are a great help, they're my 'get out of jail free' card, but a good analogy for CGI would be morphine – morphine is an incredible drug if you use it for what it was intended for, used sparingly, in the right amounts. But when it's used too much, you get addicted and it's a killer. And that's exactly what CGI is. More movies have been killed by CG than have been helped by it.

Actually, unknown to Andy and myself one of our producers, Laura Ziskin, who'd made the three previous Spider-Man movies along with Avi Arad, didn't really think it could be done, that we could make Spider-Man fly for 'real.' It wasn't until she saw the first full-scale rehearsal that she came over and gave Andy a great big hug and said, 'I've got to say I was your biggest doubter, and you've proved me wrong. You've done what we tried and couldn't do on all the other Spider-Man movies. He really is flying like a man on a web.' She had the heart to come over and say this. Laura really was a fantastic human being as well as businesswoman, she had a huge effect on the business. Tragically she died while we were on the shoot from cancer; she was a lovely lady.

Those rehearsals took place at a warehouse down in Culver City where we'd taken weeks designing and putting up these very innovative and different flying rigs. And Andrew Garfield, who plays Spider-Man, was there from day one. Although we had fantastic stunt performers and world class Parkour runners, as always what audiences *really* want to see is the actors themselves tackling the action – so Andrew Garfield came to the rehearsals facility every day and really worked hard at the physical stuff. So when you see Spider-Man first doing his swings a lot of that actually is Andrew, he was absolutely fabulous. He really bonded with Armstrong Action and the stunt team, and they didn't treat him any different from a stunt guy, he helped with the rigging and everything, even down to making tea and coffee, he was part of the team, which is very, very important. And he loved it because Andrew's one of those actors that really wants to get into the skin of the character, and he's a no-bullshit English lad, he doesn't want any of the old sycophantic nonsense. So it was great to see him really get involved with it.

Of course unlike Bond and Indiana Jones, Spider-Man wears a mask so you can cheat a little bit if you want, but the audience knows when you're faking it, so we always tried to reveal it was Andrew as much as we could. He's also got a certain way of running and moving – the stunt boys would imitate him and he'd imitate the boys, so I don't think you can see when it's Andrew and when it's not.

For some scenes we had Spider-Man swinging around New York at night. Andy

Andy and his stuntmen and riggers with the Armstrong Action mobile flying rig in New York.

went down there to set it all up on 12th Avenue, with one of our riggers, who is an engineer, Mark Dirkse. It begins where the Cotton Club was at around 130th, and goes for about six blocks along the avenue, where there's a beautiful Victorian viaduct with a road underneath it. We had Spider-Man flying above something like a hundred cars and even the people inside driving, who got to see it several times as we did two or three takes, were looking out of the windshields going 'Whoooaaaa!' without much acting going on.

There's a huge amount of planning, preparation and permissions you have to go through to get a scene like that in the can. We put up all these flying tracks, so you have to work out how you're going to shoot it so all your operating controls are out of the way of the camera. Then you have this Victorian viaduct, all cast iron metal that you have to attach your equipment to, so you have to get the city planning department's permission; there was a railway line running above us so we had to get the transport police involved, plus road safety people because you're going to shut down all these vital routes through New York. Anyway, Andy got all that organised and it went off like clockwork. A lot of that shoot ended up on YouTube which was great publicity, also the stuff we'd done earlier in down town Los Angeles. Outside the Disney concert hall there's a big overpass and it's where we had Spider-Man being chased by the police. He jumps on the back of a pick-up, then onto a semi-truck, the police block the road so Spidey webs a light pole, leaps off and swings underneath, and then you pick him up swinging into New York – that's where the cut from the LA footage to the New York shoot is. The LA shoot got a huge amount of coverage on YouTube as well, because there were people in apartments nearby videoing what was happening, and what they loved was seeing this guy leaping off buildings and jumping onto trucks for real.

Well, when I say 'real,' he's actually on wires. When he shoots a web the CGI will cover the wires that are on both of his wrists and attached to two flying rigs, but it looks like he's actually swinging from web to web. The reality is there to see: when Spider-Man swings from one direction, then turns to swing in another direction, he is actually weightless but then, when he swings down through the bottom of the arc, he's pulling three to three-and-half Gs. That's a lot of pressure on his body, and you see the arms straightening out, you see the legs straightening out and then he pulls them back up as he goes up into his flying position. Now, that kind of body language can *never* get created or simulated properly by CGI or anything else, so watching Spidey swing in that footage, you sense, subconsciously, the realism. The human computer in your head is an amazing bit of kit and it's surprising what it picks up. If something is wrong or slightly off kilter, the alarm bells go off and it can throw the whole thing out of balance. That's the danger of over relying on CGI.

To get on a big epic like *The Amazing Spider-Man* was wonderful and Armstrong Action really came into its own on that picture. As a team Andy and I work very well together, although many directors don't understand what a second unit is, or what it does. A lot of people get intimidated by the fact that I've done a lot of other big movies over the years, but that means diddlysquat really, because I'm just there as their second pair of eyes, I'm not on any takeover mission. My job is to copy the director's style and the DP's lighting and then suggest what I feel could enhance the sequences, but at the end of the day it is the director's vision I want to achieve. We had a new director on *Spider-Man* called Marc Webb and he was a little unsure at the beginning, so we'd suggest stuff, or we'd show him the 'real viz' of what we could do. Andy would shoot three or four versions of something and say, 'Look, you can do this or you can do that,' and Marc would say, 'Yeah that's fantastic,' and he would add his input, so by the end he was very confident and comfortable with the situation.

The real viz shoots that Andy does are also a great help: actual people doing the actual moves with the cameras in the correct positions, albeit on a mocked up set which Andy and his stunt crew would cobble together from whatever was available in the stunt work shop. But the director gets to see what it actually will look like on film.

The stunt team unloading the trailers across the East River with Manhattan in the background.

It was funny because Andy co-ordinated and ran the first unit with his son James and then I had my son Scott co-ordinating my unit. I think that may be a unique situation in movies, two brothers running separate units with both of their sons. Georgina was also on that show, and Nina, also Jesse Johnson, my sister's son. My other son Bruce was busy in London so he couldn't come out on it, which was a shame, but most of the clan were there, including my new son-in-law John. I remember Gary Martin, one of the top honchos at Sony, came on the set one day and there were our two 48 foot trailers with the Armstrong Action logo on the side and he said, 'Big name – big trucks.' He also said, 'There's no one else like you guys in the business.' And I guess that's true, for my kids their whole life has been an apprenticeship, and now I see them moving on in their own right, so hopefully the Armstrong name will continue. We also have another generation starting with my grandson Robert, who at nine years old is already a really good driver, plus there's Andy's grandchildren Riley and Ava, and my son Scott and his wife Zoe are expecting a baby.

It's fun working on these huge blockbusters but I've always enjoyed the challenge of smaller projects, which is why I accepted a job on the TV series *Skins* straight after *Spider-Man*. They wanted a car chase in Morocco. It was really low budget, but that's why I was so determined to do it. In fact they only had enough money for one of each car, but I managed to talk them into getting an extra car for the crash. I also persuaded the producers to go to Dave Bickers. He sent his team out there and they prepped the vehicle for the smash-up at the end of the chase. I wanted it cannoned-off, I didn't want anyone in it, I didn't want to take the risk of somebody getting hurt on such a low budget film, not that you ever want an injury. So I went out to Morocco, found all the locations and we wrote the story around those locations.

I had with me my DP Robert Binnall, who I had worked with on the Bonds, his brother Mark was our grip and Sean Connor was my focus puller. We took six Go Pro cameras with us for all the action and travelling shots. I got to work with all the actors, including Dakota Blue Richards who was the little girl in *The Golden Compass*, but is of course all grown up now, I couldn't believe it. We shot it all on the west coast of Morocco; five days is all it took, three days of prep, two days to shoot and then home, and I had such a good time, it's a real shot in the arm being able to do these smaller scale things. I just wanted to prove I could shoot a car chase without all the toys and all the bells and whistles you normally expect to have at your disposal. I would have loved to have had Scott with me for all the driving stunts, but he was busy working on *World War Z* for my great friends Simon Crane and Wade Eastwood. Simon and I go way back of course, and he was always a core member of my team, but he's now moved onwards and upwards and is I am proud to say one of the top stunt coordinators/action unit directors in the world, and along with Wade he runs things in a very similar way to which I do. They are in great demand by all the big productions, and especially by Brad Pitt and Angelina Jolie, so I was very proud that they picked Scott and his driving skills for a key position in a sequence which was shot in Glasgow (doubling for Chicago), driving a great big garbage truck that eventually wiped out between 50 and 60 cars – that has to be close to a World Record. They also shot a lot of action sequences in Malta, where Nina was also a key player.

Then I got offered *Akira*, based on the cult Japanese anime film, which was going to be shot in Vancouver for Warner Brothers. A great guy called Justis Greene, who I'd worked with on *Miracle*, a lovely little ice hockey picture I did with Kurt Russell, remembered me. The budget was I think 70 or 80 million, relatively low for what they wanted to do, stuff like enormous bike chases and a whole lot of other action. Bill Draper was the point man at Warner's and Bill is a no-nonsense, direct kind of guy that I had worked with on *I Am Legend*; he is the epitome of firm but fair, so I knew we would be properly supported by the studio.

The director was Jaume Collet-Serra, he'd done some excellent movies in Spain, and like every director was very strong and selfishly focused on his movie – he wanted everything that could make the movie better. That's really what a director has to be: you can't be Mr Nice Guy, you really do have to be utterly focused and selfish as far as what you want for your movie. What I found interesting though is that for a young director he had no qualms about accepting a second unit; he was a real team

My dear sister Diana at Stonehenge in the summer of 2011, a few months before she passed away.

player in that respect. But what quickly became apparent was that this was going to be tough to do for the money. There was going to be a huge amount of CGI, it's a futuristic, post-apocalypse world so most of the backgrounds were going to have to be CG, which costs a fortune. As far as the straightforward action went, we could have pulled it off, but I think all that CG probably pushed us over the top.

During this time my sister Diana had become ill. Wendy and I had a lovely summer in Los Angeles, my sister came out to be with Lilliana and Violet, her granddaughters, who are Jesse's children, and Andy's kids and my mum was there too: it was her 90th birthday. My daughter Georgie and her new husband John were also there. So we had a great summer together. But returning home my sister was diagnosed with bowel cancer; just dreadful.

Catching up with Harrison at the 2011 Hamilton Behind the Camera Awards, where he presented me with a lifetime achievement award.

She had been getting treatment for abscesses and her doctor had been giving her antibiotics for something like five weeks, but she had not been examined for cancer, so we missed what could have been crucial early weeks of treatment. Anyway they gave her chemo and radiology and the chemo really knocked her sideways, she has never been a terribly strong person physically. They also x-rayed her and found a couple of tiny spots in her lungs, but we thought that was probably from the asthma she had as a kid. Within five months they'd killed the bowel cancer and she went back for her final check-up only to be told by her doctors, 'I'm afraid the cancer's moved aggressively into your lungs, you've got two or three weeks left.' They hadn't been keeping an eye on her lungs, which is bizarre. And sure enough on 21st of December 2011 she died. Fortunately all her family were with her; Andy and Jesse came back from LA and I had got back from Vancouver, but it was dreadfully upsetting for everybody, especially so for my mother.

In January I was told that Warner Brothers wanted some rewrites on *Akira* so the film was put on hold. We'll see what happens. But there are other projects floating around. Emilio Estevez sent me a fantastic script called *Johnny Longshot*. It's a horse racing picture, which is right up my street: a wonderful story that reminded me a lot of my horse racing days with my dad. It's about a jockey who travels the country with his son who sort of hero-worships him, but when his career goes into decline they end up in the mid-west. At a trotting meeting they buy a horse for a couple of grand and the father trains it himself and turns it into a world champion. Sounds hokey, but it's actually based on a true story.

I had a meeting with Emilio, who I think is a really good director, and told him that I'd love to be on board, but said that if he is going to play the jockey he has to do it the right way, and that means working with the real horses just like the work jockeys do. I said, 'What I don't want you to do is to go out there and work with them at two o'clock in the afternoon as an actor coming out to have your bit of tuition with the technical advisor, you have to be there at four or five in the morning, like I used to be as a young man, you harness your horse up yourself, you ride out with the jockeys in the morning and you look after your horse before and after you've ridden it.' Because I want him to look right, so when he walks up to the horse he carries the saddle right, he looks and acts around the horse in the right way, and that's something you can't learn with just a technical advisor taking you out for a special hour or two, you've got to be immersed in it, like I used to be.

When I was shooting *Superman* I'd get up at four in the morning to be at the stables by five, I'd gallop the horses by moonlight with my dad, taking them down to the gallops, watching for the traffic with a flashlight because it was dark, then drive to the studios, have a shower and be raring to go at eight o'clock in the morning, feeling like a million dollars. That's the only way you'll learn all the nuances and little intricacies that racing people have, and that's what will make this film real. You see so many animal pictures that just don't cut it because the actor looks like a fish out of water when they're supposed to be natural. They may say the correct dialogue but they don't feel it because they have not lived it.

Anyway Emilio is really up for it, so fingers crossed that they get the money together because this picture certainly has a personal resonance for me. At the meeting I brought along some of my old racing pictures to show Emilio and told him, I'm that little kid admiring his dad. It really would be a fitting tribute to do that picture, almost full circle if you like, back to where I started all those years ago and with my whole life stretched out in front of me.

LOOKING BACK

After over four decades in this business I'm still awestruck by it. In 2003 I started directing commercials. I've done quite a few, all over the world. One was for Lincoln cars, which I shot in Tokyo. I'd never worked in Japan before, or even visited the country, so I went to see *Lost in Translation* just to get an idea about what Tokyo was like. I loved the movie, and while I was in Tokyo I went to the hotel they filmed in and sat there thinking to myself, this is amazing, 40 years-plus in this business and I'm still excited about visiting somewhere that I've seen in a movie.

Working on films, the novelty does wear off a little bit, sometimes you can't wait to go back home, but there is still something magnetic about a movie set. I've always found it bizarre when people see a movie being made in the street and they stop to stand around and watch. But then again, I was in Monrovia in California scouting for one of my commercials when Ridley Scott was shooting a commercial up there, and I must say I found it fascinating just watching them setting up and thinking to myself, how would *I* set up that shot?

It's amazing the effect that being involved in movies has on the public. You tell somebody you're a stuntman and the interest value suddenly shoots up. I'm the first to appreciate that it's a very privileged position to be in, and I've never stopped getting a kick out of it. Not long ago someone asked me, after all these years, did I still get excited about working on new projects? I said that I get excited every time I head to an airport to fly off somewhere, or when the phone rings about a new job. You can't help but get excited, it's still an adventure. I remember on *Die Another Day* when I took Pierce Brosnan down to my trailer during the hovercraft chase shoot to show how I was going to integrate him into the action, talking him through it, and he said, 'Vic, you're always so excited and enthusiastic.' I said, 'When I believe in something, I do get enthusiastic, that's part of me.'

*With my Mother at 266 South Palm Dr, Palm Springs, a special place for me now.
I'm the only action director/stuntman to be honoured by the Palm Springs Walk of Stars.*

You get a great sense of camaraderie and shared enthusiasm when you work on movies, especially when you're out in some far-flung foreign location. I think back on my films almost as much from the social perspective and the location as from the finished product itself. I've spent probably 75% of my life on location. Sometimes over the course of my career I've only spent two weeks a year at home. So it's been important that I've moved about with roughly the same group of people. The tough thing has been how my work has affected my family. My kids travelled a hell of a lot while they were young, getting shipped out around the world to lots of out of the way places, and having to mix with all the strange people that were my extended family at that particular time. It helped enormously that Wendy was in the same business, while at the same time it's been tough, because she had to give up her career to a certain degree, as did my first wife Jane, as really only one of us could be away from home at a time. But having my family around me during a film was very important. After I got established, I made it a part of all my film deals that the production company had to pay for my family to come out to visit three or four times, depending on how long the period of the shoot was (something which stuntmen had never had included in a contract before).

I've seen so many changes since I started out as a stuntman back in the '60s, some good, and some bad. You certainly haven't got the same characters you had in the old days; there isn't the same style or magic, or the same kind of fun and craziness that we used to have in the '70s and '80s. Saying that, I think by the time I entered movies, the industry had lost a lot from the golden period of the 1940s. When I read Errol Flynn's book *My Wicked, Wicked Ways*, or David Niven's *The Moon's a Balloon*, or *An Open Book* by John Huston, who's one of my favourite directors and was quite a character, people like that, that's the kind of spectacular life I would have loved to have led. The success you could achieve in those days was immense; it was like winning the lottery by getting one big movie, and they made (and lost) fortunes. There was no CGI back then either, they just went out there and did it. These people were trailblazers; they went to magical places in Africa or Asia or South America, and created their own little world. They'd employ whole armies, or buy 500 horses; they built towns to live in, or took over entire communities. And the films they made were great.

In my own way I've tried to emulate what those early film pioneers did. We have actually lived that sort of life, on films like *The Mission*, *Rambo III* and *Mohammad*. I took a group of people, good mechanics, good stuntmen, all practical people, around the world with me and we've been able to do whatever had to be done.

We could make any engine run; we could build anything. You want an aeroplane? We'd build you one by tomorrow out of scrap. And we did feel like pioneers. We went into the jungle on *The Mission*, miles from anywhere, and we just existed. We didn't have caterers, we organised where our food would come from, and the horses and the transport. You just dealt with everything because that's what you had to do to survive. It was classic filmmaking. Those days are gone, sadly, but I'm glad that I was a part of it all.

What's more, I'm still here, making movies. I'm a lucky man. I bet Dad would have been so proud.

My whole life ahead of me. About 7 months, with my Mother and sister Diana.

FILMOGRAPHY

1966
ARABESQUE
Director: Stanley Donen
Stars: Gregory Peck, Sophia Loren,
Alan Badel, Kieron Moore
VIC: Stunts/Double for
Carl Duering

1967
YOU ONLY LIVE TWICE
Director: Lewis Gilbert
Stars: Sean Connery, Tetsuro
Tanba, Akiko Wakabayashi,
Mie Hama, Donald Pleasence,
Charles Gray
VIC: Stunts/Ninja #1

1968
THE ASSASSINATION
BUREAU
Director: Basil Dearden
Stars: Oliver Reed, Diana Rigg,
Telly Savalas, Curd Jürgens,
Philippe Noiret
VIC: Stunts/Double for
Vernon Dobtcheff

CHITTY CHITTY BANG
BANG
Director: Ken Hughes
Stars: Dick Van Dyke, Sally Ann
Howes, Lionel Jeffries, Robert
Helpmann, Gert Fröbe, Benny Hill
VIC: Stunts

THE CHARGE OF THE
LIGHT BRIGADE
Director: Tony Richardson
Stars: David Hemmings, Trevor
Howard, Vanessa Redgrave,
John Gielgud, Harry Andrews
VIC: Stunts

MAYERLING
Director: Terence Young
Stars: Omar Sharif, Catherine
Deneuve, James Mason, Ava
Gardner
VIC: Stunts

NEGATIVES
Director: Peter Medak
Stars: Glenda Jackson,
Peter McEnery, Diane Cilento,
Maurice Denham
VIC: Stunts/Double for
Peter McEnery

SUBTERFUGE
Director: Peter Graham Scott
Stars: Gene Barry, Joan Collins,
Richard Todd, Michael Rennie
VIC: Stunts

1969
ALFRED THE GREAT
Director: Clive Donner
Stars: David Hemmings,
Michael York, Colin Blakely,
Ian McKellen
VIC: Stunts/Double for
Michael York

THE MOST DANGEROUS
MAN IN THE WORLD
(US title THE CHAIRMAN)
Director: J. Lee Thompson
Stars: Gregory Peck,
Anne Heywood, Arthur Hill
VIC: Stunts

ON HER MAJESTY'S SECRET
SERVICE
Director: Peter R. Hunt
Stars: George Lazenby,

Diana Rigg, Telly Savalas
VIC: Stunts/Double for George
Lazenby

ZETA ONE
Director: Michael Cort
Stars: James Robertson Justice,
Charles Hawtrey, Robin Hawdon,
Dawn Addams
VIC: Stunts

1970
FIGURES IN A LANDSCAPE
Director: Joseph Losey
Stars: Robert Shaw, Malcolm
McDowell
VIC: Stunts/Stunt Co-ordinator/
Double for Malcolm McDowell

HELL BOATS
Director: Paul Wendkos
Stars: James Franciscus,
Elizabeth Shepherd,
Ronald Allen
VIC: Stunts/Double for
James Franciscus

JANE EYRE (TV)
Director: Delbert Mann
Stars: George C. Scott, Susannah
York, Ian Bannen, Jack Hawkins,
Nyree Dawn Porter
VIC: Stunts/Double for George
C. Scott

RYAN'S DAUGHTER
Director: David Lean
Stars: Robert Mitchum,
Sarah Miles, John Mills,
Trevor Howard,
Christopher Jones
VIC: Stunts

Riding Sharkan at Stratford-On-Avon races.

Budding Bond baddie in On Her Majesty's Secret Service.

My Steve McQueen impression.

THE VAMPIRE LOVERS
Director: Roy Ward Baker
Stars: Ingrid Pitt,
Peter Cushing, Madeline Smith,
George Cole, Kate O'Mara
VIC: Stunts

1971
MACBETH
Director: Roman Polanski
Stars: Jon Finch, Francesca Annis,
Martin Shaw
VIC: Stunts/Double for Jon Finch

MARY, QUEEN OF SCOTS
Director: Charles Jarrott
Stars: Vanessa Redgrave,
Glenda Jackson, Trevor Howard,
Patrick McGoohan,

Timothy Dalton,
Nigel Davenport
VIC: Double for
Timothy Dalton

TWINS OF EVIL
Director: John Hough
Stars: Madeleine and Mary
Collinson, Peter Cushing,
Dennis Price.
VIC: Stunts

UP THE CHASTITY BELT
Director: Bob Kellett
Stars: Frankie Howerd,
Graham Crowden, Bill Fraser,
Roy Hudd
VIC: Stunts/Double for
Frankie Howerd

VILLAIN
Director: Michael Tuchner
Stars: Richard Burton,
Ian McShane, Nigel Davenport,
Joss Ackland, Donald Sinden
VIC: Stunts

WHEN EIGHT BELLS TOLL
Director: Etienne Périer
Stars: Anthony Hopkins,
Robert Morley,
Corin Redgrave,
Jack Hawkins
VIC: Stunts

1972
THE ASPHYX
Director: Peter Newbrook
Stars: Robert Stephens,

Robert Powell, Jane Lapotaire
VIC: Stunts

YOUNG WINSTON
Director: Richard Attenborough
Stars: Simon Ward, Robert Shaw,
Anne Bancroft, Jack Hawkins,
Ian Holm, Anthony Hopkins,
John Mills, Edward Woodward,
Robert Hardy
VIC: Stunts/Double for
Simon Ward

1973
BILLY TWO HATS
Director: Ted Kotcheff
Stars: Gregory Peck,
Desi Arnaz Jr., Jack Warden
VIC: Actor Harry Sweets Bradley/
Stunts/Horse Master/Double for
Gregory Peck/Desi Arnaz Jr.

LIVE AND LET DIE
Director: Guy Hamilton
Stars: Roger Moore,
Jane Seymour, Yaphet Kotto
VIC: Stunts/Double for
Roger Moore

A TOUCH OF CLASS
Director: Melvin Frank
Stars: Glenda Jackson, George Segal
VIC: Stunts

1974
11 HARROWHOUSE
Director: Aram Avakian
Stars: Charles Grodin,
James Mason, Trevor Howard,
John Gielgud, Candice Bergen
VIC: Stunts

THE ABDICATION
Director: Anthony Harvey
Stars: Peter Finch, Liv Ullmann,
Cyril Cusack
VIC: Stunts

DEAD CERT
Director: Tony Richardson
Stars: Scott Antony, Judi Dench,
Michael Williams, Julian Glover
VIC: Stunts/Jockey double for
Michael Williams

THE ODESSA FILE
Director: Ronald Neame
Stars: Jon Voight, Maximilian
Schell, Derek Jacobi
VIC: Stunts/Double for
Jon Voight

S*P*Y*S
Director: Irvin Kershner
Stars: Elliott Gould, Donald
Sutherland, Joss Ackland,
Nigel Hawthorne
VIC: Double for Donald
Sutherland

1975
BARRY LYNDON
Director: Stanley Kubrick
Stars: Ryan O'Neal, Marisa
Berenson, Patrick Magee,
Hardy Krüger, Steven Berkoff
VIC: Stunts

HENNESSY
Director: Don Sharp
Stars: Rod Steiger, Richard
Johnson, Lee Remick, Trevor
Howard, Eric Porter
VIC: Stunts

IT SHOULDN'T HAPPEN
TO A VET
Director: Eric Till
Stars: John Alderton, Colin Blakely,
Lisa Harrow, Bill Maynard
VIC: Stunts

ONE OF OUR DINOSAURS
IS MISSING
Director: Robert Stevenson
Stars: Helen Hayes, Peter Ustinov,
Derek Nimmo, Clive Revill
VIC: Stunts

SIDE BY SIDE
Director: Bruce Beresford
Stars: Terry Thomas,
Barry Humphries,
Stephanie De Sykes
VIC: Stunts

1976
ACES HIGH
Director: Jack Gold
Stars: Malcolm McDowell,
Christopher Plummer, Peter Firth,
David Wood, John Gielgud,
Trevor Howard, Richard Johnson,
Ray Milland
VIC: Stunts

CONFESSIONS OF A
DRIVING INSTRUCTOR
Director: Norman Cohen
Stars: Robin Askwith,
Anthony Booth, Sheila White,
Windsor Davies, Liz Fraser
VIC: Stunts/Double for
Windsor Davies

THE COPTER KIDS
Director: Ronald Spencer
Stars: Michael Balfour,
Vic Armstrong, Marc Boyle,
Sophie Ward
VIC: Stunts/Actor

EXPOSÉ
Dir: James Kenelm Clarke
Stars: Udo Kier, Linda Hayden,
Fiona Richmond
VIC: Actor

MOHAMMAD
(aka THE MESSAGE)
Director: Moustapha Akkad
Stars: Anthony Quinn, Irene Papas
VIC: Stunts

THE PINK PANTHER
STRIKES AGAIN
Director: Blake Edwards
Stars: Peter Sellers, Herbert Lom,
Lesley-Anne Down, Leonard
Rossiter
VIC: Stunts

RETURN OF A MAN CALLED
HORSE
Director: Irvin Kershner
Stars: Richard Harris, Gale
Sondergaard, Geoffrey Lewis
VIC: Stunts/Double for
Richard Harris

THE SLIPPER AND THE
ROSE
Director: Bryan Forbes
Stars: Richard Chamberlain,
Gemma Craven, Kenneth More,
Michael Hordern, Edith Evans
VIC: Stunts/Double for
Richard Chamberlain

TO THE DEVIL A
DAUGHTER
Director: Peter Sykes
Stars: Richard Widmark,
Christopher Lee, Denholm Elliott,
Honor Blackman, Nastassja Kinski
VIC: Stunts

1977
THE BIG SLEEP
Director: Michael Winner
Stars: Robert Mitchum, Sarah
Miles, Richard Boone, Candy
Clark, Edward Fox, Joan Collins,
John Mills, James Stewart, Oliver
Reed, Richard Todd
VIC: Stunts

With the great Donald Sutherland in Bear Island.

A BRIDGE TOO FAR
Director: Richard Attenborough
Stars: Dirk Bogarde, James Caan,
Michael Caine, Sean Connery,
Edward Fox, Elliott Gould,
Gene Hackman, Anthony Hopkins,
Hardy Kruger, Ryan O'Neal,
Laurence Olivier, Robert Redford,
Maximilian Schell, Liv Ullmann
VIC: Stunts/Assistant Stunt
Arranger

THE DUELLISTS
Director: Ridley Scott
Stars: Keith Carradine, Harvey
Keitel, Albert Finney, Edward
Fox, Christina Raines, Tom Conti,
Robert Stephens
VIC: Stunts

1978
THE FIFTH MUSKETEER
Director: Ken Annakin
Stars: Beau Bridges, Sylvia Kristel,
Ursula Andress
VIC: Stunts/Double for
Beau Bridges

SUPERMAN
Director: Richard Donner
Stars: Christopher Reeve, Marlon
Brando, Gene Hackman, Margot

Kidder, Ned Beatty, Valerie
Perrine, Jackie Cooper
VIC: Stunt Co-ordinator/Stunts/
Double for Christopher Reeve

1979
BEAR ISLAND
Director: Don Sharp
Stars: Donald Sutherland,
Vanessa Redgrave, Richard
Widmark, Christopher Lee
VIC: Second Unit Director/Stunt
Co-ordinator/Stunts/Double for
Donald Sutherland

ESCAPE TO ATHENA
Director: George P. Cosmatos
Stars: Roger Moore, Telly Savalas,
David Niven, Elliott Gould,
Claudia Cardinale,
Sonny Bono, Stefanie Powers,
Richard Roundtree
VIC: Stunt Co-ordinator/Stunts

A NIGHTINGALE SANG IN
BERKELY SQUARE
Director: Ralph Thomas
Stars: Richard Jordan,
Oliver Tobias, David Niven,
Elke Sommer,
Richard Johnson
VIC: Stunts

THE SPACEMAN AND
KING ARTHUR
Director: Russ Mayberry
Stars: Dennis Dugan, Jim Dale,
Ron Moody, Kenneth More
VIC: Stunt Co-ordinator/Double
for Jim Dale

1980
FLASH GORDON
Director: Mike Hodges
Stars: Sam J. Jones, Melody
Anderson, Topol,
Max von Sydow, Timothy Dalton,
Brian Blessed, Peter Wyngarde
VIC: Stunt Co-ordinator
(pre-production)

THE LONG GOOD FRIDAY
Director: John Mackenzie
Stars: Bob Hoskins, Helen Mirren,
Dave King, Bryan Marshall, Eddie
Constantine, Pierce Brosnan.
VIC: Stunts

ROUGH CUT
Director: Don Siegel
Stars: Burt Reynolds,
Lesley-Anne Down,
David Niven, Timothy West
VIC: Second Assistant Director/
Stunts

Few things beat the sensation of riding a horse – it's been a huge part of my life.

Wendy and myself about to jump the wall into the ocean on Never Say Never Again.

SUPERMAN II
Director: Richard Lester
Stars: Christopher Reeve, Gene
Hackman, Ned Beatty, Jackie
Cooper, Valerie Perrine, Terence
Stamp, Susannah York
VIC: Stunt Co-ordinator/Stunts/
Double for Christopher Reeve

WATCHER IN THE WOODS
Director: John Hough
Stars: Bette Davis, Caroll Baker,
David McCallum, Lynn-Holly
Johnson, Ian Bannen
VIC: Second Unit Director/Stunt
Supervisor

1981
AN AMERICAN WEREWOLF
IN LONDON
Director: John Landis
Stars: David Naughton, Jenny
Agutter, Griffin Dunne, John
Woodvine
VIC: Stunts

DRAGONSLAYER
Director: Matthew Robbins
Stars: Peter MacNicol, Caitlin

Clarke, Ralph Richardson
VIC: Stunts

GREEN ICE
Director: Ernest Day
Stars: Ryan O'Neal, Anne Archer,
Omar Sharif
VIC: Stunt Co-ordinator/Double
for Ryan O'Neal

OMEN 3: THE FINAL
CONFLICT
Director: Graham Baker
Stars: Sam Neil, Rossano Brazzi,
Don Gordon, Lisa Harrow
VIC: Stunts

RAIDERS OF THE LOST ARK
Director: Steven Spielberg
Stars: Harrison Ford, Karen Allen,
Paul Freeman, Ronald Lacey, John
Rhys-Davies, Denholm Elliott
VIC: Stunts/Double for Harrison
Ford /German Soldier

1982
BLADE RUNNER
Director: Ridley Scott
Stars: Harrison Ford, Rutger

Hauer, Sean Young, Daryl Hannah
VIC: Stunts/Photo double for
Harrison Ford

IVANHOE (TV movie)
Director: Douglas Camfield
Stars: Anthony Andrews, Sam
Neill, James Mason, Olivia Hussey
VIC: Stunt Arranger/Horse Master

1983
CLASH OF LOYALTIES
Director: Mohamed Shukri Jameel
Stars: Oliver Reed, Ghazi Al
Tickreety, James Bolam
VIC: Stunt Co-ordinator/Stunts

KRULL
Director: Peter Yates
Stars: Ken Marshall, Lysette
Anthony, Freddie Jones, Francesca
Annis, Alun Armstrong, Liam
Neeson
VIC: Stunt Co-ordinator/Stunts/
Head Wrangler

NEVER SAY NEVER AGAIN
Director: Irvin Kershner
Stars: Sean Connery, Klaus Maria

Brandauer, Max von Sydow,
Barbara Carrera, Kim Basinger,
Edward Fox, Bernie Casey, Rowan
Atkinson
VIC: Stunt Co-ordinator/Stunts/
Double for Sean Connery

**STAR WARS: EPISODE VI –
RETURN OF THE JEDI**
Director: Richard Marquand
Stars: Mark Hamill, Harrison Ford,
Carrie Fisher, Billy Dee Williams
VIC: Stunts double for Harrison
Ford

SLAYGROUND
Director: Terry Bedford
Stars: Peter Coyote, Mel Smith,
Billie Whitelaw
VIC: Stunt Arranger

1984
CONAN THE DESTROYER
Director: Richard Fleischer
Stars: Arnold Schwarzenegger,
Grace Jones, Wilt Chamberlain,
Mako, Sarah Douglas
VIC: Stunt Co-ordinator

DUNE
Director: David Lynch
Stars: Francesca Annis,
José Ferrer, Siân Phillips,
Brad Dourif, Dean Stockwell,
Freddie Jones, Linda Hunt,
Richard Jordan, Kyle MacLachlan,
Jürgen Prochnow, Max von Sydow,
Sting
VIC: Second Unit Director/Stunts

**INDIANA JONES AND THE
TEMPLE OF DOOM**
Director: Steven Spielberg
Stars: Harrison Ford, Kate
Capshaw, Ke Huy Quan
VIC: Stunt Arranger/Stunts/
Double for Harrison Ford

1985
BRAZIL
Director: Terry Gilliam
Stars: Jonathan Pryce, Robert
De Niro, Ian Holm, Kim Greist,
Michael Palin
VIC: Stunts

LACE II
Director: William Hale.
Stars: Brooke Adams,
Christopher Cazenove,
Phoebe Cates
Vic: Stunt Co-ordinator/Double
for Christopher Casenove

LEGEND
Director: Ridley Scott
Stars: Tom Cruise, Mia Sarah,
Tim Curry
VIC: Stunts/Unicorn Master

RED SONJA
Director: Richard Fleischer
Stars: Brigitte Nielsen,
Arnold Schwarzenegger
VIC: Action Unit Supervisor

1986
DUET FOR ONE
Director: Andrei Konchalovskiy
Stars: Julie Andrews, Alan Bates,
Max von Sydow,
Rupert Everett
VIC: Stunts

THE MISSION
Director: Roland Joffé
Stars: Robert De Niro, Jeremy
Irons, Ray McAnally, Liam
Neeson, Aidan Quinn
VIC: Stunt Co-ordinator

TAI-PAN
Director: Daryl Duke
Stars: Bryan Brown,
Joan Chen, John Stanton.
Vic: Stunt Co-ordinator/Actor

1987
EMPIRE OF THE SUN
Director: Steven Spielberg
Stars: Christian Bale, John
Malkovich, Miranda Richardson,
Nigel Havers
VIC: Stunt Co-ordinator/Stunts

MILLION DOLLAR MYSTERY
Director: Richard Fleischer
Stars: Jamie Alcroft,
Royce D. Applegate, Penny Baker,
Rich Hall
VIC: Second Unit Director/Stunts

THE SICILIAN
Director: Michael Cimino
Stars: Christopher Lambert,
Terence Stamp, Joss Ackland, John
Turturro, Ray McAnally
VIC: Stunt Co-ordinator/Stunts

1988
AMSTERDAMNED
Director: Dick Maas
Stars: Huub Stapel, Monique van
de Ven.
Vic: Stunts

FRANTIC
Director: Roman Polanski
Stars: Harrison Ford, Betty
Buckley, Emmanuelle Seigner
VIC: Stunts/Double for Harrison
Ford

RAMBO III
Director: Peter MacDonald
Stars: Sylvester Stallone, Richard
Crenna
VIC: Stunt Co-ordinator

1989
HENRY V
Director: Kenneth Branagh
Stars: Kenneth Branagh, Derek
Jacobi, Brian Blessed, Alec
McCowen, Ian Holm, Michael
Williams, Robert Stephens, Judi
Dench, Paul Scofield, Emma
Thompson
VIC: Second Unit Director/Stunt
Co-ordinator

**INDIANA JONES AND THE
LAST CRUSADE**
Director: Steven Spielberg
Stars: Harrison Ford, Sean
Connery, Alison Doody, Julian
Glover, Denholm Elliott, River
Phoenix, John Rhys-Davies
VIC: Stunt Co-ordinator/Stunts/
Double for Harrison Ford

WE'RE NO ANGELS
Director: Neil Jordan
Stars: Robert De Niro, Sean Penn,
Demi Moore, Bruno Kirby
Vic: Stunt Co-ordinator

Triana, a wonderful horse, seen here in Rob Roy.

1990

AIR AMERICA
Director: Roger Spottiswoode
Stars: Mel Gibson,
Robert Downey Jr., Nancy Travis
VIC: Third Director/Stunt
Co-ordinator

TOTAL RECALL
Director: Paul Verhoeven
Stars: Arnold Schwarzenegger,
Rachel Ticotin, Sharon Stone,
Ronny Cox, Michael Ironside
VIC: Second Unit Director/Stunt
Co-ordinator

1991

COVER UP
Director: Manny Coto
Stars: Dolph Lundgren, Louis
Gossett Jr
VIC: Second Unit Director/Stunt
Co-ordinator

DOUBLE IMPACT
Director: Sheldon Lettich
Stars: Jean-Claude Van Damme,
Geoffrey Lewis, Alan Scarfe

VIC: Second Unit Director/Stunt
Co-ordinator

F/X 2
Director: Richard Franklin
Stars: Bryan Brown, Brian
Dennehy, Rachel Ticotin
VIC: Second Unit Director

**TERMINATOR 2:
JUDGMENT DAY**
Director: James Cameron
Stars: Arnold Schwarzenegger,
Linda Hamilton, Edward Furlong,
Robert Patrick
VIC: Second Unit Director:
Opening Sequence

1992

UNIVERSAL SOLDIER
Director: Roland Emmerich
Stars: Jean-Claude Van Damme,
Dolph Lundgren, Ally Walker
VIC: Second Unit Director/Stunt
Co-ordinator

1993

JOSHUA TREE

Director: Vic Armstrong
Stars: Dolph Lundgren, George
Segal, Kristian Alfonso, Geoffrey
Lewis

LAST ACTION HERO
Director: John McTiernan
Stars: Arnold Schwarzenegger,
F. Murray Abraham, Charles
Dance, Art Carney, Frank McRae,
Anthony Quinn, Ian McKellen
VIC: Second Unit Director/Stunt
Co-ordinator

1994

BLACK BEAUTY
Director: Caroline Thompson
Stars: Sean Bean, David Thewlis, Jim
Carter, Peter Davison, Peter Cook
VIC: Second Unit Director/Stunt
Co-ordinator/Horse Master/Actor

RADIOLAND MURDERS
Director: Mel Smith
Stars: Brian Benben, Mary Stuart
Masterson, Ned Beatty, George
Burns, Christopher Lloyd
VIC: Second Unit Director

1995
CUTTHROAT ISLAND
Director: Renny Harlin
Stars: Geena Davis, Matthew
Modine, Frank Langella
Vic: Stunt Co-ordinator

JOHNNY MNEMONIC
Director: Robert Longo
Stars: Keanu Reeves, Dolph
Lundgren, Takeshi Kitano, Ice-T,
Dina Meyer
VIC: Second Unit Director/Stunt
Co-ordinator

ROB ROY
Director: Michael Caton-Jones
Stars: Liam Neeson, Jessica Lange,
John Hurt, Tim Roth, Brian Cox,
Eric Stoltz
VIC: Second Unit Director/Stunt
Co-ordinator

1996
THE PHANTOM
Director: Simon Wincer
Stars: Billy Zane, Kristy Swanson,
Treat Williams, Catherine Zeta-
Jones, Patrick McGoohan
VIC: Second Unit Director

1997
SHADOW CONSPIRACY
Director: George P. Cosmatos
Stars: Charlie Sheen, Donald
Sutherland, Linda Hamilton, Ben
Gazzara, Gore Vidal
VIC: Second Unit Director/Stunt
Co-ordinator

STARSHIP TROOPERS
Director: Paul Verhoeven
Stars: Casper Van Dien, Dina
Meyer, Denise Richards,
Michael Ironside
VIC: Second Unit Director/Stunt
Co-ordinator

TOMORROW NEVER DIES
Director: Roger Spottiswoode
Stars: Pierce Brosnan, Jonathan
Pryce, Michelle Yeoh,
Teri Hatcher
VIC: Second Unit Director/Stunt
Co-ordinator

1998
THE AVENGERS
Director: Jeremiah S. Chechik
Stars: Ralph Fiennes, Uma
Thurman, Sean Connery, Jim
Broadbent, Eddie Izzard
VIC: Second Unit Director

BLACK DOG
Director: Kevin Hooks
Stars: Patrick Swayze, Meat Loaf
VIC: Second Unit Director/Stunt
Co-ordinator

1999
ENTRAPMENT
Director: Jon Amiel
Stars: Sean Connery, Catherine
Zeta-Jones, Ving Rhames
VIC: Second Unit Director/Stunt
Co-ordinator

**THE WORLD IS NOT
ENOUGH**
Director: Michael Apted
Stars: Pierce Brosnan, Sophie
Marceau, Robert Carlyle, Denise
Richards
VIC: Second Unit Director/Stunt
Co-ordinator

2000
CHARLIE'S ANGELS
Director: McG
Stars: Cameron Diaz, Drew
Barrymore, Lucy Liu, Bill Murray
VIC: Second Unit Director/Stunt
Co-ordinator

QUILLS
Director: Philip Kaufman
Stars: Geoffrey Rush, Kate
Winslet, Joaquin Phoenix, Michael
Caine
VIC: Second Unit Director

2001
**CAPTAIN CORELLI'S
MANDOLIN**
Director: John Madden
Stars: Nicolas Cage, Penélope
Cruz, John Hurt, Christian Bale
VIC: Second Unit Director

THE FOURTH ANGEL
Director: John Irvin

Stars: Jeremy Irons, Forest
Whitaker, Jason Priestley
VIC: Stunts

2002
DIE ANOTHER DAY
Director: Lee Tamahori
Stars: Pierce Brosnan, Halle Berry,
Toby Stephens, Rosamund Pike,
Rick Yune, Judi Dench
VIC: Second Unit Director/Stunt
Co-ordinator

THE FOUR FEATHERS
Director: Shekhar Kapur
Stars: Heath Ledger, Wes Bentley,
Kate Hudson, Michael Sheen,
Djimon Hounsou
VIC: Second Unit Director

GANGS OF NEW YORK
Director: Martin Scorsese
Stars: Leonardo DiCaprio, Daniel Day-
Lewis, Cameron Diaz, Liam Neeson
VIC: Second Unit Director: Fight
scenes/Stunt Co-ordinator

2003
**THE LEAGUE OF
EXTRAORDINARY
GENTLEMEN**
Director: Stephen Norrington
Stars: Sean Connery, Naseeruddin
Shah, Peta Wilson, Stuart
Townsend, Richard Roxburgh
VIC: Second Unit Director

2004
BLADE: TRINITY
Director: David S. Goyer
Stars: Wesley Snipes, Kris
Kristofferson, Jessica Biel, Ryan
Reynolds
VIC: Action Director/Second Unit
Director

LAKSHYA
Director: Farhan Akhtar
Stars: Amitabh Bachchan, Preity
Zinta, Om Puri
VIC: Second Unit Director

MIRACLE
Director: Gavin O'Connor
Stars: Kurt Russell, Patricia Clarkson
VIC: Second Unit Director

With the indomitable Tom Cruise.

2005

THE GREAT RAID
Director: John Dahl
Stars: Benjamin Bratt, James Franco,
Sam Worthington
VIC: Second Unit Director:
Action Unit

WAR OF THE WORLDS
Director: Steven Spielberg
Stars: Tom Cruise, Dakota Fanning,
Justin Chatwin,
Tim Robbins
VIC: Second Unit Director/Stunt
Co-ordinator

2006

CHILDREN OF GLORY
Director: Krisztina Goda
Stars: Kata Dobó,
Iván Fenyö
VIC: Second Unit Director

THE HOLIDAY
Director: Nancy Meyers
Stars: Cameron Diaz, Kate Winslet,
Jude Law,
Jack Black
VIC: Second Unit Director: UK

MISSION: IMPOSSIBLE III
Director: J. J. Abrams
Stars: Tom Cruise, Philip Seymour
Hoffman, Ving Rhames, Maggie Q
VIC: Action Unit Director/Second
Unit Director/Stunt Co-ordinator

2007

THE GOLDEN COMPASS
Director: Chris Weitz
Stars: Nicole Kidman, Daniel Craig,
Eva Green, Sam Elliott
VIC: Second Unit Director/Stunt
Co-ordinator

I AM LEGEND
Director: Francis Lawrence
Stars: Will Smith, Alice Braga
VIC: Second Unit Director/Stunt
Co-ordinator

2008

**THE MUMMY: TOMB OF THE
DRAGON EMPEROR**
Director: Rob Cohen
Stars: Brendan Fraser, Jet Li, Maria
Bello, John Hannah, Michelle Yeoh
VIC: Action Unit Director/Action
Co-ordinator

VALKYRIE
Director: Bryan Singer
Stars: Tom Cruise, Kenneth
Branagh, Bill Nighy, Tom
Wilkinson, Terence Stamp
VIC: Action Unit: opening sequence

2010

SALT
Director: Phillip Noyce
Stars: Angelina Jolie, Liev Schreiber.
VIC: Second Unit Director/Stunt
Co-ordinator

SHANGHAI
Director: Mikael Håfström
Stars: John Cusack, Li Gong,
Yun-Fat Chow, Ken Watanabe
VIC: Second Unit Director/Stunt
Co-ordinator

2011

THE GREEN HORNET
Director: Michel Gondry
Stars: Seth Rogen, Cameron Diaz,
Christoph Waltz, Edward Furlong,
Jay Chou
VIC: Second Unit Director/Stunt
Co-ordinator

With the lovely Michelle Yeoh in Beijing.

With Brendan Fraser on the set of Mummy 3.

In my office at home with my BAFTA.

THOR
Director: Kenneth Branagh
Stars: Chris Hemsworth,
Natalie Portman, Rene Russo,
Anthony Hopkins
VIC: Second Unit Director/Stunt
Co-ordinator

2012
THE AMAZING SPIDER-MAN
Director: Marc Webb
Stars: Andrew Garfield,
Emma Stone, Rhys Ifans,
Martin Sheen, Sally Field
VIC: Second Unit Director/Stunt
Co-ordinator

TELEVISION

1969-70
NOT ONLY... BUT ALSO
VIC: Stunt Double
for Peter Cook

1972
THE ADVENTURES OF
BLACK BEAUTY
VIC: Riding double for
Michael Culver

1974
STEPTOE AND SON
Director: Douglas Argent
Stars: Harry H. Corbett,
Wilfrid Brambell
VIC: Actor 1 episode 'The Seven
Steptoerai'

THE ZOO GANG
Directors: Sidney Hayers
and John Hough
Stars: Brian Keith,
John Mills, Barry Morse,
Lilli Palmer
VIC: Stunt Co-ordinator/Actor

1975
SPACE: 1999
Director: Ray Austin
Stars: Martin Landau, Barbara
Bain, Barry Morse
VIC: Actor 2 episodes

1992-93
THE YOUNG INDIANA JONES
CHRONICLES
VIC: Director 1 episode 'Austria,
March 1917'
Second Unit Director 2 episodes
'Young Indiana Jones and the Mystery
of the Blues' and 'Young Indiana
Jones and the Curse of the Jackal'

2012
SKINS
Director: Jack Clough
Stars: Will Merrick,
Dakota Blue Richards
VIC: Action Unit Director,
1 episode 'Everyone'

My daughter Georgina rearing a horse belonging to Sled Reynolds, who provides exotic animals to the film business.